ANNA HOWARD SHAW

WOMEN IN AMERICAN HISTORY

Editorial Advisors:
Susan K. Cahn
Deborah Gray White
Anne Firor Scott, Founding Editor Emerita

*A list of books in the series
appears at the end of this book.*

Anna Howard Shaw

The Work of Woman Suffrage

TRISHA FRANZEN

UNIVERSITY OF ILLINOIS PRESS
URBANA, CHICAGO, AND SPRINGFIELD

Library of Congress Cataloging-in-Publication Data
Franzen, Trisha, 1951–
Anna Howard Shaw : the work of woman suffrage /
Trisha Franzen.
pages   cm. — (Women in American history)
Includes bibliographical references and index.
ISBN 978-0-252-03815-0 (cloth : alk. paper)
ISBN 978-0-252-07962-7 (pbk. : alk. paper)
ISBN 978-0-252-09541-2 (ebook)
1. Shaw, Anna Howard, 1847–1919.
2. Suffragists—United States—Biography.
3. Feminists—United States—Biography.
4. Women—Suffrage—United States—History—Sources.
I. Title.
JK1899.S6F73   2013
324.6'230973—dc23   2013025964

CONTENTS

Illustrations follow page 114

ACKNOWLEDGMENTS

After so many years, my debts to all the people who assisted me along the way are tremendous. I realize there is no means to adequately acknowledge and appropriately thank everyone, but I will make an attempt to recognize as many of the people who worked with me as I can.

This book would not have happened if Albion College had not kept alive their connection with Anna Howard Shaw by naming their Women's Center after her. Many additional people and offices at Albion have supported this work over the years. Within Academic Affairs, the Faculty Development monies that the Faculty Development Committee generously awarded me for this project allowed for numerous research trips and conference presentations from 1997 on. Similarly the Women's and Gender Studies supported this project with financial and multiple other levels of support.

The staff of the Albion College Library and I have become much closer as a result of this work. Mike VanHouten was always there when I had any research questions or problems with Endnotes. Not only did he find Anna Howard Shaw sources for me, but he convinced me that he welcomed all these large and small challenges. Even though we can now request interlibrary loan items via the web, I always knew that there was a person, usually Allie Moore, or Becky Markovich in the months Allie was off, in that office who would persist even when I requested another obscure item. I was frequently amazed with the materials that they located for me. While Jennie Thomas has moved on from Albion College, during her time there she made the College and Methodist Archives most accessible. Our entire library staff consistently goes beyond what is expected, for example, John Kondelik and Becky Markovich relocating the microfilm reader during renovations so that I could finish the chapter at hand. Thank you all so much.

Every one of my visits to the Schlesinger Library at the Radcliffe Institute has been an adventure and a joy. The people—especially Sarah Hutcheon and Lynda Leahy from my last visit—the collections, and the support were all invaluable assets to this project and, I am certain, many others. The Schlesinger Library is a treasure. I am always amazed with the efficiency of the staff at the Library of Congress, especially in the Manuscript Reading Room. Though this huge, public institution could be impersonal, it isn't.

Everyone is consistently helpful. And I don't know whether it was because my hair is now more white than brown, but getting a personal escort between buildings via the underground tunnels was a special treat this last visit.

Similarly, Marianne Hansen and others in the Special Collections at the Bryn Mawr College Library; Mary M. Huth at the Department of Rare Books, Special Collections and Preservation of the University of Rochester Library; Kara M. Jackman of the Archives of the School of Theology Library at Boston University; and Karen Kukil and her staff at the Sophia Smith Collection of Smith College all went beyond my requests and made sure I knew about the other items that might help my research. I am similarly indebted to Ana Guimaraes and her staff in the Division of Rare and Manuscript Collections of Cornell University Library who made special arrangements for me to receive the papers I needed. When I was getting to the end of my research and I knew I couldn't get to the United Methodist Archives Center at Drew University, Frances Lyons-Bristol generously located and forwarded to me the materials I needed. From the very warm days early in this research when I visited the Archives at the University of Kentucky through the exceptionally cold day in December 2008 when I visited the Peace Collection at the Swarthmore College Library, in each place there were warm welcomes and helpful staff members.

At the Mecosta County Historical Society in Big Rapids, Michigan, there is a group of people dedicated to remembering and honoring Anna Howard Shaw. I especially want to thank Mariann Hahn and Maxine Sofoulis for all they shared with me, from the materials in the collection and directions to the Shaw family land through a tour of the jail where Shaw's brother Jack worked. Cynthia Hall of the Osterville, Massachusetts, Historical Society opened that museum to me and allowed me to get a sense of the area where Shaw built her first home and enjoyed rare leisure and time with her family. The maps, directories, and histories that the people at the Immigrant City Archives in Lawrence, Massachusetts, shared with me gave me a much fuller sense of Shaw's life in this emerging industrial city. I am also grateful for the help I received from the Tyne and Wear (Newcastle, U.K.) Archives early in this project. It was great to have an excuse to visit Alnwick and Alnwick Castle, but more important was the information about the Castle's and Duchess's School Records that the individuals there forwarded to me. Because there are so few records from Shaw's early life, I am especially appreciative of the care all these organizations take preserving local histories.

The pastors and members of both the Dennis Union Church and the Evangelical Free Church of East Dennis welcomed me and gladly shared all the information they had about Shaw. I was thrilled to be able to hold Shaw's beautiful communion service. I especially want to thank Rev. John

Brink of the former and Rev. David E. Johnson of the latter for their help. I regret and apologize for not following up on all the leads from those visits.

Laurie Matheson, of the University of Illinois Press, has encouraged my work since I first spoke to her about it. She guided the proposal through the various reviews and processes with an impressive efficiency. Jennifer Clark and Nancy Albright have been generous and careful guardians of this manuscript. Thank you. Any remaining errors are mine. I also appreciate the helpful comments from the anonymous reviewers.

It was a case of wonderful coincidence at the Seneca Fall National Women's Rights Historical Park in 1996 that brought me into contact with some of the descendents of Shaw's family. Richard Freemen graciously responded to my assorted inquiries and put me in touch with Eleanor MacDowell Sherry with whom I had several delightful and informative conversations. Karin Curtiss contacted me when she came across information about my research. I appreciate all their help and support. I only hope that this work meets in some way their expectations.

Eleanor Sherry facilitated my connection with the Rev. Elaine Buker whose passion for keeping Anna Howard Shaw's story alive is impressive. Rev. Buker sent me files containing many documents and clippings I would never have located otherwise. Her materials made this a better book. Similarly George and Peggy Drum welcomed me and my father to Alnwick Lodge. Their stories brought the house alive. I cannot thank all of these individuals enough.

I am grateful for the encouragement and thoughtful feedback from various colleagues along the way. The Great Lakes College Association (GLCA) Women's Studies Roundtable, especially Meryl Altman, noted the importance of Shaw's identity for this biography. Several conference presentations brought instructive responses that strengthen this effort, including those from the National Women's Studies Association, the singlewomen roundtable at the 2008 Berkshire Conference on the History of Women, the 2009 Western Association of Women Historians, and the Single Women in History Conference in Bristol, U.K., in 2006. Additionally I am in debt to Helen Bannan, Robert P. J. Cooney Jr., Ellen Carol DuBois, Kimberly Jensen, and Leila Rupp who encouraged this work and generously shared sources and insights.

How do I begin to thank my family? I suspect that my siblings, nieces, and nephews know more about Anna Howard Shaw than most historians. Marie, Paul, Bill, Mark, Liz, and Val shared my enthusiasm for this project, though Marie, Paul, and Bill didn't live to see its completion. Val housed me on several of my research trips to the D.C. area. It has been so fortunate that Shaw chose to live most of her adult life in my hometown of Philadelphia so that research trips could also be family visits. My late mother Lavene Haas Franzen modeled a strong womanhood for me and all of us in our family, while my father Paul William Franzen passed on to me a deep fascination with and appreciation of history. Together they taught all of us the importance of education and hard work. Though my father recently entered his ninth decade, he has always been more than happy to accompany me as we searched out the various Shaw residences or related archives in and around Philadelphia.

Both Marlene Kondelik and Tom Hunsdorfer, wonderful friends and colleagues at Albion College, generously read and critiqued parts of this book. One of my dear friends, Pam Meitner, read the entire manuscript with the keen eye of a lawyer, catching errors that escaped others' views. Mary Collar, who, as Chair of Women's and Gender Studies at Albion College, had already supported me in my career there in many ways, was a most conscientious editor. Her close reading of the draft for both content and style was a great and generous gift. Her suggestions for clarifying the writing have made this a much stronger book.

Anna Howard Shaw has practically been a member of my family for close to two decades. I would not have persisted in this undertaking without the encouragement of both my partner, Jeanne Marie Hemond, and my daughter, Emiliana Franzen. Emiliana knew women's history from the time she was old enough to read and could name the NAWSA presidents in correct sequence as a fourth grader. Her pride in my work is perhaps its sweetest reward. There are no words that capture the breadth of support that Jeanne gave to me and this project. Her faith in my ability to bring Anna Howard Shaw's story to life was unconditional. She listened as I argued out my thoughts and critiqued what I wrote with sustaining attention. I truly cannot imagine where this project would have gone without her support.

ANNA HOWARD SHAW

INTRODUCTION

Facing Contradictions

There passed away on Wednesday a genuine American with all the qualities which in fiction collect about that name, but which are not so often seen in real life; an American with the measureless patience, the deep and gentle humor, the whimsical and tolerant philosophy, and the dauntless courage, physical as well as moral, which we find so satisfyingly displayed in LINCOLN, of all our heroes.

Forty-five years earlier, in 1874, a slight young woman with cropped hair and intense dark eyes sat silently behind the driver in an open wagon.[1] With growing anxiety, she anticipated a long night's journey through the deep forest to the northern Michigan lumber camp where she was scheduled to preach. Recently licensed as a Methodist preacher, Anna Howard Shaw had agreed to substitute for her newly married colleague before she realized that there was no train connection to his community. Now the hired driver taking her on the last leg of her trip began to taunt her by telling her in vivid terms of the grisly crimes common to that area. He assaulted Shaw with accusations about what kind of woman she must be to be alone with him in the woods and about the power he had over her at this moment. But the young traveler was prepared. "I slipped my hand into the satchel in my lap, and it touched my revolver. No touch of human fingers ever brought such comfort. With a deep breath of thanksgiving I drew it out and cocked it, and as I did so he recognized the sudden click." Shaw ordered the driver to be silent and to proceed to the lumber camp. With the gun at his back, he delivered her to the settlement where she conducted the Sunday service. Her service was exceptionally well attended, and the collection was the largest in the history of the chapel, thanks to the driver who had spread word among the lumbermen about the young woman preacher who carried a gun.[2]

These two portraits bookend Anna Howard Shaw's (1847–1919) impressive public life. An immigrant from England at the age of four, she brought a broad knowledge of her adopted country, from her childhood in the industrializing northeast through her young adulthood on the isolated frontier of Michigan, to her activism. Shaw had become an American in the new city of Lawrence, Massachusetts, where her family lived for seven years. From the age of twelve to the age of twenty-seven, she had been confined by her family's poverty and patriarchal expectations to the rural farming communities of Mecosta County, Michigan. Preaching was her calling and her escape. By her early thirties, Shaw had transformed herself into a successful ordained Methodist minister. By her late thirties she had added a medical degree, but as she reached forty, she turned her back on both of these professions to become an activist and freelance lecturer. Recognized and mentored by some of the greatest women leaders of her era—Lucy Stone, Frances Willard, and especially Susan B. Anthony—as a speaker, Shaw "stood unchallenged throughout her career as the greatest orator among women that the world has ever known, and who made more converts to the suffrage cause than any other one person" in the opinion of her suffrage colleague and putative rival Carrie Chapman Catt.[3]

In 1904 this self-made, working woman became the fourth president of the National American Woman Suffrage Association (NAWSA), the role for which she is best known. She held this position for twelve years, longer than Elizabeth Cady Stanton, Susan B. Anthony, or Carrie Chapman Catt. Sources document that she led the NAWSA's transformation from a struggling voluntary association directed by a small group of otherwise "white, middle-class and native-born" women to a professional organization headquartered in New York City with salaried executive workers and a sophisticated publicity department. Shaw presided over the years when the number of full suffrage states jumped from four to twelve, when the NAWSA finances and membership increased proportionately, and when the organization reached out and converted working women, college students, men, and many politicians to the suffragists' cause.[4]

After these years of service, after giving her health and almost her life to the cause, Shaw's retirement gave her not leisure but another tremendous opportunity to prove herself as a citizen by serving this nation and its women as the chair of the Woman's Committee for the Council on National Defense during World War I. Shaw died while campaigning for the League of Nations in 1919.[5]

With so rich a life Anna Howard Shaw deserves a major place in U.S. and women's history. Yet in one of the many contradictions involving Shaw, this exceptional leader has been generally ignored, denigrated, or marginalized during the resurgence of women's history.[6]

I first came to know Shaw's story in the 1980s when I was researching single women born between 1865 and 1890. As fate would have it, I was hired in 1992 as the director of the Anna Howard Shaw Women's Center at Albion College, one of her alma maters. In spite of my increasing fascination with Shaw's life, I could never turn my full attention to her until recently. During this volume's long gestational period, I was of two minds. On the one hand, I hoped no one else would pick up this project, because I found Shaw to be more intriguing the more I researched her. On the other hand, as no one did turn attention to her, my consternation and confusion at the historical neglect of Shaw grew.[7]

At first I was only concerned with Shaw's underexamined position within suffrage scholarship. Why did scholars ignore so important a leader? How could the histories of suffrage label the leaders of her era as "white, middle-class and native born," when she, one of the most consistent and longest-serving leaders, was an immigrant raised in poverty? Why have the years of her presidency been termed "the doldrums," when at least the latter part of her term witnessed a resurgence of the NAWSA, an almost complete enfranchisement of western women, and the media coverage needed to make woman suffrage a central political issue? What was the basis for labeling Shaw as a poor administrator? While Sarah Hunter Graham, Michael McGerr, and researchers who have focused on local and regional suffrage developments have begun revising our view of that period, still there hasn't been any significant research specifically on Shaw's life or presidency.[8]

Yet the more I researched Shaw, the more I became convinced that her life had much to tell us beyond suffrage history. Since the more accessible and numerous sources from middle-class and leisured girls and women frequently slant our understanding of gender realities in most historical periods, documents following the lives of girls and women farther down on the social hierarchy are important to balance such analyses. The materials from Shaw's early life have their problems, but her experiences of gender as a child and young adult add to our understandings of her era, particularly how survival issues frequently trumped gender norms. Shaw started life with so little. Though a sickly child, Shaw's and her family's economic realities precluded an indulged childhood, demanding instead that she take on non-traditional roles. She was an immigrant who worked to support her family from a young age before she had a chance for more than a basic education. When even privileged women had to struggle to enter colleges or professional schools, Shaw carried the greater burden of having no family support for any of her higher education. Plus she was a character who had learned early that following the rules didn't get you very far if you were poor and a girl. Sometimes her willingness to step outside the boundaries of accepted womanly decorum worked; sometimes it didn't. Shaw's life helps to uncover the weaknesses as well as the opportunities in the mid-nineteenth-century system of male dominance.[9]

Given all the fascinating questions Shaw's life raised to me, I kept wondering if there was something I was missing, something that explained why Shaw had been left on the sidelines during the incredible progress of women's history. Some feminist biographers have written about their ambivalence toward difficult subjects, but it is precisely because of her very human characteristics and foibles that I found Shaw an inviting subject. A complex figure with great strengths and serious flaws as a leader, someone who could not easily be framed as a saint or a scoundrel, Shaw was intriguing, challenging, and fun, much more radical, modern, and outrageous a subject than most of her peers.[10]

I couldn't get to the core of my attraction to Shaw until I presented some preliminary research at one of our regional Great Lakes College Association Women's Studies roundtables. My colleagues responded most to my analysis linking Shaw's non-elite background, particularly the idea that Shaw was not a "lady," to her activist standpoint. Shaw had many wonderful attributes, but none of the sedate reserve expected of the nineteenth-century middle- to upper-class white women who often argued for their political rights based on their class, race, and/or social positions as well as on their identities as the female members of the leading families. Such women contrasted their rights claims with those of immigrant, African American and American Indian men. Shaw shared neither their identities nor their sense of entitlement. Instead, as a self-supporting working woman, she had to challenge in words and actions those class- and race-based gender norms to succeed. These differences, along with all she had gained from her frontier experiences and all that contradicted the era's prescriptive womanly passivity and delicacy, recommended her to my colleagues and clarified her appeal to me. It also suggested why she was so successful as an orator and in converting her audiences to the suffrage cause. Shaw had the "common touch," a self-deprecating sense of humor, and an undeniable magic when she stood behind a podium. She knew the lives most women—and men— led, far more than most national suffrage leaders of her era. She had the ability to identify with her audiences and to have them identify with her. It made sense that Shaw led the movement from the margins to the center of American politics.[11]

Consequently, although this book is first and foremost a much-needed biography of a major figure in U.S. women's history, it is also a historiographic mystery. How and why have so few historians taken an in-depth look at Anna Howard Shaw? Why is there no discussion of the fact that she was the first and only salaried president of the NAWSA? How did Shaw become the "straw man" for both Carrie Chapman Catt's and Alice Paul's reputations? How was the energetic, charismatic, "odd woman out" among the white suffrage transformed into a conservative, ineffectual curmudgeon? And certainly the core question remains: how important was Shaw to the woman's suffrage movement?

Shaw's origins on the margins of the existing social hierarchies meant that she was far from being the typical women's rights leader. Shaw herself wrote about how she was "less like a lady than anything else in the world." What does that self-identity mean when the NAWSA leaders of her era are commonly referred to as conservative and middle-class? Without family connections or even community on this continent beyond her natal family, Shaw's was one of the immigrant families whose members gained citizenship through service in the Civil War. Not middle-class, she also wasn't part of an industrial working class, and her resulting class consciousness was as complex as her material realities. Her experiences as the daughter of a failed patriarch—it is not clear whether her father was ever able to fully support his family—made the flaws in the system of male dominance obvious to Shaw from an early age. Shaw's early opportunities and choices expand our understandings of the changing and apparently permeable gender boundaries of her era, including conceptions of women's bodies and the worth of women's traditional work.[12]

Historians have identified the intersection of class, marital status, sexuality, and waged work as a problematic site in U.S. women's history. Shaw's identity places her very much at that intersection. Her life provides an opportunity to push such an analysis in spite of the fact that we have no commonly understood term to describe that site and how women differ from each other on those factors. If we did, it would be easier to discuss how Shaw's status diverges from her colleagues. What is certain is that Shaw's life story not only reconfigures our ideas about *which* women were able to construct autonomous lives in the nineteenth century and how they achieved them, but also what should be defined as an autonomous life. How should we compare the independence of women such as Shaw to the elite women whose independence rested on inherited wealth or the women of comfortable backgrounds whose families' resources eased their journeys to self-sufficiency?[13]

This examination of Shaw's life has two distinct but interrelated parts. The first four chapters of this book cover her background and her life until 1904, and the second part covers the last fifteen years of her life, including her almost twelve years as president of the NAWSA. A major reason to focus so much on her early life is that even the historians who celebrate Shaw's incredible rise from poverty to leadership in national and international women's organizations suddenly cease to consider its influence once she becomes president of the NAWSA. This biography argues that we need to integrate the two parts of Shaw's life.[14]

The first half of the book, covering the years 1847–1903, considers Shaw's heritage and her family through her years as Susan B. Anthony's protégé and NAWSA vice president. It argues that Shaw's political consciousness, style, and strategies grew from her early experiences. The life she built was a radical departure from the one expected and proscribed for women of her era. Along with her mentors, Susan B. Anthony and Frances Willard, Shaw was one of the first publicly recognized autonomous women in the United States. Nevertheless, her family's lack of social standing; her poverty, geographical isolation, and subsequent early responsibilities; along with her consciousness as an outsider sets her apart from even those women. It is significant that Shaw never had any expectation except that she would be self-supporting, unlike a number of other suffrage leaders who were forced to shoulder the provider role after the economic failures of fathers or husbands. An analysis of how she could overcome these obstacles and create such a groundbreaking life, enter nontraditional realms, and challenge men in their own arenas while still maintaining and expanding her standing as a respected woman leader argues that the nineteenth-century gender norms were shifting and flexible. How else could this person who lived such a transgressive life come to personify the "new woman" for so many people?[15]

Shaw would redefine herself in part because, before the generally more privileged single women of the Progressive Era constituted the golden age of spinsters, she found the means to establish an infrastructure of kin-like networks. These networks stood in for those often invisible religious, political, and social connections derived as a matter of course from membership in established, white, middle-class, and stable families. These connections constitute as much of class and patriarchal privilege as actual monies. Such webs of associations have long been recognized as important vehicles in the lives of women activists. Although other "new women" used such connections to compensate for a lack of gender-based power, this early and atypical new woman needed these contacts to address her much broader and more complex lack of position and privilege.[16]

Similarly, Shaw lived before the emergence of the contemporary vocabulary on sexuality and gender. Nevertheless both her life and her analyses are remarkably modern. Shaw was gender-variant in both her personal and professional characteristics and preferences. She lived, partnered, and supported a family all outside of what we now term heteropatriarchy. Yet in a challenge to the expected order of a woman's life, Shaw named Susan B. Anthony as the great passion of her life, rather than Lucy E. Anthony, her partner for over thirty years. By placing her political mentor at the center of her emotional life, Shaw replaces the primacy of romance and the place of the romantic dyad in women's lives with a chosen family that defies definition even today.[17]

At a time when social theorists argued that sharp distinctions between women and men marked the most advanced "race," Shaw rejected such arguments in her theory and in her practice. Yet, her persona, manly or even "butch" in current terminology, appeared to enhance rather than undercut her popularity. Shaw's reputation suggests that the broader population accepted this type of womanliness, which raises questions about the emergence of a more restricted and passive feminine ideal. Was there a greater space within the concept of woman during this era than there was after? Further, the views Shaw espoused would resonate today with social construction theorists, while her success questions how widespread bifurcated gender ideals were among the general population.[18]

Much of the scholarly attention Shaw does receive is as an early woman minister. While many of the women's rights leaders sought to distance themselves from established religions or critiqued institutionalized religion, for Shaw that brief period when certain denominations encouraged women to enter the ministry allowed her entry into higher education and a profession. Shaw used the ministry. Through it she claimed respectability as well as personal and spiritual independence. It was certainly through a religious calling that Shaw and other women such as Sojourner Truth could bypass restrictions created by "mere mortal" men and claim a divine directive to preach. Religion frequently has been identified as a major obstacle to women's advancement, yet a number of suffrage leaders were pioneering women ministers. Shaw's seminary studies equipped her exceptionally well to counter the various scripturally based arguments against women's advancement that were significant over the course of her public career. After her years in the ministry, it was only a small step for Shaw to extend her pulpit to the larger public in the era of the lyceum, the social gospel, and the other reform movements to which Shaw then dedicated her life. Nevertheless, this research argues that religion ceased to be a central aspect of Shaw's life and political analysis soon after she became involved in the women's suffrage movement. Consequently, her contributions to post-1890 religious controversies are not significant.[19]

Shaw's influence as a speaker and theorist has similarly been underexplored by feminist historians. Shaw gave a remarkable number of speeches, lectures, and sermons, fifteen thousand by one estimate, reaching most probably well over a million people directly. In his 1960 dissertation, Wil Linkugel collected one thousand-plus pages of these speeches and sermons, yet these are seldom referenced as sources of suffrage arguments or feminist theory. Though it is difficult to measure the impact of one woman's speeches on a country's attitude toward women's rights, it is clear that ignoring or discounting the impact and content of a major activist's addresses leaves our scholarship incomplete.[20]

Race privilege is an unstated factor in many biographies of white women and is often undifferentiated from economic privilege. Shaw's lack of class standing allows us to see more clearly what benefits she gained as a result of her status within the dominant racial group. Clearly her struggles for independence, though impressive, would have involved significantly higher and different hurdles if she had not been white, English-speaking, Christian, and literate. Comparing and contrasting Shaw's life with other non-privileged, independent white women leaders—including Mary Anderson, Leonora O'Reilly, and Pauline Newman—and Black women leaders—such as Anna Julia Cooper and Mary McLeod Bethune—helps delineate how women's struggles for autonomy depended on race, region, and other factors.[21]

Labeled a racist, even a white supremacist, in some analyses, such conclusions fail to consider the whole of Shaw's life and the era in which she was a public figure. As an individual and as a leader Shaw was conscious of race issues and prejudices; she claims sympathy for the causes of African Americans and American Indians from an early age. She endorsed universal suffrage even when there were many calls for qualified or educated suffrage. Further, Shaw opposed efforts by white southern suffragists to expand their influence. Although Shaw never wavered from that commitment in her rhetoric, it is certainly true that she struggled to actualize her beliefs. Fearful of another race-based split in the movement, she failed to confront the reactionary racial politics and strategies of the NAWSA at the turn of the century while she was the NAWSA vice president. However, in an era when the overwhelming majority of the white American populace was convinced of their racial superiority and/or indifferent to the oppression of people of color, and when even progressive women such as Jane Addams took stands that don't stand up to today's scrutiny, Shaw's and others' stands on racial issues demand finer gradations beyond the label of "racist." Hopefully, this examination provides a more nuanced analysis of how Shaw responded to racial/ethnic oppression and the demands of African Americans and other people of color.[22]

The first fifty-seven years of Anna Howard Shaw's life are rich and fascinating for what they add to our understandings of women, gender, and the struggle for women's rights in the nineteenth century. The scholars who have considered her background have generally agreed with Aileen Kraditor that Shaw was "one of the most remarkable in a group of remarkable suffrage leaders." This author has no argument with that assessment.[23]

That agreement doesn't, however, extend to the accepted evaluations of the last fifteen years of Shaw's life when her biography and the history of suffrage almost completely overlap. This research questions the conclusions that have been widely accepted and perpetuated by feminist historians and historians of the suffrage movement since Eleanor Flexner published her

Century of Struggle in 1959. A major difficulty has been the paucity of scholarship devoted to her. Consequently, most writers simply repeat the phrases concerning Shaw that originated with the early suffrage scholars and base their subsequent analyses on the early assessments. This book questions the validity of the conclusions about Shaw and her leadership. Do the sources we have on Shaw's life support the scholarly and popular views of her?[24]

Rereading *A Century of Struggle* after researching Shaw's life, it is easy to see that there is something amiss in how Flexner views Shaw. In less than a page, using only one manuscript collection and one convention proceedings as her sources, Flexner dismisses as insignificant the over thirty years of Shaw's rhetoric and leadership, her decade as NAWSA vice president, and her eleven-plus years in the NAWSA presidency. Flexner ignores totally Shaw's 1890 work in South Dakota and the 1895–1896 work in California. Regarding Shaw's presidency (as noted, the NAWSA's longest), Flexner mentions when Shaw became president, argues that she was a difficult person and an inadequate leader, notes a few interactions with Alice Paul and Lucy Burns, and then announces her resignation. The tack that Flexner takes is that, when noting problems within the movement, especially with the NAWSA, she attributes them all to Shaw's leadership, but when covering positive results, she never mentions Shaw.[25]

Beyond her conclusions about Shaw's presidency, Flexner argued that Alice Paul and Carrie Chapman Catt were *the* important twentieth-century leaders and, by omission, that Shaw wasn't. Further, Flexner also believed that the work suffrage women did during World War I was essential to gaining victory, but Shaw receives little recognition for that contribution.[26]

Eleanor Flexner set the tone concerning Shaw when she wrote that Shaw's "gifts were many, but administrative ability was not among them." Subsequent writers have tended to emphasize the negative while ignoring any of the positives when assessing Shaw. In her 1965 book, *The Ideas of the Women's Suffrage Movement, 1890–1920,* Kraditor states that Shaw had "truly great oratorical skills," but that during her term, the "movement was stagnating, Miss Shaw's administrative deficiencies made the organization's problems worse." William O'Neill, in 1969, expands these descriptions of Shaw's abilities to include rather damning and misogynist statements about her as a person. "Anna Howard Shaw was short and fat with a broad seamed face and a disposition to match. No one else in the woman movement fitted so perfectly the stereotype promoted by anti-suffragists of the sharp-tongued, man-hating feminist." He adds a little further on, "Men admired her least of all."[27]

Most scholars since have used these three foundational texts as the basis for their own assessments. Marjorie Spruill writes that Shaw had "renown as an orator, not as an organizer"; Ellen Carol DuBois labels Shaw as "the ineffectual president of the National American Woman Suffrage Association." Linda Ford, in Jean Baker's relatively recent volume, repeats "ineffectual leader" but goes on to conclude that this pioneering minister, doctor, and orator, "unlike her nineteenth-century predecessor, did not have a militant bone in her body." The list goes on with statements of increasing certainty, yet without much, if any, additional research or recognition of Shaw's background and identity. Many scholarly and popular histories simply ignore the fact that Shaw was head of the largest suffrage organization for almost twelve years or made major contributions to the national and international movements. There have been a few exceptions to this trend, with the works of Sarah Hunter Graham, Leila Rupp, and Mineke Bosch being important among the published works. Unfortunately Graham passed away before she completed her volume. The other two books focus on Shaw's international contributions. In some cases, other authors note indicators that, if fully explored, might have changed the accepted view of Shaw's leadership, but they stop short of challenging the established conclusions about Shaw. Among the unpublished works based on primary research and focused exclusively on Shaw, writers have come to very different conclusions.[28]

Even if Flexner's, Kraditor's, and O'Neill's analyses made sense when they wrote, it is now over fifty years since Flexner published *Century of Struggle*, and the expansion of women's history was considered explosive twenty years ago. In those years, so many historians have written with such certainty about Shaw's presidency or written her off as unimportant, that it has been difficult not to imagine that there is some conclusive evidence to support their views. After over a decade and a half of research, I haven't found that material. As a result many statements about Shaw seem embarrassingly hackneyed and simplistic. They are also quite problematic since these questionable conclusions have tainted other scholarship.[29]

What I have found and what I argue for in the second half of this book is a different and a more complete and complex view of Anna Howard Shaw's suffrage contributions. Three of the last four chapters cover her years as NAWSA president, and the final chapter considers her life after her 1915 resignation. This section picks up the argument that originated with the late Sara Hunter Graham. Graham found evidence of a suffrage renaissance during Shaw's presidency that contradicted earlier conclusions about these years. Expanding on Graham's findings, this volume puts Shaw at the center of that revitalization, finding that she initiated much of this change, while acknowledging that such changes produced upheavals within the movement. Could Shaw have avoided such conflicts or handled them more adroitly? Yet beyond those concerns are other important developments that Shaw spearheaded, including the rededication to the federal amendment, the establishing of a centrally located national headquarters, the recruitment of new benefactors, a diversification of the movement's constituency, the development of novel fund-raising strategies, and the embracing of innovative publicity efforts.[30]

Additionally, a close study of Shaw's presidency brings race and class to the fore. Shaw assumed the NAWSA leadership when there was a broad trend in the United States toward support for qualified suffrage. Such views were often linked to this era's anti-Black and anti-immigration sentiments, and in the South, to states' rights advocacy, opposition to any federal voting amendment, and efforts to guarantee white supremacy. The NAWSA had begun to respond to this shift in the 1890s with the "Southern Strategy" and the courting of southern white suffragists. In 1904 when Shaw became the NAWSA president, she inherited a slate of officers that included two formidable southern leaders, Laura Clay of Kentucky and Kate Gordon of Louisiana. These two women were the national representatives of an empowered group of white women who were reformers, even progressives, on many issues, except on the issue of race and the rights of people who had formerly been enslaved. While scholars such as Marjorie Spruill document how the NAWSA and Shaw finally halted the increasing influence of these women and their bolder white supremacist efforts, neither Spruill nor others truly credit Shaw for ending the NAWSA's conservative slide. As noted earlier, there has not been a full discussion considering how Shaw's stands on race, especially how her conflicts with Laura Clay and Kate Gordon, contributed to the opposition that dogged her leadership.[31]

The second important issue has to do generally with money but includes concerns ranging from the organization's finances and fund-raising through class differences and the institution of salaries for some of the officers. One would expect that the economic backgrounds of the NAWSA and its leaders would be a major focus of research, especially for those who value a materialist analysis. The years of Shaw's presidency not only saw important growth in the amount of money raised and available for suffrage work, but they also witnessed economic transformations tied directly to the fact that Shaw was a working woman. That she receive a salary was a condition of her presidency. The Thomas-Garrett Fund, arranged by Susan B. Anthony during the last year of her life, changed the NAWSA by providing such monies to pay Shaw and certain other NAWSA officers. Instituting salaries resulted in the professionalization of the NAWSA work and opened the door for the hiring of a greater diversity of women, including single working mothers. This arrangement also forced and then fostered one of the most important relationships of Shaw's presidency, the one between her and Bryn Mawr College President M. Carey Thomas, the fund's chief administrator.[32]

Money-related issues fueled personal and professional tensions throughout Shaw's tenure. With all the other women on Shaw's original slate of officers having similar class and family backgrounds, it is important to consider whether this confrontation contained aspects of class prejudice. In this era, many of the elite were suspicious of people who had to earn their livings, believing them to be more open to influence/corruption than the rich were. Documents suggest that some of these officers questioned the appropriateness of having a wage-earning woman as head of the NAWSA. Tensions reached such a level during Shaw's presidency that on several occasions certain women charged Shaw with either misuse of funds or actual corruption.[33]

As noted, much of suffrage scholarship states that Shaw was an ineffective administrator, but seldom defines the basis for this conclusion. Further, such views may come from the contrast between Shaw, who didn't centralize power and decision-making, and Carrie Chapman Catt, who did but at the expense of democratic processes. Was money at the core of this difference also? Catt, by 1915 a wealthy widow, came into the presidency controlling the fortune Mrs. Frank Leslie had left to suffrage work. Twelve years earlier, at the start of her presidency, neither Shaw nor the NAWSA had any comparable personal or institutional monies. Shaw's lack of financial clout may have encouraged her to maintain democratic structures within the NAWSA, a factor that Graham viewed in a positive light. Further, Shaw was willing to take risks and have faith in other suffragists' abilities. In many cases her faith and trust were justified when women and men at various levels of "the cause" proved capable of the type of creative and sustained efforts needed for victorious state campaigns, innovative publicity efforts, and numerous other new and ingenious political strategies. There were problems during Shaw's presidency, some Shaw could have avoided. Yet conflicts are not inherently negative, and some shouldn't or can't be avoided.[34]

Among the repeated conclusions about Shaw is the view that she fulfilled the stereotype of the shrill suffragist and that she alienated men. Shaw was "sharp-tongued," but writer after writer from her era comments on her quickness, her humor, and her warmth. In appearance, her prematurely gray and then white hair, lively eyes, dimples, ready smile, and generous, matronly figure in fact contradicted the general characterizations of women's rights activists as angular, severe, intense, and haughty. Throughout her career Shaw knew that she needed to convert men, even more than women, to the cause. She not only spoke directly to men in her speeches, but reached out to male allies and politicians with significant success. In one example from late in her life, no less a figure than President Woodrow Wilson held her in such high esteem that he twice requested her help, once to head women's efforts during World War I through the Woman's Committee of the Council for National Defense and after the war to help garner support for the League of Nations.[35]

Shaw is regularly acknowledged as the movement's greatest orator—even those who opposed Shaw acknowledged the power of her oratorical "magic."

Given the fact that she was a master of reading her audiences from her long and successful years at the pulpit and podium, Shaw's talent as a publicist should be studied. Of what significance were the new media and technologies, including film and automobiles, and Shaw's popular autobiography?[36]

In challenging and rebutting what appears to be fifty years of misinformation and superficial analyses, compounded by the lack of research on Shaw mentioned earlier, it is a struggle to keep a balanced view and tone. My goal is not to replace one set of conclusions with another, but to urge us to consider two core changes to Shaw scholarship. First we must consider what the sources actually tell us. Certainly many of the best documents on Shaw are compromised. Shaw's executors destroyed the one thousand letters between Susan B. Anthony and Shaw as well as the thousands of letters between Lucy and Anna. M. Carey Thomas edited her letters and papers before her death. Yet Shaw was a prolific letter writer and traveler. I have no doubt there are sources out there still to be discovered. So this first goal is to present the best current data on Anna Howard Shaw and to assess what we do know about her, what stories aren't supported by current sources, and what we can't know. Wanting to avoid adding to misinformation, I have resisted filling in the narrative when I don't have solid sources.

The second goal is to open up the analyses and consider the possibility of other views of Shaw. Consequently, this biography should be considered a first, if very overdue, step in rectifying and rehabilitating Shaw as a significant woman in suffrage and U.S. history. What this book isn't is a history of the movement or even the NAWSA, as much as it might contribute to those studies. Hopefully, future studies will further pick up from here.

Anna Howard Shaw was an extraordinary woman who constructed a singular life. Her full story is so rich and complex that integrating its lessons into our current scholarship deepens and enlivens U.S. women's history. Shaw was everywoman; she was also an uncommon woman. In the liminal space that she inhabited she presents a deep critique of hegemonic beliefs about nineteenth- and early-twentieth-century womanhood. This research fundamentally questions the currently accepted narrative and conclusions about her leadership of the woman suffrage movement along with suggesting major revisions in suffrage history generally. Hopefully, these challenges are provocative enough to spur further studies into a movement and its leaders, all of whom are too frequently dismissed as only bourgeois and racist. As the opening quotation makes clear, Shaw was esteemed during her lifetime and even up until the 1950s, yet ironically she has been marginalized by scholars of women's history since then. Forty-plus years after the reemergence of the field of women's history, our scholarship needs to revisit the story of Anna Howard Shaw.

CHAPTER I

The Development
of a Dissenter (1847–1870)

> B orn of an overworked mother burdened with the entire care
> of six children at a time when even for the well-to-do there
> were but few conveniences and little labor-saving machinery
> to lighten the load. . . . Can anyone wonder that mothers bore
> offspring wearied at birth, looked upon life without joy and filled
> early graves. . . . So I came into existence a tiny, underfed child,
> robbed before birth of the vigor and health which are the
> birthright of every human being.

Anna Howard Shaw faced an uphill battle from the start.[1] She was born on St. Valentine's Day in 1847, in Newcastle-Upon-Tyne in northeast England, the sixth child and the third daughter of a bankrupt Scottish family. While all members of such struggling families in the mid–nineteenth century faced bleak and limited futures, girl-children, if they survived, had even fewer opportunities. Most would see lives that reproduced their mothers' existences of the inevitable marriage, uncontrolled maternity, and domestic drudgery. Nothing in Shaw's background set her apart from the millions of other baby girls born to poor families. Nothing suggested that this child's life would not follow the expected course given her class, race, sex, and family—nothing except perhaps her will to survive. Yet, through some combination of factors, this one girl-child found other possibilities and created a different script for her life.[2]

Certainly Shaw was born into a time of change. The old stone row house her family occupied at her birth was fewer than two hundred yards from where workers were finishing the great Newcastle Railway Station that would transform this expanding northern industrial center. Perhaps some spirit of this innovation of travel imprinted itself on her. Or perhaps she sensed her family's yearning for something else, something better. Although the Shaws could give this girl baby little in the way of material goods, they did instill in her a pride in her heritage. The stories of "fighting Shaws" of northern Scotland from her father's heritage and the Grants and Stotts on her mother's side who were religious dissenters and nonconformists may have inspired her to believe that she had the right to determine her own destiny.[3]

Re-creating Shaw's early years is a challenge. While many of the middle-class girls who would be her colleagues years later in the suffrage and other struggles were encouraged to keep self-reflective journals, Shaw hardly had the leisure or inclination to sit and write. Her father, mother, and siblings, though literate, were too poor and too busy to leave personal documents, diaries, or even portraits. Little beyond public records, a few photographs, and Shaw's own recollections from later in her life provide documentation of her first twenty-three years. Certainly, by the time Shaw produced her autobiography, she was an accomplished speaker and storyteller who knew how to create a dramatic tale. As a result it is difficult to verify the accuracy of many of her stories.[4]

We do know that the birth certificate from the General Records Office in Newcastle states that this child was named *Ann* Howard Shaw. She was called Annie by her family and most everyone else during her early life; the more dignified "Anna" came later. "Ann" probably came from one of her mother's sisters, but "Howard" remains a mystery. While there is a story still believed among some of her supporters that she took Howard as a middle name to suggest that she had been married (and the *New York Times* among other papers often called her "Mrs. Shaw"), the earliest record of her existence states otherwise. "Howard" was on her birth certificate. Neither older sister had such a distinctive middle name, nor are there any Howards in her known genealogy except a nephew born years later.[5]

Whatever the explanation might be, it was quite a name for this infant whose welcome into this desperate family could easily be questioned. It is not that she wasn't loved—she remembered both of her parents with the great affection of a cherished child—but for her mother this was yet another birthing to survive and, if so fortunate, from which to recover. By the time of Anna's birth, the Shaw family was already on a downward spiral from a promising, if marginal, middle-class position, where they had been able to give their children educational opportunities and a modest home, to a bleak and hungry life in a few dark crowded rooms. In 1847, Thomas and Nicolas (a feminine Scottish name, accent on the second syllable) Shaw already had five children: Eleanor, James, Thomas, John, and Mary.[6]

Thomas Shaw (1813–1895) was born in Radcliffe, near Manchester, in Lancashire. His class status is hard to determine. Anna's autobiography tells us that her paternal grandfather had been a "gentleman" who had squandered the family's resources and abruptly died, leaving the widowed Eleanor Robinson Shaw to raise her two sons. The younger son, Thomas, trained in the wallpaper embossing trade. Though Anna provides little background on her father's immediate family or her father's early life, she proudly traced his paternal family back to the Shaws of Rothiemurchus and their stern castle on the island of Loch-an-Eilan in the northern Highlands. These Shaws migrated to England in the hard times that hit Scotland in the 1690s, but the specific journey of Anna's ancestors is lost. Records suggest that Thomas's mother, Eleanor Robinson, was born and raised in Alnwick, Northumberland.[7]

Shaw's most quoted description of her father succinctly captures her views of him: "Like most men, my dear father should never have married." She goes on to remark on his sweet and thoughtful nature but notes that he was so idealistic that he was irresponsible in practical matters. Although his youngest daughter portrayed Shaw as a failed patriarch, he was fondly remembered by others as extroverted, gregarious, and intellectual. He loved to read to others and was a master storyteller who could captivate and hold an audience—hints of the source of his daughter's great talent. A Big Rapids, Michigan, newspaper, many years later, commented on his presence at a wedding reception, stating that his "genial face and ready wit made fun for all." A photograph of his Civil War Company captured an image of a serious and dignified officer, and the photograph in Shaw's autobiography shows a man still handsome at eighty.[8]

In contrast to her silence on her father's family, Shaw wrote at length about her mother's family, honoring her maternal grandmother as a righteous and heroic dissenter. Anna's grandmother, Nicolas Grant, had married James Stott of Ellingham, a parish of seven hundred and forty people located eight miles north of the Northumberland country seat, Alnwick. Soon after, the Stotts settled in Alnwick, a medieval town of cobblestone streets and city gates dominated by Alnwick Castle, home of the Duke of Northumberland for seven hundred years and now famous as the Hogwarts in two Harry Potter films. Alnwick was and is in the borderlands between England and Scotland. It is north of Hadrian's Wall and only thirty miles south of the current boundary of Scotland. James Stott first appears on the public records of the militia for 1798. The church records from this period document various Stotts as active leaders within the town's many nonconformist or dissenting churches.[9]

Anna's grandfather, James Stott, was a driver of the royal-mail stagecoach between Alnwick and Newcastle, a position that gave him a lower-middle-class status in that era. Starting in 1798, Nicolas and James had seven children, including her namesake, Nicolas, who was born in 1810. While the children were still quite young, James Stott died in a stagecoach accident. In an era before regularized social welfare, his widow and their children became part of Alnwick's "Established Poor," who received a weekly allowance from the town coffers. Nicolas also received a position at Alnwick Castle.[10]

In spite of, or perhaps because of, these hardships, Nicolas Grant Stott was an independent thinker and activist. Unitarian at a time when such believers could not legally follow their faith, Widow Stott adamantly refused to pay tithes to support the Church of England. Consequently local tax collectors confiscated a portion of her belongings each year in what became a ritual that the entire community observed. From this, her resistance to intolerance, Nicolas Stott became an inspiration and role model for her granddaughter.[11]

As a result of her father's death and her mother's subsequent employment at the castle, Nicolas and her siblings entered the Duke's and Duchess's schools where "attendance . . . was dependant [*sic*] on a parent being an employee of the estate." The Duchess's school, founded in 1808 by Duchess Julia three years before the Duke's school opened, emphasized "needlework, along with the basics of reading, writing and mathematics" for the young women in its charge. At this school, the younger Nicolas not only gained a basic education, but she also mastered the skills of the seamstress, one of the few positions open to women. She would call on this training at a number of crucial points in her life and pass her skills on to her daughters.[12]

None of the ambivalent feelings that Anna had toward her father clouded her memories of her mother. Throughout her life Anna practically canonized the women she loved; her mother and grandmother were the first among these women. To her youngest daughter, Nicolas Shaw was as beautiful in spirit as she was in appearance. The line drawing of Nicolas Stott at eighteen in Shaw's autobiography shows a delicately pretty, dark-haired young woman. Though physically frail—a semi-invalid by the time her family settled in Michigan—she was, to Anna, the powerful emotional foundation of the family. While Anna's father was by tradition and law the head of the family and its intellectual leader, Nicolas Shaw was the one who had to temper the dreams of her impractical husband and stretch whatever resources they had to ensure meeting the material needs of the family. Anna saw the great physical and psychological burdens her mother and other women bore, giving her a deep knowledge of the significance of all the types of unrecognized work that women did. In spite of the hard life she led, Nicolas Shaw also passed to her children an optimist's view of the world. Anna wrote that she benefited from "the cheerful and brave spirit inherited from my mother, who rarely ever lost courage or loosed her hold on a sunny, hopeful disposition."[13]

Anna leaves no story, romantic or otherwise, about how her parents met. She simply states, "My father and mother met in Alnwick, and were married in February 1835." Though Nicolas Stott and Thomas Shaw were "dissenters," their marriage had to be registered in the Church of England. It is listed in the records of St. Andrew's Church, Newcastle-Upon-Tyne, on entries of the last day of January, 1835.[14]

The 1841 British census has the Shaws as residing on Blenheim Street in the Westgate section of Newcastle, the oldest "suburb" of the city, up from the River Tyne and outside the ancient city walls. With Thomas and Nicolas were their first three children—Eleanor, 5; James Stott, 3; and John, known as Jack, 1, who had all been baptized at the Hanover Square Unitarian Chapel, a famous congregation whose records date back to 1752. Anna's paternal grandmother, Eleanor Robinson Shaw, lived close by on Westmorland St.[15]

On this census Thomas is identified as a wallpaper embosser, yet soon he quit this trade. In spite of the political unrest of the 1840s that saw the Chartists riots and demands for electoral reform, the continuation of the Corn Laws and the positive economic outlook of this decade were enough to push Thomas to start his own business as a grain dealer. Unfortunately this was a case of bad timing. He had barely established his enterprise when the repeal of the Corn Laws that had subsidized the price of grain undercut his trade and brought about financial difficulties for the Shaw enterprise. By the mid-1840s, Thomas Shaw declared bankruptcy.[16]

Forced to sell their home and most of their possessions and end their sons' educations, the Shaws began to look beyond Newcastle for a new beginning. The family first tried London, but the capital was no kinder to them. They returned to Newcastle where there were at least some extended family members for support. Finally, Thomas decided they should migrate to the United States, continuing his family's search for economic opportunity and religious and political freedom, but there could be no exodus until Thomas cleared his debts.[17]

It was into this family, now at its lowest ebb materially and emotionally, that Anna was born, six years and two more children after the 1841 census. Anna was not a healthy infant. One can only imagine the state of Nicolas's health given their financial stress and the fact that she had birthed six children in twelve years. With the maternal and infant mortality rates of this period and the epidemics that swept Newcastle, the fact that the six children and their mother lived was remarkable. Throughout her life Anna would return to that fundamental question, wondering why she did survive. Yet it is also possible that she was more cherished and more indulged because she had to struggle from the start.[18]

By 1849, Anna's family sensed that they were beginning to emerge from their Dickensian existence. Nicolas bore another child, Elizabeth Nicolas, in 1849, a birth that coincided with the end of the family's indebtedness. Thomas Shaw, with the help of his family, had succeeded in paying his creditors. Leaving his wife to care for their seven children, Thomas sailed for the United States. The 1850 U.S. Census locates Thomas working as a paperstainer and living in a boarding house in Lynn, Massachusetts.[19]

Thomas may have found a new beginning, but his wife and children faced two more hard and sad years in Newcastle working to save enough money to pay for passage to the United States. The stereotypic image of nineteenth-century Newcastle as a dark and dank environment fits their lives. At fifteen, Anna's oldest sister, Eleanor, was a servant for a family on Blenheim Street, their old neighborhood. Nicolas is listed in the 1851 census as the "lodging housekeeper," while earning additional income by hand-sewing shirts for the local clergy. The Shaw family was sharing their quarters with Stott relatives, Arthur and Charles, as well as another family from Alnwick. While these cousins are listed as "scholars," none of the Shaw children were in school. This census report captures the strains and sorrows of their last months in Newcastle. Anna was again the youngest child since not long after Thomas left, the baby, Elizabeth, had died. Because she was a Unitarian, Nicolas had to travel back to Alnwick with the body of her baby on her lap to bury her; in Newcastle there was no place but a paupers' graveyard for a baby not baptized in the Church of England. Soon after, Anna's grandmother, the indomitable Nicolas Stott, passed away.[20]

Before the family could turn their faces and their hopes westward, they endured one final wrenching separation. Thomas Shaw was his mother's only surviving child. The elderly Eleanor Shaw couldn't accept the idea that she wouldn't see him or any of his family again. On the night before the group was to leave for Liverpool, she hid two of her grandsons in a hollowed out tree close to her home. Even when they were discovered, their paternal grandmother clung to them.[21]

In August 1851, Nicolas Shaw and her six children boarded the *Jacob A. Westervelt* in Liverpool, bound for New York for what was to be a seven-week passage. So horrendous was this transatlantic voyage that Anna dreaded ocean travel for the rest of her life. Any journey across the Atlantic for steerage passengers in the middle of the nineteenth century meant misery—the crowding, the food, the sanitation, the sea, and the weather. On the *Westervelt,* the Shaw family faced the additional challenge of a storm so strong that the ship lost all its power and needed to be towed back to Queenstown (Cork), Ireland, for repairs. Yet this trip also found the young Anna working and singing with the sailors who doted on her. This is an early hint of Shaw's lifelong ability to tolerate, even find some respite in, the hardships of travel and the first indication that she was at least as much of an extrovert as her father.[22]

Thomas Shaw was not there to meet the exhausted but relieved travelers when they finally disembarked in New York. Having received the erroneous report that the ship had sunk in the Atlantic, leaving no survivors, the grieving Shaw had returned to Massachusetts to prepare for his own journey back to England to arrange whatever service was held for those lost at sea. Fortunately his nightmare didn't last as long as theirs. After hearing that his family had survived, he rushed back to New York. Many years later Anna could recall her father's joyful face as he scooped her up and hugged her. He then gave her two gifts. "I can see, too, the toys he brought me—a little saw and a hatchet, which became the dearest treasures of my childish days. They were fatidical gifts, that saw and hatchet; in the years ahead of me I was to use tools as well as my brothers did, as I proved when I helped to build our frontier home."[23]

Anna used these child's tools long before the family moved to Michigan. In their first American home in the old whaling town of New Bedford, Massachusetts, Anna befriended a shipbuilder who allowed her to use her father's gifts when she accompanied him to work each day. Eventually dressed in a boy's suit appropriate for her labors, she discovered the joy of working with her hands and the satisfaction of contributing to the family's income. Her friend and mentor allowed her brothers to take all the scraps of wood from the shop for the Shaws to use as fuel, all in exchange for the pleasure of little Anna's company.[24]

Many years later, when she wrote her autobiography, Shaw suggests that by this early age, she had created an unusual identity for herself. Out in the public rather than by her mother's side within the home, Anna moved among women and men with a precocious self-confidence. Not only was she a productive person who could make an economic contribution to her family, but she was already demonstrating her preference for nontraditional activities. She enjoyed work, particularly the hard physical labor associated with the artisans and laboring men, rather than the genteel and domestic endeavors generally expected of white, middle-class women, or even the commercial or intellectual pursuits of privileged men. If Shaw felt any pressure to conform to the nineteenth-century ideals of "true womanhood," she left no record of those concerns, nor was there any Aunt March to challenge the behavior of this real life Jo. While many of her sex who became independent women recalled having tolerant families who allowed them wide freedoms during their childhoods—today we would call them tomboys—none felt or assumed economic responsibilities at such a young age. All these experiences formed the foundation of Shaw's gender identity and analysis.[25]

As industrialization was transforming Massachusetts, economic developments soon pushed the Shaw family to move from New Bedford on the coast to a new mill town, Lawrence, in the North on the Merrimac River. Lawrence would be their home for the next seven years, during the nation-changing decade of the 1850s. Here the Shaws experienced the energy and instability of a new city. Founded in the 1840s when several industrialists determined the optimal site for a dam on the Merrimac River, Lawrence already had 3,577 residents in 1847 when it received its name. Although

1851 brought a short depression, by 1853, the opportunities created by its factories had attracted 13,000 people, including the Shaw family. Textile mills dominated, but the city included a wide range of industries including several paper manufacturers.[26]

If Anna ever had what might be considered a typical childhood or a stable home life, it would have been during these years. The family lived on Prospect Hill, located on a bluff above the river in a section of the city that was thinly populated by a diverse cross section of the city's residents from manufacturers to operatives, shoemakers to papermakers. This was a semirural area, removed from the factories and immigrants' housing that lined the river banks; the street where the Shaws lived didn't even have a name until the late 1850s.[27]

While the Shaws were rebuilding their lives, they were becoming Americans. Once again they were on the verge of middle-class status. Unlike the many Irish immigrants settled in Lawrence who were kept apart by their religion as well their ethnicity, the literate and religiously liberal Shaws could join the most prominent community leaders at the local Unitarian church and other community events. Anna celebrated the Fourth of July with the rest of the city, learned of garden parties from the wealthier neighbors, and ate her first banana, including the peel, experiences she shared with her sister, Mary, only two years her elder.[28]

Most retellings of Shaw's youth highlight her years on the frontier and suggest, in perhaps a Lincolnesque parallel, that she was primarily self-taught. Such stories ignore the Lawrence years. For seven years, Shaw had access to one of the most innovative public school systems in the country. By the mid-1850s, Lawrence had ten grammar schools, nine middle schools, and a high school. Anna as well as some of her other siblings probably attended the Prospect School, located within a few blocks of the Shaw home, a school building still standing today. Here her curriculum was at least equal to that of most children in the United States of the time, when many children, especially those of immigrants, were fortunate to be able to complete a few years of education. Though Shaw left few records from this early schooling, there is one surviving comment. Shaw was an attentive and diligent student, but she had no gift for spelling.[29]

The Massachusetts years introduced Anna, and all the Shaws, to the unsettled politics of the United States in the 1850s. In Lawrence, Anna heard and read about the issues and opinions of the era, especially the debates over slavery and race. The publication of *Uncle Tom's Cabin*, talk of war, and debates among abolitionists reached Anna and the rest of her family. One day she found an African American woman hidden in their basement, though when the excited Anna told her mother of her discovery, her mother worked to convince Anna that she had only imagined seeing the fugitive woman.[30]

In her autobiography, Shaw wrote of how her knowledge about women's realities broadened when she became intrigued by another woman in the neighborhood, a "beautiful and mysterious" lady who lived in the house closest to them and about whom the adults spoke "only in whispers." The fascinating woman was a prostitute.[31]

When this woman noticed little Anna's keen observations of her as she went out riding, an unlikely friendship developed. After careful negotiations, Anna was allowed to visit this woman. Anna never saw any of the other women who lived and worked in that house or the men who "called" there. Of this time, Shaw wrote, "My second friendship, and one which had a strong influence on my after-life, was formed in Lawrence . . . but the memory of her in after-years, and the impression she had made on my susceptible young mind, led me first into the ministry, next into medicine, and finally into suffrage-work." Unlike her later colleagues who might have seen prostitutes as "other," as a result of this early friendship Shaw saw them as individuals, women forced to work when there were few options for women to make a decent living. To her, prostitutes were part of the diversity of the female experience.[32]

Had Anna's family stayed in Lawrence with its proximity to a range of educational and industrial opportunities, her life might have developed quite differently. Perhaps she might have found herself part of the industrial army of young women in the textile mills, or if the economy smiled on the fortunes of her family, she might have entered one of the women's colleges opening in the state. Those possibilities all disappeared when Thomas Shaw again decided to uproot his family. Possibly concerned by the economic difficulties sweeping the country that forced the closure of many of Lawrence's factories, the threat of war, or the impulse to seek greater opportunities, in 1857 Thomas Shaw purchased one hundred and sixty acres of land in the wilderness of western Michigan.[33]

One wonders what the senior Shaw thought as he made this decision. From the earliest years of European settlement, the great expanse of putatively open land lured people for whom land ownership had marked freedom and full citizenship. But Thomas and Nicolas were well into middle age when Thomas decided they would now become farmers in the "old northwest." The land Shaw purchased in Mecosta County had magnificent forests—maples, pines, and other species that were hundreds of years old and not infrequently one hundred and fifty feet high. This resource would fuel the economy of this region for years as lumbermen clear-cut section after section, sending the logs by roads and rivers to the mills and furniture factories, supporting each part of the economy in turn. What this land was *not* was farm land. If Thomas Shaw had seen his land before he claimed it in 1857, he might have realized this. But he was a dreamer. One hundred and sixty acres of Michigan land must have held great promise in spite of the fact that he had not one bit of farming experience in his life. Coupled with his age, Thomas must have expected this would be a family endeavor.[34]

In her autobiography, Anna recounts the family move with dramatic detail, suggesting that even fifty-five years later she still sharply felt the trauma of the whole experience. As he had done when the family left England, Thomas went first, this time with two of his sons. The three men traveled a thousand miles to claim their land in the northwest quadrant of Michigan's Lower Peninsula. Sparsely populated even today, the homestead was over sixty miles from the closest rail connection in Grand Rapids (population eight thousand in 1860) and fifty miles inland from Lake Michigan with its prevailing winds and winter blizzards. These three men cleared just enough land to erect a basic but decent-sized log cabin—four walls, a roof, a fireplace and spaces for a door and windows—before Thomas Sr. and Jack headed back to Massachusetts. They left James to guard and maintain the homestead.[35]

Perhaps reasoning that the non–wage-earning members of the family could be of more use in Michigan than in Massachusetts, Thomas sent his wife, three daughters, and youngest son west while he, Thomas Jr., and Jack stayed in Massachusetts earning wages for the next eighteen months. Whatever the logic, Nicolas, now fifty-one years old and a semi-invalid; Eleanor, a young woman of twenty-five; Mary, fourteen; Anna, twelve; and Henry, the youngest Shaw at six, stoically set off. They joined the many families who set out to settle the Midwest and West. Their one consolation might have been that they could travel by rail over most of their journey.[36]

That relative luxury ended in Grand Rapids. James met his mother, sisters, and brother there. The brave band loaded the rented wagon, which Anna thought resembled a hearse, with all they had brought from Massachusetts and all they could purchase in Grand Rapids. On some level they knew that they were venturing "in(to) the wilderness," for they tried to bring everything they would need for the next year, including a box of piglets. With their mother and supplies in the wagon, the children and oxen began to walk through old growth forests, among trees over one hundred feet tall, without settlements, often without paths, searching for detours to traverse deep ravines and streams. They walked for seven long days, finding shelter at night at some farmhouse or crude travelers' hut.[37]

The family maintained a degree of optimism as they journeyed, however slowly, toward their new home. Only James knew what waited for them. Anna and her younger brother Henry were still young and innocent enough to feel a sense of adventure. This environment was a new world for them. On the other hand, the older girls and their mother must have begun to question any expectations they had of tidy fields bordered by hedgerows or villages linked by paths or roads, such as those they had seen in the rural areas of England.

When the family arrived at their destination, an incredible rush of shock probably coupled with exhaustion hit Nicolas Shaw. Whatever hope she might have had that a true farm awaited them left her when she finally saw the homestead her husband had prepared for her. This was no home. It was a crudely built cabin with no floors or windows. There was no well, no crops to sustain them over the winter, and no land cleared for a spring planting. After their long and harrowing journey, this reality crushed Nicolas.[38]

Anna remembered this moment vividly half a century later. Hours passed as their mother remained huddled against the wall of the cabin with her face buried in her hands, unmoving and unresponsive, her consciousness apparently far from her confused children. The day turned to night while the forest came alive with the sounds of animals and the wind. Finally James built a fire for some solace and protection. After what seemed to the children an eternity, their mother finally emerged from whatever state she had entered, but, in her youngest daughter's eyes, she was transformed and aged by this stunning disappointment.[39]

This event was Anna's first painful step into adulthood and a consciousness that patriarchal power could be dangerous. Before this point Anna had a carefree if eventful childhood in which she never doubted that the adults in her life would care for and protect her. Now she saw the horrific effects of her father's questionable decisions. When she wrote her autobiography, Shaw still felt the sense of abandonment keenly. She portrayed her father's attitude as one where "It remained for us to strengthen our bodies, to meet the conditions in which he had placed us, and to survive if we could."[40]

Anna had no choice but to share the responsibility for her family's survival and to shoulder the anxieties. All the expected hierarchies and structures of the traditional family were superfluous at this point, as they were for many female-headed kin groups, even though in this case the physical absence of the father was temporary. The whole family realized just how hard they would have to work just to feed and shelter themselves. In their own version of a democracy, the Shaw family assessed their situation and divided the work. While Anna's mother and two older sisters were responsible for the "inside" work, she chose to work outside with her oldest brother James. Young Henry joined them. Anna embraced the rigorous challenges. "I loved work—it has always been my favorite form of recreation—and my spirit rose to the opportunities of it which smiled on us from every side." In this struggle Anna forged a lifelong bond with James.[41]

Soon another crisis challenged these pioneers. James, the only adult male among them, became ill and needed to return east for medical care. Now onto the shoulders of the two youngest Shaws, Anna and Henry, fell all the responsibilities for procuring food and water. Through some combination of naïveté, energy, and luck, they managed to make it through the first winter by fishing, gathering, hunting, and hauling water from the local stream. In the spring they took up the actual farming. All the hardships she faced later in life must have paled next to her memories of her first Michigan winter and spring, of trying to plant a crop among the stumps of huge trees, or of trying to remove those stumps when she knew her family's survival depended on her work.[42]

It was in these unexpected responsibilities that Anna discovered that she was not only capable of sustained physical labor but that she thrived on it. With only the help of a young man from a neighboring farm, Anna dug the well that would serve the family for the next twelve years. She was particularly proud of this accomplishment since a consistent source of decent water was critical for the whole endeavor. She and Henry tapped the maple trees in the spring and produced one hundred and fifty pounds of sugar and a barrel of syrup for the family. The girl who had been a sickly and undersized infant was now a strong and capable worker.[43]

In these months Anna built on her nascent analysis of women's status and gender norms, though, of course, she would never have used those terms. Anna realized that she was just as skilled in this work as her brothers and the other young men of the area. In this frontier world, there were no pedestals for idle women, little time for self-reflection, and no dearth of meaningful labor. Even her invalid mother worked as she could, making and maintaining the clothing for the family. Anna's conclusions, based in her own realities, were certainly at odds with prevalent nineteenth-century theories that increasingly posited that women and men were biologically more different than they were similar, or at least the "more evolved" were, and that women were physically inferior, but more moral. She hardly found all men were bodily and intellectually more robust than women. As a result of her father's decisions, she understood that many women had no choice but to be strong and that they couldn't rely on male protection.[44]

Nor were Anna's observations limited to those of white settlers. In Massachusetts, Anna and her family had been involved in one aspect of the American racial landscape, the national struggle over the position of free and enslaved people of African descent. In Michigan the Shaws came to own land that had, until recently, been part of the domain of Native Americans. As a child of settlers in northern Michigan, Shaw and her family had had a range of interactions with the native peoples, the Potawatomi and Ottawa. Though she started with the traditional fears, Anna and her family soon had positive contacts with native women and men, including exchanging foods and sharing celebrations. The frightening experiences were limited to times when native men had alcohol, and in Shaw's writings this is the earliest mention of the problem of alcohol abuse. On the other hand, Shaw saw that the work done by women of these tribes and the responsibilities of the homesteading women were similar; in both cases women's labors were essential to their families' and communities' survival.[45]

Thomas Shaw Sr. and his whole family are listed on the U.S. Census taken in June of 1860, one of thirty-seven households in Green Township, Mecosta County, Michigan. Almost exclusively farmers with a few hunters and trappers and one schoolteacher, the township's residents had real estate estimated as being worth from $200 to $2000, with Thomas Shaw's valued at $500. His personal property's value was $30. Though the family appears on the census as if they were all physically together in Michigan, that record reflected hope more than reality. Most likely it was still the small band of women and young Henry who were actually present on the enumeration day. At least two of the Shaw men show up on the Massachusetts census. James was among the patients in the Massachusetts General Hospital, while Tom was among those recorded as living in Lawrence.[46]

By the end of 1860, the senior Thomas Shaw had physically joined the rest of his family in Michigan. However, Thomas's lack of knowledge of farming combined with his preference for intellectual rather than physical work hardly eased Anna's duties. At thirteen, Anna saw herself as an adult, a full and productive member of the family, and she had little patience for her father's foibles. She was frustrated by his failures, failures that kept the family enterprise from being much of a success. To what extent the rest of the family shared in this strained dynamic isn't clear. The only hint is that James never rejoined the family in Michigan after he recovered from his illness.

These tensions produced the next formative event in young Anna's life. With the knowledge that her contributions to the family's survival while her father was still in Massachusetts had not earned her Thomas's respect, Anna increasingly resented how her father could do what he wanted and indulge in his preferences for contemplative activities and social exchange while the rest of the family had to struggle to pay for his choices. This all boiled over one day in a confrontation between Anna and her father.

Anna had spent the day in the woods with *her* books and *her* dreams. This day, alone with the trees and her thoughts, she felt the call of a vocation. She was awed by the experience of feeling God's will, telling her to preach and lead people to salvation. Still lost in the wonder of this insight, she rushed home to share this amazing development with her family.[47]

When Anna, radiant with excitement, finally entered her home, she found a cold welcome. Her father was furious because she hadn't been there when her mother had needed her help. "Father reproached me bitterly for being beyond reach—an idler who wasted time while mother labored. He ended a long arraignment by predicting gloomily that with such tendencies I would make nothing of my life." The unfairness of this rebuke stung Anna; her father often spent his days engrossed in his books while she labored. In her equally heated response she threw her hopes to preach and join the ministry at her father as a challenge. She finished with the announcement that one day she would go to college and that she would be worth $10,000—the largest amount she could imagine—before she died. In this exchange, Anna's wonderful dreams became encased in a hard bitter anger, and she held onto them with a level of desperation precisely because they seemed hardly plausible for this daughter of a poor Michigan farmer.[48]

Soon external developments added to these tensions and forced more changes on the family. Undoubtedly this family with abolitionist sentiments closely followed the events surrounding the election of Abraham Lincoln. The years of the Civil War were long and difficult for almost all American families, and the Shaws were no exception. When the Civil War started in April 1861, Jack volunteered immediately, enlisting in May. The younger Thomas joined the war effort in July of the next year, while Anna's father volunteered in 1863. Both Eleanor and Mary married during the war years— Eleanor to Colton Carpenter in December 1861, and the seventeen-year-old Mary to George W. Green. As her husband fought for the Union, Eleanor died giving birth to her son, Arthur.[49]

Over these years, Anna felt her plans, her hopes, and her health fading as the war dragged on. She had no choice but to remain on the homestead. She, her mother, and young Henry consoled each other in their grief over Eleanor's death, even as they faced desperate economic times. Throughout the community, there were few adult men to plant or harvest the crops. Food became a scarcer and dearer commodity, and the prices of all goods increased tremendously as the war went into its third and then fourth year.[50]

Only sixteen, Anna again shouldered the responsibility for her family's survival. In 1862, she had qualified as a schoolteacher. Her earnings from her first year of teaching, before her father volunteered, had been hers to keep. The following years, as more of the men, including the elder Shaw, left for a war that seemed endless, her family needed whatever she earned from the two thirteen-week school sessions. Even with all her mother could earn from sewing and taking in boarders and all she and Henry could produce from the farm, they could hardly keep themselves fed and pay the taxes to hold on to the land. The Shaw women faced what so many women did during wars: they labored to do the work that had always been theirs to do as well as the work that the men of the family had done. They were almost too tired to worry, but they did. While news of battles came quickly, they understood that it could take weeks to hear if Thomas or his sons had been injured, or worse. Hunger, anxiety, and exhaustion took their tolls. Anna felt herself weakening as the burdens became almost too much.[51]

Finally the war ended in 1865 with a Union victory. In spite of all their sacrifices, the Shaws counted themselves lucky. Though Thomas Shaw and Thomas Jr. had been injured, both, plus Jack, returned to Michigan. The men resumed their roles, though so much had changed during the long conflict. Anna's father, who had risen to become an assistant surgeon during the Civil War, "entered upon the practice of medicine, which he pursued for two years, but was obligated to abandon it from the inability to perform the necessary duties of the profession at night, and he resumed farming." Tom and Jack were grown men and war veterans who were now anxious to begin their own families. Since her sister, Mary, had married, Anna was the one daughter left at home to tend to those domestic responsibilities that were beyond the capabilities of her mother.[52]

Anna chafed in this role. Though she humorously retold the story of one marriage proposal, that tale was the last mention of any type of heterosexual romance. She had long known that she wanted none of traditional woman-hood, but she had few alternatives. While it is hard to envy men fighting in the bloodiest war of our history, Anna did resent her own confinement. Though most independent women of this and succeeding eras had to face breaking the "family claim," the poverty, isolation, and health issues of Thomas and Nicolas Shaw made Anna's dilemma especially difficult. Her father might ignore the work she did on the farm, but he counted on the income she contributed from her schoolteaching.[53]

The earliest images of Anna Howard Shaw survive from this post–Civil War era. One small portrait shows a dark-haired, dark-eyed, somber young woman with her hair parted in the middle and piled in curls on the top of her head. She is attractive, but her eyes are her compelling feature. Another picture includes a full-length view of Anna, with another of her sitting next to an unnamed young man. In these, Anna already sports the cropped hair that she wore for a number of years. Although her slight figure is overwhelmed by the voluminous skirt of her fashionable dress, there is still a reserved quality about her presentation with her high neckline, a small collar, and dark tie or cravat. These photographs document her appearance, her hair, her face, and her dress, but with the set poses and unwaveringly neutral facial expressions, these early images hardly capture the lively energy that already set her apart from her peers. In spite of her internal struggles, Anna was recognized as a charismatic individual and a leader among the young people of the area around Big Rapids.[54]

Another set of photographs documents the beginning of Shaw's lifelong friendship with Clara Osborn. The Osborn family arrived from upstate New

York in 1868 and took up residence in Big Rapids, close to the home of Anna's sister Mary. Two years apart in age, Clara and Anna quickly became inseparable both in town and out at the Shaw farm. In one photograph, Anna and Clara posed with two additional young women, most probably their sisters. Clara found Anna to be the best of companions, always lively, adventurous, and fun. Together they wandered the farm lands and forests between Big Rapids and Green Township. With Anna as the acknowledged social leader, in their free time they attended whatever events this town offered. They confided in each other, replacing perhaps for each other the sisters who had married and set up their own homes.[55]

Anna's friendship with Clara provided an important refuge in what must have been a tremendously frustrating era of her life. Anna had expected that the end of the war would allow her to pursue her dreams, but she found that day after day, month after month, and then year after year she remained cyclically fulfilling the responsibilities that her sex and family position dictated. She taught school when she could but found it hard to save much money. Between sessions she farmed, chopped wood, and did whatever was required to assist her father, while also sewing, cooking, and doing what she could to help her mother. As she faced each new school year, she found herself no closer to having enough money to go to college. The years passed, and Anna turned twenty, twenty-one, and then twenty-two, and she now had not left this rural county for over a decade.[56]

The stark contrasts between her early years in Lawrence with all its opportunities and its connections to many of the era's social and political developments and the limited possibilities of her rural Michigan homestead fueled Anna's impatience and her ambition. She read the newspapers; she knew what was happening in the rest of the country. She already believed she could be part of the country's changes. Throughout the United States, women had expanded their roles during the war. In the postwar activism, women were teaching in Freedmen's schools in the South, opening women's seminaries and then colleges, speaking out on various reforms, and expanding their spheres of influence. Women were organizing and among their causes were temperance and suffrage. Anna believed she belonged among these pioneering activists.[57]

With only Shaw's own words written over four decades later as the source for her early life, it is hard to know exactly how she weathered these years. Over time, her analyses of women's lives certainly grew in sophistication, but it is clear that at an early age Shaw understood the bases of women's critiques. And she had her own experiences of gender that informed her views. On a private level, Anna had seen and felt deeply the patriarchal power of a good and loving man. Thomas Shaw's American dream of becoming part of the landed gentry had failed. Perhaps Anna had benefited from her father's choices after all. Having to assume nontraditional adult responsibilities at the age of twelve kept her from entering a restrictive womanhood; puberty marked the end of tomboy freedoms among a number of women of her cohort. In contrast, between the ages of twelve and eighteen, Shaw shouldered responsibilities that were both beyond her years and outside her gender role. Further, she succeeded—succeeded in her view better than her father did. There is a power in knowing that you can survive, that you have the skills and strength to sustain a homestead on the edge of the frontier. This resulting self-knowledge set Shaw up well for her future. Shaw learned what she could handle. Each patriarchal abandonment strengthened her consciousness as well as broadened her survival skills.

Anna also had the lessons from the lives of the women in her family, from the economic hardships her widowed grandmothers faced through her mother's burden and her sister's death in childbirth. Increasingly she had experiences in which she saw the ranges of women's realities—fugitive Black women, American Indian women, and perhaps most unusually a prostitute. That her mother, at least, allowed Shaw to be friends with this woman gave young Anna the ability to see her as more than simply "other" or a victim. Shaw could understand women's limited economic choices. By the age of twenty-three, not only had she seen a diversity of women's choices, but she faced them herself. She had concluded that the role of "wife" would never suit her.

In the post–Civil War years, the Shaw family mourned Eleanor's death, but they also celebrated the marriages and new families of Mary, Thomas Jr., and Jack, as well as James's beginning of a medical career. Anna, energetic, ambitious, and charismatic, remained confined to the homestead by the physical and economic needs of her aging parents and by her lack of money and opportunities. Yet she never resigned herself to the fate that her future would be in this isolated farm in Michigan. She loved her parents, her whole family, but she knew she couldn't allow these domestic demands to hold her forever. Though frustrated, Shaw remained resolved to find some opening, some means to take those first steps away from the farm and away from Mecosta County and toward her own vision for her future.

CHAPTER 2

The Road to Independence (1871–1880)

The members of my family, meeting in solemn council,
sent for me, and I responded. . . . We had a long evening
together, and it was a very unhappy one. At the end of it I was
given twenty-four hours to decide whether I would choose my
people and college, or my pulpit and the arctic loneliness of a life
that held no family circle. It did not require twenty-four hours
of reflection to convince me that I must go my solitary way.

When the U.S. Census enumerator visited the Shaw family on their
farm outside of the village of Paris, Michigan, in 1870, the Civil War had been
over for five years.[1] For Anna Howard Shaw these had been five frustrating
years. From 1865 to 1870 Shaw had struggled against external realities as
well as internal conflicts. She had a vision, shaped by that early epiphany in
the woods, that God had called her to a larger life. She would not resign
herself to a world bounded by Mecosta County, Michigan; by the school
district where she had earned her license; and by the people who still arrived
by horse or by wagon to "settle" this region. In her refusal to accept the
hand that life dealt her, she was her father's daughter, the child of a dreamer
whose imagination could see better and bigger achievements. The question
was whether this daughter, whose aspirations hardly had names or shapes,
would be any more successful in realizing them than her father had been.
This youngest daughter of an immigrant farmer could conceive of a grand
future, but the means to that larger world eluded her.[2]

Given this inner turmoil, it is ironic that the census of this decade listed
Anna as a twenty-three-year-old unmarried daughter who was "at home."
That phrase conjures up ideas of a sedate young lady, in a parlor, engaged
in needlework when she wasn't receiving visitors, a young woman waiting
perhaps until the proper suitor appeared. This was not Anna's life in 1870
or ever. Clearly capable of handling traditional and nontraditional work,

Anna loved and chose any action over waiting. Her environment did not allow her the pretensions of refined domesticity; for the last eleven years a log cabin had been her home and her responsibilities had included digging wells and pulling stumps as well as teaching school. A realistic reading of the census record would suggest that Anna was between teaching sessions and occupied with all those domestic responsibilities that women generally had but which were increasingly excluded from contemporary definitions of productive work. Since her parents were in late middle age, she probably also managed much of the farm work that her father had consistently avoided. One has to wonder who labeled Anna's occupation for the permanent and official record of her in the census report.[3]

The societal barriers Shaw faced were gendered expectations modified by race and class. With no independent means of wealth, Shaw's choices appeared to be limited to marrying or resigning herself to struggle along as a respectable though impoverished schoolteacher, living in her parents' home and helping them maintain their homestead. College and entering a profession might have been emerging choices for her more privileged sisters, but pursuing that path was unrealistic for most women in Shaw's situation.

She knew if she stayed on her parents' farm, she had a home, as basic as it might have been, but she was cut off from waged work beyond the teaching positions she had held for eight years. Yet the teaching wasn't getting her anywhere. To gain access to any formal education for herself, she would have to leave that home, but go where? And how? There was no extended family—she had no grandparents, aunts, uncles, or cousins nearby or anywhere else in the United States with whom she could live. She had no entry into any other type of community that might have opened doors for her. There was no Unitarian Congregation in Big Rapids, and neither Thomas Shaw nor any of his sons had any position of significant influence at this point. Shaw's lack of opportunities highlights all the unseen but assumed resources that separated her from many of the elite or even middle-class young women of her era who were also searching for autonomy and meaningful work. Certainly many middle-class and wealthy young women were struggling against traditional expectations, pushing for educational and professional openings, and demanding the right to some measure of their families' wealth to support them as they pursued unknown futures. However, their families, unlike Anna's, had some material, familial, and social resources that these women might claim. Shaw, if she left her family, was on her own.[4]

However incongruous that 1870 census record was, it provides a definitive starting point against which to measure Shaw's achievements and an indication of how hard it would continue to be to put a name on her status. As the country faced major upheavals, including the emergence and growth of the women's rights movement, Shaw searched for ways to become part of those changes and to transgress the familial, class, sex, and geographical boundaries that had limited her. In the end, what she actually accomplished might well set the 1870s as the most remarkable period of Shaw's impressive life.[5]

At this point Anna turned to the only resource she did have beyond her own dreams, ingenuity, and determination—her sister Mary. Perhaps it was prescient that her sister, rather than her father or brothers, provided Anna with her first opportunity to break the family claim. Perhaps only Mary could understand the depth of Anna's determination. Mary could offer Anna a home, of course, because she had married a successful entrepreneur. So it was that Anna made the difficult and seemingly selfish decision to leave her parents' home, face whatever consternation this brought from other members of her family, give up teaching, and move in with her sister to seek her options in the small town of Big Rapids, Michigan, population 1600.[6]

Anna's first goal was money. In her analysis, she had to earn enough money to attend college. She knew she could do any type of work to earn that money, but the most lucrative work was closed to women. "I would have preferred the digging of ditches or the shoveling of coal; but the needle alone persistently pointed out my way, and I was finally forced to take it." In Big Rapids, this meant serving as a seamstress for other local families, using skills she had undoubtedly learned from her mother.[7]

History was on Shaw's side this time. Her move into town coincided with the coming of the railroad to Big Rapids and the town's subsequent transformation from an isolated small town to a regional center for local industries. Though primarily used by the lumber and mining industries of the region, the train now tied Big Rapids to the rest of the country, an expansion repeated throughout the whole country as the growth of the railroad connected so many small, formerly remote, communities. The weeklong trek that Shaw and her family had made on foot from Grand Rapids to their farm in 1859 was now reduced to less than a day.[8]

Shaw could have no idea how important the railroad would become for her life. The expansion of the rail system created a generally underexplored gendered revolution in transportation. The trains were faster and cheaper than previous modes of travel, and importantly for white women, they were considered physically and morally safe. The benefits of this development did not extend equally to all women; discrimination and abuse by the railroads would be a major issue for African American women for many decades. In this period of the Chautauquas and the speakers' bureaus that sent educators and lecturers throughout the country to lecture, educate, and entertain, the women activists took advantage of the transportation boom.[9]

Concurrently, Michigan was in the midst of an educational reform. While the smallest communities continued to struggle to maintain and staff their one-room schoolhouses, in more urban parts of Michigan, public and private institutions now offered secondary and postsecondary education. Big Rapids, influenced by Michigan's commitment to educational progress, had built and opened a high school in 1868. This development put secondary education within Shaw's reach.[10]

Transportation and education innovations ended Shaw's isolation. Next, four people—three women and a man—each connected in some way to the early women's movement, came to Big Rapids and further expanded Shaw's world. Together they presented Shaw with options and opportunities that brought her dreams into the realm of the possible.

Among the many women activists already using the railroads to create a new enterprise, the postwar lyceum, was the Reverend Marianna Thompson, a Pennsylvania Quaker who became a Unitarian minister and women's rights supporter. When she appeared in Big Rapids, she personified the life to which young Anna aspired. Here was an educated, professional woman, traveling, speaking, and earning her own way. To Anna, the physical presence of this type of woman, not the content of her talk, mattered. This young schoolteacher turned seamstress needed to know how to join this new womanhood, so, after the lecture, she approached Reverend Thompson and boldly confessed her own ambition, especially her goal of entering the ministry. With a few encouraging words, Reverend Thompson gave the push Shaw needed. Urging Anna to follow her dreams, Thompson also gave her strong and clear direction—get her education first.[11]

Hardly needing any more of a push to drop the dreaded needle, the next day Anna presented herself at Big Rapids High School. Shaw had not been to school formally since she arrived in Michigan at the age of twelve and had found that she was better educated than the local schoolteacher. Now she was twenty-three. Though her future colleagues were finishing seminary or college by this age, education was hardly regularized on the frontiers. Plus Anna had always read voraciously. Nevertheless it was a tremendous step to be able to enter a free public high school with formally trained teachers.[12]

Heading this school was a young woman graduate of Albion College, a recently accredited Methodist institution in south central Michigan. Lucy Foot, "preceptress" of Big Rapids High School, immediately recognized that this young woman was no ordinary student. Foot saw Shaw's character and her talents. While Thompson encouraged Shaw to actualize her dream and gave her key words of advice, Lucy Foot was her instrumental mentor. Taking Anna under her wing, Lucy worked with her on a daily basis, directing her curricular and cocurricular work to develop her skills as a speaker.

Eventually Foot would identify and open doors that allowed Anna to enter the world beyond Big Rapids.

After years of living with and supporting a family who took her and her work for granted—a family that may have recognized her hopes but was unable to help her move toward realizing them—Anna had found a supporter who could provide what her family could not. With these first instances of nonfamilial support, Anna saw the opportunities she had long dreamed of begin to take a shape. Though she did not yet have to make the choice between maintaining her ties with her family and following her dreams, she realized the need for friendships and alliances beyond her kin.[13]

These connections brought new decisions and occasional compromises. Lucy Foot could help Shaw, but all Foot's connections were within the Methodist Episcopal Church network. As Unitarians, the Shaws had not had the opportunity to be part of any such congregation since they had left Massachusetts; even today there is no Unitarian Church in the Big Rapids area. In contrast, the Methodist Episcopal Church was very active in Michigan. It was expanding rapidly, causing the West Michigan Conference to organize a Big Rapids District. The church appointed Dr. H. C. Peck as the presiding elder.[14]

Among the broad religious debates and changes occupying scholars and leaders across the country were the Methodists who were part of an energetic and evangelical wing of Christianity and the social gospel movement. Denominational arguments ranged from how they governed themselves to the role of the churches in the political and social issues of the day. This era of dissent and schisms was not unlike that known by the Stotts and Shaws several generations before in England. Already in the years between the 1790s and the 1830s, during the period of the Second Great Awakening, several reform groups had split off from the Methodist Episcopal Church, forming Free Methodist, Wesleyan, and other Churches.[15]

Simultaneously, women had claimed roles as preachers and exhorters in many dissenting religious groups. Religious historian Catherine A. Brekus argues that women were most likely to assert their right to speak on religious matters under three circumstances: when they were members of marginal groups rather than established religions; when they were poor/lower-class women; and when they were in those areas considered frontiers, from the back countries of the upland South through the recently settled rural areas of the old Northwest. In many cases, local congregations, elders, and/or reform groups recognized such women, formally or informally sanctioning their work. The Methodist tradition provides many such examples. Jarena Lee had been an exhorter and prayer leader in the African Methodist Episcopal Church in 1817. By 1866, Helenor M. Davison had been ordained deacon by the Methodist Protestant Church, and in 1869, Margaret Newton Van Cott was the first woman to receive a local preacher's license in the Methodist Episcopal Church. While the Quakers had long recognized that women had an equal claim to the pulpit, other Christian traditions had vacillated on granting women public religious roles, often allowing for such irregular or exceptional cases while they were struggling as new sects. They then silenced women when they wanted to establish their respectability.[16]

We know little about the man who first decided that women should preach in the Big Rapids District; Dr. H. C. Peck appears to have been both a supporter of women's rights and an ambitious man who was determined to be a pioneer on this issue. After Lucy Foot, his first choice, made it clear that she had no such aspirations, Peck accepted Lucy's recommendation of her young protégé Shaw, who believed she had such a calling. Although she knew what this move would mean to her family, Shaw chose to convert and was accepted into the Methodist Church. With this formality accomplished, in 1871, Dr. Peck scheduled Shaw's first sermon for Ashton, Michigan, fifteen miles north of Paris.[17]

How much Shaw's conversion was about faith, about opportunity, or about taking another step away from her family is difficult to know. Shaw had long abandoned any concerns she had about denominational differences when she wrote her autobiography so many years later. Becoming a Methodist meant having to give up dancing—the other prohibitions of no drinking and card playing weren't part of her life, but Shaw had the reputation of being the leader at the local dances. Shaw doesn't mention struggles over doctrinal issues.[18]

Anna had fainted the first time she spoke in public at her high school, but once revived, she had returned to finish her recitation. Now the thought of preaching to people—friends, family and strangers—rather than the trees on her father's land brought a similar combination of terror and resolve. On the occasion of her first sermon, Shaw trembled so violently that the pulpit shook.

"Faith is letting go of all other dependence and falling into the arms of Jesus," Anna urged the crowd at Ashton. It was an appropriate image. With this first sermon, Shaw was publically declaring that she would always be ready to step off that cliff, trusting that she would survive, or not, as God determined. It is ironic that this view, in many ways, echoed the attitude her father had taken when he sent the family off into the wilderness. Dr. Peck deemed Shaw's first sermon a success. With his support but in opposition to her family's wishes, she preached in all thirty-six of the district's locations that year. Finally, after over a decade of searching for the means, Anna had possibilities.[19]

Could this be the path that could lead her to the life she had envisioned? As had many women before her, Shaw argued that she had been called to preach and to the ministry by a higher power that she was morally compelled to obey. She dismissed all opposition as God's tests of her worthiness. But this justification was probably all the more powerful since it was also a means to expand her world and explore options beyond the usual fate of women of her background. It was a means to an education, to economic autonomy, and to professional status, dreams as big as Shaw could imagine at the time. When this dream came to include ordination and full ministerial standing, it isn't certain, yet each step Shaw took during this decade indicates her determination for that credential.

With her prodigious energy, Shaw threw herself into her new responsibilities. This shift shocked her family and community. As they saw her determination, they all became engaged in a rigorous debate over the propriety of her efforts and in an active effort to dissuade her from this course. And there were dangers far beyond offending community norms. Shaw may have been prepared to face the risks, as she demonstrated when she defended herself with a handgun, but her family still had no understanding of her ambition.[20]

It isn't clear whether the core of her family's opposition came from the fact that she was speaking in public, that she planned to become a licensed preacher, that she would face situations that respectable women should avoid, or some combination of these and additional concerns. Tensions were so strong that Anna's beloved sister, Mary, stopped talking to her, though they continued to share a house. Her brother-in-law, George Green, now a prominent businessperson, published a statement in the local paper urging her "true friends" to oppose her efforts. Her "family"—probably George Green since only he had the means—even offered to pay for her education at the University of Michigan if she gave up the pulpit.[21]

It was too late. Already Anna had demonstrated that resistance only fueled the fire of her determination. It may have been painful, but Shaw knew she needed a clean break from her kin. She had made her decisions and now stubbornly stood her ground. In school during the week, and traveling to preach throughout the region on weekends, she pushed to prove herself and make up for lost time. This feverish pace was so demanding that the health she had recovered since the hungry days of the Civil War was once again in jeopardy.[22]

At this critical point, Mary Aston Livermore, one of the most popular women speaking on the lyceum circuit, came to Big Rapids. Best known today for her work organizing the Sanitary Commission during the Civil War, Livermore was active in women's rights and in temperance. A remarkably effective and successful lecturer, she was promoted by the premier speakers' agency, the Redpath Bureau of Chicago. She was also a gentle and generous mentor.[23]

Always seeking whatever advice and support such prominent guests might offer, Anna presented her hopes to Livermore. Just as Thompson had, Livermore urged Anna to follow her heart regardless of the challenges she faced. This time, Anna's friends, arguing from the other point of view, noted that Anna had all but ruined her health. "Mrs. Livermore turned upon me a long and deeply thoughtful look. 'Yes,' she said at last, 'I see she has. But it is better that she should die doing the thing she wants to do than that she should die because she can't do it.'" Vindicated by this famous stranger, Shaw kept her eyes on her goal: the ministry.[24]

This was a heady time for Shaw. Traveling throughout western and northern Michigan and earning a respectable amount of money, Shaw found that she could survive outside the circle of her family. On August 26, 1873, the Big Rapids District Conference of the Methodist Episcopal Church enthusiastically licensed twenty-six-year-old "Annie Howard Shaw" as a local preacher. Her first nontraditional professional credential signaled her membership in a larger community, one where she and her work were valued.[25]

The same railroad lines that had brought Mary Livermore and Mariana Thompson to Big Rapids now took Shaw south to the small town of Albion at the forks of the Kalamazoo River. As a licensed Methodist preacher, Shaw was eligible for a free college education at Lucy Foot's alma mater, Albion College. With the church supporting the academic side of the college, Shaw had to cover only her room and board. Though she arrived alone with no family or friends to help or welcome her, this quiet event was nevertheless a triumphant celebration for Shaw, her dream of going to college actualized. The sacrifice of her family's approval and the separation from her beloved friend Clara were the prices to be paid for autonomy. Shaw may not have even seen such choices as remarkable. It is impossible to know the level of her ambition or self-confidence when she first trudged up from the railway station onto Albion College's campus. Nevertheless, she was now on her own. After fourteen years of rural isolation, Shaw felt she had reentered the larger world, and she didn't look back.[26]

Shaw arrived on the educational scene, specifically at Albion College, at a time that was auspicious for women. Feminist researchers have built an impressive scholarship on the history of women in education in the United States. A key area has always been the contrasting experiences of women of different classes, races, and regions. While the emergence of parallel elite colleges for women followed the refusals of (men's) colleges in the Northeast and New England to open their doors to women, in many other regions, coeducation was the norm at private as well as public colleges.[27]

The history of the school to which Shaw traveled in 1873 paralleled such trends. A small group of Methodist leaders in south central Michigan, knowing that educational institutions were essential to any territorial development, had petitioned for a charter for a seminary in 1835. They built the Wesleyan Seminary in the mill town of Albion. The Seminary was coeducational from the start and even had an Indian Department for several years. This Methodist school that existed on the verge of financial ruin during its first two decades was further threatened when Michigan's support for free public high schools began to undercut the need for private seminaries. The trustees, prompted by the University of Michigan's refusal to admit women to its degree-granting programs at the time, took the unusual step of offering formal degrees to women first. With "Female Collegiate Institute" added to its name, this institution offered MSA (Mistress of Science and Arts) degrees to young women starting in the late 1850s. Albion College, as a liberal arts college granting BA degrees to women and men, came into existence in 1861.[28]

By the time Shaw arrived on its campus in 1873, the college, under the guidance of Dr. George Jocelyn, was entering its most stable period since its founding. The Albion College Catalog records her as a member of the Preparatory Department in 1873. She entered the regular college course in 1874.[29]

These collegiate years were ones of comparative peace and personal growth for Shaw. The physical demands were certainly the lightest she had known since her family came to Michigan. She could manage her studies while preaching or lecturing enough to support herself. Her immediate concerns were reduced to the comparatively minor issue of her wardrobe. One day Shaw stood too close to the fireplace in a classroom and singed the back of her dress. This incident caused her a minor panic since she had only one good outfit. Fortunately, when she was chosen to give the major student address at the college, her family relented in their disapproval long enough for her mother to make her a special gown for the occasion.[30]

Overall, status differences based on class and sex that might have been issues in larger and more established colleges were not issues among her fellow students or the faculty and administration. The minor exception involved her confrontations with the men in the all-male literary society when she challenged the assumption that a man would always give the most important student oration. But even this conflict led to triumph and perhaps Shaw's first successful experience of organizing for women's rights. In the end, everyone insisted that Shaw give the speech for her year.[31]

Albion College also gave Shaw some objective assessment of her talents. Certainly she had been a leader among her peers in Big Rapids, but at Albion she realized that she had that difficult-to-define gift of charisma. The combination of such a personality, with her voice and her intellect, brought her repeated success and recognition. By the spring of 1874, the Albion College *Annalist* gave her lecture on women's role in the temperance movement in Albion's Opera Hall a most positive review. The same source also celebrated her effectiveness when she spoke from the pulpit. In 1875 she was president of the women's literary society, the Atheniaedes. A classmate and longtime friend, Dr. Della Pierce, recalled Shaw's influence and a professor's early identification of the skills that later would propel Shaw to international acclaim: "She soon became a leader in many ways. . . . I remember a professor saying she was possessed of a wonderful personal magnetism which gave her perfect control of her audience almost from the very first." In the congenial environment of Albion College, Shaw began to sense that she really did have something special to do in this world.[32]

A picture of Shaw as an energetic personality, as well as a bold and ambitious young woman, emerges in this period. Yet in the few surviving letters to her friend, Clara, we also hear how her plans were couched in the language of an evangelical Methodist. God had chosen her path, and she had no choice but to follow. But the persona of the dignified Methodist preacher could not completely mask Shaw's charm or her penchant for humor. Shaw wrote, "I never mix in any of their fun but even as a Methodist and preacher I can laugh once in a while."[33]

Although Albion was a small school in a small town, Anna was on her own there, living and studying with young people from a greater range of places and backgrounds than she had known in Mecosta County. In Shaw's own words, "Even if I had my education now my character is not well rounded nor am I sufficiently versed in the ways of the world to be able to battle with it single-handed and alone. God requires these years to make a woman of me. I am praying for patience to wait and grow higher in the scale of womanhood before I strike out into deep water."[34]

In the summer of 1874, after her first year at Albion, Anna assessed the "deep water" when she traveled outside of Michigan for the first time in sixteen years. Her brother James now lived in St. Johnsbury, Vermont. With Mary, with whom she now had a type of truce, she went to visit James. As the only member of her family who didn't oppose her preaching, James had arranged for Anna to preach at area churches almost every Sunday of that summer. Though this plan threatened the peace between the sisters, in the end Mary dropped her active opposition to Anna's work. The immediate result was that Anna earned enough money from her work that summer to enter her second year at Albion College with a financial cushion. That summer also gave her the opportunity to survey the climate for women preachers among the Methodist leaders of New England.[35]

During her college years, Shaw fully regained her health. The images of her from this period show intense dark eyes as her dominating feature. Shaw's face is still narrow and her hair dark and rather short. Although it is assumed that all nineteenth-century women kept their hair long—the "bob" didn't become fashionable until the 1920s—at least some had rejected this tradition. The very popular and celebrated woman speaker Anna Dickinson cropped her hair during this period. Both the young Willa Cather and Elizabeth Cady (later Stanton) had short hair at some point in their lives. It might have been this haircut that led her Albion classmates to nickname Shaw "Annie boy," though her look was more handsome than boyish. In contrast to her earliest photographs, which betrayed an awkwardness and a discomfort with the camera, in her *carte de visite* from her Albion years Shaw's steady gaze and composed face argue that already she was controlling her image, and that image was serious and determined.[36]

Balancing the responsibilities of a college student with those of a preacher and a lecturer—Shaw was noted as having preached three sermons one Sunday—set the new norm for Shaw. Already she demonstrated her disdain for moderation; she believed in seizing the day. She was the daughter of the frontier who, like so many women from these regions, had been socialized to handle the long preindustrial hours of hard labor and had developed an essential tolerance for the demanding conditions, from the seemingly unending winter cold to the monotonous diets of rural homesteads, farms, and ranches. Her experiences once again contradicted the idea that rigorous activities were detrimental to women's bodies and health, a belief popularized by physicians, psychologists, and educators such as Edward H. Clarke and S. Weir Mitchell. The world of separate spheres for women and men, and the genteel pedestals of her more privileged sisters, were not Shaw's realities. That ideology held less power on the frontiers.[37]

Shaw faced several more years before she could complete her degree. While she still looked the part of a schoolgirl, she was already twenty-eight years old. During the fall of 1875 Shaw debated, "Should I devote two more years of my vanishing youth to the completion of my college course, or, instead, go at once to Boston University, enter upon my theological studies, take my degree, and be about my Father's business?" Impatient after all her years of waiting, Shaw had gained the confidence from her years at Albion College to take the latter path. In February 1876, she left Albion for Boston, Massachusetts.[38]

When Shaw left Albion College and her family and friends for Boston, she was taking the greatest risk of her life. Compared to Albion and Albion College, Boston was a new world, and the Boston University Seminary was an impersonal and rigid institution. Shaw had left Massachusetts as a twelve-year-old. When she returned as a twenty-nine-year-old, her personality reflected the ideas and attitudes of the rural frontier rather than the norms of urban New England. The tests Shaw faced in her first few months in Massachusetts came to rank among the most severe and retold of her trials.

Shaw had assumed that she could now support herself anywhere. When she tried to find preaching opportunities in Boston and the surrounding areas, she found that there were so many male seminarians that she was not in demand. The novelty of her status worked against rather than for her. Further she had no mentors and none of the networks she had in Michigan. During the hard economic times of the late 1870s, when she did find opportunities for preaching, she never knew if she would be paid or only thanked. This situation was acute because Shaw was excluded from the room and board arrangements that the school provided for the male seminarians. The inadequate compensation that she did receive left her cold, hungry, and weak in the only housing she could afford—an unheated attic room. In this supposedly tolerant region and institution, Shaw came to understand de facto discrimination.[39]

As the lone woman in her class at the Boston University School of Theology, officially a coeducational school, Shaw faced what might best be described as a very hostile tolerance. She had no companions with whom to share this chilly climate or with whom to develop strategies for sustaining herself. The emotional stress from such antagonism and loneliness might not have been so overwhelming if it had not coincided with a time of material deprivation. As a result of her early deprivations, Shaw was not naturally healthy. She found that she had to work to maintain her vigor. As her desperation became overwhelming, she made a pact with herself. She concluded after only a few months that even God didn't expect her to continue without heat, without food, and without a decent pair of shoes. If no relief for her health-threatening poverty came soon, she would give up the seminary.[40]

Though Shaw viewed these challenges as God's tests, the tests were in the form of men and their policies. Her salvation came in the form of women. The first was a grateful grandmother whose grandson Shaw "saved" during a weeklong revival for which she received no pay. Shaw juxtaposed the five dollars this poor woman pressed into her hand with the meager verbal gratitude from the minister who had organized the revival. Next were the women of the Methodist Women's Missionary Association who recognized Shaw's dire straits and arranged for a weekly allowance from an anonymous donor. The University had granted Shaw a $2/week allowance for room and board at a time when even women factory workers were earning more. The donor provided for an additional $3/week on the condition that Shaw not work and focus on her studies. Anna's first reaction was to have a good meal and buy new shoes to replace the ones that had split open.[41]

Relieved, Shaw felt God had answered her doubts. Now freed of the need to take every preaching opportunity with the hope that some percentage of them would provide financial remuneration, Anna could attend to her studies and listen to, rather than give, sermons on Sunday. This also freed Shaw to minister to the "women of the streets." Shaw hadn't forgotten the woman who had befriended her in Lawrence. "I went into the homes of these women, followed them to the streets and the dance halls, talked with them, prayed with them, and made friends among them. Some of them I was able to help, but many were beyond help; and I soon learned that the effective work in that field is the work done for women before, not after, they have fallen."[42]

In 1876 a new type of woman entered Shaw's life. Persis Crowell Addy (1837–1878) was a college graduate, former schoolteacher, and now the wealthy widow of Captain John Addy. Addy's husband had died from an illness contracted when the young couple was shipwrecked during their honeymoon in the South Pacific in 1867. In addition she was the daughter of Prince S. Crowell, a prominent retired sea captain and bank owner, and a member of an old and large Cape Cod family. Their paths first crossed in the summer of 1876, when Shaw went to East Dennis, a mid–Cape Cod seaport, as part of her summer circuit of substituting for vacationing pastors. Anna's and Persis's connection with and affection for each other must have been immediate, for Shaw states that only after that summer, Persis Addy returned with her to Boston and that they lived together.[43]

Addy's friendship marked a wonderful turning point, after which Shaw saw what her life could be as a single professional woman, single in the sense of being unmarried rather than alone. Addy's wealth alleviated Shaw's financial struggles as well as her loneliness. The young widow introduced Anna to the theater and other cultural offerings. What had been the hardest of times became "my first experience of an existence in which comfort and culture, recreation and leisurely reading were cheerful commonplaces." This was Shaw's first exposure to a woman who fit in some ways the dominant ideology of the era, but who had been raised and nurtured among the strong women of the Cape who had often had to assume familial and financial responsibilities during the absences of their seafaring husbands and fathers.[44]

Shaw was destined to have only a taste of such a life. This year of companionship and calm, the brief respite from her years of struggle, came to a shocking close when Persis became ill the next summer. She was eventually diagnosed as having a brain tumor. During her final year of seminary, Anna had to balance a stressful array of responsibilities that not only included caring for Addy and finishing her studies but also serving as pastor for the Methodist Episcopal Church in Hingham. Persis Crowell Addy died on March 6, 1878.[45]

We have few writings from this era from which to measure Shaw's grief. Perhaps the clearest indication of Shaw's grief comes from her diaries. For the rest of her life, Shaw noted the anniversary of Addy's death in each.

Persis Addy became part of Shaw's personal pantheon. She wrote, "If I am not a good woman it is because I will not be, for God has done all he can for me and given me the purest person I ever knew to love me better than she did her own life, for I know she would have given her life for me."[46]

This was also Shaw's first experience of a type of relationship the full nature and name of which scholars still debate. While she already had shown that she was capable of strong and loving friendships, with Addy, Shaw found not just love and companionship but something that could have been a life partnership, a "Boston marriage" to use the term Henry James coined a decade later. Of course it is impossible to determine the level of intimacy they shared or what terms they would have used to describe themselves; nevertheless, with Addy, Anna gained a brief view of what life as an unmarried woman could be, that it did not necessarily mean a lonely existence. Addy's death left Shaw with an aching awareness that work alone could not complete her life.[47]

Death didn't end Persis's influence on Shaw's life. In her will, Addy left Anna $1500. The two women had planned a European tour as a celebration of Anna's graduation and had spent many hours planning this trip. When Persis realized that she would not survive to take that voyage and tour, she gave Shaw the means to take it herself. When the time came, Anna had little desire for such a trip, but to honor Persis's last wish, she began to make the necessary arrangements. At this point, Addy's father, Prince Crowell, stepped in and gave Shaw what amounted to her introduction to finance and investments. She would be better off if she invested the money in railroad bonds and borrowed what she needed for the trip against the principal, he explained. That way the $1500 would serve as Shaw's safety net. Just as the emotional aspect of Shaw's relationship with Addy changed her expectations of her life, this gift introduced Shaw to an economic world that was entirely new to her also.[48]

In June of 1878, only eight years after the 1870 Census had recorded her "at home" in Green Township, Mecosta County, Michigan, and four years after she had left Michigan for the first time in sixteen years, Anna Howard Shaw sailed for Europe. She had earned her education and possessed her first investments. This thirty-one-year-old daughter of impoverished immigrants returned to tour the great sights of the continent. Such a grand tour of Europe in one form or another was an increasingly common event in the lives of young women of privilege, but it was not something expected for the daughter of a failed Michigan farmer. Although many of Shaw's accomplishments of this decade allowed her to enter new worlds, the European tour marked a major transition in her life. This was not a finishing of her education as a prelude to entering society as an eligible woman; it was a bittersweet culmination of her struggles to become an independent professional.[49]

Persis Addy and Crowell's influences on Anna Howard Shaw continued. Shaw had realized as her graduation approached that the school's leaders would not support her as a candidate for ordination. For her part, Shaw was adamant that her goal was ordination and that she was part of the effort to "overthrow the monopoly of the pulpit." While she was willing to go anywhere—whether to the poor rural parishes of the United States or to the foreign missions of South America—she would not go in the traditional female role of a teacher; she would go only as a full elder. As a result, no position within the Methodist Episcopal Church waited for her upon her return from Europe. Instead Shaw assumed the leadership in the church where Addy, Crowell, and many of their extended family worshiped in East Dennis, Massachusetts. This had been a Free Methodist Church, one of the groups that had split off from the larger Methodist movement early in the nineteenth century as a result of conflict over issues such as the role of women and the church's response to slavery and racial segregation. Now it was completely independent. The Methodist Episcopal Church seemed to have determined to keep Shaw and other women on its margins.[50]

Shaw arrived in East Dennis, a small town of shipyards and cranberry bogs, in September 1878. Her church stood on the town's highest point; its tall steeple could be seen for miles. But within the walls of this scenic place of worship her congregation was in upheaval. The leaders of the conflict were stubborn, older men, many of whom had been sea captains working out of this port and shipbuilding center. They were using the church services as a vehicle for attacking each other. Young and looking even younger, and a woman to boot, Shaw knew that she had to establish her leadership if she was going to have any success in this parish. It was not easy to confront the wealthy pillars of this community, but somehow these men were more familiar to Shaw, more like the men she had preached to on the frontiers than the men who had failed her at Boston University. With her characteristic fearlessness she gave them a choice. They could accept and respect her authority, or she would resign. Though she lost some of her parishioners at least temporarily, the majority of the congregants supported her because she had the backbone to exert her authority. This they could respect. Similar difficulties led Shaw to offer her resignation two more times, but each time the leaders refused to accept it.[51]

Pastor Shaw found her work among the people of East Dennis to be congenial. Her memories of this time involve anecdotes about the interesting people of the Cape, and the records of the church confirmed that her years were successful. A measure of the calm and relatively undemanding nature of this work was Shaw's ability to take on a second parish, a Congregational Church in nearby Dennis.[52]

Now established as an economically independent, respected minister, Shaw still felt the lingering shadow of her failure to achieve her goal of ordination, without which she could not baptize or take members into her church, and in her eyes, fully and equally serve her parishioners. With her usual determination and established success at overcoming sexist barriers, Shaw set out to remedy this situation. From the two versions of her struggle for ordination, it is possible to assess both the facts and Shaw's analysis of this next milestone in her life.[53]

On the basics, the two versions agree. Shaw had come to Boston University when Bishop Gilbert Haven, who was sympathetic to the woman's rights movement and the idea of women in the ministry, was the presiding elder. Shaw might have met Bishop Haven on her earlier trip east, but it is fairly certain that she knew of his position on women when she decided to enter the Boston University Seminary. Unfortunately, Bishop Haven fell ill during a trip to Africa in 1876–1877 and never fully recovered. His replacement, Bishop Andrews, held the opposite view on women and ordination. Under his jurisdiction, Shaw and all other women had little hope for advancement. Nevertheless, Shaw and Anna Oliver, another pioneering woman minister and graduate of Boston University School of Theology, would not give up their struggle without a spirited challenge to their exclusion.[54]

Methodist protocol demanded that each woman start at the local level. Shaw appeared for questioning before her conference. Her papers contain a report "to certify that Sister A. H. Shaw appeared before the Examining Committee of the M. E. Conference of 1880, as a candidate for Local Deacon's Orders, and that she passed a *very Satisfactory Examination*, and was duly recommended to the Conference." With this recommendation, Shaw faced Bishop Andrews. He rejected any consideration of both Shaw's and Oliver's petitions.[55]

This rejection stopped neither of these fearless women. Together they took an appeal to the 1880 National Conference in Cincinnati. At this point, Anna Oliver took the lead, writing a strong and personal justification for why women should be ordained. Though her words found support among certain sectors of the denomination, they didn't convince the presiding authorities. In the end, the National Conference not only sustained Bishop Andrews's decision, but also revoked the women's licenses as local preachers.[56]

The decision at Cincinnati was the final straw for Shaw. She had enough of fighting with the Methodist Episcopal Church. On the advice of a young minister, Mark Trafton, Shaw petitioned for ordination with the smaller and less prestigious Methodist Protestant Church. She went to their national meeting in Tarrytown, New York, where she was subjected to another rigorous round of examinations. However, as a recent graduate of a leading seminary, Shaw was more than prepared to answer all challenges. Once again, Shaw had to change churches to advance, converting from Methodist Episcopal to Methodist Protestant. Finally, however, on October 12, 1880, Anna Howard Shaw was ordained as a deacon in Tarrytown, New York.[57]

Methodist women remember and have celebrated this event ever since. Shaw is often awarded the honor of being the first woman ordained in the Methodist Church. Though that honor probably belongs to Eleanor Davison who was ordained in 1866, Shaw was a major figure in women's efforts in the Methodist Church. Even when her suffrage contributions are underplayed, she is recognized for the triumph that her ordination truly was. Shaw's congregation acknowledged her achievement at the time. When she returned to Massachusetts, she received a beautiful silver communion service from her very proud parishioners. In her autobiography, Shaw tells this story with a mixture of amusement—at the hurdles the denominations had put in her way—and reverence for what this really meant to her.[58]

What is missing from that public account was her vestigial outrage and disgust that comes through in her second, more private account of the events. Shaw never forgot how badly the men of the cloth treated her throughout the entire episode. Apparently even after she was ordained, the young men in the Methodist Protestant Conference went out of their way to make her week there miserable. While Shaw maintained her ministerial credentials for most of the rest of her life, she never returned to a single Conference gathering. It was, after all the years of struggle, a hollow victory. After years of fighting to become what she believed God wanted her to be, Shaw concluded that there was no future for her within organized religion.[59]

These were remarkable years for women in the United States as they were challenging their roles and the limits imposed on them by law and tradition. As activists sought means to right the wrongs that had been articulated at Seneca Falls over twenty years earlier, poor and middle-class women found or created opportunities for waged work. Fewer women were marrying, challenging conceptions of womanhood based on legal and presumed economic dependency, though there had long been women who had to support themselves. From Freedmen's Schools in the South through coeducational colleges in the Midwest, women turned to education at all levels. But it was an opening in the religious arena that gave Anna Howard Shaw her first opportunity to escape a life defined by her family, her class, and her place. More quickly than even her active imagination might have allowed, she was on the cusp of becoming part of the leadership of this movement of women.[60]

To have moved from a family that provided her with so little, to achieve all she did in so short a period of time, gives some sense not only of how permeable gender boundaries were in this era, but also how ambitious and fearless Shaw was. Shaw *was* confident; she had investments, credentials, and work that was rewarding. She pushed herself physically, taking risks that most "respectable" women would have eschewed. Yet her struggles had left scars. Shaw had remarkable stamina, but she also knew that she had limits. The public saw her charisma, but privately her fears about money and her health haunted her. For all her accomplishments, for all the mentors she gained and admirers she earned, she always felt on some level that she was working without a safety net.

CHAPTER 3

Finding the Cause
(1881–1889)

In every land the voice of woman is heard proclaiming the word
which is given to her, and the wondering world which for a
moment stopped its busy wheel of life that it might smite and jeer
her has at least learned that wherever the intuitions of the human
mind are called into special exercise, wherever the art of persuasive
eloquence is demanded, wherever the heroic conduct is based
upon duty rather than impulse, wherever her efforts in opening
the sacred doors for the benefit of truth can avail—in one and all
of these respects woman greatly excels man.

Ordination, national coverage by the *Woman's Journal*, two parishes, and financial independence—by 1880, Anna Howard Shaw had not
only achieved her specific goals, but she had redefined herself.[1] The 1870
unmarried, "at home" daughter of the Michigan frontier was now a thirty-
three-year-old "clergyman," in East Dennis, Massachusetts. Yet the changes
recorded in the 1880 census don't begin to capture the physical and figu-
rative space Shaw had traversed. In those ten years, she had crossed state
and national borders, but perhaps more importantly she had challenged
the less tangible boundaries of gendered institutions and professions by
attending college, graduating from seminary, and achieving ordination.
She had entered the rarefied world of the nation's leading intellectuals and
activists in Boston and was serving as pastor to one of the country's oldest
communities. She had ministered to the poor, preached to Native Americans and lumbermen, and worked among the "women of the streets." She
was in the vanguard of establishing a new womanhood, one in which she
could have professional status and economic autonomy along with deep
friendships, love, and an extended community apart from the patriarchal
and heterosexual arrangements recognized and sanctioned by the state.[2]

But Shaw had hit what we now call a "glass ceiling." Her inspiration for twenty years had been her call to the ministry. Armored with the belief that God guided her life, she had pushed through all levels of hardship—family opposition, material deprivation, and the decrees of her church—to gain her education and win full membership as an elder. Now what? After all this, Shaw had concluded that there was no future for her within the institutional structures of the Methodist denominations. Nor did the life of a small-town pastor satisfy her aspirations. She was still young and expected to live a long life. Her world had become ever so much broader than the one she had known in Michigan, and consequently her sense of her possible place in that world reflected her new understanding. Unlike most women, she was in control of her life.

Living only eighty miles from Boston, Shaw witnessed many of the changes that were creating a new United States. What was this world in which Shaw now felt she could play a role? Closing was the era dominated by the causes, realities, and aftermaths of the Civil War. The Progressive Era, a response to the excesses of capitalism, was beginning. In this supposed Gilded Age, shifts in class and race relations were taking place that would influence the women's movement and Shaw. The emergence of a complexly racialized society came in 1877 as the end of Reconstruction heralded the start of a period when the constitutional guarantees of equal citizenship were abandoned in the name of states' rights. Freedmen, freedwomen, and their allies were still struggling to respond to the post-Reconstruction efforts as white southern legislators began to put Jim Crow laws on the books.

As class disparities grew and regional differences marked the country, race remained a defining factor in individual lives and political struggles. Shaw saw industrialization dominate the changes in New England and the Mid-Atlantic States. The South remained agricultural and dependent upon the labor of poor sharecroppers and tenant farmers, Black and White. Newspapers documented Chicago's rise as the great city of the Midwest— receiving, processing, and shipping the products of the heartland. Beyond the Mississippi, in the sparsely settled territories, the U.S. government used military force and its economic power to subjugate Native Americans, forcing the numerous tribes onto reservations mostly on marginal lands. Easterners, claiming free land through homesteading, superimposed their transported lifestyles over people who had previously been part of the Spanish colonial empire and then independent Mexico. On the West Coast, railroads recruited Asian immigrants, and their cultures added to that region's diversity.

Women were redefining their roles and responsibilities and seeking new avenues to respond to their changing situations. While the daughters of native-born, middle-class or elite families were finding new options in education and professional work, working women, many from the varying waves of immigrants, were becoming part of the labor force in factories and sweatshops. In the aftermath of the controversy over the Fourteenth Amendment and the failure of the constitutional challenge known as the "New Departure," the women's rights movement faced the reality of a long-term state-by-state struggle for the franchise. Though generally led by white, middle-class women, more men and African American women had national leadership roles during this era than they would later. Women constructed their local and regional associations in response to the new racial landscape. In suffrage as well as in many other areas, African American women, sometimes by necessity and sometimes by choice, organized separate societies.[3]

From the Woman's Christian Temperance Union (WCTU) and the Women's Department of the Knights of Labor through mothers' clubs with varying foci, women formed increasingly formal groups throughout the country. Scholars have designated this period as the "Women's Era" or a "Maternal Commonwealth." For many, these were the vehicles for extending their influence beyond the literal boundaries of the home while maintaining the guise of domesticity; however a minority of women rejected the separate spheres view of the sexes and embraced a radical view of gender.[4]

Shaw was one of that minority. Her experiences informed her theory of women's capabilities. Though the fight to enter the ministry, a traditionally male profession, had been difficult, Shaw saw no intellectual, physical, or biblical reasons why women should be excluded from such positions or from other professions. Her life reflected her views. She was economically independent. From an early age she had seen that almost all women worked, but without wages they were at the mercy of patriarchal power, both individual and institutional. As a minister of the Wesleyan Methodist Church, she had started with a salary of $425/year. Not long after, she accepted an invitation to the pulpit in another local church, an added responsibility she found she could easily handle. Although her income was modest, it was enough to lead a respectable life. In reserve, she had the $1500 she had inherited from Persis Addy.[5]

Before Shaw could fully consider any new directions for her life, a stunning loss pulled her back to her family in Michigan and complicated her decisions about her future. On May 11, 1881, Mary Shaw Green, Anna's last surviving sister and the one to whom Anna had been closest, died at the age of thirty-six. Though Mary had been the traditional daughter in contrast to the rebellious Anna, they had been each other's childhood companions. Mary had provided a home for Anna so that she could pursue her dreams; she was the one who followed James in accepting Anna's choice to preach. Anna had already been traveling to Michigan when she received this news.

When she reached home, Shaw conducted her sister's funeral service with a deep sorrow that can only come from losing one's closest sibling.[6]

Anna and her family had reconciled. Over the years, Anna consistently returned to visit with her aging parents and her siblings. She relished the role of "Auntie," corresponding with each new member of the family as she or he became able to read and write. Now with this death, Shaw and her family faced change as well as grief; Mary's death left her children—Grace, 14, Lola, 8, and George, 4—motherless, and Thomas and Nicolas Shaw without a home. Further complicating this situation, the children's father, George Green, had various business interests that kept him frequently on the road.[7]

In view of this new family crisis, Anna had to reconsider her autonomous, apparently solitary, life. She was torn. As the sole surviving daughter, she felt again the "family claim," but returning to Big Rapids was out of the question. Her first attempt to resolve this involved bringing Mary's children and her mother back to East Dennis. Anna arranged a home for them close to hers, and they stayed over the summer of 1881. Unfortunately this solution wasn't satisfactory over the long term; Shaw's mother wanted to return to Michigan. The immediate issue was solved when George Green found a new wife, one from among Anna's Cape Cod parishioners. Shaw presided over his marriage to Ellen Kelley in East Dennis in October 1882. Though this resolution eased Anna's responsibilities, her relationship with her sister's children had changed. In the future her nieces would live with and depend on her. So too would her brother Jack's daughters after their mother died and their father remarried.[8]

Mary's passing came just three years after Persis Addy's death. Two years later her brother Henry died. Before she was forty, Shaw had lost the siblings closest to her, and with Persis's passing, her first beloved companion. Even though her nieces and nephew soon had a new stepmother, Mary's death added more considerations to Shaw's search for a new direction and vocation.

This was Shaw's period of discontent. In spite of her disillusionment with the institutional churches, Shaw was still first and foremost an ordained Methodist minister. She was an activist, more concerned with ameliorating people's lives than debating theological doctrine or the latest intellectual development. Her vibrant and rebellious Christianity consistently needed to challenge the status quo and established institutions. Promoting justice was a core part of her religious duty, and that contributed to her belief that her calling extended far beyond the walls of her churches. While her colleague, Anna Oliver, would continue to battle for a place within orthodox Methodism, and many other women would attempt to alter the male dominance of the clergy, Shaw now abandoned that quest and searched for another mission. Though Shaw would remain a licensed minister, she positioned herself increasingly outside such religious and other patriarchal organizations.[9]

Shaw's first step in a new direction defies easy explanation, perhaps high-lighting her own uncertainty. Shaw decided to attend medical school. She asked and received permission from her churches to commute to Boston each week for classes and clinical work. Why study medicine at this point? There are a few hints. According to the 1880 census, she had shared a house with a woman doctor. Both her brother James and his wife, Sarah, had graduated from Boston University Medical School in 1876 and 1877, respectively. They urged her to enter the medical field. The 1883 *History of Mecosta County* quotes her father stating that she was in medical school preparing for mis-sionary work. While the missionary field was one option open to women ministers and doctors, Shaw made no mention of this intent when she wrote her autobiography. Of the choice, Shaw wrote, "[P]artly as an outlet for my surplus energy, but more especially because I realized the splendid work women could do as physicians, I began to study medicine."[10]

Fortunately the Medical School of Boston University was far more sup-portive of women than the Theological School had been. No male-only enclave, the school had retained core women faculty members and main-tained a focus on women's health issues after the merger of the New England Female Medical College with the Boston University unit in 1873. It was a homeopathy medical school.[11]

The primacy of applied health care in her training also appealed to Shaw. In this era before our modern idea of emergency rooms, Shaw and other medical students practiced their skills while responding to medical crises in several poorer communities in Boston three nights a week. Anna delivered babies to women burdened with poverty, doctored to immigrant working-men, and cared for their undernourished infants and children. Again she worked with prostitutes and learned that alcoholism occurred with women as well as with men.[12]

A determined Shaw persisted through graduation in 1886, but just as she had rejected the ministry after achieving her ordination, so too did she con-clude that practicing medicine was not her vocation. She was glad to have the medical knowledge, but medicine was not the answer to her restlessness. Many pioneering women doctors struggled financially and professionally while the field was still so male-dominated. Shaw may have realized that missionary work as a woman doctor would be no less constrained than mis-sionary work as a woman minister.[13]

In justifying this change of course, Shaw wrote "There is a theory that every seven years each human being undergoes a complete reconstruction, with corresponding changes in his mental and spiritual makeup. Possibly it was due to this reconstruction that, at the end of seven years on Cape Cod, my soul sent forth a sudden call to arms. I was, it reminded me, taking life too easily." "Too easily," is, of course, a relative assessment. Shaw did have abundant energy. On one hand, from her work among poor women, women in the industrial workforce, and prostitutes, she concluded that neither the ministry nor medicine could help them because those efforts didn't get to the "foundation of social structure." She felt charged to join in the "great battles" of suffrage, temperance, and social purity. All this was consistent with her earlier religious calling, but Shaw was undoubtedly ambitious. By this time, she may have concluded that her greatest talent, her oratory, could best be used in the political realm.[14]

Although Shaw's voice in her autobiography frames this dramatic telling of the next significant transition in her life as a moral calling, it is clear that Shaw fully understood the power of her particular political gift. Shaw's life path already had proven that she had the drive and self-confidence to achieve what to others might have seemed to be unrealistic and unattainable goals. Shaw had a strong sense of herself as someone special. She knew that she possessed a gift that could change people's beliefs. This was a weighty and awesome power. Beyond this was a belief in her physical stamina as well as her intellectual gifts. She knew she could work harder than most people, men and women.[15]

Actually, Shaw had begun setting the foundation for this move years earlier. She had already debuted on the suffrage stage with the Massachusetts Women Suffrage Association in January 1881. Throughout the early 1880s, Shaw had consistently lectured in and around Boston while also cultivating relationships with many of the great women leaders of this era—Mary Livermore, Lucy Stone, Frances Willard, Julia Ward Howe, and Anna Garlin Spencer. Further, she had worked with such writers and activists as the Emersons, William Lloyd Garrison, Bronson and Louisa Alcott, Wendell Philips, and her favorite among this group, John Greenleaf Whittier. Undoubtedly she had observed the opportunities of the lecture circuit. Though the lyceum movement was waning by this time, Shaw believed she could succeed.[16]

In 1885, Shaw resigned as pastor from both of her parishes. She was not abandoning her religious vocation; at her core she remained a progressive Christian who increasingly valued good works on a large scale over a particular evangelical experience of conversion and personal faith. But the particulars of Methodism were far less important to her than the greater themes of Christ's teachings. She now planned to move her application of the social gospel onto new issues and to make a life for herself on a larger stage. She wanted the freedom to devote herself to a public political career. Shaw doesn't credit any particular mentor with urging her to follow this path, but Frances Willard was among her closest friends at this time.[17]

When Anna Howard Shaw chose the public stage and political organizing as her career, this was still a risky career move for a self-supporting woman. Could she duplicate the successes she had had in Michigan and on Cape

Cod? Yet Shaw was hardly a pioneer as a woman speaker. The claims of women of European heritage to speak on spiritual issues and in religious spaces date from the first century after colonization. Women had somewhat different struggles in secular forums. With their 1837–1838 tour, Sarah and Angelina Grimke were the first women to raise the issue of women's rights within the lyceum. Though women were not common on that circuit before the Civil War, Susan B. Anthony, Lucy Stone, Lucretia Mott, Ernestine Potowski Rose, and Elizabeth Cady Stanton were among the pioneers willing to take to the public stage for women's rights. After the Civil War and especially with the expansion of the rail system, the lyceum merged with the Chautauqua movement to include everything from eminent writers such as Charles Dickens and Mark Twain to musical performers and mystics. This expansion included increasing numbers of women.[18]

James Redpath accelerated the process through which public speaking by women became accepted and respectable. In 1868 this political journalist and activist had founded his lecture bureau after he saw how haphazard the arrangements for foreign speakers were. Redpath convinced many of his acquaintances from the reform movements he had supported, including the leading progressive figures Henry Ward Beecher, Anna Dickinson, and Mary Livermore, to lecture under his guidance. His talent in this arena brought him success, and from his first office in Boston he later expanded to New York and Chicago. Though Beecher famously earned $1000 per lecture and Dickinson earned over $20,000 in one year, most of the people on Redpath's roster followed a grueling schedule, speaking five to six nights a week for about $50/night. As Tetrault's research demonstrates, many suffragists took to the circuit in the postbellum years. However, as early as the 1870s, the initial novelty of this form of education and entertainment had diminished. Lyceum courses were also on the decline at this time though Chautauquas flourished into the 1900s. Redpath wrote that "The only way to 'revive' the lecture system (if it needs reviving) is to get orators to adopt lecturing as a profession instead of law, and medicine, and the pulpit." By the time Shaw embarked on her career, the public had come to expect entertainment as well as education from these speakers. This was the state of the field when Shaw chose to make her living as a speaker.[19]

Soon, consciously or unconsciously, Shaw was crafting the public image she needed for the next stage of her life. Perhaps because Shaw was a minister, even as a young woman she was never described as a romantic or sexual figure as her sister orator, Anna Dickinson, had been. Dickinson, the fiery young Quaker, had lectured to huge audiences on abolition, radical Republicanism, and the rights of Freedmen while in her late teens and early twenties. While Shaw certainly benefited from mentoring from men as well as women, there is no hint of romance in any of her friendships with men. It is impossible to know whether Shaw had learned to avoid any involvement that could be wrongly interpreted or if she simply never had any such inclinations. On the other hand, she did casually repeat an accusation that all the women of her parish were in love with her. Shaw was much younger than Mary Livermore had been as "Queen of the Platform" in the post–Civil War era. Shaw's parishioners referred to her as a "gal" preacher, an expression that recalls both youth and frontier toughness. That latter attribute remained even as Shaw created the sedate and dignified persona seen in her ordination photograph.[20]

That portrait presents a pleasant-looking young woman with a soft but still resolute expression. With none of the delicate beauty of her mother, Shaw, with her now solid build, left the impression of sturdiness. Shaw had abandoned her earlier experiment with short hair, which seems to have been her only recorded nod to the dress reform movement. Shaw wrote of that decision that "I learned that no woman in public life can afford to make herself conspicuous by any eccentricity of dress or appearance. If she does so she suffers it herself, which may not disturb her, and to a greater or less degree she injures the cause she represents, which should disturb her very much." In her new image Shaw arranged her now long hair into a basic chignon on the top of her head. It was loose enough to avoid the impression of severity, but it was devoid of any fussy details such as curls or bangs.[21]

In dress, too, Shaw found a middle road between high style and Quaker plainness. While no public woman could escape judgments based on her appearance, she could determine the impression she made through a judicious choice of the cut of her gown, the length of the train, and the colors and fabrics she used. The young looking Shaw leaned toward gravity in her clothing: dark gown, heavy but not extravagant fabrics, basic but not unfashionable cuts, and few adornments. Her conservative dress was often relieved by a white lace collar and a pin at her neck or on her shoulder. This gravity in clothing would always stand in contradiction to her lively wit and nonconformist attitude.[22]

Nevertheless, establishing a career as a lecturer did not come easily even for someone with Shaw's rhetorical gifts. Until she could build her reputation, she needed some reliable income. It was at this juncture that Shaw accepted a paid position with the Massachusetts Woman Suffrage Association (MWSA). With this move, she now officially entered the struggle that would shape the rest of her life.[23]

By 1886, the movement that started from early individual calls for an expansion of women's opportunities and the initial gathering in Seneca Falls, New York, in 1848, had grown into an autonomous movement by and for women. Without recapitulating its history, it is clear that two significant developments had shaped the landscape Shaw entered. The first was the post–Civil War split in the movement that led to the parallel growth of the

Massachusetts-based American Woman Suffrage Association (AWSA) and its focus on state-level reforms and the New York–based National Woman Suffrage Association (NWSA) and its focus on a national constitutional amendment. The second was the failure of the NWSA-initiated legal challenges, known as the "New Departure." The backdrop to the former was the differing positions the leaders had taken over the Fourteenth Amendment that had inserted the word "male" into the constitution for the first time and extended the electoral franchise to African American men but not to women of any race. The failure of the latter legal challenges forced the NWSA to accept that the movement would have to fight on the state level first, even if the NWSA members held to their goal of a federal woman suffrage amendment. Nevertheless, it was geography more than ideology that made the Massachusetts-based group Shaw's first suffrage alliance.[24]

Just as women's activism in this era included far more than suffrage, Shaw's connections and commitments extended beyond the struggle for the franchise. Most prominent among the other causes was temperance. A movement that had long roots in the United States, it had been male-dominated until the 1870s when women joined the crusade. These activists formed a woman-led organization in 1873 and called it the Woman's Christian Temperance Union. Though its first president, Annie Turner Wittenmeyer, had limited her vision for the WCTU to one that could be reconciled with the ideas of separate spheres for women and men—women's moral superiority and the power of women's moral persuasion—her successor, the brilliant organizer Frances Willard, linked temperance to a far wider range of reforms including women's suffrage.[25]

Willard, elected president of the WCTU in 1879, had more in common with the "new women," than with the older Crusaders. She was single, well-educated, and the primary wage earner of her family; her closest relationships were with women. Drawn to the WCTU because it allowed her autonomy, Willard had been frustrated when male leaders had questioned both her abilities and her right to claim leadership when she had tried to work within male-controlled institutions. In 1883 Willard created a Franchise Department within the WCTU after the organization adopted the equal suffrage plank. Willard also claimed Shaw as a protégé and recruited her to work with the WCTU.[26]

Shaw juggled commitments to Willard, the WCTU, and various organizations during this period, but only the MWSA offered her the security of a salary. Their first proposal to Shaw included a salary of $100/month, twice her highest salary at the East Dennis Wesleyan Church. Wanting to make sure that she could live up to expectations first, Shaw hesitated to accept that level of salary. She settled on $50/month for the first year with a job description that included lecturing, organizing, and writing for the

Woman's Journal. Shaw must have been satisfied with her work for that year because she accepted the higher salary in 1886. At the same time she expanded her role and began to serve as the unpaid associate superintendent and lecturer for the WCTU.[27]

A photograph from this era captures a stylishly dressed Shaw as she works on the *Woman's Journal* with Alice Stone Blackwell, though Shaw is often cropped out of the photograph. In a way this is emblematic of Shaw's association with the Stone-Blackwell family. Few scholars acknowledge this connection. Shaw mentions her position with the MWSA in her autobiography, but she doesn't say much about her connection with the Stone-Blackwell family. Complicated from the start, it remained so throughout Shaw's life. But Shaw was quite close to the family at one point, documented by other surviving images of Shaw attending a Stone-Blackwell family reunion on Martha's Vineyard and relaxing while camping with Alice in Canada. All indications are that she started with a close and positive relationship with Alice Stone Blackwell.[28]

On the other hand, Shaw never established an easy collegiality with Alice's mother, Lucy Stone. Shaw's penchant for sarcasm is evident in her remark that she was tempted to steal something from the Stone-Blackwell home because Lucy Stone watched her as if she expected such a transgression. Further, Shaw soon felt undervalued by the MWSA. As her reputation as a speaker and organizer grew and larger and larger audiences came to her lectures, the MWSA refused to increase her salary beyond the original offer of $100/month. Other materials from these years suggest that Shaw was unwilling to be controlled even by a women's organization and especially if it meant limits on her ambition and her ability to earn money.[29]

By the summer of 1886 Shaw was freelancing beyond New England. In August and September, Shaw spoke throughout her home state of Michigan, including several engagements in her hometown of Big Rapids, making her own arrangements and probably calling on her old connections within the Michigan Methodist network. On August 26, 1886, the *Big Rapids Pioneer* printed a glowing review of "Annie" Shaw's talk entitled "The Field of Women's Usefulness," in which Shaw urged young women to look beyond material gain to see how they could serve the public.[30]

Early in 1887, Shaw realized the limits of handling her own arrangements and decided she would benefit from professional assistance. Her preference was to go right to the best and work with the Redpath Bureau. When she turned to friends and colleagues for advice, her mentor from years before, Mary Livermore advised patience and urged her to establish her reputation first before approaching Redpath. Shaw then began to gather endorsements from such names as Clara Barton and Frances Willard to promote her talks. Though she eventually did work with the Redpath Bureau of Chicago, she first settled on the Slaton Lecture Bureau.[31]

If Shaw ever struggled financially during her years as a freelance lecturer, she made no mention of it in her autobiography. She states that she earned $300 the first month. "Later I frequently earned more than that, and very rarely less." This development further strained the power dynamics with the MWSA and the Stone-Blackwells as she now negotiated her arrangements with the MWSA more as an independent contractor than as an employee. A particularly tense correspondence between Shaw and the Stone-Blackwells illustrates these strains as Shaw worked to redefine her position with those who had been her mentors and who had eased her entry into the women's movement. After several letters in which the AWSA leaders tried to gain firm speaking commitments from Shaw, Shaw agreed to certain specific weeks with the MWSA, stipulating fifteen lectures a month at $10 each, plus another $100 per month for two months if she organized the Association's bazaar. Shaw had negotiated her way around the salary limit the MWSA had imposed just months earlier. After all these arrangements were settled, Shaw felt the need to calm the waters. She wasn't about to burn any bridges with this part of the movement. Writing that she hoped they could soon talk face-to-face, Shaw stated, "I thank you for all the kindly thoughts and sentiments expressed for me in your letters, and I trust you may always have reason to feel the same sympathy with and in me." For the time, this seemed to work. This same year she was named one of two National Lecturers for the AWSA.[32]

These seemingly small details from the earliest days of Shaw's public speaking career illustrate how thorough a negotiator Shaw was. At a time when women were expected to be removed from the masculine world of money, the reality was that Shaw was probably not that unusual in having to be vigilant about economic matters. Whether they had direct control over their finances or not, few women could ignore the details of their families' incomes or the costs of food and clothing. Further, as Tetrault's 2010 article argues, many apparently "middle-class" women had to become families' wage-earners when husbands died, became ill, or failed in their businesses. Though few other scholars and biographers have explored additional economic questions such as how wealthy women came to have access to the fortunes they seldom had earned themselves, who actually controlled the finances in middle-class homes, or exactly how single women of varying classes supported themselves—though scholars of single women are beginning to address the latter—it is impossible to understand Shaw's life without examining such issues. Shaw consistently had to attend to the minutiae of fees, collections, the cost of train tickets, and her other expenses. Not only did she have to convince herself and others of what she was worth, but she also had to demand payment for her political work. This need to earn her living would complicate the relationships she had with her colleagues throughout her entire suffrage career. The seemingly innocent phrase "plus expenses" would end up taking on a meaning far greater than might have been imagined.[33]

Still, Shaw negotiated these years during which she established herself as an independent speaker and leader with remarkable self-assurance. Undoubtedly she already envisioned herself as the equal of these leaders. She must also have been on solid financial ground. At a time when few women could set their own fees or salaries, Shaw learned to ask for what she felt she was worth and what would make a venture profitable enough to provide a reasonably comfortable life.

Publicity flyers capture how Shaw covered her multiple positions in the late 1880s. Her address is listed as 5 Park St., Boston, the AWSA address, and her titles are "Associate Superintendent and Lecturer of the Franchise Department of the National Woman's Christian Temperance Union" and "State Lecturer of the Massachusetts Woman Suffrage Association." Her advertised lecture topics reflect the WCTU influence in "The Temperance Problem," "The Relation of Woman's Ballot to the Home," and "True Manliness or Social Purity," while "Woman's Enfranchisement" and "The Fate of the Republics," addressed suffrage issues. Though most of the endorsements included on her press release are newspaper reviews from Massachusetts or Michigan, the last paragraph belongs to Frances Willard. "[B]ut her address before the Bay View Sunday School Assembly on Woman's Christian Temperance Union Day was a revelation. For basis and breadth, for plan and perspicuity, for logic and humor, it merited that choice word, 'masterly.' In calm strength and dignity of tone and manner, Miss Shaw reminded me of Mary Livermore." At least in Willard's eyes, Shaw already had earned the right to be positively compared to the "Queen of the Platform," the woman who had first inspired and encouraged her to follow her dreams. Nevertheless, Shaw's fees were still modest at this time, at least for her temperance lectures—$20 for one day and $35 for two.[34]

Such support from Frances Willard made sense. In the 1880s the Shaw and Willard bond was much stronger, closer, and more comfortable than those Shaw had with the Stone-Blackwell family. Though Willard had come from a solidly middle-class family who had supported her education, both were single Methodist Midwesterners who worked best and formed their closest ties with other activist women. Willard was eight years older than Shaw and fashioned herself as Anna's "older sister," while Anna was Willard's clerical "confessor." Although Willard was definitely grooming Shaw to take over the WCTU Franchise Department, at least one passage from an undated letter between Willard and Shaw indicates that Willard was even hoping that Shaw would eventually succeed her in the WCTU presidency. For a few years, Shaw kept open the possibility of a future in the WCTU leadership.[35]

Then in 1887, a new and even more powerful force entered Shaw's world in the person of Susan B. Anthony. Shaw first met the veteran organizer in Newton, Kansas, on October 14, 1887, when she, representing the AWSA, spoke on the same platform as Henry Blackwell, Susan B. Anthony, and Rachel Foster. A reference to that event marks the first time that Shaw's name appears in the *History of Woman Suffrage*.[36]

Susan B. Anthony hardly needs an introduction to today's readers, though the images most have of her probably capture little of the power and charisma of the best-known American suffrage leader. Anthony, with her Quaker father and Baptist mother, could trace her family's arrival in America to 1634. Though her family's fortunes had risen and fallen with the economic crises and booms of the early nineteenth century, Anthony had earned her education in local and Quaker boarding schools before a family financial crisis forced her into wage-earning. Anthony had devoted almost all of her life to the struggle for equal rights with the focus increasingly on women's right to vote. Single, without a permanent home or a regular source of income, by this time "Aunt Susan" was understandably venerated by the younger generation of suffrage activists. Few could ever match her selfless devotion to "the cause."[37]

Elizabeth Cady Stanton was Anthony's first and most important compatriot in the struggle, but Stanton, married with a large family, had never adopted Anthony's peripatetic lifestyle or exclusive devotion to suffrage. She did continue as titular leader of the NWSA (and later, the NAWSA) mostly at Anthony's insistence. As Anthony continued to lead a life focused on women's rights, she consistently recruited younger women to her circle, adopting them into a type of kinship over which she presided. One of her first "nieces" was Rachel Foster (1858–1919), later Avery. This Quaker heiress, who had joined the movement in 1879, had become Anthony's companion, assistant, and often benefactor. As Anthony turned many responsibilities over to Foster, Susan B. Anthony's niece, Lucy E. Anthony, in turn became Foster's secretary.[38]

Shaw was already forty when she first met Susan B. Anthony. Shaw was also single and certainly committed to the life of a political activist even if not exclusively devoted to suffrage. Anthony quickly recognized Shaw's potential. Anthony was in her late sixties and especially concerned about who would lead the next generation. Her current lieutenant, Rachel Foster, adopted a baby in 1887. Foster would go on to marry Cyrus Miller Avery the next year, and soon they had two more daughters. While Foster Avery assured Anthony that her commitment to the suffrage movement would not change, Anthony probably knew better than even Foster Avery that their partnership already had.[39]

Shaw's star was in the ascendance when Elizabeth Cady Stanton convinced her American coworkers and several international leaders that the fortieth anniversary of Seneca Falls was the occasion to launch a new organization, the International Council of Women. They agreed the NWSA would convene representatives of the leading women's organizations in Washington, D.C., on March 25, 1888. "Formal invitations requesting the appointment of delegates will be issued to representative organizations in every department of women's work." This was not an open convention, but Anna Howard Shaw was invited as president of the Wimodaughsis Club of Washington, D.C. On Sunday, March 24, 1888, on Susan B. Anthony's recommendation, Shaw preached the sermon at the inaugural religious service. A transcription of "The Heavenly Vision" fills five pages of the *History of Woman Suffrage*, accompanied by a photograph of the Rev. Anna Howard Shaw.[40]

If Anthony had any doubts about Shaw, this sermon ended them. Reading the extant text of this sermon, it isn't hard to imagine why. The vision Shaw constructed was of an inclusive, global, and ecumenical women's movement. Believing that anyone who could imagine such a movement was one who could commit to the struggle, Anthony now decided to actively but carefully recruit Shaw to the NWSA. Though Shaw had just become head of the WCTU's Franchise Department that January, Shaw wrote that after the first ICW, Anthony "soon swung me into active work with her."[41]

Soon after, another Anthony family member entered Anna Howard Shaw's life, someone who would be as important to Shaw as Susan B., though in an entirely different way. Lucy E. Anthony was the daughter of Susan's brother Jacob Merritt Anthony. Both of Susan B. Anthony's brothers had settled in "Bleeding" Kansas during its turbulent pre–Civil War history. Daniel Read Anthony first became a military hero and then a wealthy newspaper editor. Jacob Merritt Anthony lived in his brother's shadow, managing a lower-middle-class living as a seller of sewing machines. He had married Mary Elmira in Kansas, and together they had three children; Lucy, the oldest, was born in 1859. Sometime before 1880, Lucy had been sent east to join the Rochester household of her Aunts Susan and Mary.[42]

Lucy had none of her aunt's confidence or vigor, but she was dedicated to "the cause." Soon after Shaw met Lucy Anthony, Susan B. Anthony urged Shaw to hire Lucy as her business manager. Very quickly she became much more than that. Even their earliest letters have a tone of flirtation. "So you are fond of me," Shaw wrote to Lucy in one of these. Starting in the late 1880s, Shaw developed a complex personal and professional partnership with Lucy that persisted for the rest of her life.[43]

Shaw was now dead center in the rivalry between the NWSA and the AWSA. Lucy Anthony had written to her aunt that she wanted to pay for a lifetime membership in the NWSA for Shaw. Although Susan B. Anthony found this to be a "lovely" thought because she too wanted Shaw as a leader of the NWSA, Anthony felt she had to tread carefully because Shaw was still aligned with the AWSA. "I do not want to call anybody before she is sent by herself but I do hope she'll soon send herself over to us, head, heart and hand."[44]

It took some time, but by February 1889, the Anthony forces had made Shaw a concrete offer to become a NWSA organizer. Wherever Shaw's heart might have been, the financial pragmatist or perhaps the negotiator in her dominated. The NWSA offered $1000 a year and $200 toward expenses. Shaw responded matter-of-factly, "My expenses are about $1000 a year. I have had a standing offer for three years which I can take any time, of $100 a month and all my expenses and a room in Boston. The past year I have earned about $2800, but my expenses have been high." But Shaw went on to state that this was a financial not a political hesitation, declaring that she has "already gone over to Woman Suffrage, head, heart and hand" and that "there does not live, not excepting Aunt Susan, a more thoroughly radical suffragist than I am."[45]

As Shaw's loyalties and her future remained unsettled, she joined the AWSA and NWSA leaders who began working to reunite these groups in 1889. Concurrently, Shaw was still committed to the WCTU and hoped to bring Lucy Anthony and Alice Blackwell into her franchise department of the WCTU. "I think that would be a kind of poetic uniting of the old names of Stone and Anthony, and as I had perhaps as much as anyone to do with bringing the two societies together, I would like to have the privilege of bringing the younger generation together with me in my official capacity in the W.C.T.U." Susan B. Anthony was trying to convince her to publicly declare that suffrage was her first priority and move to Philadelphia where Lucy E. Anthony and Rachel Foster Avery lived.[46]

During these years of transition, Shaw may have found the cause to which she could and would dedicate the rest of her life, but she still had no real home base. She was in Michigan and Boston regularly, but as would be the case for the next fifteen years, she was frequently in a railway car or in some small town hotel. The only consistent address for her correspondence was the AWSA office, 5 Park St., Boston.

Soon this changed and Shaw began to call Philadelphia her home. While Susan B. Anthony's advice to move to the City of Brotherly Love might have been based as much on her wish to separate Shaw from the AWSA base of Boston as it was to ease the organizational complications among her nieces, in the end it seems pretty certain that it wasn't the place but the person who determined Shaw's home. In October 1889, her letter to Lucy stated, "I do so long to get our rooms settled in Philadelphia or anywhere else on earth where you and home are. I am so fond of thinking of the blessed rest of it when I am away and take perhaps as much comfort in the thought of you in the midst of it resting from your work as in anything else. You are a blessed comfort to me, my Balance." Although the final agreement that brought the AWSA and NWSA together as the National American Woman Suffrage Association (NAWSA) and resolved Shaw's institutional identity would take another year, Anna's friendship with Lucy was settled in far less time.[47]

Over this decade Shaw had journeyed back to Michigan frequently, but one trip, the one in 1885, had been special. That year she and her surviving siblings and their families gathered with her parents to celebrate Thomas and Nicolas's fiftieth wedding anniversary. This would be the last time she and her three brothers would be together until 1911. Gradually Shaw's ties to this hometown and to this patriarchal family lessened as her ties with her new family, a new type of family, strengthened.[48]

In the years since she had left Big Rapids and Mecosta County, Shaw had taken all that had frustrated her from that life—her limited options, her mother's powerlessness, her father's and brothers' freedoms and privileges, the geographical isolation, the poverty—and used it as fuel to first educate herself to be able to enter the male-dominated professions and then to find the means with which to earn a decent and respectable living. Making a living, though, was not making a life, and Shaw wanted a life with meaning and a life with love, companionship, and family. Over the course of the 1880s Shaw willingly gave up the comfortable but limited life of a small town minister to dedicate herself to changing the inequalities of the social structure in ways that she believed would better women's lives more than any work she could do as a minister or medical doctor. Fortunately for Shaw, she turned out to have many of the talents, skills, and attributes that the leaders and the constituencies of the woman suffrage and women's temperance movements needed and valued. By 1888, Shaw would state to Lucy Stone, "I have registered a vow that I will from this time forth *never* work for any political party, never give one dollar to any religious body, home or foreign, never listen Sunday after Sunday to the preaching of any man, never give one ounce of my strength of body or purse, or mind, or heart to any cause which opposes the best interest of women."[49]

Fortunately, Shaw achieved the independence to make those decisions. Shaw had found that she could make a very good living serving this cause, lecturing as much as she needed to for financial security and organizing during the rest of her time. As a single woman she could travel as far and for as long as her commitments needed. She answered to no boss except the leaders she valued. Her only constraints were her stamina and health.

Only after she allied herself with Susan B. Anthony, Anthony's niece Lucy, and, to a great extent, Rachel Foster Avery, Anthony's adopted niece, did

Shaw find that she could have a life as well as make a living. Probably no one outside such relationships can understand how certain people just "click." Shaw, the Anthonys, and Avery found that they could work together in harmony, not necessarily always agreeing but trusting each other enough to always be able to move forward together. Sources suggest that Shaw struggled with the Stone-Blackwell–led organizations over finances, yet Shaw chose to work with Anthony when the NAWSA could not pay her a set salary. Obviously the issues were respect, autonomy and probably those intangible qualities that allow people to connect this strongly and which Shaw valued more than money.

CHAPTER 4

Apprenticeship in the National American Woman Suffrage Association (1890–1903)

All human beings are under obligations first to themselves.
... The abominable doctrine taught in the pulpit, the
press, in books and elsewhere, is that the whole duty of women
is self-abasement and self-sacrifice. I do not believe subjugation is
woman's duty any more than it is the duty of a man to be under
subjection to another man or to many men. Women have the right
of independence, of conscience, of will and responsibility.

South Dakota was not a welcoming landscape for Anna Howard Shaw when she joined Susan B. Anthony and other suffrage workers in 1890 for her first state suffrage campaign.[1] While the Wounded Knee massacre of December 1890 dominates the history of South Dakota's initial year of statehood, the earlier part of that year witnessed a campaign and a referendum on woman and Native American suffrage. The debates among the white male politicians were intense. These politicians made promises to their constituents and the petitioners that they casually abandoned with the next round of debates. Adding to the tensions was the ease with which white immigrant men could gain citizenship and consequently the vote in this thinly populated state.

In this rugged region, suffrage activists struggled to find a decent hotel or boarding house, purchase an edible meal, or locate a laundry to wash their clothes. The weather compounded the challenges that the women and their allies faced. The record heat and drought of that summer was relentless. The resulting dust and grit swirled up with each hot breeze before settling back on the houses and the people, on the water and the food. As accustomed as she was to adapting to travel and unpredictable environments, Shaw doubted her decision to sign on for this campaign where she joined the now seventy-year-old Anthony, Henry Blackwell, Anthony's other new recruit, Carrie Lane Chapman Catt, and numerous local suffragists. Unlike

Anthony, who seemed as oblivious to physical discomforts as she was impervious to political slights and rejections, Shaw keenly felt the heat and the other discomforts.[2]

Shaw also chafed at the slights coming from both the leading men of the state and the armchair suffragists back east. Anthony's new disciple stayed in a low-level rage as she watched the veteran campaigner weather both the conditions and the rebuffs of the state's political leaders. Susan B. Anthony had become part of Shaw's pantheon, and consequently this loyal partisan bristled at treatments Anthony had long learned to tolerate.[3]

Further, Shaw, with her consciousness as an outsider and working woman, noted who was shouldering their share of the struggle and who wasn't. The unification of the two leading suffrage organizations—the Massachusetts-based, Stone and Blackwell–led American Woman Suffrage Association (AWSA) and the Stanton-Anthony–headed National Woman Suffrage Association (NWSA)—was ratified, but there were residual resentments on both sides. The AWSA had always been assumed to be the richer of the two organizations, and in a letter to Lucy Anthony, Shaw raged as she could when tired and homesick against those who were not there and not helping them financially. "I wish some of the rich Massachusetts suffragists could endure it a little. I think these Wianno people would prefer to smell the salt air and fan themselves and talk palmistry and hypnotism and ethics and Emerson and agnosticism and their idea of woman suffrage, while they neither subscribe a dollar nor get anyone else to do so to enable us to stop at decent places while we do the work they dream about." Shaw, who had worked closely but not always congenially with the AWSA people, did not keep her complaints just between herself and Lucy. She wrote testy notes to Alice Stone Blackwell until finally Blackwell's mother and suffrage pioneer, Lucy Stone, sent out a request for monies for South Dakota.[4]

Though the rigors of this campaign tested even Shaw's adaptability, at forty-three, Shaw was at her peak in terms of health and vigor. She had a still smooth and pleasant face, but with her prematurely gray hair and conservative clothes, she looked "womanly." Sturdy and strong from years of physical and emotional struggles, she clothed her radical, irreverent, and nonconformist spirit in the garb and style of a respectable minister, a dignified image of the "Reverend Shaw" for the photographs that accompanied her publicity brochures. It was a necessary camouflage for a single woman who was actively challenging in words and in actions the current hegemony that women were the "weaker sex," naturally suited for hearth and home.[5]

Overall, Shaw embraced her new calling, her new pulpit, and her new form of ministry. She was quickly becoming the movement's new voice, a leader whose nonelite origins gave her a remarkable ability to translate women's demands into appeals understandable to a diversity of Americans.

Shaw's strengths as a speaker and the depth of her commitments to women's causes were put to the test here, but she toughed it out as a true daughter of the frontier.[6]

In reality, only a few elite women, especially in places such as South Dakota, had ever had the luxury of the frailty or the delicacy that was being proclaimed and promoted as the feminine ideal by this period's pundits, a group that included many men and some women and ranged from college presidents through politicians, writers, and journalists. Yes, the Gilded Age had brought extraordinary wealth, luxury goods, and leisure to a small number of women; many more knew the economics of domestic work in the homes of those women or of industrial labor in the factories such families owned. Of course more and more frequently, young middle-class women were attending colleges, entering professions, and rejecting marriage. These women and their choices were the topics of much debate about the future of womanhood, but few such women knew the conditions that the majority of women faced. Though Shaw shared certain characteristics with the new middle-class cohort of college-educated single women, she knew better the challenges of the average homemaker.[7]

The preponderance of women in South Dakota, in fact in all of the United States, lived on farms—their own or as tenants—where wives and daughters had long shouldered the myriad responsibilities that kept their rural families fed, clothed, and sheltered in the best of times. Shaw understood how these women and their families faced the threats of droughts, diseases, or collapsing markets that could undermine their survival in any season. Many of these women had confronted frontier conditions, given birth "on the prairie," and shared the experiences of living on seemingly endless plains, on mountains, or on marginal lands whose climates and conditions were almost unimaginable for those raised east of the Mississippi River. From a wide range of cultures, they created homes and communities even as they faced brutal winters and debilitating summer heat in log cabins, sod houses, or other minimal shelters on lands that had been populated for thousands of years by various indigenous groups. The women in the western states had known hard and uncertain times, and Shaw understood their lives.[8]

Nevertheless, Shaw was writing a new script for a woman's life. Her early experiences may not have differed from most women's realities, but her subsequent choices were a drastic departure from what was expected of women. In her autobiography, Shaw made her public career sound exciting. She regaled her readers with thrilling stories of venturing across a railroad trestle on foot over a flooded river to keep a speaking commitment and of outrunning pursuing wolves in a sleigh to catch her next train one winter midnight. Fortunately at this point in Shaw's history, we have letters and diaries, sources that tell the other side of this life. With the adventures came loneliness, uncertainty, and hardship. This was the "job," the career Shaw willingly chose believing she had the stamina, the toughness, and the tolerance to live such a life at a time when concerns about women's delicacy were only beginning to shift.[9]

Shaw needed her fortitude and optimism; the 1890s were hard years. The economic depression that started with the collapse of the railroads in 1893 lasted until 1897. Conservative turns in politics, economics, race relations, and foreign policy produced resistance and reactions ranging from Progressive Era reforms, anti-imperialist activities, early civil rights organizing, and labor protests to the rise of anti-immigrant and racist political groups. Through their decisions at the end of the nineteenth century, the U.S. courts permitted states to ignore the rights of citizens of color and the voting rights of African American men. With the 1896 *Plessey vs. Ferguson* decision, "separate but equal" became the standard in many parts of the country. Protests, or success in spite of such restrictions, resulted in harassment, violence, and lynchings. It was not uncommon in this era for reformers, including suffrage leaders, to hold extreme racist and reactionary views. Many otherwise liberal Progressive Era activists held to paternalistic beliefs that their class, their race, their nationality, and their religion positioned them to direct the betterment of their "inferiors," both the nonelites at home and the increasing number of people under U.S. control as it joined the imperial age.[10]

This decade brought the annexation of Hawai'i, the Spanish-American War, and a greater U.S. role in the Caribbean and the Philippines. Scholars are beginning to link these empire-building policies with concerns about gender and the changing definitions of masculinity. Missionaries, including increasing numbers of women, spread out across the globe preaching a Christian message that combined the social gospel with social Darwinism. The great Columbian Exposition in Chicago in 1893 presented a spectacular visual of the supposed global divide between the "civilized" and the "exotic."[11]

The woman suffrage movement was hardly immune to these larger political developments. As the first generation of activists abdicated their power to new leaders, the next cohort included more conservative women and fewer African Americans. Calls for universal suffrage competed with the louder and broader discussions about "qualified," educated, or limited suffrage. Anti-Black and anti-immigrant positions became commonplace and were found even among such prominent women as Elizabeth Cady Stanton and Charlotte Perkins Gilman. Although the states that approved woman suffrage—Wyoming, Colorado, Utah, and Idaho—were in the West, the NAWSA also believed the movement needed to work in the South. With such efforts, the NAWSA stepped into the quagmire of racial and states' rights politics. These issues framed the grueling 1890 campaign in South

Dakota, but they persisted as challenges for Shaw and the suffrage movement well into the twentieth century.[12]

The other outcome from the South Dakota campaign that would shape the newly reunited movement was the friendship between Shaw and Anthony's other new recruit, Carrie Chapman Catt. Both Shaw and Catt proved their mettle to Anthony and each other in an area where the widely scattered settlements could be reached only by long train rides. Amid the harsh conditions with water so brackish that they couldn't even brush their teeth, Catt and Shaw forged a lifelong respect for each other.

These women and many other organizers gave it their all, and yet this long and demanding campaign ended in defeat for both the Indian and the woman suffrage efforts. Shaw was outraged that the women lost by the greater margin. When Shaw, herself an immigrant, railed against the "ignorant laborers newly come to our country" who defeated the bill, one wonders if she wasn't also protesting her own exclusion from the rights her brothers now enjoyed. She continued to be irate over the treatment Susan B. Anthony received at the Republican State Convention when the white male leaders had barely acknowledged the venerable suffragist while honoring a delegation of American Indian men as "Distinguished Guests."[13]

According to the *History of Woman Suffrage*, Shaw turned her anger and frustration into "wit, satire and pathos" when she took to the stage in an address inspired by the South Dakota incident. She gave her talk "Indians versus Women," at the 1891 NAWSA Convention not long after the South Dakota campaign ended. While this is certainly not the most coherent of Shaw's addresses, with its various parts presenting contradictory messages, nevertheless it is significant because it is Shaw's first public statement involving race. Further, it is the most recognized and discussed Shaw address in feminist studies, a strong example of the strange twists evident in much scholarship concerning Shaw. This address is often used to label her a racist, even a white supremacist. For these reasons it is worth considering in depth.[14]

In this speech, Shaw challenges South Dakota's men to explain why they questioned women's qualifications for citizenship more than those of other men, giving the example of how newspaper editors doubted women's preparedness for suffrage but not Indian men's. Shaw then expresses outrage over the fact that 8 percent more of the white men of South Dakota supported Indian male suffrage than supported woman suffrage. In this section Shaw is unquestionably condescending toward Native Americans, even attributing the caricature "Ugh" response to an Indian she engaged in conversation.[15]

Then, abruptly, Shaw ends this line of argument and demonstrates her understanding of the realities of frontier women, elaborating on the hardships women faced and the sacrifices they made in South Dakota. She bemoans the fact that the women had no laws to protect themselves, not even their right to their children or the lands where their presence settled a claim. Shaw protests that the women get "nothing" from the state. To her it was plain and simple misogyny that produced the disparate treatment in the vote. Men valued and honored men while ignoring all women. Shaw makes it clear that she is including all women, naming pioneer, immigrant, and Native women.[16]

Continuing, Shaw then asks what the Indian gets from the current government. Now sympathetic to the indigenous people of the Dakotas, she argues, "He gets something though he does not get half that belongs to him." Shaw reminds her audience of how Native Americans have been forced into a dependent relationship with the government. Building to an emotional climax, she proceeds to retell the horrors of the Wounded Knee massacre that took place at the end of 1890. She names as murder the killing of women and children, re-creating with her words the image of infants found after surviving through three days of a blizzard in the shawls of their dead mothers. Shaw asks what rights these murdered Lakota Sioux women had. Contrasting this treatment from the U.S. government with the various examples of how Indians treated white settlers, Shaw describes the murals in the nation's capitol that show Native Americans acted with love and generosity to the colonists. Given the history of white men's oppression of Indians, Shaw suggests that white women would do much better. Referring to how Pocahontas saved John Smith, Shaw continues, "We only ask that the white woman may do for the Indian what the Indian woman did for the white man." Shaw closes with a plea for justice for all.[17]

Beyond the opening, this isn't a particularly racist, white supremacist, or elitist speech, especially in the context of its time. Shaw states the shared disenfranchisement of women and American Indians and never demands more rights for white women than she did for the native people. As Shaw would throughout her long career, she advocated for universal equal rights. This speech might have faded from history as have most of Shaw's from this era if African American educator and writer, Anna Julia Cooper, hadn't taken note of it. Cooper responded with her statement, similarly titled, "Woman versus the Indian," included in her *A Voice from the South* (1892).[18]

Cooper opens her essay by praising Shaw and Susan B. Anthony. She refers to an incident that took place in Washington, D.C., when Shaw was the president of a women's organization, Wimodaughsis. Cooper describes how the organization's secretary, an unnamed woman from Kentucky, refused to allow an African American woman (Cooper?) to join one of the organization's classes for working women. Cooper tells how, when this incident came to Shaw's attention, Shaw gave the club an ultimatum—fire the woman from Kentucky or she would resign. The woman from Kentucky left, and Wimodaughsis was open to women of all races.[19]

With this opening, Cooper clearly establishes Shaw as someone who would not see herself as racist. Cooper then proceeds to argue that white women, especially "ladies," have the power to establish the behavioral norms of the society. In the main part of this essay, Cooper focuses on the current state of race relations in the United States with special attention to the oppressive treatment of African American women by the railroads. Cooper challenges white reformers to address this issue. Only at the conclusion does Cooper return to the specifics of Shaw's speech.[20]

Near the end, Cooper writes "This, too, is why I conceive the subject to have been unfortunately worded which was chosen by Miss Shaw at the Women's' Council and which stands at the head of this chapter." It is difficult to assess whether Cooper was responding to the actual content of Shaw's speech or just the concept behind Shaw's title. Both Cooper and Shaw seem to argue for the same thing, so much so that the endings of each statement seem to echo each other. One stated, "Let all of us who love liberty solve these problems in justice; and let us mete out to the Indian, to the negro, to the foreigner, and to the woman, the justice which we demand for ourselves, the liberty which we love for ourselves. Let us recognize in each of them that One above, the Father of us all, and that all are brothers, all are one." And the other argued, "For woman's cause is the cause of the weak; and when all the weak shall have received their due consideration, then woman shall have her 'rights,' and the Indian will have his rights, and the Negro will have his rights, and all the strong will have learned to deal justly, to love mercy, and to walk humbly; and our fair land will have been taught the secret of universal courtesy which is after all nothing but the art, the science, and the religion of regarding one's neighbor as one's self, and to do for him as we would, were the conditions swapped, that he do for us."[21]

Nevertheless, Cooper presents a remarkably prescient critique of the shifting racial politics of the women's movement and warns against the NAWSA's southern plans and its leaders' acquiescence to the culture's conservative shift. It captures the tensions between Shaw's patronizing and problematic language and her commitment, at least in her public speeches, to equal rights regardless of race, sex, or religion—a stand that, as noted, put her at odds with increasing numbers of her sister suffragists. Nevertheless, Cooper's essay is significant because it demonstrates the gap between Shaw's and Cooper's understandings of the issues facing women of different races. While Shaw saw herself as an ally of women of color and as a reformer who believed in equality and would act against racism as an individual, as in the Wimodaughsis incident, she was limited by both her own analysis of how racism worked and by the decisions of the organizations to which she gave her allegiance. Shaw might have held to the earlier ideal of universal suffrage, but in this era of increased segregation, Shaw and the newer suffrage leaders lacked the experience and subsequent insights that came from working side-by-side with African American leaders, experiences that Susan B. Anthony, Lucy Stone, and especially Lucretia Mott had known. Nevertheless, what Shaw learned from her first major address on racial issues since becoming a national figure was that African American women were organized, that they were listening, and that they would respond.[22]

Religion was another contentious arena for woman rights activists in the 1890s, but Shaw, secure in her knowledge of contemporary religious exegesis, generally relished confrontations over biblical interpretations of women's appropriate roles. Though Susan B. Anthony discouraged drawing attention to Shaw's ministerial credentials, she certainly encouraged Shaw's challenges to any arguments against women's rights that were based on the Christian scriptures. Of course, the later controversy over the *Woman's Bible* demonstrated that Shaw didn't welcome all religious controversies.[23]

Shaw joined a long line of suffragists who challenged the mainstream Christian interpretation of the *Bible* when she spoke on "God's Women," in February 1891 for the National Council of Women, shortly before she gave "Indians versus Women." In this speech, which Shaw gave in some version hundreds of times, she used the rhetorical and logical device of juxtaposing the actual words and stories of the *Bible* with men's interpretations of them. Shaw challenged men on their right to define who "God's women" were by recalling the divinely directed leadership roles and independent actions of such women as Deborah, Moses's mother; Miriam; Ruth; Rachel; the Marys of the New Testament; and her own personal heroine, Vashti, the disobedient wife, who chose self-respect over following the wishes of an unworthy husband. Shaw challenged not just husbands but also ministers on the issue of wifely obedience and countered the argument that motherhood was women's "greatest crown of glory." These figures from the *Bible* stood as examples of "true, noble, strong, healthy, spiritual womanhood." Their glory didn't come from submission or motherhood. During the decade when Elizabeth Cady Stanton and her revising committee of women critical of the latest version of the *Bible* began researching and writing the *Woman's Bible*, Shaw chose this route to bring to the public her views on what the Christian religion said about women.[24]

Both of these speeches illustrate how Shaw used her new pulpit, and the podium was the most consistent aspect of Shaw's life during this period. Over these years, Shaw developed the rhetorical strategy of first honoring mainstream values on various issues, such as motherhood and marriage. Only after she was well into her speeches would she develop her critiques. This was successful. Throughout this period reporters gave her more positive reviews than they had generally given suffrage speakers. They noted Shaw's quickness, her warmth, and particularly her wit, which was sarcastic but never so biting as to alienate her audience. "Friend and foe of the vexed question of Woman Suffrage alike admire her. Even the man who quivers under her blows, smiles, applauds and admires." During these years, between her paid lecture tours and her direct NAWSA work, Shaw spent well over 50 percent of her time "on the road," most frequently speaking in smaller venues, learning to handle both hostile audiences and indifferent organizers. Over these years the number of different locations Shaw visited ranged from a high of 170 in 1893 to a low of 101 in 1901. Not infrequently she would give two or more lectures on a given day.[25]

Shaw seems to have always been away from home for longer periods than she had planned or hoped to be. Given the difficulties of this life, it is not surprising that the word "home" took on a mystical meaning for Shaw. Starting in the late 1880s, Shaw spoke of "home" as an emotional space rather than a physical location. While her aging parents and one brother remained in Big Rapids, Shaw's official address in Philadelphia changed eight times between 1888 and 1902. What was constant was that home had become wherever Lucy E. Anthony was.

The letters of this early period concerning Anna and Lucy's relationship are remarkable for the intertwining of emotional and financial terms. The latter issue set this relationship apart from many such partnerships. In 1890, only two years after they met, Shaw told Susan B. Anthony that she was going to start paying Lucy a regular salary, but Shaw went further and stated that from now on half of whatever she had would be Lucy's. It almost sounds as though Anna was proposing a community-property marriage. Aunt Susan seemed to understand that Shaw was describing more than a business agreement, but she questioned this arrangement. "I don't understand it, you a strong, self-reliant, energetic woman, and she a sick young creature without experience." Anna was adamant, arguing that this was both the "right" and the "just" thing to do. Over a decade had passed since Persis Addy's death. Shaw had gained strong friendships in that time, but she had no companion to fill the void Addy's death had left. Now Shaw had decided that Lucy, though younger, shyer, and far from being her peer as a leader, had both the business skills and moral qualities that were compatible with her needs. Just as Susan B. Anthony had become Shaw's public and political partner, Lucy became her life partner, as well as the woman whose work allowed her both to have a home and lead the nomadic life she had chosen.[26]

This interdependence of feelings and finances in Shaw's conception of her relationship should not be surprising. As someone who was first and foremost a working woman, Shaw understood money. Lucy may have been Shaw's "beloved," but also Shaw recognized that it was only fair that Lucy receive a regular salary to ensure her a measure of autonomy. In many ways this was Shaw's way of putting her own theory about traditional women's work into practice. Additionally Shaw decentered romance. From her earliest letters, Shaw had emphasized other emotions over "love." "I wish I could let you see the inside of my love for you, but, better still, that you could know the depths of my trust and faith in you." Long before there were feminist analyses of the economic basis of heterosexuality, Shaw had a materialist perspective, one still not fully explored in LGBTQ theories or discussions of single women. Additionally, though she, or perhaps any of her generation, never uttered the phrases "same-sex marriage" or "nontraditional family," Shaw had envisioned a new type of "family," one neither constrained nor endorsed by the state.[27]

This family extended beyond Shaw and Lucy E. Anthony. In the early 1890s, when Shaw was gone for so much of each year, Lucy continued to reside with Rachel Foster Avery and Avery's family, first in a large brick row house at 748 N. 19th St., in the Spring Garden section of Philadelphia. After the death of Avery's sister and a lawsuit that disinherited her brother, Avery was the sole heir to the wealth her father had accumulated. In 1891 Avery purchased a large tract of land on the northeast edge of Philadelphia called Somerton. On this land she built a home that could accommodate not only her immediate family but also her sister suffragists. Lucy and Anna used this address from 1892 to 1896. So close were these women that Anna referred to one of Rachel's daughters, probably Rose, as "my baby."[28]

In spite of the benefits and apparent ease of this arrangement, Anna and Lucy clearly yearned to have some place of their own. They especially sought one that could be their refuge during the summer months when Shaw tended to travel and lecture less. At first these were just future dreams. "I have so many happy thoughts of that little house we are planning. It shall be yours to furnish just as you want it." Soon, though, Shaw and Lucy decided to act and not wait "five years." "We will begin the month we bargain for the place, which will probably be next month." Shaw contacted her friend, suffragist Ellen Dietrick, who suggested some land on the southern Cape. Given her earlier criticisms of the people who lived in Wianno, it is ironic that Shaw chose this spot on Cape Cod as the location of her first home.[29]

Shaw chose a secluded location for "The Haven," as they fittingly named their summer retreat. For years their spot was the last on the road in the colony started by reformers such as William Lloyd Garrison. The land faced the Nantucket Sound in a newly developed part of Osterville in Barnstable County. With pine forests and bluffs overlooking the ocean, inlets, and ponds, it was both an idyllic rural escape and an easy train ride from Boston, seventy miles north. The house, a cottage of two and a half stories with dark cedar shingles and a large porch, couldn't be seen from either the beach or the road. By November 10, 1892, she was inviting her old friends from Big Rapids "down to the cottage." This would be Anna and Lucy's first home, the first place they shared with their biological and created families. Shaw's life had a fullness now that she could only have imagined when she had set out on her new path in 1885.[30]

Other very different transitions came that year. In the NAWSA Elizabeth Cady Stanton retired from the position of president at age seventy-six, participating for the last time at a national gathering of the movement she had inspired, organized, and directed for over forty years. She did not leave, though, without one final inspired oration in the form of her "Solitude of Self." Lucy Stone similarly stepped down from her position as head of the executive committee. Both retirements and Stone's death a year later reminded the delegates of the passing of the pioneer generation. From among the younger women, Shaw was the one the NAWSA elected vice president, stepping into the second spot that Susan B. Anthony vacated when she became president. In this ascension, Shaw bypassed many women with far greater seniority in the struggle. Not all of these women welcomed Shaw's rise or her closeness to Anthony. So public was some of this jealousy that Carrie Chapman Catt wrote Shaw urging her to ignore such gossip. This is the first public recognition that not all suffrage workers welcomed Anthony's new protégé.[31]

Susan B. Anthony was conscious of these reactions, but they hardly diminished her delight in having a loyal companion and a suffrage speaker who was the oratorical equal of the most prominent men of the day. She quite deliberately arranged several highly visible events to showcase Shaw's talent. One of the most significant of these confrontations came in the summer of 1892. The Chautauqua organization agreed to schedule Shaw to speak on suffrage at their center in Lily Dale, in western New York. Dr. J. M. (James Monroe) Buckley, prominent editor of the *Christian Advocate* and longtime opponent of woman suffrage, would give the rebuttal the following day. Shaw had her own reason to take on this contest; Buckley had been a very harsh opponent to Anna Oliver with whom Shaw had fought for ordination.[32]

In her lecture "Woman's Right to Suffrage," Shaw demonstrated her consistent opposition to essentialist arguments about women's nature. She strongly and methodically emphasized the commonalities that linked women and men. "One thing is forgotten, and that is, that before woman is woman she is human. We are always talking about womanhood in women, but back of womanhood is humanhood, and whatever is good and wise and best for humanity in man is good and best and wisest for humanity in woman." Sex should not be an excuse to limit women's potential.[33]

Shaw's quite explicit belief in what we call today the social construction of gender set her apart from many thinkers and writers, suffragists included, who grounded their profranchise arguments in women's supposedly natural moral superiority and maternal nature. Shaw believed that if women were allowed to grow physically, they would develop muscles and become strong. Further she argued that there could be no valid basis for intellectual comparisons until women had several generations of equal education and other intellectual activities. "Until that time comes we shall never know whether women are the weaker or stronger sex." Echoing her argument from "God's Women," Shaw stated unequivocally that to limit women is to go against God's will. An enthusiastic suffrage audience heartily applauded her lecture.[34]

Buckley faced a less than receptive audience the next day. He had gotten off on the wrong foot with this prosuffrage group and had hurt his cause before either had spoken by predicting that Shaw would be a failure as a public speaker, stating that either she would have to scream or she would not be heard. When he finally did begin to speak, he was heckled by an elderly man in the audience and subsequently lost his temper. He never recovered either his composure or his listeners. It was a day when the suffrage leaders felt they had challenged a renowned and powerful opponent and won. Anthony, Shaw, and many of their supporters gleefully celebrated this triumph. For years they recalled this event as a turning point.[35]

Anthony arranged an even greater opportunity for Shaw a year later at the great Columbian Exposition of 1893 in Chicago. This monumental celebration of the 400th anniversary of Columbus's arrival in the Americas displayed all the social tensions of the era. African Americans had been excluded from the planning by the exposition's organizers. Susan B. Anthony had worked behind the scenes to ensure a Board of Lady Managers and a Women's Building, but there were no African American women involved in these efforts either. Shaw was scheduled to preach on May 21, 1893, before the huge audience of the World's Congress of Representative Women in the Hall of Washington on the Exposition grounds. Adding to Shaw's concern was the fact that her still skeptical eighty-year-old father was to be in attendance.[36]

Shaw most often spoke extemporaneously. Although she planned her speeches, she would commit only the main points of her lecture to memory. Shaw's talent was in being able to sense the mood of her audience, adapting and altering her points and the tone of her presentation to respond to the particulars of each setting and each population. This time, according to Shaw, in recognition of this event's importance she had written out her complete sermon. She wanted to give a great speech for the movement—and for her father. The evening before the event, Shaw persuaded Anthony to listen to her practice run.

The result was disastrous. As Shaw told the story, Anthony's face grew longer and longer as Shaw gave the constructed speech. It would not do, Aunt Susan told Shaw. By planning out each word, each phrase, Shaw left no room for the spark that made her so effective. As the demanding mentor she was, Anthony told Shaw to start over with a new text. Anthony then went off to bed, leaving an uncharacteristically panicked Shaw facing a long night of composing a fresh sermon.[37]

Next morning a tired but inspired Shaw urged women to "Lift your Standards High." The ecumenical call was exquisitely appropriate for the day, while subtly critical of the sexist, racist, and ethnocentric prejudices that were a subtext to the Exposition. Shaw opened with passages not only from the *Bible* but also from Zoroaster, Buddha, and leaders from other religious traditions. She urged women to see that they all shared a truth, one under which all women should be able to struggle together for freedom. This was Shaw's genius and her gift. Before even the largest audience, Shaw could sense the message that would work, name the ideals that would inspire them, remind them of the best in themselves, and call them to action. As pleased as Shaw was with her sermon—she came to consider it as one of only two truly satisfactory efforts—it meant even more because it convinced her aging father that long ago Anna had made the right decision for her life.[38]

Over the next few years, as Elizabeth Cady Stanton focused more and more on religious issues and, with certain of her colleagues, wrote *Woman's Bible*, Shaw devoted less and less attention to such concerns. Though she is recorded as voting for the resolution disassociating the NAWSA from Stanton's work, it is surprising that Shaw left none of her thoughts on the issue. Even in unedited correspondence from the days when the NAWSA was debating the resolution, Shaw doesn't mention it.[39]

Such triumphs as the one at the Exposition sustained Shaw, but these moments that brought her acclaim from many and jealousy from a few were rare events. For most of the days from September through June of each year, Shaw earned her living through public lectures. In 1893, one of the first years for which we have complete records, we get a shape of her life during this period. After having spent a few days with Lucy and her nieces, getting her accounts and wardrobe in shape, and attending a few dinner parties and theater performances in Philadelphia, Shaw left home on January 10th. She gave a few regional lectures and then headed west to Ohio, Kentucky, Michigan, and New York. She wasn't back in Philadelphia until February 20th and that was for only one night. Again, she started off with a few Pennsylvania engagements before going back to Ohio, New York, and Pennsylvania and then moving on to Ontario, Canada. Shaw continued to cover the Mid-Atlantic and Great Lakes states with twenty-four stops in March, fourteen in April, and eight in May. June then had fifteen dates with some as far west as Missouri. July was a quiet month, probably spent at Wianno, with only two dates, but Shaw started again in August with thirteen. From September until the end of the year, she had fifty-nine more engagements. Though other years may have had fewer dates, they might also include longer and more distant travels that Shaw coordinated with her NAWSA work on conventions or campaigns.[40]

In spite of the hard economic times of the 1890s, these were the years when Shaw made good money, up to $3700 a year. In the early years her typical rate was only $20–$25 a lecture or $100 for a work week of six days, plus expenses, when Shaw spoke as part of a suffrage campaign. She charged up to twice that amount for regular lectures. In most cases a group or organization guaranteed Shaw's fee, but would take up a collection after her speech. Any monies over her salary and expenses stayed with the organization. Occasionally an opponent or rival accused Shaw of taking exorbitant fees, but there is no evidence of this. Her rates for suffrage organizations were much lower than the $50 per event Redpath biographer McKivigan notes as the lowest rate for Redpath lecturers of the era. With the Brockway Lecture Bureau a few years later, her rates were still modest, $35 to $50 per night. Further, when her sphere extended to Europe, Shaw followed the other American suffrage leaders' principle of never charging any fees when they spoke in other countries. Shaw argued that she could have been rich if she had spoken on topics other than suffrage and temperance. Nevertheless, when the average woman worker was making less than $5 a week, $260 a year if she was lucky enough to have full-time employment, this daughter of an immigrant farmer earned an exceptional income for a woman. Shaw may have portrayed herself as a dedicated crusader for women, but she was also a successful entrepreneur who was following the path of early suffragists who had populated the postbellum lyceum circuit.[41]

Although this was an impressive income for a self-supporting woman who had "pulled herself up by her own bootstraps," Shaw had moved into circles that included people whose financial resources, whose incomes and trust funds, and whose lines of credit allowed them a stability that Shaw didn't and never would know. In almost all of these cases, men had earned the money from which these leading reformers benefited—from Jane Addams of Hull House and Margaret Dreier Robins of the Women's Trade Union League through Harriet Stanton Blatch, Elizabeth Cady Stanton's daughter. Ellen Carol DuBois argues that these women should be termed "elite." Others, such as Charlotte Perkins Gilman and Frances Willard, had known the financial vulnerability that resulted from patriarchal failures, but they still had claims to social positions and networks through their extended families and social connections. Shaw was very conscious that she had no safety net and no hereditary status. Consequently she never stopped fretting over financial issues and never stopped expanding her roster of contacts. She kept careful records of her income, lived frugally and saved money "in preparation for the 'rainy day' every working-woman inwardly fears." According to Shaw, these were the only years when she could build her savings. Aware that her ability to earn a living depended on her continued good health, Shaw worried about her physical well-being as much as she worried about money.[42]

As 1893 proceeded into 1894 and 1895, Shaw's life had a regular pattern, some parts of which she appreciated and some parts that she hated. Her home base was with Lucy E. Anthony at Philadelphia most of the year and Wianno in the summer; her political home was the NAWSA with its President, the now venerable Susan B. Anthony. The reunification of the suffrage movement did not produce any new energy. Innovations during these years were few. Shaw continued to play a major public role at each NAWSA Convention and its annual hearings before Congress. With Susan B. Anthony, Shaw traveled to many state conventions; to other suffrage, temperance, and political gatherings; to Lily Dale in western New York State for an annual Chautauqua speech; and to whichever state(s) undertook an effort to extend the ballot to women. On her own she had various lecture tours or other paid engagements. When she could, she visited her aging parents and the family in Michigan, and in some of the summer months she invited her extended group of kin to her summer home at Wianno to join her there to hike, fish, and swim and generally escape the limitations of a very public life.[43]

In 1895 the NAWSA bowed to the traditions of the old AWSA and held its annual convention outside of Washington, D.C., for the first time. The NAWSA convened in Atlanta, Georgia. The anti-Black backlash was now so strong and accepted in the country that at this convention AWSA founder and former abolitionist Henry Blackwell publicly argued for a suffrage strategy by which the South could ensure white supremacy by enfranchising women. Though Susan B. Anthony and Carrie Chapman Catt, who had toured the southern states evaluating the level of support for woman suffrage among the southerners before the Atlanta Convention, never explicitly endorsed this plan, neither did they openly repudiate it. As with almost all other white suffrage leaders, they were unwilling to acknowledge the obvious: they were choosing to abandon their Black supporters and allies by embracing this Southern Strategy. Anthony had personally asked Frederick Douglass not to attend the Atlanta Convention. Douglass died the same day that Anthony visited with him after this Southern NAWSA Convention. Both Anthony and Shaw spoke at his funeral.[44]

Suffrage issues in the western states were seemingly less treacherous in terms of race, regional tensions, and established political powers. Women gained their first victories west of the Mississippi: women in Wyoming and Colorado now had full suffrage. Though the NAWSA officers were all based in states east of the Mississippi, with increasing frequency they boarded trains that took them west, over the Rockies, to the states on the Pacific coast. Among the many wonderful photographs that documented their journeys is one from Yosemite Park taken in 1895. At the center, with the tall pines in the background, is Susan B. Anthony, erect and comfortable on a mule at seventy-five, still as stately as she was when Elizabeth Cady Stanton first met her in the 1850s. To her right is Shaw, who, though she had hoped to be a bareback rider in her youth, now looked less than at ease astride her mule. The pioneer-style bonnet doesn't improve her dignity. The occasion of this image was a trip to California to attend the Woman's Congress in San Francisco, one of many organized in response to the success of the one at the 1893 Columbian Exposition in Chicago. In this case the effort was headed by one of the leading women of San Francisco, Sarah Brown Ingersoll Cooper.[45]

California was a revelation to Shaw: she fell in love with the "Golden State." Shaw relished the warmth of California and the promise of the outdoor life she loved as only someone who had the unrelenting cold of her early Michigan years scarred into her memory along with the continuing dread of winter travel in the Midwest and Northeast. On four separate trips in 1895 and 1896, Shaw spent over six months in California's sunshine, all for the cause, of course. This unusual period of her life is especially well documented; in addition to the typical letters and other sources, there survives intact an almost daily correspondence between Shaw and Sarah Cooper's daughter, Harriet, an enthusiastic suffrage worker a few years younger than Shaw. These letters provide an exceptionally clear and complete record of how Shaw conceptualized the NAWSA's and her own work in California, as well as how Shaw attempted to mentor this young suffragist.[46]

After their first trip, Anthony and Shaw were enthusiastic but exhausted. They thought the Congress in San Francisco, which focused on both politics and the home, had been splendid. The newspaper coverage of their speeches and appearances had been thorough and generally positive, but the best result was the suffrage referendum planned for 1896. Shaw wrote to Harriet how, once settled in their sleeper cars, she and Aunt Susan started planning their strategy, listing each community in the state with a population of one thousand.

Yet the adrenaline carried them only so far. The usually indefatigable Anthony was beginning to feel her age, and once home, she needed several weeks of rest. That certainly was to be expected for a seventy-five-year-old. But Shaw, a mere forty-eight-year-old, faced a very serious health crisis for the first time in her adult life. By the time the train reached Chicago, Shaw had pneumonia, an illness that would haunt her for the rest of her life. Alerted by Shaw's telegrams, Lucy had Shaw's brother, Dr. James S. Shaw, join her to meet Shaw's train in Boston, and together they took the now gravely ill orator to The Haven. In this preantibiotic era, there was little anyone could do for Shaw except care for her and allow her to rest. For weeks Shaw could do nothing for herself. It was several more weeks before Shaw could walk or write letters on her own. Fortunately Shaw always found her time at the Cape and the physical work she did at The Haven restorative. Slowly she regained her strength, and soon she returned to her normal Haven routine. Nevertheless, Shaw knew this illness was a warning.[47]

Her home on Cape Cod always served this function in Shaw's life. Her life experiences had convinced her that the rigorous physical activities—wood chopping, fishing, hiking, and others—were an antidote to all the unhealthy conditions she tolerated much of the year. At her secluded Haven, freed from the heavy restrictive clothing required in polite company, Shaw donned a modified bloomer outfit while her nieces and the other younger women wore knickerbockers.[48]

This year, while The Haven was full of family and friends, a young woman reporter, who had heard "rumors about our carefree and unconventional life," came to interview Shaw. Though the entire household dressed and behaved as conventional "ladies" while the reporter was there, the front page story in the *New York World* on Sunday, August 25, 1895, included a sketch of The Haven with Shaw in her short skirts, i.e., above her ankles, and the other six women in knickers, all heading off to fish. The headline was "An Adamless Eden of Women in Bloomers," followed by comments about how scandalized the "select" Wianno's founders would be by "summer suffragists who discard skirts and wear bathing suits just like a man." Shaw uncharacteristically took great offense and considered the article "almost libelous." Although Shaw didn't bring any legal action against the paper, it is clear that the careful boundary she had constructed between her public image and the life she could lead in her private retreat had been breached. Was it anxiety about the image of the movement that made Shaw wary of showing her unconventional side to the public in 1895? Nineteen years later, long after the movement had moved into the mainstream, Shaw happily shared this story in her autobiography.[49]

Professional and familial demands were crowding in on Shaw, so she couldn't dwell on this violation for long. As she was preparing to return to California for a long season of campaigning, Shaw received news that her father was failing. She traveled to Michigan to help as much as she could. Her parents were both now in their eighties. Her father was nearing the end of his life, and Shaw also found that her mother was no longer the joyful soul she had always been. Shaw had been a consistently solicitous daughter, arranging for nurses when they needed them or for home repairs. Now there was little she could do except sit with her father, trying to make him as comfortable as she could for as long as she could stay.[50]

This was her last visit with her father; she was in California when he died in October 1895. Anna was able to manage one more trip back to Michigan before her mother's passing the next year. In spite of the earlier estrangement,

Anna had loved both of her parents, and she mourned them deeply. Yet her devotion to her mother had a special quality. Years before she had noted that "the thought that I am a comfort to my mother settles everything, and I feel content to live for her sake if I had no other reason." It was terribly painful for Anna to be so far from her mother in those last days of her mother's life. She considered her absence from her mother's deathbed one of the greatest sacrifices she ever made for the cause.

Now for all intents and purposes, Shaw's Michigan home was gone. Her brother Tom, his family, and her dear friend, Clara Osborn, still lived there, but it became hard for Shaw to take herself there to face the void left by these deaths. Her nieces and nephews, the children of Jack and Mary, increasingly became her family. Shaw often had Lola and Grace Green and Nicolas and Eleanor Shaw with her; Willard Green visited but less regularly. She merged this part of the Shaw clan with Susan B. Anthony's actual and adoptive families, including Susan's sister, Mary, and of course her niece, Lucy, and Rachel Foster Avery and her husband and daughters. For most of the next decade, Shaw headed the younger branch of this blended family.

Many women, from middle-class professionals through factory workers, became "self-supporting" in these last decades of the nineteenth century. Many never married. Few studies focus on the extent to which some of these women shouldered the financial burden of supporting impoverished parents, partners, or other relatives. Consequently it is difficult to know how unusual Shaw's provider role was. Records indicate that Shaw from an early age almost always contributed to her parents' care. Lucy was her employee as well as her partner. As Mary and Susan B. Anthony had taken in their nieces for periods of time, Shaw and Lucy now housed various combinations of Shaw's four nieces over these years. Certainly Shaw was well equipped to take care of herself and her dependents. On August 4, 1896, Anna noted that she was now worth the $10,000 she had told her father she would be. Nevertheless, being the one on whom so many others depended contributed to Shaw's financial responsibilities.[51]

Shaw also had a new suffrage role when she returned to California. Susan B. Anthony chose not to make the arduous return trip to California in 1895, so for the first time, Shaw was the senior NAWSA officer for a state campaign. As part of this, Shaw had to convince other NAWSA women to commit to the California campaign of 1896. Even at this early date, Mary Garrett Hay, who had recently relocated from Indiana to New York and joined Carrie Chapman Catt's NAWSA Organization Committee, was acknowledged as the best organizer of the movement. Shaw, recognizing Hay's gifts, convinced Hay along with Lucy Anthony to take on coordinating the state effort.

This was Shaw's chance to prove herself as an administrator, and she devoted herself to the California campaign in a way she never would to any other state. Many in the NAWSA felt a momentum with California, Utah, and Idaho all possibly joining Wyoming and Colorado as suffrage states that year. Further, this type of concentrated campaign offered Shaw certain financial benefits. By staying in one state for months at a time, she could use her time more efficiently, not wasting days in traveling from one venue to the next. In California she could give multiple lectures on any given day and then travel a short distance and do the same thing the next day for several weeks at a time. Even though Shaw charged the campaign her lower rate, the work was steadier. And she got to be in California's sunshine.[52]

The Shaw/Cooper letters capture Shaw's work ethic as well as her personality as a correspondent. In spite of her best efforts to be a lively and attentive mentor in her letters, Shaw's default topic and focus was the work. When she was relaxed, her letters could be charming, full of humor and amusing stories, but very often Shaw bypassed the niceties and dived into the organizational details. These letters show how hard Shaw worked and how single-minded she could be; it also shows how frugal Shaw was. Her letters were often written on paper that she collected from her frequent hotel stays or on the backs of used flyers and envelopes. She regretted each night she had to pay to stay in a hotel rather than stay free in a supporter's home. She recorded the cost of each meal and each train or carriage ride. She so appreciated the railroad pass given her by Mrs. Leland Stanford that she kept it for the rest of her life (and it is part of her papers). On the other hand, nothing appalled her more than when her young protégé Harriet Cooper sent unnecessary or wordy telegrams. Shaw knew the worth of not only every dollar, but of every nickel and every penny. With so little discussion of how women handled money or about the class differences among them, it is hard to determine whether Shaw was "careful" or a bit obsessed with finances. On the other hand, concerns about the problems and tensions among the various California suffragists are missing from Shaw's letters. Was she oblivious to or dismissive of them? Later events suggest that Shaw was a little of both in the area of interpersonal conflicts.[53]

The NAWSA and California women suffrage activists covered the state from San Diego to the border with Oregon, from the Pacific to the mountains and the central valley. Shaw spent five months in California in 1896, after two preliminary trips in 1895. Some campaigners visited every town with a population over one thousand. It was an amazing effort, but it wasn't without its shortcomings, as Rebecca Mead chronicles in her recent volume. In addition to differences among the California women, some of the state's activists came to resent the directives of these eastern women. The California women had cause for this reaction for not only had they raised all the money for the drive, but in many cases they were experienced activists in their own rights. Shaw, along with her mentor, Anthony, may have been so accustomed to going into unorganized regions that she (and other women from the NAWSA) was slow to realize the changing capabilities of state leaders. It was a sign of the growth and maturity of the movement that capable and experienced organizers now ran the state associations.[54]

All this work was for naught; the 1896 California woman suffrage referendum lost. The complex demographics and politics of California proved to be too much for this effort. Mead found that the suffrage leaders failed to reach across class and racial lines. Yet as she increasingly learned to do, Shaw found positives even in defeat. She saw that the women had made a good showing of which they should be quite proud, but she concluded that grassroots, house-by-house, and community-by-community organizing was more significant than voter education. Her strength, providing inspiration, was great, but all the rousing speeches would never be enough to gain women the vote. It was an important lesson to Shaw that the California effort that received so much support from the NAWSA lost, while women gained suffrage in Utah and Idaho without much outside assistance.[55]

California would never seem as golden to Shaw as it had been those two years. Tragedy followed defeat when Sarah Brown Ingersoll Cooper and her daughter Harriet committed suicide at the end of the campaign. These were Shaw's closest friends and suffrage colleagues in California. Sarah had survived illnesses, financial difficulties, the deaths of three of her children, relocation, and her husband's suicide to become one of the leading women reformers of San Francisco. Her daughter, Harriet, had stepped in to help ease her mother's responsibilities in the 1890s, but as the decade progressed, Harriet increasingly became convinced that she was doomed to suffer from the same mental instability that caused her father's premature death. Shaw couldn't keep up with Harriet's correspondence in 1895, but by the summer of 1896, it was Shaw who was cajoling Harriet with frequent letters of concern and encouragement. On the night of December 12, 1896, the date of Shaw's last letter to Harriet, the mother and daughter appeared to have agreed to end their lives. With all their legal affairs in order and the windows all shut, they turned on the gas jets in their home. By morning they were both dead.[56]

These were beloved friends, and Shaw had mentored Harriet intensely. This loss followed closely the deaths of Shaw's parents. Now as the end of the century approached, Shaw realized that her beloved "Aunt Susan" also felt her mortality. Increasingly Anthony resisted traveling, working instead at home on the next volumes of the *History of Woman Suffrage*. It wasn't that she abdicated her responsibilities; she pushed herself just as strenuously as she had through all those years of campaigning, but assorted health issues made the journeys and the public speaking harder. Sometimes she had throat spasms, and Shaw would step in and finish Anthony's speeches. Anthony once fainted on stage leading to the premature publication of her obituary in quite a few newspapers. After years when Aunt Susan and Anna traveled and campaigned together, now Shaw traveled alone. Lucy would arrange Shaw's schedule to allow frequent, if brief, stops in Rochester. Both Susan and Mary Anthony inevitably pampered the travel weary Shaw when she stopped, even drawing Shaw's bath for her while she shared the latest suffrage news.[57]

Yet it seemed that no amount of hard work was enough to counter the difficulties that came at the end of the 1890s. The general mood of the country was focused elsewhere, and woman suffrage stayed on the margins. After the wonderful successes in Wyoming, Colorado, Utah, and Idaho, and numerous other energetic campaigns, women added no other suffrage states over the rest of the decade. Friends and family had lost money in the economic crises, and Shaw worried about their and her own finances. Unnamed problems forced Rachel Foster Avery out of her beautiful home in Somerton, outside of Philadelphia. In 1898, the same year that the entire suffrage movement celebrated the 50th anniversary of the Seneca Falls Convention, Frances Willard, the great leader of the Woman's Christian Temperance Union, died at the age of 59.[58]

As the United States became a global power, spreading its domain in the Pacific and the Caribbean especially, suffrage activists split over support for these efforts. Most within the women's movement, including Elizabeth Cady Stanton, supported U.S. imperialism. These voices echoed the same racial and class consciousnesses that positioned the white, middle- to upper-class leaders as appropriate to define the needs of all women. Once again Shaw's views were at odds with the majority of the suffragists and perhaps the public. In "White Man's Burden," Shaw argued against U.S. imperialism. Positioning herself as she frequently did, as both a patriot and a critic, she argued that the United States was a country of great but unfulfilled promise, where politics and prejudices had as yet prevented the actualization of the founders' ideals of true equality and real democracy. For Shaw, "The loyal citizen seeks the truth."[59]

Shaw's 1899 speech linked militarism, masculinity, and imperialism with the denial of suffrage, a basic right of any citizen in a republic. Shaw asked, "How can we expect men to respect the citizenship of other men when they fail to see the justice of its application to their daughters?" Shaw was unconvinced that the U.S. military might and rule would bring a civilizing effect to the Philippines, arguing rather that the United States would be much more effective a force for democracy if it led by example through extending rights, including voting rights, to all its adult citizens. In what could have been a comment on recent U.S. wars, she found, "Such an exhibition (of military prowess) cannot but awaken in other nations' scorn, derision and hatred, even though they may be coupled with fear, but it can never arouse feelings of increased respect for American principles and a desire to adopt them into their own life." Hers might have been the views of a minority, but they demonstrate that there remained a diversity of views within the NAWSA. Further, it never seemed that these expressions harmed Shaw's popularity or efficacy.[60]

Shaw's anti-imperialist views were reinforced during a tour of the Caribbean taken in the winter of 1901–1902. On the only purely private vacation she ever took after becoming an activist, Shaw spent two months primarily in Cuba and Jamaica with University of Rochester naturalist Dr. Ward, and his suffragist wife, Lydia Coonley Ward. Shaw left little explanation for this trip; in her letters from it, she refers to it as a "spree." Though not without its challenges in terms of food, travel, and accommodations, this was a restful change for Shaw, who always enjoyed warm weather, sunshine, and unhurried days.[61]

Shaw wrote numerous letters to "home folks" from the Caribbean. While these suggested a pretty standard tourist's agenda, her descriptions of the land, the flora, the cities and towns, and the people often diverged into comments upon the more serious political issues. Shaw was observing the results of U.S. imperialism firsthand. For once she wrote of issues beyond suffrage, discussing tariffs, annexation, the sugar industry, and militarism. She was outraged with how the American presence was spreading racism and exploiting the beautiful land.[62]

These transnational issues coincided with Shaw's growing influence beyond the U.S. borders. In 1899 Shaw was a delegate to the International Council of Women in London. While Susan B. Anthony was certainly the American star of this event, Shaw began to construct her own network within the international women's movement. At the 1900 NAWSA Convention, Shaw spoke with her usual self-deprecating humor about how she had to "enter society," and argued that "traveling up and down the country with a gripsack in hand was hard enough; but it is child's play to handshaking and hob-nobbing with duchesses and countesses." Europe would later draw Shaw on an almost annual basis, fostering both personal friendships and significant political exchanges.[63]

The 1890s were truly the apprenticeship years for Shaw. Through her national and international travel she came to know a far broader range of people and they, in turn, came to see her as a leader in the generation that would carry on this work after Stanton, Stone, and Anthony. Within the NAWSA, at their annual meetings—the seven in Washington, D.C., 1895 in Atlanta, 1897 in Des Moines, and 1899 in Grand Rapids, Michigan—audiences greatly anticipated Shaw's speeches, and she was a consistent presence on the stage and at the podium. Aside from the times she had at The Haven or at home, these gatherings were the best parts of Shaw's year, where she was among friends and supporters, with "Aunt Susan" and Lucy. The work she did to support herself and her family continued to be grueling. Seldom did a year go by that Shaw did not at some point in her travels sink into a depression and write to Lucy that she would have to quit such a life. Yet the same steely will that had gotten her this far kept her climbing onto the next train and onto the next venue.[64]

As these activists entered the new century, the prospects for progress were not good. Shaw acknowledged that her audiences still weren't enthusiastic about woman suffrage. The Southern Strategy was not bringing the expected results, and the NAWSA continued to be strapped for time, money, and energy. The NAWSA was stagnant, dependent upon the same financial resources—dues and bequests and the mostly voluntary labor of its middle-class and upper-class leaders. Carrie Chapman Catt tried to use her work within the NAWSA Organizational Committee to push for reforms to confront suffrage opponents who were now better organized and financed than they had been before this time. The question was whether the movement could change to meet the challenges of the new century.[65]

At this critical point, the now eighty-year-old Susan B. Anthony "retired," resigning from the active presidency of the NAWSA to become another "Honorary President" with Elizabeth Cady Stanton. Writers then and historians since have debated how and why Carrie Chapman Catt rather than vice president Shaw succeeded Anthony as the president of the NAWSA. In the official story captured in *History of Woman Suffrage*, Ida Husted Harper wrote that while Catt became Anthony's choice to succeed her, "The Rev. Anna Howard Shaw, who for a number of years had been vice-president-at-large, could have had Miss Anthony's sanction and the unanimous vote of the convention if she would have consented to accept the office." In her *Life and Work of Susan B. Anthony*, Harper added that Anthony had felt that Catt and Shaw were equally capable of leading the NAWSA, but that Shaw, believing "that her best work could be done in the lecture field, had declined to be a candidate."[66]

These passages contradict the commonly accepted and repeated story that Susan B. Anthony chose Carrie Chapman Catt as her successor *over* Shaw. True, some partisan voices later argued that Anthony thought Catt was the better choice. Mary Gray Peck, Catt's great admirer, friend, and biographer, stated that Catt was the only logical choice and that Shaw "simply was not in Mrs. Catt's class as a creative leader—which nobody knew better than Miss Anthony." But Peck, who was not involved in the NAWSA in 1900, was neither objective nor an actual observer. She denied and denigrated Shaw's contributions to the movement at every available opportunity. And she was certainly no confidante of Anthony's. What was certain was that Shaw was in no position to assume an unpaid full-time office. She was not only self-supporting but also the primary breadwinner of a complex and nontraditional family. And at this point in time, the NAWSA expected women to have their own money.[67]

Carrie Lane Chapman Catt was a tremendous organizer and strategist. An able if reluctant speaker, Catt was most impressive when constructing the broad plan for suffrage success and then determining all the components needed to make that plan work. A meticulous manager, Catt had honed her skills rising through the ranks in her home state of Iowa before coming to the attention of Susan B. Anthony. Never as personally close to the great leader as Shaw or Rachel Foster Avery were nor as open or as passionate in her personal and political expressions, Catt was just as fully committed to the struggle as those Anthony considered her "family." Widowed and now remarried, Catt had worked as a teacher, an administrator, and a journalist but was now wealthy enough to be able to take on this office without remuneration.[68]

In her version of the story, Shaw maintains that she fully supported Catt as Anthony's choice. At the same time she states that it had been one of her life goals to succeed Anthony. It must have been a bitter decision on Shaw's part to give up that opportunity. The reality was that the organization didn't have the funds to pay Shaw nor the will to find such monies.

While the NAWSA constituency heartily welcomed Catt as the new head, her election didn't reflect a major shift within the organization. She inherited Susan B. Anthony's board, a core group of officers who had been stable through most of the 1890s. Catt found that, in spite of the support for the general membership, the executive committee of the NAWSA that met just after the convention immediately resisted her plans for reform. The very first meeting of her presidency, one that left several officers in tears and caused Catt to bolt from the gathering in frustration, may have foreshadowed the problems Catt would face during her first presidency. As in many of the intraorganizational conflicts, personalities as well as political strategies mattered. Some writers have argued that the sentiment was that the Executive Committee felt that the Organization Committee had usurped too much power; others name Catt's good friend, Mary G. Hay, whose managerial gifts were frequently undermined by her abrasive personality, as the root of the problem. This was also the period when the friendship between Shaw and Catt was most strained. In fact Catt was stunned by how hostile Shaw was to her in the first months of her presidency. As much as Shaw later maintained that she endorsed Catt as Susan B. Anthony's successor, at the time she couldn't control her jealousy.[69]

By 1903, between the organizational difficulties and these personal challenges, Catt began to experience the suffrage struggle as a Sisyphean labor.

Catt's difficulties were complicated by her caretaking responsibilities; her husband was seriously ill and the stress of this took its toll on Catt's own health. In an acknowledgment of the burden the position was on Catt, the NAWSA agreed to move the headquarters of the organization from the World Building in New York City where Catt lived to Warren, Ohio, to be under the direction of NAWSA Treasurer Harriet Taylor Upton.[70]

This was a trying period of transition for Shaw as well. She was still the vice-president-at-large, but she was no longer the closest ally of the president. Shaw's connection to the center of power had changed. Catt had her own close circle of colleagues. Additionally, the physically and emotionally challenging life she had chosen was beginning to wear on Shaw as she moved into her late fifties. In April of 1903, her doctor ordered her to rest, yet Shaw was back on the road shortly after the middle of the month. Nevertheless, this episode marked a change after which Shaw did have more serious illnesses. She never did learn to pace herself, but her resilience had changed. She would be stopped cold by a serious illness more regularly.[71]

It was during this leadership crisis that the NAWSA bowed to pressure from numerous white southern suffrage leaders and scheduled their annual convention for New Orleans. In most histories of the suffrage movement, the 1869 split that led to the creation of the AWSA and the NWSA is considered the nadir of race relations in the suffrage movement, but it is hard to look at the overall record of the NAWSA Convention in 1903 in New Orleans without believing that it really was the low point for suffrage racism. The Louisiana convention was a segregated convention. Although a number of women who could pass did attend and report on the convention, no African American women officially gained entry. The NAWSA, in trying to accommodate the white Louisiana hosts without blatantly abandoning the principle of universal suffrage, produced major obfuscation on the race issue. Accused by the local media of promoting racial equality, the NAWSA responded with a strong states' rights position. Mississippi's Belle Kearney's speech on how woman suffrage would ensure white supremacy was a "leading feature" of the convention and enthusiastically received. Carrie Chapman Catt's response never directly confronted this call to racial domination.[72]

All of the NAWSA leaders toed this same line, including Shaw. Shaw addressed the decisions the NAWSA made concerning race and the New Orleans Convention more directly in her autobiography than Ida Husted Harper did in *History of Woman Suffrage*. Shaw recalled that they all understood, "that we must take every precaution to avoid being led into such a (race-related) discussion. It had not been easy to persuade Miss Anthony of the wisdom of this course; her way was to face issues squarely and out in the open." For her part, Shaw tried to avoid responding to a submitted question about how the NAWSA advocated political and social equality. After this query appeared for the third time, Shaw decided to answer it. Shaw started by noting that through disenfranchisement the South had already made Black and White women politically equal. She went on to state how through the vote, the South had made "former slaves the political masters of their former mistresses," and that men from all races and all nations were able to "govern American women." It seemed that Shaw too had put organizational unity above her principles.[73]

Though Catt would preside over the 1904 convention, 1903 marked the real end of this short period of her leadership. In spite of her significant abilities, Catt had not been able to make any major positive changes. In her heart Catt was more of a strategist than an ideologue. In the name of expediency rather than principle, she had been willing to court White southern women at the expense of African American women. When she let the association know at the gathering that she would not stand for reelection the next year, she left it burdened with this shift. In 1904, the NAWSA would have to find its fourth president.

Between 1890 and 1904, Anna Howard Shaw established her reputation and her position not just among national and international women's organizations, but also among the U.S. public. Shaw had hoped to succeed her longtime mentor, Susan B. Anthony, when Anthony retired from the NAWSA presidency in 1900, but her need to earn a living had kept her from seriously considering assuming that position. The NAWSA wasn't ready to accept a leader who was a self-supporting woman, so Carrie Chapman Catt became the new NAWSA leader instead. Now, after four years, Catt was refusing to stand for reelection. The National American Woman Suffrage Association and Shaw were again at a crossroads.

Anna Howard Shaw had led a remarkable life. The sickly infant girl from a large, bankrupt family had experienced a range of nineteenth-century U.S. women's realities from immigration to homesteading. Shaw had farmed, taught, and sewed to support herself and her family before entering the ministry and gaining a medical degree. Gifted with a voice that could change people's lives, backed by and following in the footsteps of some of the leading women of the era, Shaw now employed that talent to earn a living while also fighting for equal rights for women. Shaw knew America: she traveled to urban industrial centers and small towns, through all its regions. In many ways Shaw embodied the solitude of self that Stanton had argued for women. Certainly she chose a hard life, but Shaw knew that her life was not nearly as hard as the lives that most women led. That knowledge fueled her resolve to continue to give all that she could to further the cause that had become her life's work.

Yet Shaw was confronting another contradiction in her life. While she was formally a freelance lecturer, she was also the vice president of the leading suffrage organization. As long as the NAWSA didn't take an official position on an issue, Shaw was free to express her views as she did on gender, religion, and imperialism, to name a few of her lecture topics. But the more she identified herself with the NAWSA the more she felt restricted by her responsibilities to the organization, as shown by the 1903 convention. It was one thing to follow the party line when the NAWSA was headed by Susan B. Anthony. It was much harder since Anthony resigned. Shaw increasingly found her views to be at odds with the rest of the association's officers. Shaw and the U.S. suffrage movement were facing some difficult times.

CHAPTER 5

Compromised Leadership
NAWSA PRESIDENCY, PART I (1904–1908)

Aunt Susan, love for you is all that would make me do this. You
have borne so much and been to me more than a mother, and
after your letters came I could not let you have one more hour of
anxiety on my account. I only hope my acceding to your request
will not make more anxiety in the end. I hope for the best and yet
fear it is very unwise in me to even try it.

Anna Howard Shaw had dreamed of succeeding her mentor, Susan B.
Anthony, as leader of the National American Woman Suffrage Association
(NAWSA).[1] That hope had crashed against the economic realities of Shaw's
life. In 1900 and still in 1904, she was in no position to assume the unpaid
position of the NAWSA presidency. In 1900, however, Anthony and the
NAWSA had another choice in the independently wealthy Carrie Chapman
Catt. But personal and political stresses had worn Catt down to the point
where she felt she had no option but to refuse reelection. As 1904 opened,
Anthony, soon to be eighty-four, immediately started a campaign to convince
Shaw that she had to take the post.

The last years had been hard on the entire suffrage movement. They had
been hard years for Shaw too. The usually robust leader was physically tired
and emotionally drained from two decades of constant traveling, speaking,
and campaigning for woman suffrage. Though she usually greeted each New
Year with an optimistic prayer, this year that prayer was accompanied by the
worst headache of her life.[2]

The United States was in the middle of a transformation, but not one
that favored the reforms Shaw, Anthony, and their colleagues envisioned.
Theodore Roosevelt had become the country's youngest president in 1901
after the assassination of President William McKinley in Buffalo. Although
Roosevelt was willing to confront the monopolies and trusts, he was pro-
growth and a great backer of U.S. expansion. It wasn't clear whether dealing

with the country's increasing racial, ethnic, and class tensions was high on his list of initiatives. What was most important as far as Shaw and her colleagues were concerned was that Roosevelt was not a supporter of woman suffrage at this time.[3]

Tensions between the established and new Americans as well as rich and poor citizens had hardly abated. Immigration, industrialization, and urbanization challenged the rural and Protestant identity of the nation. The current European immigrants were predominantly from Italy, Austria-Hungary, Russia, and Poland, yet continued migrations from Ireland, Germany, and Great Britain, as well as Mexico, Japan, Canada, and the West Indies, added to the new demographics of the country. The percentages of Jewish and Roman Catholic Americans increased, challenging the Protestant hegemony. New industries producing ready-made consumer goods kept workers in the cities, leading to the emergence of urban ghettos and sweatshops that employed immigrant fathers, daughters, and sons. Labor unrest highlighted the broadening wealth gap and the questioning of the "American dream." Racial violence—lynchings, harassment, and sexual terrorism against African Americans—women, and men—and economic limitations that followed the disenfranchisement of African American men in the South and disempowerment of African Americans generally in that region were pushing individuals and families toward the cities of the north.[4]

American women had established themselves in the public sphere, addressing these societal problems. However, most of these organizations were racially segregated. African American women, who had long organized their own clubs on local levels, had founded the National Association of Colored Women in 1896. Working-class women, who had been organizing since joining the Knights of Labor, participated in both union activities and women's organizations such as the Women's Trade Union League, founded as a cross-class coalition in 1903 by Jane Addams, Mary Anderson, and others. Women's history has traced the activities of middle-class white women as they founded clubs, schools and colleges, settlement houses, and other social organizations.[5]

Though its origins had been as part of earlier reforms, the movement to extend the franchise to women had taken a conservative turn. In what the leaders felt was a move essential for success, during the 1890s the NAWSA followed the Southern Strategy. As a result of this courting of southern white women along with other efforts to become respectable and mainstream, it had abandoned controversial positions and marginalized African Americans. Yet this plan brought no tangible results. The years without a new suffrage state had stretched to eight. There were no new monies coming in; the suffrage constituency as a whole was aging; and the now entrenched officers were split by both ideology and personal styles. The national movement seemed stalled. Catt, the most accomplished organizer among this generation, had found that the majority of her officers resisted her efforts for reform. With no consensus among them and strengthening opposition throughout the country, the NAWSA verged on becoming ineffective and irrelevant.[6]

These next chapters follow Shaw's life and her NAWSA presidency. With little scholarship on Shaw's leadership, most historians follow the position originated by Eleanor Flexner that Shaw's tenure was chaotic and Shaw an ineffective administrator. The only major challenge to this view comes from the late Sarah Hunter Graham and her argument that these were the years of a suffrage renaissance. This research leans more toward the latter, finding that the growth and transformation of the NAWSA and movement as a whole between 1904 and 1915 are undeniable. The tensions and conflicts under Shaw's leadership were essential for the change that revitalized the NAWSA. Key challenges involved economic and racial issues, the focus on the federal amendment, and what the move to New York and the professionalization of the staff meant. Feminist suffrage scholarship generally has concluded that a conservative and racist NAWSA and Shaw were finally challenged (and in Shaw's case, ousted) by younger, more radical leaders. This close examination of Shaw's presidency finds that the dynamics within the NAWSA and the suffrage struggle to be far more complex.[7]

Initially, Anna Howard Shaw's personal solution to the suffrage problems was to work ever harder for the cause. Even into her sixth decade, Shaw had yet to learn moderation as she juggled the demands of her paid and her political work. Her pattern was to work until she couldn't do anymore. In the culture at large, fifty-seven-year-old women may have been considered old or elderly, but among suffrage women she was still part of the younger generation. Yet, as the NAWSA faced this succession crisis, she was so exhausted that her doctor told her that she had to take a real break from her demanding schedule. Shaw's response was to plan an extended trip to Europe during the summer of 1904, with her suffrage family—Susan B., Mary S., and Lucy Anthony. They were to attend the International Council of Women in Berlin and remain to be part of the founding of the International Suffrage Alliance. Their beloved friend, Rachel Foster Avery, was moving to Switzerland with her family, and they looked forward to spending time there with Rachel and her daughters. In between the meetings and time with the Avery family, they would tour the British Isles and other sites. The trip would start in Italy, where Shaw could fulfill her childhood dream of seeing Pompeii.[8]

Plans changed. On January 29, 1904, Susan B. Anthony wrote to her longtime friends and fellow activists William Lloyd Garrison Jr. and his wife, Ella, "Now dear friends I am going to tell you what is at present a secret with the business committee only. Mrs. Catt has in a formal letter, declined to stand for the presidency another year." Catt insisted that it wasn't because of the organization, but her "nerves" that necessitated rest, and that she must be freed from all responsibilities. Anthony's letter to the Garrisons continued, explaining why, among all the officers, only Anna Howard Shaw could be president. But, Anthony continued, Shaw was a working woman and needed a salary to take the job. Anthony was pleading with the Garrisons. Garrison controlled the Mrs. E. K. Church Fund, one of the sources for suffrage funding. She needed him to make a commitment to help pay Shaw.[9]

Shaw was now the suffrage star. For so many reasons she stood out among the movement's leaders. Most of the current leaders came from genteel backgrounds, so taking up the suffrage cause was a radical step for them. For Shaw, who had embraced nontraditional roles since childhood, the suffrage movement at the turn of the century was a comparatively tame choice of activism. And Shaw's public persona, especially her humor, certainly contradicted the suffrage stereotype. Over the last fourteen years, Shaw had grown a bit grayer, having more white hair than dark now, still pulled up into the basic coil on the top of her head. She had grown stout in the decade that had been prosperous for her, but she was still physically agile and strong for the most part. She was a woman for whom leisure meant chopping wood, gardening, long walks, and home repairs rather than reclining on the divan. This energy and her irreverent wit endeared her to her followers and entertained most of her audiences. Tough, frequently blunt, passionate, and mercurial, Shaw embraced those aspects of her identity that separated her from the other suffrage leaders. She proudly wore her identity as a working woman. At home and among her closest friends, she happily tolerated the nickname "Ladee," a sarcastic nod to what she certainly was not. As she later explained the nickname to young Eleanor Garrison, "I am less like a lady than anything else in the world."[10]

In her fifties, Shaw did have to face some of the inevitable consequences of her hard life and of pushing herself physically, traveling through heat and cold and surviving on little sleep and questionable food. The headaches—they might have been migraines—and other ailments came with increased frequency. When tired or unwell, Shaw worried, mostly about her health and money. Every worker knew how connected these were. Though always presenting an optimistic and energetic face to the public, in private she tended toward pessimism, perhaps even episodes of depression.[11]

Given her very real differences from the other national and often international leaders, Shaw felt removed from whatever tight circles of friendship formed among her colleagues. Her extant letters are devoid of the gossip and unsubstantiated rumors common among some of the suffrage leaders. Throughout her life she had always relied on a few very close friends, mostly women. Since she had dedicated herself to women's rights, she had been a deeply loyal, though not unquestioning, apprentice to Susan B. Anthony.

She had come to know the leaders Anthony had recruited and cultivated. Most importantly she most trusted the people Anthony trusted.[12]

Now her beloved Aunt Susan needed her to take the leadership of the NAWSA. Shaw's diaries from the beginning of 1904 until the NAWSA Convention in Washington in February give little hint of her reaction to this inevitable change. The first mention of Catt's decision came from Iowa when Shaw wrote to Lucy for her thoughts on this. As usual, her schedule was so tight that she had to travel all night just to get to Washington, D.C., in time for the preconvention meetings. "Reached Washington two hours late, but before Lucy was up; found Aunt Susan in our bed at Shoreham and Lucy in hers. . . . B.C. [Business Committee] meeting called at 10 am."[13]

Shaw was not convinced about taking the presidency, but in the end, she could not resist Anthony's pleas. She agreed to stand for the office for one year, as a placeholder until Catt was again well enough to retake the reins. Since she would be gone for four months that summer, she refused to accept any compensation for this year. Harriet Taylor Upton, who now ran the headquarters that had been relocated to Upton's hometown, Warren, Ohio, a small town in eastern Ohio, was already handling much of the routine office work. The general NAWSA constituency was more than happy to elect Anthony's choice and their favorite speaker.[14]

The aging Anthony might have imagined that the presidency would allow or force Shaw to take a break from her traveling, but the presidency only added to Shaw's responsibilities. After the 1904 convention, Shaw went right back out on her lecture schedule. Maybe she really had convinced herself that this was only a one-year or, at the most, two-year position and that she really didn't need to change her life; maybe she saw no other option. From the end of the convention in February until a few days before she sailed for Europe in April, she stayed on the road, visiting and encouraging state leaders and local organizations, speaking in New Jersey, New York, Connecticut, Massachusetts, and Pennsylvania. On April 9, 1904, she returned home to Philadelphia with only four days to prepare for the four-month trip to Europe. In addition to all the necessary packing, between April 10 and April 13, she and Lucy worked at a hectic pace to send out over one hundred and forty letters. Finally on board, she collapsed, sick and exhausted. She remained confined to her bed for the first five days of the voyage.[15]

Now, as the official leader of the U.S. movement, Shaw needed to represent the NAWSA at various international meetings. There would be no more summers at The Haven, her summer home on the south shore of Cape Cod, but these trips abroad were something of a break from her usual routine. Shaw, most often accompanied by Lucy, combined business and leisure on what became annual voyages. In 1904, the ruins of Pompeii and the visits to Naples and Rome all delighted her. In June, Anna and Lucy joined Susan B.

and Mary S. Anthony in Berlin for the meetings of the International Council of Women and the celebratory founding of the International Suffrage Alliance. From the end of those meetings until they sailed for home three months later, Lucy and Anna split their time between visiting friends and suffrage colleagues and touring continental Europe, London, and Scotland. Though this was certainly one of the longest breaks Anna had ever taken from work, suffrage issues were never far from her consciousness. With each trip Shaw drew closer to various European women leaders, developing friendships that she sustained through a correspondence that merged business and personal concerns.[16]

Only upon her return did the new president gather all the NAWSA officers at their headquarters for one of their regular Business Committee meetings. Warren, Ohio, was hardly an impressive site for the headquarters of the leading woman suffrage organization, but it was the best the organization could manage at this point. This small-town location was symbolic of the state of the movement; woman suffrage hardly seemed to have a presence as a national issue. Though there is no record of any substantive discord, as had marked Catt's first such meeting—perhaps the continuing presence of Susan B. Anthony as the Honorary President forced a surface cohesion—it isn't clear whether this group of women agreed on many issues beyond some basic dedication to woman suffrage.[17]

Of course there were no shrinking violets among the NAWSA leaders. Each was formidable in her own right, though Alice Stone Blackwell was more forceful with her pen than in person. Alice, with her delicate health and rather severe demeanor, was most comfortable and talented as the editor of the *Woman's Journal*. Shaw had known Alice from her days as an organizer with the Massachusetts Woman Suffrage Association. Though once close and probably still closest in terms of their political views on issues of race and universal suffrage, Blackwell's reserve and resistance to change grated on Shaw. Shaw complained of Alice's "New England cussedness." In return, Blackwell tended to be hard on Shaw, perhaps never having forgiven or again fully trusted Shaw for shifting her allegiance from the AWSA to the NWSA shortly before the union of the two associations. Blackwell's greatest power came from the *Woman's Journal*, where she controlled what was published and what was not.[18]

The treasurer, Harriet Taylor Upton, was generally remembered as a large and competent woman whose laughter was loud and frequent. Married but childless, this daughter of a Republican congressman was gregarious and known as the NAWSA's biggest gossip. She was hard-working and dedicated but not particularly intellectual or creative.[19]

It is interesting that by temperament the Republican Upton was drawn most to the two single southern women, Laura Clay and Kate Gordon, who constituted that region's representatives on the Official Board. It was in the letters that passed among them that many of the personal opinions and candid views among the board emerged. The tall and imposing Clay was a member of one of the leading political families of Kentucky. Her father was related to Henry Clay and had served as ambassador to Russia. After her parents' divorce, Clay had used her family inheritance to establish herself as an independent businesswoman. She knew herself to be part of the Kentucky aristocracy and carried herself with a sense of noblesse oblige, always supporting philanthropic efforts for the less fortunate. The pleasantly attractive appearance of Louisiana leader Kate Gordon masked a fiery and determined personality. One of three active Gordon sisters who were all involved in community improvement efforts in New Orleans, she was an unapologetic racist. Carrie Chapman Catt, vice president, and Dr. Cora S. Eaton, in the one office that saw yearly turnover, filled out the board of officers that Shaw inherited. In Susan B. Anthony's estimate these women were all good workers in their positions, but none was of presidential caliber except Catt or Shaw. Although labeling any suffrage leader as "conservative" in 1904 is problematic, with the exception of Shaw, these women, all of the same generation, were far less radical in their views and lifestyles than the earlier suffrage cohort of women that included Olympia Brown, Abigail Duniway, and Matilda Joslyn Gage, to name a few.[20]

Though Kentuckian Laura Clay has generally been remembered as a moderate voice from the South, something in her bearing and political positions put off both Susan B. Anthony and Shaw. Certainly her racial politics and states' rights positions clashed with Anthony's and Shaw's commitments to equal suffrage via a federal amendment. It had been Clay who had most adamantly pushed to hold the NAWSA Conventions away from Washington, D.C. And, with equal fervor, she had argued down a consideration of Black women's issues at the 1899 NAWSA convention. In a handwritten postscript to her January 1904 letter to the Garrisons, Anthony, after praising all of the other longtime officers, had stated that Clay could not be considered for the NAWSA presidency because of her "negro equality-hating": "We should never have another colored woman on our stage if she could have her way." Clay, perhaps with the goal of leading the organization herself, would prove to be a frequent thorn in Shaw's side for years.[21]

Now Shaw was the leader of this group. Unlike Catt who had come into her presidency full of ideas for reforming and modernizing the NAWSA, Shaw leaves us no evidence of a grand vision for change. Her first letter to the state presidents was hardly inspiring. She solicited their concerns and suggestions while urging them to work to increase the number of members and local organizations, an approach in keeping with Hunter Graham's assessment of Shaw as an egalitarian leader. Then Shaw was back on the road earning her living. From September through the end of the year she kept up a rigorous travel schedule, attending numerous state suffrage and WCTU conventions. In December, for two weeks, she worked in Oklahoma during their Constitutional Convention, but once again the advocates of woman suffrage faced defeat.[22]

Anthony soon recognized that Shaw's original agreement with her and the Business Committee was void. Any realistic expectation that Catt would resume the NAWSA presidency in 1905 had been dashed when the founding convention of the International Suffrage Alliance elected Catt president. Catt refused to stand for reelection in the NAWSA, even as vice president. As Anthony's health deteriorated, she became increasingly adamant that Shaw continue in the office.

Yet with Shaw on the road most of the time and Harriet Upton handling the day-to-day responsibilities at the NAWSA Headquarters in Warren, most people within the organization, including Upton and maybe even Shaw herself, might have conceived of Shaw as the titular and ceremonial head of the organization but not the real power. Yet the person who was still the most powerful voice in the struggle didn't see it that way. Anthony believed in Shaw even if Shaw didn't have a full belief in herself. Determined that Shaw would be the true leader of the NAWSA, but knowing that Shaw needed a regular income, Anthony's focus in 1905 was finding the needed money. A resolute Anthony was still formidable.

Anthony didn't have to just raise the money, a significant task for the ailing leader, but she had to convince the NAWSA that this step was justified. For the NAWSA to consider paying its officers was a radical step. Most women's organizations were still voluntary associations, the domains of elite women. If a woman didn't have a father, husband, or even brother to support her, she might find a benefactor, become a writer or journalist, or lecture, as Shaw did. Ladies assumed that a class difference separated them, women who didn't need to work, from the women who had to earn a living. Now for Anna Howard Shaw to be its president, the NAWSA could no longer follow such a model. Shaw's economic situation disrupted this old arrangement and forced twentieth-century realities onto the veteran suffrage organization. Yet suffrage scholarship has left this major organizational dilemma largely unacknowledged, almost completely glossing over the fact that the NAWSA instituted salaries for certain officers beginning in 1907.[23]

Shaw wasn't just a working woman, she was an immigrant. In an era when class and immigration tensions remained high, what did it mean that such an individual was leading the U.S. suffrage movement? To the most broad-minded women such as Catt, Anthony, and Anthony's closest allies, it meant nothing. In fact Anthony was indignant that it was so hard to get the money for Shaw's salary. "It is a disgrace to the Association that Miss Shaw has to work through the heat and swelter of the dog days to earn her living expenses. There are plenty of rich women who ought to enable her to give her whole time to the needs of the Association." Yet to others it brought their unexamined class prejudices as well as long-standing jealousies to the fore. Although few left direct comments about her status at the time, over the course of her presidency, Shaw's financial relationship with the NAWSA was the basis of some of the nastiest attacks against her.[24]

The issue of salaries is also significant because it did allow other working women to hold offices in the organization, changing further who held power in the NAWSA. Among the women who would be salaried officers in the next years were several divorced, single mothers. The growth of the organization and the growth of paid positions within it were interdependent. Yet tensions between paid and unpaid leaders were never fully resolved.[25]

This was background when, in June 1905, Shaw visited Catt at her home in Bensonhurst-by-the-Sea (now Bath Beach, Brooklyn). Catt was charged to act on behalf of the Business Committee to find out what salary level Shaw would need to continue leading the NAWSA. In a confidential letter to the committee, Catt described how she finally forced Shaw to name the income she would need to continue as the NAWSA President. "We badgered her so much that she was driven to take counsel of her account books, and to think what she could do. Then she hated to speak of it. So, I abused my hospitality, drove her in a corner, and at the point of a bowie-knife, metaphorically speaking, succeeded in getting this very reluctant information." At this point and for this reason, Shaw's private finances became the business of the organization.[26]

Anna Howard Shaw was willing to make great and deep sacrifices for women's rights. She regretted needing to be paid, but she was not willing to impoverish herself. Shaw was not a poor woman by this time in her life, but she never felt financially secure. Her frequent expressions about money-related anxieties argue that she not only was haunted by her memories of poverty, but also that she had a consciousness that others were dependent on her. She was the financial foundation of her extended family. This type of economic awareness was one that most of the newer leaders, with their comfortable lives, their substantial homes, and numerous servants, could avoid.[27]

Shaw also knew that the NAWSA never had surplus funds and suspected that any salary granted her would be given grudgingly and that she would be viewed as a drain on the organization. Nevertheless, Catt persisted and after much resistance, Shaw admitted to average yearly earnings of $3600 over the previous decade with expenses of $1000 annually. Shaw paid Lucy's salary, which had been $600/year in 1889, out of what she earned. Shaw told Catt that she could maintain her current lifestyle on $2400 a year. Why she agreed to this low amount isn't clear. Maybe she didn't want to burden the NAWSA or thought that she could forgo savings. The great irony was, after all these intense discussions, practically forced disclosures, and hard-argued agreements, the NAWSA still didn't have the money for this salary anyway. With Anthony promising to find the money, Shaw agreed to stand for reelection. With this agreement hammered out, the NAWSA leaders boarded a transcontinental train and headed for Portland, Oregon.[28]

Shaw would never have chosen Oregon as the first NAWSA Convention under her leadership. This was the home turf of Abigail Scott Duniway, the longtime suffrage powerhouse of the Northwest. The formidable, irascible Duniway seldom got along with anyone for very long, but her animosity toward Shaw was extreme even for her. Believing that the suffragists' association with the temperance movement, especially with WCTU, had and would continue to doom the movement in the West, Duniway had always objected to Susan B. Anthony's close friendship and working partnership with the former WCTU organizer Shaw. Nevertheless it was in Oregon where Shaw would have to prove that she was Anthony's worthy successor. One can only imagine what each was thinking when the veteran Duniway faced Shaw, each a tough pioneer, to extend the official welcome and give her the gavel made of Oregon wood on June 28, 1905. By all accounts, all the women were on their best behavior at this convention. Possibly they realized just how vulnerable the whole organization was.[29]

At the western boundary of the country, Shaw gave her first presidential address. In "Our Ideal," a speech that runs sixty-five typewritten pages, Shaw defined the values that would guide her presidency. Using the belated honoring of Sacajawea, whose statue the women dedicated here, as an example, Shaw sought to frame her analysis with the question of "how do great republics reward the toil and sacrifices of women?" Shaw argued that, in spite of women's broadening involvements in the republic, women's work, paid and unpaid, in the domestic sphere, in the public marketplace, or through voluntary civic organizations, was ignored, undervalued, or even condemned. Echoing Stanton's argument from "A Solitude of Self," Shaw noted the "reactionary movement against women's economic independence" that denigrated women workers "who are simply following their work where changed industrial conditions have taken it." In terms of women's familial responsibilities, Shaw was no sentimentalist, but argued that, "motherhood is a service to the State," and the state should realize its debt "to the citizen who rears children." Though European feminists used this argument to fight for social welfare legislation, Shaw only asked for the ballot.[30]

As the length of Shaw's speech suggests, she covered a wide range of topics from education and prostitution to marriage and divorce. She returned again and again to the issue of citizenship and the importance of women having full rights. Shaw praised the idea of the "School City" where public schools taught the rights and responsibilities of being part of a republic.[31]

In a critique of "sordid materialism and corruption," Shaw condemned "Corporate power [that] has so blocked the wheels of national legislation that the people and their interests are subordinated to the greed of millionaire lords." She called upon the suffragists to "guard against the reactionary spirit which marks the present time" and stand "unfalteringly for the principle of perfect equality of rights and opportunities for all." While she did not argue that women alone would change this culture, she believed women could and should be a part of this change, that women could help create a true republic. In a closing that challenged the racist and anti-immigrant sentiments of many of even her own colleagues, Shaw asked women to dedicate themselves to a society "in which men and women together shall in perfect equality solve the problems of a nation that knows no caste, no race, no sex in opportunity, in responsibility, or in justice." These were Shaw's beliefs.[32]

Shaw may have envisioned and articulated change but, officially president or not, she was only one voice. When the NAWSA elections took place, almost all of the same women were reelected, including most importantly both Laura Clay and Kate Gordon. While scholars have seen the long tenure of many of the officers as indications of stability, it could also indicate the inertia of the organization. The one surprising addition to the board was the remarkable scholar/activist Florence Kelley, who replaced Catt as vice president. Kelley had the same sort of class background as many of the other officers—she was a member of a Progressive Quaker family and the daughter of a congressman—but she had a broader education and was a more radical thinker and progressive reformer than any of the other women of her generation serving with the NAWSA. Far from new to suffrage work, Kelley came from a family of suffrage supporters and had been a voice and a presence at annual gatherings for years. Head of the National Consumers' League and a persistent voice for workers, especially child laborers, Kelley's election marked a shift toward the inclusion of more progressive women on the NAWSA Board. No one ever used the adjective "conservative" to describe Florence Kelley, who would serve from 1905 until 1910.[33]

Now that the office was truly hers, Shaw began to address some of the concerns that she believed were limiting the movement, especially the lack of age and racial diversity among the membership. Shaw wrote, "I very much like Mrs. Parke's [sic] plan of organizing the college women. . . . She is just the one to put at the head of the college work in our association, and I am going to try to have that department made with her at its head at the next national convention." In a note to Emily Howland, Shaw discussed asking Anna Julia Cooper, who had so strongly challenged her fifteen years before, or "Mrs. Booker T. Washington" to speak at the next convention. "However

I shall do my best to have the colored women represented." While a decade earlier many of the suffragists, Shaw among them, had feared the vote of Chinese American men, Shaw hoped to have Chinese and Japanese women at the next NAWSA. "I would like to have a representative there from all the races."[34]

One wonders what happened to these goals. Were these just words to reassure one of the more progressive suffragists or were Shaw's honest intentions blocked by her NAWSA colleagues? Certainly the next NAWSA gathering, the 1906 convention in Baltimore, did not have representatives of all the races, though it did have its inaugural College Night. On racial issues the NAWSA continued to bow to the concerns of southern women, so a diverse representation of women would have been remarkable in this conservative southern city where few of the leading citizens supported suffrage.[35]

The 1906 NAWSA Convention became one of the most important conventions in suffrage history for a broad range of reasons, the most obvious being that it was Susan B. Anthony's last. Those closest to her knew that Anthony's heart was weak. After so many years of dedication to the struggle, of ignoring the physical demands of her body, and of eschewing the comforts of home and leisure, Anthony knew she couldn't carry on much longer.

Susan B. Anthony had one last job to finish before the 1906 convention. In the seven months between the Portland meeting and the gathering in Baltimore, Anthony finalized an arrangement that would have far-reaching consequences for Shaw and the NAWSA. What Anthony did was create a fund that would pay Shaw's and other officers' salaries as well as finance other suffrage activities. This fund would pay Shaw as head of the premier suffrage organization, but it was a fund that was controlled not by the officers of the NAWSA, but by two women who had no official connection to the NAWSA before that year: President M. Carey Thomas of Bryn Mawr College and her partner, Mary Garrett. There was no smoking gun proving that Anthony deliberately engineered all the changes this development produced; Anthony may simply have done what she could to ensure that Shaw remain as leader of the NAWSA. Nevertheless, power follows money, and this new arrangement would change the NAWSA.[36]

M. Carey Thomas, another of the fascinating and original women of this era, had struggled to have her family support her education, which eventually included a PhD from the University of Zurich. Even before she had completed that degree, Thomas set her sights on the new women's college her Quaker relatives helped to found outside of Philadelphia. Dean at the age of twenty-seven, Thomas became president of Bryn Mawr College in 1894 at thirty-seven. Thomas had learned how to assess and use power when the founders of Bryn Mawr had resisted her ambitions. Once in office, Thomas pursued her vision of women's education with an almost single-minded focus. In 1906, though a very visible leader in women's educational circles, Thomas was not a public suffrage supporter. Unlike Vassar's President Taylor, she had however welcomed suffrage leaders as speakers to her campus. Anthony and Shaw had visited Bryn Mawr together a few years earlier.[37]

The official narrative of this process is that Anthony, in the process of planning for the 1906 NAWSA Convention in Baltimore, had called on Thomas and Garrett, heir to the impressive B&O Railroad fortune, to ask these native Baltimoreans' assistance in persuading the society women and men of that city to embrace the NAWSA during their time there. In the course of their discussions about the convention, the women had expressed surprise at the antiquated methods the NAWSA used to raise money through convention pledges and solicitations to established supporters. They volunteered to demonstrate a better approach. Thomas and Garrett proposed that they would raise the monies to pay the NAWSA officers. They set a total of $60,000 over five years as the goal of this fund; annually the NAWSA would have $4500 for salaries and $7500 for other expenses.[38]

What this story doesn't capture is how Anthony converted Thomas and Garrett from women who had zero involvement in the NAWSA to major players in the organization and the overall struggle. Although Thomas's biographer attributes Thomas's emergent interest in suffrage to her acquiescence to Garrett's stronger suffrage sentiments, given the college president's life and her life's work it makes sense that she could have had an interest in women's rights and woman suffrage. Perhaps she only needed Susan B. Anthony to persuade her. On the other hand, Thomas was an incredibly independent leader with an already demanding set of responsibilities. Garrett also had diverse commitments. It makes sense that she and Garrett accepted their new roles only with guarantees that they could run this fund as they saw fit. Both women were experienced in what Garrett's biographer calls "coercive philanthropy." What they then held was the power to support, in many ways, Anthony's protégé.[39]

The official story also fails to address how Anthony sold this concept to the rest of the NAWSA leadership, if she did at all. The *History of Woman Suffrage* states that the rest of the board could never agree to guarantee Shaw's or others' salaries. Perhaps the carrot was that the fund would provide for two additional salaries beyond Shaw's. One of those was for the treasurer, at that time Harriet Taylor Upton.[40]

After much work, the Baltimore Convention was both a tremendous success and a bittersweet trial, especially for Anna and Lucy. At one point, it seemed Susan B. Anthony might not be able to make it to Baltimore. In the end she rallied enough to make the journey, but once there she was too ill to attend the opening session. Thanks to the efforts of Thomas and Garrett, the program was elaborate with impressive attendance from the leaders of the city, suffrage elders, and college leaders. Mary Garrett opened her mansion to the leaders, especially for Susan B. Anthony, who grew frailer with each day. Garrett arranged for round-the-clock nurses to care for Anthony, while other honored veterans, Clara Barton and Julia Ward Howe, gave a sense of continuity to the first night's proceedings. A determined Anthony attended the second night, the NAWSA's first "College Evening," with numerous college presidents and students in attendance. At this changing of the generations with such a large show of college women, Anthony spoke her last public words, "Failure is impossible."[41]

Shaw's speech, only thirty-four pages this time, continued the focus on education as well as on women in industry. Shaw also responded to the debate among male "oracles"—former President Cleveland, President Roosevelt, Reverend Lyman Beecher, and others—about how women should not stray from their empire, the home. Shaw noted how women around the world were responding to changing realities by demanding the right of self-determination. She argued that while many women were homemakers, they were first individuals and citizens, a frequent refrain in her talks.[42]

From the Baltimore Convention, Shaw moved on to the annual congressional hearings while the ailing Susan B. Anthony returned home. For the next three weeks Anna and Lucy anxiously waited on each day's mail, receiving one day indications of Aunt Susan's recovery and then the next, news of a relapse. Anthony never wanted visitors when she was ill, but finally an anxious Shaw had reached her limits; she needed to go to Rochester. Her decision was prescient; while she was en route, Mary S. Anthony sent for her to come.[43]

From March 8th until Anthony's death on March 13th, Shaw kept a vigil. She recorded the days in her diary. "Another day full of loving little visits with precious Aunt Susan. Oh, how can we let her go?" Anthony was intermittently conscious, and when she was, Anna sat at her bedside. "This is more than I deserve and the sorrow of it is so hard to bear. It will inspire my life with a longing for the cause I have never known before." It was during one of these deathbed exchanges that Anthony demanded from Shaw that she stay at the head of the struggle as long as she was physically able. "She asked me if I could promise to never give it up and I gladly made the promise. . . . In the night she pressed my hand and laid hers in blessing on my head kissing me three times. It was my work's benediction and charge."[44]

On March 13th, the end came. Shaw wrote, "Early this morning, in the darkness, the spirit of the greatest woman and most noble patriot flickered like a fading light. Slowly her life ebbed away and dark as the night darker still is the night of our sorrow. What shall we do without her?"[45]

The whole nation mourned the passing of this great woman leader, joined by supporters of women's rights from around the world. In Rochester the flags were at half-mast and ten thousand people passed by her bier. Ida H. Harper described Shaw sitting at the service for Susan B. Anthony with "a white face and tremulous lips, showing more plainly than others how she was bereaved." After the addresses of some of Anthony's closest and most famous allies in the struggle, Shaw gave the final and now well-known eulogy.[46]

One can only imagine the depth of Shaw's grief. Susan B. Anthony had been the single most important person in her life, her only great passion, her model and her mentor. There was hardly then, and probably still isn't now, an adequate term to describe so complex a connection that was an all-encompassing love based equally in personality and politics. Yet once again, Shaw had little time to reflect on her loss. She had to move on with the work, and in many ways, this was the most appropriate way to mourn "Aunt Susan."

Shaw left Rochester soon after the funeral to resume the life she had led since 1886, one of boarding trains, traveling at least half the year, and staying in a different place almost every night of those months. Even more so than Anthony, Shaw needed to be in the field, talking with leaders, addressing the wide diversity of people who came to her lectures. And as she traveled she observed the changes in their lives and attitudes. One of the realities Shaw pondered in 1906 was how to modernize the NAWSA now that Anthony was gone.

Susan B. Anthony had predicted that her death would change the power hierarchy within the suffrage movement and warned Shaw to expect more intense jealousy and challenges. As she imagined, without her dominating presence and especially her support for Shaw, soon other longtime leaders began to position themselves as the next NAWSA president. Anthony's friends and foes alike may have been waiting for such an opportunity for years. Yet Shaw was the anointed successor, and she felt deeply her promise to Anthony to stay in the office. Consequently, rather than hesitate without her guiding spirit, Shaw claimed the leadership of the NAWSA. Predictably, the reactions against her and the resistance to her initiatives grew. At a time when the NAWSA needed all its energies to reinvigorate the struggle, when it needed to decide its course for the new century and find new methods and new constituencies, the leaders fell into a period of internal dissention. Shaw was the most common target of these complaints, but challenges came from all sides and all political positions.

Often the complaints were personal. The first rumblings came from Harriet Taylor Upton. Upton wrote to other board members, as she was wont to do with her complaints, that Shaw didn't stay in close enough touch with her and that Shaw had treated her "terribly" in Baltimore. Given all the tensions and pressures on Shaw to hold the organization and herself together during the 1906 convention, it isn't surprising that she failed to show sufficient public appreciation for the work that had been done at the Warren Headquarters. Or possibly Shaw was trying to distance herself from Upton.[47]

Next came Florence Kelley's criticisms. Kelley was impatient. She wanted to see more new women in the leadership and more activity in Washington. Shaw agreed on both points but felt a bit bullied. To Lucy, Shaw confessed, "Your letter to Mrs. Kelley was all right. I just do not like her attitude toward our people. She does not know much about us and our work and jumps at conclusions." Shaw also worried that Harriet Upton was "dazzled" by Kelley.[48]

The next challenge was far more serious than the others and could have changed the course of the movement. The white suffrage leaders from the South, emboldened by the NAWSA's support for the Southern Strategy under Catt's leadership, wanted the NAWSA to endorse their plan for a new southern-based organization. This would be a white organization, of course, because its explicit strategy was to gain woman suffrage in the South by linking it to a guarantee of white supremacy. This wasn't a new idea. There had been talk of this plan for over a decade. Now the women thought it was time to act, perhaps expecting that Anthony's death had removed a final barrier. The fact that the southern suffragists approached the NAWSA speaks to the power they believed they had in the movement.[49]

On this, Anna Howard Shaw and the NAWSA drew a line in the sand. Finally Shaw had the power to act on her principles, so there was no equivocating. After years of the NAWSA retreating on the issue of racial equality, Shaw gave an immediate and unconditional refusal. Shaw was clear: "[I]t would be impossible for us to be allied with any movement which advocated the exclusions of any race or class from the right of suffrage."[50]

Shaw's unambiguous decision ended the expansion of influence and power of this cohort of southern white suffragists and the NAWSA's slide away from supporting universal suffrage. It wasn't quite a complete turnaround, but it set a boundary. Though a number of the women behind this proposal continued to be active and often opposed to Shaw, never again during Shaw's presidency could they presume that they could dictate the NAWSA's policy in the South. And there were other active suffragists in the South who had less extreme positions. Nevertheless, Shaw still had to work with two of the women who were in sympathy with this plan, Clay and Gordon, on the Official Board. This would not be the last confrontation between Shaw and her southern colleagues—not by a long shot. So, two years into her presidency, Shaw had challenges from Kelley, Clay, Gordon, and Upton, representing ideologically left, right, and center.

Anna Howard Shaw celebrated her sixtieth birthday presiding over the 1907 NAWSA Convention in the city of Chicago. The celebration, focusing on the fact that more women than ever before were enfranchised and that the

NAWSA's membership was the largest ever, was tempered by the mourning for both Anthony sisters—Mary S. Anthony had died eleven months after her sister and just days before the convention. The next day, February 15, 1907, what would have been Aunt Susan's eighty-seventh birthday, was devoted to the deceased leader. Rachel Avery Foster, who had returned from Europe the previous year, announced a plan for a $100,000 Susan B. Anthony Memorial Fund. An additional vice presidency was created to allow this longtime leader to rejoin the board. As would be expected in Chicago, social and labor issues were front and center. The program included tours of Hull House, a day devoted to Industrial Conditions of Women and Children, and a eulogy to Susan B. Anthony by African American leader, Fannie Barrier Williams.[51]

During this period when tensions between Shaw and veteran officers were growing, Shaw was constructing a new network of allies. Her most deliberate and effective outreach efforts were to college and working women's organizations. Harriot Stanton Blatch, Elizabeth Cady Stanton's daughter, had returned from England full of ideas for the American suffrage campaign. By 1907, Blatch had organized the League of Self-supporting Women and, through this group, pressured the NAWSA to give greater recognition and support to wage-earning women. Shaw was personally fond of "Hattie," though she found working with her difficult. Nevertheless Shaw strongly supported Blatch's efforts to reach out to and include working women in the New York State and national associations and conventions. Shaw went so far as to direct that her usual pay and expenses be used for the expenses of getting the working women to the conventions. To Shaw this was both the right and smart thing to do.[52]

As would be expected from someone for whom working was the most consistent aspect of her life, Shaw had definite views on women and work that varied little over her lifetime. Central to her analysis was the idea that became very familiar to many in the contemporary women's movement—almost all women worked even if only a percentage of those women worked for wages.

> There are more men doing the work which women formerly did than there are women doing the work which men formerly did; all the carding, weaving, and spinning, all the churning, cooking and table waiting, the washing, the knitting, the preserving and baking, the dressmaking and millinery, every industry of the home men have taken to the factories and shops of the country, and when women start out to find their grandmothers' work, ten to one, they find a man doing it. It is not that men object to women working, for they have always worked,—ceaseless, grinding toil has been their lot, and no one complained until they set a price upon their labor and demanded payment for their service. We have never been denied work, it is only the pay to which objection is made.[53]

In Shaw's analysis women weren't supported by their husbands. Reflecting a preindustrialization view of women's domestic work, she believed that women contributed as much to a family's maintenance through their unwaged work as men did through their waged work. This analysis of the value of women's labor had lost ground during the nineteenth century with the emergence of an urban, middle-class ideal in which women were seen as too delicate to engage in strenuous or productive activities. The work of most women was invisible.[54]

College women were the other targeted constituency. The College Equal Suffrage League (CESL) was now officially affiliated with the NAWSA. Part of its increased strength and visibility came from the energy of M. Carey Thomas. An organizational powerhouse, Thomas took the lead of the CESL at this time, a move that was not appreciated by its founder, Maud Wood Park.[55]

At the same time that Thomas was positioning herself to be the leader of the CESL, she was also completing the fund-raising for the Thomas-Garrett Fund. By the May 1, 1907, deadline, the pledges were in, and Thomas could telephone Shaw and tell her that her salary of $2500 for the next five years was guaranteed. Few things rattled Shaw, but she was overwhelmed by this news. Not since her brief stint with the MWSA in 1886 had Shaw had the luxury of a guaranteed income. At sixty, Shaw now had some degree of financial stability. Further, Shaw, Thomas, and the NAWSA were now bound together for at least five years in a complex relationship involving power, politics, and money.[56]

As if to complete her lifelong struggle for economic stability and a middle-class lifestyle, Anna and Lucy moved into their first full-time permanent home on Lucy's forty-eighth birthday. Twenty years after they first started living together, they finally had the home they had wanted, the domestic refuge Shaw had dreamed of on all those journeys around the United States and abroad. Shaw had purchased this tract of land back in 1905. For $8500 she gained twenty acres in Rose Valley, Upper Providence Township, in Delaware County outside of and to the west of Philadelphia. It was close to a train station, of course, and not far from Swarthmore College. After engaging in some minor land speculating, selling off sections of this land, including a parcel to Rachel Foster Avery, Shaw retained a little over two acres for herself. At that time the Wianno cottage had been on the market for over a year, but it had not yet sold.[57]

That it took this long for Anna and Lucy to build the home of their dreams suggests again just how cautious Shaw was about her finances. The first architect they employed was told to design a home that would cost no more than $9000, but she brought in a plan for a $20,000 home that the women knew they couldn't afford. Another plan of a less expensive design was completely unsatisfactory to the two women. A third plan, one that fulfilled their requirements, was affordable after Mary Anthony left the two women $5000 each.[58]

Shaw's and Anthony's emotional investment in this home was great. Numerous photographs of it at its various stages of construction make up a significant part of the Schlesinger Library Anna Howard Shaw photographic collection. The Dutch Colonial house sits, as Shaw had required, on a hill overlooking woods and a creek. Though the area was quite underdeveloped at the time, Shaw ensured that it would remain as private as possible, removed from the demands of her work and eyes of the world. The house was at the end of a long curved driveway with a large lawn separating it from the road. The front entry had only a small covered portico. This was a home that definitely faced away from the public.

The back of the house was as homey as the front was austere. A large porch spanned the entire length of the house. So spacious was the porch that it could function as several additional rooms, accommodating numerous chairs and tables, both an outdoor living room and dining area. A smaller second-floor porch looked out from the space Shaw called "Peter Pan," since standing there she felt she was in the treetops. This was the gracious home of Shaw's dreams, one with a big kitchen, a large living room, and numerous bedrooms with lots of light and air. Anna's own touches were a play space for visiting children and a separate room where their housekeeper could visit with her guests. Anna and Lucy had settled on the name "Alnwick Lodge" after the town in Northumberland where Shaw's grandparents had lived and her mother had been born.[59]

One month after the completion of their home, Lucy and Anna hosted a memorable family Christmas that Shaw gleefully described to her old friend Clara Osborn. "When the packages were taken off the Christmas tree yesterday yours was taken off among the first, and I opened the package at once and found a splendid great apron. I immediately put it on and wore it the rest of the day . . . and carved our turkey in it. . . . We had a family of twenty-four and for two nights we had fifteen sleeping in the house, so that you see for spinsters we are doing pretty well."[60]

Among the guests were Rachel Foster Avery and her family with whom Shaw and Anthony had boarded in Swarthmore while they were waiting for their home to be completed. At this point these women were still very close. In fact, a map at the Delaware Court Archives from 1908 identifies the land adjacent to Shaw's as belonging to "Mrs. Avery," though the local courthouse records contain no documentation of a sales transaction between Shaw and Avery.[61]

After four and a half years in the presidency and as the sixtieth anniversary of the Seneca Fall Convention approached, on one level, Shaw's leadership seemed to be gaining some solid footing. The movement had new members if not new suffrage states. Shaw accepted that the struggle would have to develop new tactics. While in London in June, Shaw was among the women who led one of that city's large suffrage parades. She found this expression of support for the franchise exhilarating and believed it would be useful in the United States. In October of 1908, in the unlikely locale of Boone, Iowa, Shaw backed the Iowa Equal Suffrage Association leaders' decision to hold a march on the last day of their state convention. This may have been the first such march in the United States, although a small march of about twenty-three women occurred earlier in 1908 in New York City. Though much suffrage scholarship has cast Shaw as opposed to such innovative strategies, her own words and the historical records argue otherwise.[62]

The 1908 annual convention of the NAWSA's theme was the progress woman had made since that meeting at the Wesleyan Church. Scheduled for Buffalo, New York, in October 1908, it had been almost twenty months since the association members had gathered. While much of the movement was in an optimistic mood, Shaw remained unsettled about the future direction of the NAWSA, but she rose to the occasion as she usually could. As the local newspaper reports remarked, "The Rev Anna Howard Shaw has set a new standard for womanhood. She is one of the most wonderful women of her time, alert, watchful, magnetic, earnest, with a mind as quick for a joke as for the truth. . . . Even unbelievers are carried away with her brilliancy, eloquence and mental grasp."[63]

Appropriately, Elizabeth Cady Stanton's daughter, Harriot Stanton Blatch, had a major presence at this convention that marked the sixtieth anniversary of the Seneca Falls Convention. In addition to speaking on her mother's vision on the opening Pioneers' Night, she spoke as president of the League of Self-supporting Women. Among these working and celebratory aspects of the convention, the internal conflicts of the organization emerged into the public only in Upton's treasurer's report, where she sounded a strong note of caution and concern. Pledges and contributions were less than they had been in previous years, and Upton expressed the fear that some felt that the NAWSA had "unlimited funds" and that the planned $100,000 Anthony Fund had already been raised. Though Shaw supported Upton's plea for contributions, she was also able to announce that she had received a $10,000 check from Mrs. George Howard Lewis of Buffalo, a wealthy and consistent supporter of Susan B. Anthony and now Shaw. The rest of the convention had no serious controversy or drama. All the longtime officers were reelected.[64]

This was the last harmonious convention of Anna Howard Shaw's NAWSA presidency. Shaw was already well aware of the growing tensions. In November she noted that Mrs. Blatch was "furious" over the "$10,000 going to the National out of the State of New York." Shaw sensed that the support she had among her board was eroding even more; none had expressed their appreciation of her work from the previous year. Shaw herself was angry with Harriet Taylor Upton for voting for some unspecified New York measure, which Shaw had opposed. Finally she wrote, "I am so tired of being bossed and bullied by Miss Clay who does not digest a thing but hops at anything to get out of organization." What isn't clear is whether Shaw still wanted the support of this board, or if she wanted a new board.[65]

By 1908 the once hesitant Shaw had accepted the burden of her office, honoring her promise to the dying Susan B. Anthony. The money raised by M. Carey Thomas and Mary Garrett financially allowed her to keep this commitment. With Lucy maintaining the home Shaw had long dreamed of, her presidency still popular among the general NAWSA constituency, and her reelections uncontested, Shaw at sixty-one seemed poised to stand as the new elder stateswoman of the woman suffrage movement. Such a static view of Shaw and the movement would have been misleading. Shaw was never satisfied with the status quo, and she was willing to risk the apparent accord among the leaders if that was what was needed to make progress. She knew she had the power and some level of means with which to truly change the NAWSA.

Annie Howard Shaw as an Albion College student, circa 1874. Courtesy of Schlesinger Library, Radcliffe Institute, Harvard University.

Annie Howard Shaw (right front), her friend Clara Osborn (left front), and probably their sisters, Big Rapids, Michigan, circa 1875. Courtesy of Schlesinger Library, Radcliffe Institute, Harvard University.

Rev. Annie Howard Shaw around the time of her 1880 ordination. Courtesy of Schlesinger Library, Radcliffe Institute, Harvard University.

Anna Howard Shaw (middle), Lucy E. Anthony (left), Alice Stone Blackwell (right), and an unidentified child camping in Canada around 1890. Courtesy of Schlesinger Library, Radcliffe Institute, Harvard University.

Anna Howard Shaw, with paintbrush, and her partner, Lucy E. Anthony, at The Haven, Wianno, Massachusetts, about 1895. Courtesy of Schlesinger Library, Radcliffe Institute, Harvard University.

Anna Howard Shaw (left front), Susan B. Anthony (right front), and three German women in Berlin from the International Council of Women, 1904. Courtesy of Schlesinger Library, Radcliffe Institute, Harvard University.

Anna Howard Shaw and her three surviving siblings at Alnwick Lodge,
August 5, 1911. Courtesy of Schlesinger Library, Radcliffe Institute, Harvard
University.

Shaw (third from left), Lucy E. Anthony (far left), and four young women, probably Shaw's nieces, in about 1914. Courtesy of Schlesinger Library, Radcliffe Institute, Harvard University.

View of the front of Alnwick Lodge, the home that Shaw and Lucy E. Anthony built in Moylan, Pennsylvania, in 1905. This photograph is from about 1915. Courtesy of Schlesinger Library, Radcliffe Institute, Harvard University.

View of the back of Alnwick Lodge including the second story porch that Anna and Lucy called "Peter Pan." Courtesy of Schlesinger Library, Radcliffe Institute, Harvard University.

Anna Howard Shaw and a young girl exchanging a nest or plant at Alnwick Lodge in 1915. Courtesy of Schlesinger Library, Radcliffe Institute, Harvard University

CHAPTER 6

Creating Her Vision

NAWSA PRESIDENCY, PART II (1909–1912)

T he old battle cries no longer stir our souls. Give us new
banners for our times, let us have new leaders, and what
we need most is undoubtedly a new battle cry to stir the
dormant souls of American men and women. . . . In the past
they called this spirit by one name and in another period they
called it by another, we, today are calling it by a new name and
that name is Democracy.

On September 18, 1909, five long years after the membership of
the National American Woman Suffrage Association (NAWSA) first elected
her President, Anna Howard Shaw celebrated a major victory. The victory
wasn't adding another suffrage state or securing a large fund for the cause.
On this September day the NAWSA opened its new national headquarters
at 505 Fifth Avenue in Manhattan.[1]

This was a major symbolic as well as material triumph for Shaw and the
NAWSA. Woman suffrage was now part of the political mainstream. Opening the New York headquarters helped bring it there and keep it there.
Journalists and politicians could no longer ignore this cause. Reestablishing
a strategically located national presence truly marked the end of a period of
exile and stagnation for the movement. Positive press coverage increased
substantially, and the next year brought promising developments in the
western states. It is easy to argue that the momentum that carried the movement to final victory started with this event. Certainly opening the New
York headquarters was a pivotal point of Shaw's tenure. Just as the Warren,
Ohio, headquarters had represented a marginalized association, the suite
of offices on Fifth Avenue in the media and financial center of the country
signaled a new beginning for both the NAWSA and its leader, part of the
growth and transformation that Shaw spearheaded. This was a personal
triumph for the veteran orator.[2]

Without a doubt the first five years of Shaw's NAWSA presidency had been frustrating. A reluctant president at first, taking the helm only at Susan B. Anthony's insistence, Shaw often stated that she remained in office only to fulfill her promise to the dying Anthony. But gradually at times, and at other times with a sudden jolt, her grip on the leadership tightened. The jolts came mostly when others tried to grab the position and power from her—those "others," at this point, being mostly from within the old guard of the NAWSA leaders. This opposition appears to have inspired Shaw to be a more creative and energetic leader. Certainly Carrie Chapman Catt had similar internal opposition and dissension when she tried to revitalize the NAWSA. Yet even as her colleagues doubted her program, Shaw was gathering new alliances, new leaders, new strategies, and new sources of funds with which to actualize her vision for the organization. Shaw began not so much by turning away from many of the women with whom she had worked for over a decade, but by turning toward those with new ideas and energy. Shaw knew the risks of being a change agent, but some of the consequences were beyond what even she could have imagined.

These middle years of Shaw's presidency—from planning for the 1909 NAWSA Convention in Seattle through the 1912 convention in Philadelphia—deserve a closer look than they have received from suffrage scholars. While analyses critical of Shaw's presidency have most frequently used the upheavals of these years as the basis for judging Shaw as a failure as an administrator, the gains of these years as well as the full context and origins of these organizational conflicts have received scant in-depth attention.

Class and race issues are especially significant for analyzing both Shaw's legacy as a leader and the positions of the suffrage movement as a whole. Money tensions had always haunted the NAWSA, but the fact that Shaw drew a salary for her presidency and had access to monies beyond the control of the NAWSA treasurer raised suspicions among the privileged leaders who linked financial need with corruption. That Shaw was also the strongest and most consistent supporter of universal suffrage brought additional resistance from those who were opposed to or willing to compromise on the extension of the franchise to African American and immigrant women. Yes, there were personal grudges and tensions, but we need to ask how often they were linked to the substantive political struggles taking place within the NAWSA.[3]

The year 1909 opened with a public debate between Shaw and Charlotte Perkins Gilman. Sponsored by the Women's Trade Union League and mostly attended by working women, this forum presented two gifted speakers who took very different positions on women's domestic work. Gilman's frames of reference were the nineteenth-century ideal of separate spheres and the white, middle-class family. Shaw's views were grounded in the preindustrial gender system of rural America where women were conceived as productive helpmates. These class, family, and experiential differences help to explain both the content and the general reactions to the debate that was held at the beginning of January in the Carnegie Lyceum (now the Zankel Hall of Carnegie Hall) to a packed house.[4]

As reported by the *New York Times* and other newspapers, Shaw argued the side that stated that women more than earned whatever monetary support their husbands provided. Gilman argued that women were kept by their husbands. Referring especially to women who had housekeepers and servants, she called such women "parasites." While Gilman argued that women's emancipation would come from their entry into the waged workforce and the severing of their financial dependence on men, Shaw argued that women and men were economically interdependent and that the belief that women were supported by men denied the value of women's domestic work. Having been in the waged workforce since fifteen, Shaw understood the limits of this path to liberation for most women. Shaw's position was consistent with her earlier statements in which she had called for governments to recognize how mothers serve nations, a position close to that of Ellen Key, the Swedish feminist who advocated state payments to all mothers. As the *New York Sun* noted, Gilman gave the more scientific arguments while Shaw's "common sense" examples more effectively caught the audience's sympathy. Similarly, while historians have credited Gilman with the more progressive analysis, by all contemporary accounts of the event, the working women in the audience agreed far more with Shaw's views.[5]

Such public debates gained publicity for the suffrage cause. Though both the contemporary media and later historians have set this up as a confrontation, this debate was not between two rivals, but between two suffrage colleagues who respected each other and often shared a stage. Charlotte Perkins Gilman was a consistent presence at the NAWSA Conventions for many years. At least once when Shaw had to cancel her speaking engagements, she recommended Gilman as her replacement. Further, Shaw was never so naive as to expect that all suffrage supporters would agree on policies and analyses. Shaw and Gilman were the two suffrage leaders who had grown up in poverty; both knew women's vulnerability within the prevailing familial structures. Yet their identities and experiences differed in that Gilman was a member of an old and prominent New England family.

Shaw would never have engaged in a truly contentious debate with a sister suffragist. The press would seize with glee any hint of a split within the movement and exploit the conflict as a means to denigrate it. Shaw feared another split that would set the struggle back decades. While Shaw was not skilled as a peacemaker—possibly she had worked alone for too many years to have learned the subtleties needed to keep fragile alliances working—she was constantly aware that with growth came such a danger.[6]

Soon Shaw was again on the road. Travel was still the most constant aspect of Shaw's life. In spite of being in a salaried position, she continued to travel almost as much as she had when lecturing was the only source of her income. Needing to be in motion may just have been part of Shaw's makeup now. There was no set model for the NAWSA presidency, and travel may have been Shaw's solution to the awkward delays of conducting business by mail. The positive sides to this were that Shaw earned money for the NAWSA and local organizations from her talks, and she gained firsthand knowledge of local progress from state and local organizations, suffrage leaders, and legislators. The problem with this approach was that Shaw wasn't handling the day-to-day business of the association.

Increasingly, Shaw was building her analysis that the current leadership of the movement was out of touch with a changing society. The NAWSA Board continued to be dominated by the wives and daughters of white established middle-class and elite families. Certainly some were more progressive and others more conservative, but this was not a representative group of women in terms of class and race. Not happy or comfortable with the changes in the American population, some of these privileged women had been rethinking their views of democracy. Considering themselves the true Americans who were best suited to determine the policies that controlled the workers, the immigrants, the American Indians, the African Americans, and the other people of color, many of these women and men, even Charlotte Perkins Gilman, were influenced by Social Darwinism and, in this era of increased immigration, had turned away from the earlier commitment to universal suffrage, promoting in its place a limited and educated electorate.[7]

Increasingly M. Carey Thomas became Shaw's political confidante. As Shaw's frustration with the NAWSA's inertia, the growing conservative attitudes of particularly the southern women, and the lack of board support for her, she relied more and more on newer converts to the cause for counsel. There is no easy way to characterize this relationship since Thomas, with her partner Mary Garrett, always had control over the monies that paid Shaw, the funds for various NAWSA initiatives, and the budget of the CESL. A congenial relationship with Thomas was absolutely necessary for Shaw as she moved forward with her plans. As a result, it is impossible to disaggregate the professional relationship between the two from their personal friendship.[8]

Thomas was one of the new NAWSA power players. Shaw trod more carefully in her relationship with Thomas than she did with her other friends. One indication of this comes from the tone and the level of formality in the correspondence between Thomas and Shaw, which contrasts with the humor and teasing Shaw often inserted even in "business" letters with many suffrage colleagues. Years into the friendship, while Thomas declared that they didn't always agree on strategies and that she always deferred to Shaw on suffrage issues, Shaw confessed to Thomas that she was still at times in awe of the Bryn Mawr president. Nevertheless, in spite of the inevitable and unequal power dynamic between them, Shaw and Thomas appeared to have recognized kindred spirits in each other. No rift ever threatened their partnership.[9]

In early 1909 Shaw wrote to Thomas about her desire to have a NAWSA headquarters in Washington, D.C. Shaw saw this as another preparatory step for the ultimate goal of federal action and recommended reformer and educator Sophonisba Breckinridge to head such an office. The NAWSA hadn't had such a presence in the capital since 1891 when they had rented two rooms at the Wimodaughsis Club for several years. Shaw wanted a permanent office, building on the temporary presence the NAWSA already had in the capital where former NAWSA President Catt was leading the last great petition drive, aiming to gather one million signatures to present to Congress urging the passage of the federal suffrage amendment.[10]

The core of the NAWSA leadership had never abandoned the goal of the federal amendment, in spite of much scholarship that argues that they had. But the NAWSA was split on this issue. To Shaw, Catt, and many other leaders, the state-by-state approach was what they had to do until they gained enough congressional support to get the federal amendment moving. Most certainly the two southern leaders would oppose any real action in the direction of a federal amendment. To them, the federal amendment was only a strategic tool with which to threaten their male conservative, states'-rights politicians. Predictably, as soon as Shaw pushed for a permanent D.C. office, the other NAWSA officers responded with protests to her and complaints among themselves. At this point and on this issue, Shaw could not change their minds and in the end accepted a merging of the petition work with a temporary headquarters in the nation's capital. Rachel Foster Avery added heading the Washington office to aid Catt on the national petitions drive. It was, however, a step in the right direction in Shaw's view.[11]

Shaw realized she needed a stronger base of support if she was going to be able to circumvent the board and implement her ideas. That meant money. That spring, while attending the International Suffrage Alliance, she met Alva Smith Vanderbilt Belmont, the ex-wife of William Kissam Vanderbilt and the widow of Oliver P. Belmont. As a member of the nouveau riche Vanderbilt family, Alva had built her reputation as a maverick by challenging the established New York social hierarchy. In 1909, after a divorce, remarriage, and the death of her second husband, Alva Belmont was ready for new causes. Courted by Shaw, Ida Husted Harper, and other suffragists, she soon became one of the major New York society matrons to join the suffrage movement. Over the course of several long meetings, Shaw used her gifts of persuasion to convince Belmont to fund a national NAWSA headquarters. Shaw acquiesced to a New York City location since Belmont also agreed to support a headquarters for the New York Woman Suffrage Association there.[12]

Such a triumph! Shaw could hardly contain her exhilaration. In June 1909, from the International Council of Women gathering in Toronto, she wrote to Lucy that she was "so full of plans for the new Headquarters that I cannot think of anything else." The entrenched officers were less thrilled, viewing with suspicion this development and the initiatives of women such as Belmont or even Thomas. Since Shaw was no automatic insider herself, the shift of power from the older families to the new social, industrial, and corporate leaders didn't threaten her status. Of course, Shaw hoped that moving the headquarters would also lessen Harriet Taylor Upton's control over the NAWSA activities.[13]

Since the announcement and approval of the New York headquarters were set for the annual convention, Shaw urged as many women as possible to attend the NAWSA Convention. Unfortunately this gathering was scheduled for Seattle, Washington. One of the contradictions Shaw and the NAWSA faced still was the reality that much of the suffrage momentum was in the western states, while the NAWSA was dominated numerically and financially by women from east of the Mississippi. Further the political, financial, and media powers of the country were along the Atlantic seaboard.[14]

As a result few women from the College Equal Suffrage League planned to attend; the CESL was dominated by colleges from the Northeast. To remedy this, Shaw set about recruiting various leaders to speak on the now established College Night. In the process of recruiting CESL women for the convention, Shaw focused more and more of her attention on Professor Frances Squire Potter from the University of Minnesota. Potter had been active in Minnesota suffrage work and the College Equal Suffrage League, under whose auspices she first appeared on the national suffrage stage in 1908. By late spring of 1909, Shaw was promoting Professor Potter as a major speaker for College Night at the National Convention to be held in July. Shaw was so anxious to have Potter in Seattle that she persuaded Thomas that the CESL should pay Potter's expenses, along with those of several other women.[15]

All of these developments brought out Shaw's recklessness. In her excitement over the new headquarters, she made one questionable decision after another. As the convention approached, Shaw decided that Potter was the person to run the New York City NAWSA Headquarters. To say that this was an impulsive decision for both women would be an understatement; all evidence suggests that Shaw and Potter hardly knew each other. Next, Shaw was so anxious to entrust this new headquarters to Potter that Shaw agreed to be responsible for the difference between the official salary and the one Potter needed. She also agreed to have Potter's good friend, Mary Gray Peck, become the headquarters secretary. This plan was finalized before Shaw ever met Peck. Nevertheless, Potter and Peck resigned from their faculty positions at the University of Minnesota and planned to relocate to New York City.[16]

The daughter of an upstate New York physician, Frances Squire Potter had earned her BA and MA degrees from Elmira College. She then married and had four children, but she separated from her husband when her youngest was only two years old. In 1900, at the age of thirty-three, she joined the faculty of the University of Minnesota while also continuing her own writing, which included plays, a novel, and other publications. There is no evidence that she had had any administrative or press experience, but she had more than a touch of the bohemian in her. In a similarly incongruous career change, Potter's close friend Peck sacrificed an academic faculty post to take what was essentially a secretarial position. What connections these two women had with suffrage or other political leaders outside of Minnesota before they agreed to the positions at the new headquarters isn't clear. Perhaps they wished to return to their home state; both were from upstate New York.[17]

Just how keyed up Shaw was is clearly seen in the speech she gave in New York in June. It was the most militant speech of her long career. As a prelude to a spectacular torchlight march, Shaw's impassioned exhortation included a declaration that she was willing to die for suffrage, if such an action would further the cause. The *New York Times* sensationalized her talk with the headline, "Urges Suffragists to Become Militant: The Rev. Anna Shaw Calls on Them to Adopt the Methods of the English Women." "She'd Die for the Cause: Cheers Greet Her When She Declares She'll Be Fighting the Police When the Time Comes." If Shaw really was ready to fight the police, this position was uncharacteristic of her. Over the next years, she was far more likely to condemn such violent methods.[18]

With this heightened level of energy, Shaw headed to Seattle. Suffrage activities were heating up in California, Oregon, and Washington, and the city on Puget Sound was hosting the Alaska-Yukon-Pacific Exposition that summer. The leaders boarded the special train in Chicago, holding business meetings and meeting supporters and the curious as they made their way across the northern plains and over the Rockies into Washington.[19]

NAWSA conventions were now covered by newspapers across the nation. Anticipation of the upcoming move of the national headquarters to New York City dominated the discussions, reports, and talks at the convention. As had been the case since the NAWSA had been formed in 1890, the leaders presented a unified front even as a number of them harbored deep misgivings about the move. And as was also the practice, few such tensions were recorded in the official history or the convention proceedings. The exception again came from Harriet Taylor Upton, who had the most to lose with this move. Newly reelected treasurer, Upton still did not directly admit her concerns but took an oblique approach by warning the constituency to make sure that they paid close attention to the finances and not simply trust the officers.[20]

What were the bases for Upton's warnings? She had been handling the NAWSA finances for years. Upton felt she was the guardian of the NAWSA's treasury and handled the monies via her own very informal processes. When, for example, there were budgetary shortfalls, she kept them to herself. In her small town, she could cover them by approaching the local banker for a personal loan. With the move to New York and the increasing complexity of the organization's monies, she knew she could no longer personally manage problems in this individualistic way. But now, along with the official treasury, there were the Susan B. Anthony Memorial Guarantee Fund, aka the Thomas-Garrett Fund, plus the monies left to the movement in Mary S. Anthony's will, and finally the proposed Susan B. Anthony Memorial Fund. Further, the College Equal Suffrage League was an independent organization with its own finances, officers, and workers. With Shaw ally Alva Belmont funding the headquarters and the Press Bureau, Upton most probably realized that the financial reins of the organization were now held by the Shaw camp. Did Upton not trust Shaw and her supporters?[21]

There were other changes in the air. Frances Squire Potter, the presumptive corresponding secretary, gave a powerful speech at the "most brilliant session," of the College Evening. Yet part of Potter's speech was both surprising and confrontational, another indication of the regional tensions within the national organization. Professor Potter referred to the single-sex colleges of the East as "nunneries" and the "last entrenchments of the middle ages," while championing the superiority of the coeducational institutions of the Midwest and West. CESL President Thomas wasn't present at the Seattle Convention. The women and men who led and represented the women's colleges left no record of how they received this message. Nevertheless, this assertion might have indicated that Potter had a very strong streak of independence and believed in speaking what she saw as the truth to power. The CESL, which had been founded by and was still dominated by women from single-sex colleges, had paid for her trip to the convention.[22]

Still, at this point, Shaw could only see the positive. She was so impressed with Potter's talents that she declared that Potter's addition to the leadership was even more important than the headquarters in New York City. Her enthusiasm seemed to pervade the gathering; the convention concluded its program, its elections, and work sessions in a general spirit of congeniality and optimism.[23]

If one believed in troubling omens, Potter's impolitic remarks at the convention might have been the first. Next, Shaw sprained her ankle in Minneapolis when she stopped to visit with Potter on her way back from Seattle. This injury forced Shaw to remain there for several weeks, pushing back her other commitments for the summer. During this time Shaw uncharacteristically was out of contact with Lucy, who had also been traveling back from the convention separately. This might have been a deliberate move on Lucy's part. There were already signs of tensions between Lucy and Professor Potter. For Potter, having the incapacitated Shaw under foot in her home for weeks as she was arranging to move to New York City may have strained the new friendship. Shaw wrote only that Frances seemed tired. At this moment, Shaw would not allow her vision of the future of the NAWSA to be clouded by any of the obvious or subtle signs of discord.[24]

The major suffrage developments and the roles of socially prominent suffragists were attracting new and positive attention from the media. Alva Belmont opened her Newport, Rhode Island, home to a large suffrage gathering with Shaw as the featured speaker in August 1909. The press eagerly followed both the gathering and the surrounding controversy as other residents of the exclusive neighborhood took sides over the suffragist invasion of their summer resort. Photographs of this event are the only extant images of Shaw in a formal evening gown.[25]

Finally, in September, Shaw welcomed reporters from the various New York City media to a preview of the 505 Fifth Avenue offices. Shaw and Lucy had worked with various other women, including Potter and Peck, to furnish and organize the rooms they would occupy on this spacious floor. The *New York Times* article mentioned the rooms of Mrs. Belmont; Dr. Shaw; Mrs. Crossett, head of the New York Association; and that of the Press Department, which Ida Harper headed. There was no mention of Potter or Peck or their offices, though Shaw described the highlight of the upcoming work in words that described "suffrage settlements," an idea generally attributed to Potter. Shaw further noted that there would be four campaigns in the coming year in Washington, Oregon, South Dakota, and the Arizona Territory.[26]

With this move to Manhattan, the NAWSA and Shaw stepped into the increasingly complex suffrage politics of New York City and New York State. As the home of Elizabeth Cady Stanton and Susan B. Anthony, New York State, especially the upstate "Burnt Over District," had long stood as a stronghold of the NWSA and then the NAWSA. Shaw had inherited the support of many of Anthony's surviving friends, a few of whom, such as Seneca Falls organizer Martha Coffin Wright's daughter, Eliza Osborne, gave consistently and generously to the suffrage organization. The power of the region was now increasingly challenged by the activism that was growing in the New York City area, as DuBois has described in her biography of Harriet Stanton Blatch. Carrie Chapman Catt had established her home in this metropolitan area as well as had Blatch, when she returned to the United States from Great Britain. This was also the base of society leaders such as Belmont and Katherine Duer Mackay.[27]

Additionally, Manhattan was the center of working-class women's activism. Shirtwaist workers, mostly young women immigrants who worked long hours in sweatshops, were struggling for better wages and better working conditions in varying coalitions with unions, socialist organizations, and wealthier women, especially through the Women's Trade Union League (WTUL). The fall of 1909 was a long season of walkouts. The climax came at the end of November with a call for solidarity by the young leader, Clara Lemlich. What followed was the "Uprising of 30,000," a truly remarkable demonstration of solidarity and nonviolent militancy among the diverse women in the needle trades. In a historical moment of sisterhood, numerous groups of women, including the NAWSA, joined the working women and the WTUL allies in support of their activism and demands. On December 6, 1909, Belmont rented the Hippodrome and opened it for a meeting of the striking women where Shaw, among others, spoke.[28]

While this historic struggle was taking place on the streets and in the great halls of New York City, within the new NAWSA headquarters a far different type of power struggle was in progress. What might have been the expected adjustments to the major administrative shift of establishing a full-time central office with salaried professionals as well as support staff, many of whom had never worked in such an arrangement before, was growing into a major power struggle. On one side were Shaw and Lucy Anthony; on the other, Potter and Peck. Compared to the issues of the women garment workers, the emerging conflicts among the NAWSA leaders appear trivial. As much as it can be traced back to a single event, it seems that Potter and Peck strongly objected to Lucy's presence and, in their view, her interference in their running of the headquarters. They may really have been frustrated with Shaw, but Lucy was a less threatening target.[29]

Again, Shaw either ignored or was oblivious to the earliest tensions; she hardly mentioned any problems to M. Carey Thomas as the first months of the new arrangement passed. She may not have wanted to admit that she had been mistaken about Potter, or she may have just had a high tolerance for discord. As well as Shaw was able to read her audiences, she seemed at times equally unaware of interpersonal stress. Nevertheless, during October and November, gossip about headquarters problems reached suffrage leaders who lived far from the New York offices courtesy of Mary Gray Peck's frequent notes to Harriet Taylor Upton, who then passed the stories on to other officers. By early November, Thomas reported to Mary Garrett on a meeting she had with the corresponding secretary. "Mrs. Potter was *very* nice but they are in trouble at Headquarters." Potter had many complaints about Shaw and about money. Potter was so persuasive and effective in telling her version of the discord that she had Thomas convinced that Shaw and Anthony were the problems.[30]

Other NAWSA officers appeared only too happy to jump in with their complaints. Harriet Taylor Upton blamed and condemned Shaw, Lucy Anthony, Ida Husted Harper, and Alva Belmont for the problems. Kate Gordon in turn criticized Upton to Laura Clay. "If Mrs. Upton was a woman who raised any money by her own initiation she might be credited with earning her salary." Gordon also concluded that the NAWSA should get rid of Rachel Foster Avery because of her "total incompetency and unfitness for office." This was not a copacetic or productive team of leaders.[31]

Now the discord reached a boiling point. Issues of contention ranged from money and salaries through the allocation of office space and the use of stenographers' time. Antagonisms ran so high that Shaw uncharacteristically lost her temper with Peck and publicly argued with her. Potter stopped consulting or even speaking to Shaw. More and more of the national leaders were drawn into this conflict. Shaw wrote to NAWSA legal advisor, Catherine Waugh McCulloch of Chicago, for her opinion on the responsibilities of the various officers. Florence Kelley and M. Carey Thomas both tried to mediate the dispute. Potter then pulled Carrie Chapman Catt into the picture, meeting with her in early December. By this time, Thomas had reversed her position, finding that Potter and Peck "had openly defied Miss Shaw and refused to do anything she asked them to do, Mrs. Potter claiming that she was in entire charge of Headquarters and of the policy of the Association." If this was true, it is understandable that Shaw was alarmed. Whatever the origin of the disagreement or the truth in the various charges, it was clear that, in spite of Shaw's great hopes, Potter and Shaw could not work together in any harmony.[32]

The extant sources are not broad enough to determine whether this was basically a personality clash and/or an orchestrated struggle for the leadership of the organization. What is clear is that this conflict was the catalyst through which all the jealousies and divisions among the NAWSA leaders that had accumulated over the years flooded into the open. This seems the only logical explanation for how two relative newcomers to the national suffrage politics could disrupt the NAWSA and find internal support against a popular and democratically elected president. While Shaw and Upton had struggled over control of the NAWSA for several years, these two women had years of friendship, knowledge of each other's personalities, and shared work that seemed to have kept their conflict at a low level and out of the public eye. Potter, Peck, and Shaw had no such history with each other.

Shaw was stunned when Potter, the woman in whom she had put so much faith, turned out to be, in her view, both disrespectful of and disloyal to her. Certainly Shaw had never worked so intensely or in such close quarters with anyone but Lucy. The split became increasingly defined as one between those who supported Shaw and those who wanted to see her ousted, between the mass membership of the NAWSA and the small cohort of presumptive successors to Shaw.[33]

The NAWSA Board gathered for an emergency meeting to handle this crisis in mid-December 1909. Held behind closed doors, with no minutes, this meeting ended the open hostilities at least temporarily. There were some acrimonious moments. Shaw apparently faced intense challenges to her leadership that took a toll on her health, though it isn't clear whether the ailments were physical or emotional. Shortly after the meeting, she fell ill, canceled the rest of her engagements for December, and entered a rest sanitarium. On the other hand, her opposition felt vindicated. Laura Clay expressed satisfaction with the results and the role she played. Harriet Taylor Upton penned a rather mean-spirited rhyme about the session, celebrating the fact that Clay had brought Lucy to tears. Among the documented outcomes was an agreement that Lucy stay out of the headquarters, that Shaw give more responsibility for the headquarters to Potter, and that Shaw and Anthony take an apartment in New York City. It appears that Shaw had lost this round.[34]

Few of Shaw's personal writings from this period survived. It makes sense that Lucy would have destroyed documents from this painful period, but some letters survive. In a January 1910 letter to Catherine McCulloch, Shaw was conciliatory, highlighting the positive and stating that she believed the board did what they thought was right. Yet this meeting appears to have broken whatever trust remained between Shaw and the rest of the current board. They may have imagined that they could outlast Shaw, forcing her to resign as they had Catt. For her part, Shaw now had to confront the reality that the NAWSA might, in the end, have to choose between her and the current board.[35]

There was no turning back. Upton, in particular, continued to fan the flames of discontent through many letters to Laura Clay. Upton wrote that Lucy was "the most harmful person we have in our ranks" and that "if Miss Shaw is reelected president, we simply must have Headquarters taken away from her or take her away from Headquarters." Given that Shaw had been the one who had convinced Belmont to fund the headquarters that had been functioning for less than six months, Upton's assumption that the board could make such a change was unrealistic. Upton went so far as to predict the demise of the NAWSA as they had known it.[36]

Shaw certainly internalized the stress even as she returned to her regular schedule after the first of the year. During the long week of lobbying in Albany, she mentions using prescription medication to sleep. She was dreading the NAWSA Convention to be held in Washington, D.C., in April. Florence Kelley, whose role in this struggle is hard to determine from available sources, had quietly quit the NAWSA board, having written that she would not stand for reelection. For Shaw the best hope was that Potter and Peck would similarly resign without fireworks.[37]

This was not a good time for such an internal conflict. Across the country and in the nation's capital, suffrage issues were in the media spotlight. The opening of the New York Headquarters had brought the desired increase in media coverage. As the Washington, D.C., convention approached, Shaw had her hands full. President William H. Taft had agreed to address the gathering—the first U.S. head of state to do so. At the request of the board, the convention as a whole would vote on adopting the *Woman's Journal* as the official NAWSA publication. Finally, as part of the convention, Shaw would head the delegation testifying before both houses of Congress and presenting petitions containing over four hundred thousand signatures. As the convention progressed, only the incident when one participant hissed at Taft's failure to endorse woman suffrage marred an otherwise productive gathering.[38]

As the last work session approached and the election of new officers took place without any controversies, Shaw might have imagined that she had dodged a bullet. But she hadn't. On Tuesday, April 19, the last day of the 1910 convention, Potter, who with Peck had chosen not to run for reelection, rose to read the resolutions of the convention. There, the official minutes, without explanation, record a vote to go into executive session.[39]

According to press coverage Shaw emerged from that session visibly upset. The other officers presented the following resolution:

Whereas, the undersigned members of the Board, feeling respect and gratitude for the Corresponding and Headquarters' secretaries, both in their official capacity and as private individuals, regret singly and collectively the loss of Mrs. Potter and Miss Peck to official positions in the National American Woman Suffrage Association, therefore be it resolved "That we herewith tender to the outgoing secretaries our esteem and friendship and ask that this statement be read to the convention now assembled and be spread upon the minutes."

The signatures of Rachel Foster Avery, Florence Kelley, Ella S. Stewart, Harriet Taylor Upton, and Laura Clay were listed after the statement. This was not an ideologically based action. These women may have been united on this issue, but they represented a range of political positions otherwise.[40]

Shaw, standing alone, gave her rebuttal in a "minority statement," stating that the resolution was read at a public meeting by Florence Kelley before she (Shaw) ever knew about it or was given the opportunity to sign it. In her statement, she continued, referring only to Mrs. Potter, "I conscientiously believe that the aforesaid statement in regard to Mrs. Potter's official efficiency is not in accord with the facts as I know them." After hearing this statement, Shaw's old friends, Upton and Avery, who had just been reelected officers, announced their immediate resignations.[41]

For the first time since the NAWSA had formed, a major internal controversy reached the newspapers. Media accounts quoted Potter as confirming that she had instigated the resolution and that she had refused to allow Shaw to see or sign it. Then Avery and Upton stated that they tendered their resignations because they had discovered that "injustices" in the headquarters they had worked to rectify still existed. Shaw left no surviving statements about the actual event.[42]

The NAWSA Board's unanimous support for Potter and Peck constituted an overwhelming vote of no-confidence and a humiliating rebuke for the popular leader who had just been reelected for the seventh time. That these mostly longtime colleagues of Shaw's essentially stood united in support of two women they really didn't know and of whose work they had only secondhand evidence strongly supports the analysis that this confrontation was about far more than Potter and Peck. The question at the time might well have been whether Shaw's presidency could survive.[43]

What was really going on here? More importantly, was it of any major significance to the suffrage struggle? After a century it is hard to bring clarity to this sequence of events. Carey Thomas concluded that this whole process was undertaken to embarrass Shaw, while Shaw believed that this brouhaha resulted from Upton's hurt feelings and Avery's resentment that Shaw wouldn't resign and allow her, Avery, to be president. Later Thomas wondered whether Avery had been in her right mind. When Potter died only four years later, Shaw similarly wondered if Potter has been ill even then. An analysis of available sources strongly suggests that Florence Kelley, Potter, and Peck, the women most aligned with progressive politics, led this effort, but that they drew on underlying anti-Shaw feelings to bring in the other officers.[44]

On one level, this confrontation doesn't seem to have had long-term consequences. Quickly Shaw, the NAWSA, and most of the women involved in the NAWSA moved on. Potter soon had a position with the Women's Trade Union League. Carrie Chapman Catt urged Peck to become a full-time writer. Upton and Avery returned to Ohio and Pennsylvania, respectively, to head their state suffrage organizations. Yet the conflict didn't die. Most of the women who opposed Shaw would organize against her for the rest of her presidency. Mary Gray Peck may have been the most unrelenting adversary. Generations of readers have been exposed to her point of view through her writings. Her influence on Eleanor Flexner's analysis of Shaw is clear. And the repercussions of the 1910 convention events reached across the Atlantic because Shaw and Avery had shared many friends and colleagues in Europe.[45]

Shaw was certainly thick-skinned. She was accustomed to opposition. For her, it was the disloyalty of Rachel Foster Avery that pained her the most. For twenty years they had been family to each other. So intertwined had been their lives that this split significantly disrupted both women's plans. Avery's daughters had been scheduled to attend Bryn Mawr College, but that plan was abandoned. Shaw had loaned Avery money and held the mortgage for the part of Shaw's land where she probably had hoped to build a home. While Shaw worried about these financial deals, her diary and letters record her profound hurt and confusion over Avery's actions.[46]

It is logical to believe that a number of the women who had voted against Shaw—Upton, Clay, Kelley, perhaps Avery—along with Potter and Peck, expected that their action would derail the Shaw presidency. Their frustration with Shaw is undeniable, but what was the basis of their discontent? Was it personal? Was Shaw too much of a lone wolf? Was she lacking in interpersonal skills? Or were there truly some political differences? Unfortunately, the sources that might have made this clearer are gone, if they existed. For the NAWSA and the movement, the longer-term result was that Shaw persisted and shaped the NAWSA policies for the next five years.

Shaw survived this crisis because she had the support of the membership and an alternative network of supporters—most importantly Thomas and Belmont. Her popularity among the average NAWSA members was as strong as ever as a result of a long history with the NAWSA, her association in their minds with Susan B. Anthony, her incomparable ability to convert and inspire through her oratory, and her personal contacts as a result of decades of travel. So, while women such as Upton predicted the end of the NAWSA if Shaw continued in office, Shaw, though terribly pained by the 1910 events, saw opportunity.[47]

As had been her practice, she now moved forward. With Thomas's assistance, she began to build a new leadership team, one more to her liking. Even before she sailed to England that summer, she coordinated the elections to fill all the board and headquarters vacancies. Chicago lawyer Catharine McCulloch became first vice president, with Kate Gordon as second VP. Mary Ware Dennett and Ella Stewart were corresponding and recording secretaries, respectively. Jessie Ashley became treasurer, and Laura Clay and Alice Stone Blackwell stayed as the auditors. At this point, the conservative southerners remained in leadership while the most radical board member, Florence Kelley, left. At this time, as if to reinvent herself, Shaw dropped "Rev." and became known as "Dr. Shaw."[48]

Does this support the argument that the NAWSA was becoming increasingly conservative? Or that Shaw was a conservative leader? What conservative or radical meant within the NAWSA or the suffrage movement is not easy to define. In an oft-repeated quote, Elizabeth Cady Stanton had argued that she was more radical than Susan B. Anthony. She might have been so on religious and some other grounds. Yet Stanton was quite "conservative" or elitist on issues of race, imperialism, and universal suffrage. Similarly, Shaw is cast as a conservative minister, but most Americans would have seen any woman minister in this era as a radical. In these and other cases, without more specificity or explanation, such terms are only confusing.[49]

This new slate of officers included women with vastly different points of view. Given that 1910 does mark a major change in status of women's suffrage, it is worth considering what roles these women played in that transition. Jessie Ashley, though not as well known as Kelley, also identified as a socialist. Mary Ware Dennett was progressive generally but would come to be seen as a radical on sexual education. Mary Ware Dennett, of all these women, would play the greatest role in the work of the NAWSA and Shaw's remaining presidency.

Dennett came to New York at the urging of Thomas and Shaw. Descended from old New England families, she had pursued artistic interests before her marriage. After that union fell apart, this now single mother of two was at the beginning of a new life for herself and her family. Dennett took over the NAWSA headquarters under very difficult conditions but quickly proved that she possessed impressive administrative and interpersonal talents. Never afraid to confront problems directly—in her first months she rebuffed Peck, who tried to convince her to join the anti-Shaw "insurgents"—Dennett became the headquarters' executive Shaw had hoped to find. Though Dennett and the new treasurer, Jessie Ashley, were much younger and much more involved in the political, social, and cultural movements of the Progressive Era, they worked smoothly with Shaw for years even when they had political disagreements.[50]

In the end, Shaw's leadership survived, and in many ways, both Shaw and the NAWSA thrived in the aftermath. This middle year of Shaw's presidency was part of the suffrage renaissance. Shaw, with Dennett and Ashley, immediately began to re-create the NAWSA, bringing it more in line with the "new women" of the era, the working women, the college women, and all the women involved in the multiple reform activities in the country. Together they strengthened their alliances with the more progressive political and social groups and individuals. They successfully raised new monies, garnered more press attention, and oversaw incredible growth in the organization. It is impossible to know how much of this should be credited to Shaw or to Dennett and Ashley.[51]

Concurrent with this second beginning of the headquarters in New York City was the increasing popularity of new suffrage propaganda tactics, many originally tried in New York City under the leadership of Harriot Stanton Blatch. Shaw was front and center for the first great New York City parade on May 21, 1910. That summer, in London, she participated in the British women's demonstration in Hyde Park. One other major campaign innovation came with the availability of automobiles. It wasn't just young women who took to these new vehicles, setting up meetings in those parts of the country not easily reached by the trains. After traveling in England with Ray Costelloe, a young expatriate suffragist and niece of M. Carey Thomas, even the sixty-three-year-old Shaw was ready to learn to drive.[52]

On her return from Europe, Shaw resumed her roles as both the workhorse of the leadership and the star of the U.S. movement. With a corresponding secretary whom she trusted and who was, in return, loyal to her, Shaw was freed to do what she did best. Though Catt was by far the superior organizer, she didn't shine in the limelight as Shaw did, a difference Catt was large enough to celebrate rather than resent. Harriet Stanton Blatch, an energetic innovator in the struggle for the franchise, never had the national presence of Shaw and Catt. Shaw persisted as the face and the voice of the suffrage movement in this era after the passing of Susan B. Anthony. Additionally, as if getting the tensions among the board members into the open had relieved her of her greatest source of stress, from the time of her vacation in England in 1910 until 1914, Shaw enjoyed a significant period of good health.[53]

While many historians do limit the dates of the so-called "doldrums" to 1896–1910, others ignore the gains of the remaining years of Shaw's presidency. There were major victories. As if to validate the idea that Shaw, the NAWSA, and the movement as a whole were on the right path, on November 8, 1910, Washington became the first new state since 1896 to grant women full suffrage. Though accompanied by defeats in Oregon, South Dakota, and Oklahoma, this was still great cause to celebrate. This generation was used to defeats, far more than to victories, but the success in Washington confirmed Shaw's belief that the NAWSA's role had changed. The national organization's most effective work in the states was to help them build their local groups and promote local leaders who knew which strategies would work best in each location. Victories would come under strong state and regional leadership that the NAWSA could support but not direct. Shaw had a keen ability to predict whether a state would succeed based on the quality of the organization in place before she or other national leaders ever came to the state. She also understood the importance of a coordinated effort, adopting the principle that she and other NAWSA workers should go only where they had been invited by the official state campaign. This was the new NAWSA policy. And as this year of turmoil ended, Shaw continued to lead the NAWSA as best as she knew how, keeping her vision on the ultimate goal and trusting her colleagues until proved wrong.[54]

Fortunately for Shaw and the NAWSA, after the turmoil of the previous eighteen months, 1911 proved to be a comparatively calm year. For whatever reasons, perhaps to preserve her health, perhaps to keep close to the headquarters and the New York City and State activities, or perhaps to make sure that the headquarters did run smoothly, Shaw concentrated her efforts on the eastern states during 1911. Ida Husted Harper maintained that since Shaw and the NAWSA had relocated to New York City, Shaw was never able to fulfill all the requests that came in for her to speak, even within the city. She would travel no farther west than Illinois, and her only southern trip was to the NAWSA Convention in Louisville in November.[55]

The downside of this plan was that women from other areas of the United States felt excluded from the core suffrage work. Though Shaw, Dennett, Ashley, and the other members of the headquarters staff were working together harmoniously and productively, criticisms from other members and ex-members of the board continued. Again, these conflicts seem small and reinforce the idea that certain NAWSA officers were simply bickering; it may also have been the case that the other officers objected to the more progressive direction of the association.

Shaw wondered what could have been accomplished if these women had put all the energy they expended on questioning the headquarters decisions into constructive suffrage work. Finally, on April 17, before she left for Europe, Shaw had had enough. She sent out a letter giving her assessment of the accomplishments of the New York office and her strong defense of the work of Dennett and the headquarters.[56]

Still the internal sniping continued. The self-proclaimed insurgents continued to believe that the NAWSA would be better without Shaw at its head. On June 6, 1911, Kate Gordon wrote to the corresponding secretary, arguing in support of a new tactic to achieve this end. She wanted to limit the term of the president. "I think two successive terms, of two years each, is long enough for any one woman to administer the affairs of the Association." Next, while still in Europe, Shaw had to mediate between Alva Belmont and board members when the latter objected to Belmont's offer to continue to fund the headquarters only if Shaw were reelected president. Looking ahead, the passionate and impulsive Gordon worried about "some plan afoot by Miss Thomas" and urged Catherine McCulloch and Ella Stewart to stay on the board the next year. She was concerned that Laura Clay would be the only "opposition" voice remaining on the board since she planned to be away in Europe for the entire year. But what did the opposition represent at this point? Were they united only in their opposition to Shaw?[57]

Shaw didn't escape controversy on this European trip, but what she faced there was a very different and very public dispute over women's rights. Shaw had been invited by women of Norway and Sweden to speak at their state churches. She was to be the first woman to preach in the Swedish church, but what would have been momentous became sensational when the Church of Norway denied Shaw a similar right to preach. As Shaw spent weeks fulfilling her full agenda of meetings and speaking engagements across Europe, the controversy and the media coverage grew. The members of the public who were interested in hearing the Rev. Dr. Shaw preach in Stockholm increased tremendously, while Shaw felt the pressure to deliver an extraordinary sermon. Never before, in all her years on the public stage, had she so felt the eyes of the world on her.[58]

Shaw found the means to exceed even these expanded expectations. In the end, the ceremony during which she preached was such a powerful and beautiful service that Shaw described it as an otherworldly experience in which her spiritual self fully directed her physical being. Of all her sermons and lectures, this was one of only two in which she was completely satisfied. Unfortunately, no transcript of this speech exists.[59]

After such a triumph, returning to the United States to face a still recalcitrant board was quite a letdown, but a few positive events sustained Shaw. Unexpectedly, Anna had a reunion with her three surviving siblings at her home in Moylan. The press delighted in this picture of Shaw with her three Civil War veteran brothers. The best surprise, though, came when Anna opened a letter on August 13 to find a $20,000 check from a supporter who wished to remain anonymous. After her death it was revealed that Boston philanthropist and activist Pauline Agassiz Shaw (no relation) had given this money to Shaw with explicit instructions that it was for her to use as she saw fit. Shaw's reaction was, "I will never lose heart again."[60]

Not surprisingly, when Shaw shared this good news with the rest of the board, they didn't share in her celebration. Apparently suspicious of Shaw's money-handling, certain members complained about the anonymity and demanded to know who the contributor was. Shaw was finally pushed to the limit of her tolerance for what she saw as petty discord. Perhaps it was the power that came from that check or the endorsement of her work that it represented, but a renewed Shaw finally confronted the "insurgents." More strongly than she had ever done before, she reprimanded the board about their consistent efforts to make mountains out of molehills, pass gossip among themselves, and focus on internal strife rather than the larger cause.[61]

Again the influence of place in politics played out in the NAWSA, this time at its 1911 convention in Louisville, Kentucky. As state president and gracious hostess, Laura Clay coordinated many of the arrangements for this gathering in her home state. Just before the meeting, the women received word of the suffrage victory in California. Buoyed by this news, the NAWSA publicly touted and celebrated its growth, from the two new suffrage states through the increased media coverage and press work. Although a tremendous range of individuals spoke and many organizations sent their endorsements, as would be expected in this southern locale, the history left no record of any participation by women or men of color. On the other hand, Madeline McDowell Breckinridge kept the idea of an educated electorate alive with her analysis of the problems caused by the extension of voting to "illiterate voters." Privately, the organization continued to struggle with finances, with the *Woman's Journal* at the top of the list of expenses.[62]

Since the events of the 1910 convention seemed to have taken Shaw and apparently her supporters by surprise, Shaw's close friend Thomas was determined that Shaw not again be blindsided. Consequently, the great drama of the 1911 convention occurred with the elections. Vice president McCulloch and recording secretary Stewart had decided before the convention not to stand for reelection in spite of Kate Gordon's urgings. While McCulloch urged the Kentucky and Illinois delegations to support Laura Clay for first vice president, they were completely stunned to find out that the large eastern state delegations all supported the nomination of the eminent Jane Addams of Chicago for that office. The Illinois and Kentucky leaders could not believe that this internationally known leader from McCulloch's hometown could have agreed to run without McCulloch's and their knowledge. When they questioned Addams's willingness to serve, the Illinois women were again startled to find that Addams had so agreed. This was a tremendous coup for the NAWSA—Jane Addams brought new prestige and credibility to the suffrage struggle. Her alliances throughout the world were extensive, but for the NAWSA it was her record on race that stood in sharpest contrast to Laura Clay's stands. After the nominating ballot, as was the long NAWSA tradition, the minority candidates moved to make Jane Addams's election unanimous.[63]

The full extent to which Clay and her allies were outmaneuvered did not become apparent until the next nominating vote. This one was for the position of second vice president. The same bloc of delegations who had voted for Addams now gave Kentucky-born, Chicago-based educator Sophonisba Breckinridge, another progressive and a friend of Addams, the plurality of votes. Clay received some votes for every other open office but never enough to gain any position on the board. At the end of the 1911 convention none of the long-term leaders other than Shaw remained in office. Alice Blackwell continued to have a role but only as editor of the *Woman's Journal*. The elections were only one of the difficult issues at this convention. There was a long and rancorous debate over moving the headquarters to Chicago and an accusation against Shaw that she had misused the monies from the Susan B. Anthony Fund.[64]

The changes of 1911 are at least as confusing as, and certainly related to, those of 1910. Someone had organized the move to oust Laura Clay and bring in Jane Addams and Sophonisba Breckinridge, but at the time many of the women didn't know who. Florence Kelley could be considered since both Chicago women were her Hull House colleagues and friends. Yet Kelley had been behind the anti-Shaw resolution at the 1910 gathering, and Clay had supported Kelley. If Kelley and her allies were promoting Addams, they did so at the expense of Kelley's former ally, Clay. And was Addams brought in to support progressive changes, oppose Shaw, or both?

In a letter from McCulloch to Breckinridge explaining how Breckinridge came to be elected in opposition to her fellow Kentuckian Clay, McCulloch stated that she didn't believe even Shaw knew who was being nominated. Clearly someone in the NAWSA was playing hardball politics. Other evidence gives M. Carey Thomas a role in this transition.[65]

Even if she didn't have a hand in the ousting of Clay, Shaw was relieved to have the board changes. In October she wrote that she was sleeping better and "I think much of my depression will pass if I can sleep more." She wrote to Thomas, "The Official Board meeting of the eleventh was delightful and we got through with more business that one day than we usually do in two. Miss Clay was not there to talk four hours out of five." Shaw was effusive in her praise for Thomas, thanking her in many ways for her friendship and her loyalty. The NAWSA now had a new slate of officers that included an impressive group of women, several with national and international reputations as leaders of the Progressive Era, women who had long worked for racial and class equality. Absent from the board were the women who opposed the federal amendment, universal suffrage, and Anna Howard Shaw.[66]

What did these events say about Shaw and her leadership? This election again questions the easy labeling of the NAWSA as being conservative. Addams, Breckinridge, Ashley, Dennett, and Shaw should all be considered more left/progressive even than moderate. Further, when historians have discussed the NAWSA during this period, they have almost unanimously used the events of 1910 and 1911 to question Shaw's abilities. But a surprisingly different interpretation of the events comes from none other than Carrie Chapman Catt. Catt had missed much of the discord and changes that had taken place in the NAWSA. In 1910, she had minimal involvement in the internal battles and in 1911 she was on her global suffrage tour. Nevertheless, all the news reached her via Dutch suffragist Aletta Jacobs as well as her friend and admirer, Mary Gray Peck.[67]

At first Catt agreed with the opposition that Shaw's administrative deficiencies were the source of the disputes and that she should step down as president. However, by December 1911, Catt reversed her overall assessment of Shaw's leadership. Now Catt consistently countered Peck's relentless and clearly biased criticisms of Shaw and Shaw's talents. She wrote to Peck,

"I am glad the National is quarreling: it betokens life and alertness. A few years ago nothing could rouse the convention from a dead calm. . . . I am beginning to think AHS is more executive and a better politician than I thought her! . . . Our cause is certainly arriving." Later the same month from Egypt she continued her analysis. "Here is the NAWSA with a Board of dead wood. All very nice women, but contributing nothing new. Their friends could not put them off. Along comes M. Cary [*sic*] Thomas and performs the much needed surgical operation, willy-nilly. I say we ought to be grateful." Though Catt was and remained somewhat ambivalent about Shaw as NAWSA president, her assessment is important. She agreed that the old board had been a major part of the problem, and she was now celebrating Shaw and her allies as important change agents.[68]

And Catt was right that woman suffrage was "certainly arriving." The presidential election year of 1912 would turn out to be a remarkable year for both Shaw and the movement. The accelerated rate of suffrage activity is measured by the number of states that had this question on the ballot. Five states—Ohio, Michigan, Wisconsin, Oregon, and Kansas—plus the Arizona Territory (soon to be a state) were all submitting the suffrage question to their voters. The January 9th scene where Shaw spoke to an immense crowd in the Broadway Theatre set the tone of the year. The public support for suffrage was building.[69]

Shaw knew this would be an exceptionally demanding year. To prepare, she took three weeks to rest in Florida in January and February before entering into the whirlwind of campaigning. She headed south after seeing off the British suffrage leader, Mrs. Pankhurst, after her U.S. tour. It was Shaw's first visit to Florence Villa, a small settlement in the middle of an orange-growing region of the state not far from Orlando, where her old friend Dr. Mary Jewett had settled. Shaw still craved time outdoors and reveled in this respite from the cold and snows of the Northeast. Yet before she could become a total "model of laziness in hammocks and novels," she returned to the North, arriving on February 11, just before her sixty-fifth birthday.[70]

Shaw took a new vigor into the year's work. March brought Shaw to Washington for another series of congressional hearings, and then to Chicago for the Mississippi Valley Conference to face the discontented southern and western suffragists. In May she participated in the New York City Suffrage Parade that had twenty thousand suffrage supporters marching in what had become almost regular displays of support for the enfranchisement of women. In June she agreed to star in the first suffrage foray in the new medium of film. Somehow Shaw found time to pen what became a widely discussed article for *McCall's* June 1912 issue entitled, "If I Were President," in which Shaw names the women and men she would appoint to her cabinet and names her policy priorities.[71]

When Theodore Roosevelt decided to run as the candidate for the Progressive Party, the NAWSA faced a new test. The organization had always had a policy of nonpartisanship, but first vice president Jane Addams publicly supported Roosevelt and seconded his nomination at the Progressive Party Convention. Many, especially those who had opposed Addams's election, believed this stand violated the NAWSA policy of nonpartisanship. Shaw didn't. She gave Addams her support and praised the speech Addams gave at the convention. While Shaw did not support or even trust Roosevelt herself, she mediated this conflict as adroitly as she could.[72]

As the fall election season opened, Shaw, a veteran of so many campaigns, set off again with her trunk and train schedule for a ten-week sweep of Ohio, Michigan, Wisconsin, Oregon, Arizona, and Kansas, with a stop in California. Her first engagements brought her into the semihostile home turf of Harriet Taylor Upton. Upton apparently put her personal grudges before the cause as she relegated this premier propagandist to small towns and cities that were hardly organized while arranging for Frances Squire Potter to speak in the largest venues. The results in Upton's Ohio were a disappointment.[73]

The leaders of Michigan gave Shaw a friendlier welcome, and she took the opportunity to visit her childhood home and her alma mater, Albion College. As Shaw reminisced with her nephew and remaining friends, this visit reminded her of where she had started and how far she had come. Politically she felt Michigan was hopeful on the suffrage issue. By mid-September she was off to Wisconsin. Shaw felt the discord in this state and had little hope for Wisconsin this year. This state visit did leave us a wonderful photograph of Shaw cranking her own car. When her work in Wisconsin was complete, she was halfway through her swing of the campaign states, and the rest lay west of the Mississippi. At this point, Lucy joined Shaw in Chicago, and they headed to Oregon together.[74]

To Shaw's great relief and joy, she found that state, home to her old nemesis Abigail Scott Duniway, well organized and the leaders unified. Shaw's friend and Oregon leader, Esther Pohl Lovejoy, argued that the women of this state had learned to cooperate through loose coalitions that gave local leaders significant autonomy. While the vast majority of the work came from these leaders, the Oregon leaders now appreciated the support the NAWSA and its president gave them. Mrs. Solomon Hirsch wrote to Shaw, "We feel that in a very great measure the women in this state are indebted to you for your very able efforts in helping us to victory. Your ceaseless energy and unselfish devotion dispelled antagonism and convinced the voters of the justice of our cause." Through the rest of October, Shaw spoke in Arizona and Kansas, breaking only to travel to the Grand Canyon where the great orator was so overwhelmed by the beauty and majesty of this natural wonder that for once she was at a loss for words.[75]

Shaw had to wait only two days after she returned home to begin to see the results of her and so many other women's efforts. On November 4, 1912, Kansas, Oregon, and Arizona moved onto the suffrage map while Michigan hung in the balance for a few days. Though that wait ended in a defeat, Shaw maintained, as many others did, that a victory there had been stolen from them. All suffrage supporters celebrated this unprecedented set of successes. The New York City organizations held their victory parade on November 9 where, according to the *New York Times*, four hundred thousand spectators viewed the twenty thousand suffrage marchers.[76]

Enormous crowds and a new and exhilarating conviction that the woman suffrage movement had turned the corner in its struggle met the NAWSA as it convened in Philadelphia just days after the 1912 national election. From the convention announcement and the Art Nouveau–themed graphics and program to the press coverage of the number of men attending, this gathering argued that the NAWSA was new, modern, and progressive. Forty women speakers on five different platforms took over Independence Square. Special publicity and stationary highlighted the fact that Jane Addams would preside. The audiences at the Philadelphia Convention were huge. Over thirty-five hundred delegates and six thousand members of the public packed the halls the NAWSA had hired for the event. The local press gave wide coverage of the events of this suffrage gathering with large photographs accompanying the articles. The organizers had added a men's night to the schedule in recognition of the twenty-thousand-member strong National Men's League for Woman Suffrage.[77]

Not all was harmony and good news. The Association finally gave up on finding a means to profitably support the *Woman's Journal*. The drain it had been on the NAWSA budget was settled with the help of the funds given to Shaw by the then anonymous donation. The ownership returned to Alice Stone Blackwell. The constituency debated and passed a constitutional amendment that allowed a more direct method of voting for officers, possibly as a reaction against the election maneuvers of the previous year. On an issue that would continue to split the movement, the most heated discussion came over the issue of partisan support for political candidates. The convention ended with a memorable evening and speeches by Baroness Bertha Von Suttner, the first woman to win the Nobel Peace Prize, and by Carrie Chapman Catt, who had just returned from her two-year world suffrage journey.[78]

Historically the most significant aspect of this convention was that W. E. B. Du Bois gave the keynote address. It is also the most underexamined. In spite of Shaw's triumphs and the addition of more progressive and liberal women to the national leadership, race remained an issue over which the movement stumbled. As previously discussed, the *History of Woman Suf-*

frage and Shaw were notoriously evasive on racial issues. Not only did these sources ignore or erase the level of support and organizing among African American women, but they failed to acknowledge how Black activists continually attempted to force a public discussion on their issues. Although Shaw and her ally, Thomas, had worked to oust the southern leaders who supported states rights and other efforts to achieve woman suffrage without challenging white supremacy, the National Association for the Advancement of Colored People (NAACP) President and *Crisis* editor, Dr. W. E. B. Du Bois, had taken up the cause that Black women had spearheaded. Du Bois had publicly challenged Shaw on the acceptance of African Americans in the NAWSA based on the actions taken and not taken before and during the Louisville Convention.[79]

One specific charge brought against Shaw and the NAWSA was that she had refused to allow a resolution linking woman suffrage with the cause of those disenfranchised on the basis of color to be offered in Louisville. There is some dispute about who refused to bring forward this resolution, but as president, Shaw was ultimately responsible. The NAWSA, still fearful of splits, was trying to walk a line that would placate both sides. This was the foundational event through which Du Bois forced open a new space for a rhetorical confrontation, one the leaders of the NAWSA had worked to avoid for two decades. In 1912, the *Crisis* published an entire issue devoted to woman suffrage in a continuation of the dialogue. It was in response to that issue that the NAWSA invited Dr. Du Bois to speak at the 1912 convention.[80]

Though the official *History of Woman Suffrage* contains nothing beyond the title of Du Bois's speech, the 1912 leaders must have felt it was important; they published it themselves as a pamphlet. In "Disfranchisement," this leading Black activist and intellectual linked the struggles of women and people of color. He argued that no democracy could truly serve all its citizens if it did not give all those citizens equal voice in the government. "The real argument for democracy is then that in the people we have the real source of that endless life and unbounded wisdom which the real ruler of men [*sic*] must have." Du Bois stated that men could not know and represent women anymore than white men could know and represent the interests of people of color. The highly publicized presence of W. E. B. Du Bois and the publication of his address, while not marking a complete conversion of the suffrage community, did signal a major opening in the communications among the white leaders and the African American leaders who supported woman suffrage. Undoubtedly this was a significant directional change for the NAWSA that had held a segregated convention nine years earlier. Nevertheless there is hardly a mention of this event in any publication on U.S. women's history.[81]

Shaw entered the postconvention board meetings with a sense that the NAWSA had been revitalized, that woman suffrage was truly in sight, and that this was the organization that would lead the way. The greatest concern the board had was raising enough money to fund all their work. With the rest of the country, the suffragists wondered just how progressive this new president, a Democrat born and raised in the South, would be on woman suffrage.[82]

And was the NAWSA now progressive also? Jane Addams was vice president. The leading Black activist and intellectual W. E. B. Du Bois had headlined the convention in Philadelphia. The southern suffrage stalwarts, Clay and Gordon, were still active but without national positions, while Dennett and Ashley apparently controlled the work of the headquarters. This certainly was a different organization than the one that had met in 1903 in New Orleans. How much credit does Anna Howard Shaw deserve for this change?

In 1912, as Shaw was about to begin the tenth year of her presidency, she remained the most charismatic woman in the movement as well as the "odd woman out" among the other women leaders who were split between those who admired and celebrated her and those who resented and questioned her leadership and even her morality. Among most suffragists she was still the inspirational star whose humor and ability to connect to a wide range of people made her their best recruiter and propagandist. Though the conflicts of 1909–1911 had been ugly at times, they allowed a suffrage renaissance led by Shaw and her supporters. Personally Shaw entered 1913 in great spirits and wonderful health. She could see the end of the struggle and was willing to give whatever she could to reach that goal.

CHAPTER 7

Unanticipated Challenges
NAWSA PRESIDENCY, PART III (1913–1915)

I have but one thought and one desire, and that is to win the
vote, and whatever I do, I do with that one thing in view, and
am as utterly indifferent to the effect of what I do, upon myself
personally, as if I did not exist. In fact I do not exist apart from
woman suffrage. With it I want to go up or down, and for it, every
bit of strength, every bit of ability, every bit of loyalty in my nature
is given, and will be given until the last of my life, as it has been in
the last forty years, regardless of any criticism or of any antagonism
which may be leveled against me.

By 1913 Anna Howard Shaw could see the end of the struggle. The
movement to extend that basic right of equal citizenship—full suffrage—to
all women now had sufficient momentum to see it through to the final victory.[1] After years of slow progress and the efforts of generations of women,
Shaw was leading "the cause" with new leaders and organizations, extensive
financial resources, regular attention from the media and politicians, and
finally new suffrage gains in major western states. Within the expanding
NAWSA office, Shaw had a team of innovative and efficient administrators
building an increasingly powerful political organization. After the 1912 electoral gains, this vigorous campaigner, now sixty-five and in her tenth year at
the head of the NAWSA, shared with most suffragists a sense of optimism
about the Susan B. Anthony Amendment.

Yet political roads and pioneering paths are seldom smooth or predictable.
Though she believed the success was inevitable and near, the final years of her
presidency threw up hurdles that complicated Shaw's leadership and administrative efforts. This period, during a tremendous period of suffrage activism,
Shaw confronted new difficulties and made occasional, but significant, missteps
in her efforts to close the final chapter of the suffrage struggle.[2]

A core belief among Shaw and most suffrage leaders was that a victory in any one of the large eastern states would provide the tipping point that would put woman suffrage on the fast track for congressional action. Now rid of the southern leaders who opposed the federal amendment, the NAWSA could prepare for that shift from the states to federal level work. Shaw had consistently pushed the NAWSA to put more if its focus on and devote more resources to federal work since 1908. Sustained by an almost religious belief in the cause that had occupied her life for thirty years, Shaw continued her personal involvements in international, federal, and state work with a schedule that would have challenged the stamina of many younger women.[3]

On January 1, 1913, Shaw prayed for her usual blessings for the future, for herself and for the cause, but one issue from the previous, generally triumphant year, hung on her heart. Though she would have to be "out in the wide world for the rest of the winter," she first went to upstate New York and sought some solace in the homes of several of the movement's oldest supporters, women who had been Susan B. Anthony's friends. For once, gossip had truly wounded Shaw. Harriet Taylor Upton, the former treasurer of the NAWSA and friend of Shaw's, had written a vicious letter about Shaw, stating that "as long as she was fighting for principle, she was a powerful woman, but the money she made and which was handed to her, caused her to prostitute these principles . . . she has grown more and more self important and degraded all the time." Those are pretty vicious words, especially for that era, especially from a longtime suffrage leader. Though Upton had written this diatribe to a West Coast suffrage leader, it had been passed through the activists' network until it reached its subject. Shaw in turn shared it with Susan Look Avery and her daughter, Lydia Ward-Coonley, and Katherine Bell Lewis. Did these women still support her leadership? These wealthy women joined her in condemning Upton's letter, and reassured her that they still believed in her. After several days of visiting, they sent Shaw off with gifts and financial contributions.[4]

Knowing that these core supporters of Susan B. Anthony still backed her sustained Shaw over the next hectic month; she lectured and met suffrage leaders in New England and New York before journeying to Kentucky, Indiana, Missouri, Nebraska, and Kansas. Shaw found the trip, although exhausting, exhilarating because the audiences, especially in Missouri, were so large that even the largest available halls couldn't accommodate everyone who lined up to hear her speak.[5]

New suffrage developments soon eclipsed this one distraction. The great parade planned by the NAWSA's Congressional Committee for the day before Woodrow Wilson's inauguration was garnering an increasing amount of press coverage even as Shaw moved from meetings in the Northeast to a swing through Michigan. One group of women had fashioned themselves as an army under "General" Rosalie Jones and was marching from New York to Washington. Various other hints about the upcoming spectacle showed up, especially in the Washington newspapers. Though Shaw, as president of the NAWSA, the official sponsor of the event, received the most credit for this work in newspaper coverage at this time, the true creators were Alice Paul, Lucy Burns, and the committee of volunteers that had gathered around them. At this point Paul and Burns were working as members of the NAWSA's Congressional Committee. For Shaw, who had long wanted more activity at the federal level and who knew the movement needed younger activists, Paul seemed a godsend.[6]

Alice Paul, an independently wealthy young intellectual from New Jersey, had become a life member of the NAWSA when she returned from London after having been active in Emmeline Pankhurst's organization. She was among the women who had been arrested and, while on a hunger strike in prison, had been force-fed. Her name first shows up in the *History of Woman Suffrage* when she addressed the 1910 Washington Convention on the "militant" suffragists of England. Soon after she began to contribute in behind-the-scenes ways to the NAWSA work. In September of 1911, for example, she had organized a successful open-air meeting on Independence Mall in Philadelphia, quickly showing her genius for organizing bold public statements.[7]

The 1913 Washington, D.C., parade has become tremendously important in suffrage history, but not because it was the first or even the largest such event. This gathering of women garnered attention in part because of its place and bold timing, staged to deliberately divert attention from Wilson's arrival in Washington. However, what ensured its significance in history was not the beauty and size of the women's demonstration but the behavior of men, both the spectators and the police. When some of the rowdy crowds that were inevitable at such great public celebrations began to heckle the women and block their parade route, things turned ugly. The police stood by and failed to intervene and keep the peace, so numerous women were injured and taken to the hospital. As NAWSA president, Shaw soundly condemned the actions of the D.C. force and called on women to demand that Congress investigate what had happened. As always, she noted how this treatment only highlighted once again why women needed the vote.[8]

The parade also recorded the public debut of Alice Paul as a major player in the women's struggle. Though a number of historians have argued that conflicts between the old NAWSA leadership, including Shaw, and Paul and her allies date from this event, there is no clear evidence of this. Shaw had backed Alice Paul's work in Washington and the general plan for this parade, though her preference would have been for a less extravagant demonstration. Shaw believed that the movement needed young, dedicated, and creative workers even if she wasn't quite ready to turn over serious leadership positions to such women just yet. For quite a while before this and continuing through the next few months after it, Shaw and the young Quaker worked together harmoniously within the NAWSA. Even later when Shaw began to receive complaints about the activities of the Congressional Committee, such as reports that the group had adopted the purple, green, and white colors of the Pankhurst movement rather than displaying the yellow of the NAWSA, Shaw was reluctant to chastise the young women too harshly. Just as Anthony had mentored her, Shaw hoped to bring these women along within the NAWSA. In this case, Shaw underestimated the power, the determination, and the true intentions of this new group of young activists.[9]

Another reason this march was important was race. The Washington pageant witnessed the infamous incident at the 1913 D.C. parade when African American leader Ida B. Wells-Barnett's own state delegation acquiesced to the parade organizers' request that all Black women march in a separate segregated section, a request Wells-Barnett and a few of her allies quietly but determinedly ignored. In spite of the minimal support they received from the NAWSA, African American women continued to organize in support of women's suffrage, join local and national organizations, and push the NAWSA on these issues.[10]

Chicago and the state of Illinois became centers of this continuing controversy when Ida B. Wells-Barnett organized the Alpha Suffrage Club. At a time when the political forces in the state were in flux, the far-from-unified suffragists nevertheless came together to push forward a partial suffrage bill. On June 26, 1913, Wells-Barnett and the other women of Illinois became voters. Such progress highlights the increasing independence and strength of state organizations.[11]

Shaw was already in Europe when the Illinois legislation became law. She received this update along with the news that the Senate made the first favorable Senate report on woman suffrage in twenty years. Alice Paul and her allies immediately claimed responsibility for the progress and hoped for more quick progress. However, to the disappointment of the young Congressional Committee leaders, there was no further action at the federal level in 1913.[12]

Having long represented the NAWSA at the meetings of the International Council of Women and the International Suffrage Alliance, some of Shaw's closest friendships were now with European women leaders. She moved easily among the diverse groups that constituted the European suffrage leadership. In 1913, American and Dutch women, including her dear friend, Dr. Aletta Jacobs, welcomed Shaw when she landed in the Netherlands. Though her opponents consistently criticized her trips to Europe, Shaw generally did a great amount of work while abroad. In this case, en route to Vienna, her entourage held two-day conventions in Berlin,

Dresden, and Prague. It was in Prague that Shaw enjoyed a tremendous welcome, what she considered her equivalent to the Berlin ovation given to Susan B Anthony.[13]

On this occasion, Shaw actually allowed herself a week of vacation and escape. At the invitation of Countess Iska Teleki, head of the Hungarian woman suffrage movement, Shaw enjoyed a stay at the Countess's home in the Tatra Mountains. In this beautiful setting, these two women from very different worlds spent much time out of doors, "tramping," as Shaw called one of her favorite activities, through the forests, over mountains, and along streams. As was her habit, Shaw packed up a basket of tiny fir trees that she carefully nursed for the rest of the trip though Florence and Genoa. They would become part of her "Forest of Arden" at Moylan when she returned. Though initially intimidated and concerned about her acceptance, as a working woman from a modest background, by the aristocratic leaders of the European women's organizations, Shaw appreciated the diversity among them and was close to Aletta Jacobs, from a Dutch Jewish family, and women such as the Countess.[14]

While some international friendships strengthened, others faltered. When Shaw returned to the United States, she faced a difficult situation involving Emmeline Pankhurst. Up to this point, the NAWSA had cordial relationships with almost all of the international suffrage leaders, hosting them and helping arrange speaking tours, even when the NAWSA didn't completely agree with their methods. Shaw was well aware of the tensions between the Pankhursts and the other British suffrage organizations. Shaw's and others' attitudes changed that summer when Pankhurst began a tour of the United States. Shaw wrote "I feel her coming is the most unkind thing that could be done." Pankhurst wanted American women to help her conduct a *money-making* tour. American women had never charged for their lectures in Europe, and this change offended Shaw. More importantly, however, Shaw didn't want the increasingly violent militant actions of Pankhurst's organization to reflect on the U.S. movement. Shaw's anxiety indicated that there were increased tensions between Alice Paul, a protégé of Emmeline Pankhurst, and the Official Board of the NAWSA.[15]

This was one more concern for Shaw as she prepared for the 1913 NAWSA Convention. Now wary of each national gathering, Shaw consulted with Carey Thomas to see if her ally knew of any unexpected developments among those who persisted in opposing her. For once, Thomas could report that she knew of none. And this gathering in Washington, D.C., proved to be calm and productive in spite of Upton's continuing quest to oust Shaw. The introduction of the Suffrage School for training activists indicated how even the NAWSA conventions had changed. No longer did the participants sit through a combination of pageantry, reports, and inspirational lectures.

Now experienced leaders from among the already enfranchised through the veteran campaigners, from working women and college presidents, shared their knowledge and trained each other. Most of the convention included workshops on everything from running meetings and fund-raising to how to lobby and how to utilize the resources the national office produced. Not only were there more suffragists than ever before, but they were better trained for all aspects of the work.

On the money front, the NAWSA approved the sale of $50,000 of stock in the Woman Suffrage Publishing Company, another attempt to address the ongoing budget deficit. Money difficulties were chronic, but this caused Shaw little anxiety. She expected political organizations to function on a financial edge. This year the organization debated constitutional changes and another new election system. The constituents passed a new constitution. The NAWSA's outreach to working women brought "labor women" Rose Winslow and Mary Anderson to the NAWSA stage for the first time. Shaw and most of the officers were reelected by significant margins.[16]

Nevertheless, as the year progressed, Alice Paul and Lucy Burn's leadership on the Congressional Committee kept complicating all the work that the NAWSA had planned. For Shaw and most of the NAWSA, woman suffrage activism had certainly become an insider's game. The NAWSA was working as hard to convert individual senators and congressmen as they were on public demonstrations, grassroots organizing, and state actions. It became increasingly clear that Paul and Burns believed in a more confrontational approach. It is in that context that Shaw reprimanded, though mildly, Lucy Burns for her arrest for "chalking the side-walks." Shaw urged Burns to plead ignorance of the law and pay the fine quietly. "We do not want to do what the English militants have done, and that is to arouse the bitterness of those who have the power to grant or to withhold the submission of our amendment." Still, complaints about the Congressional Committee's tactics increased. Shaw had to admit finally that there was a real problem.[17]

The tensions peaked when Paul founded the Congressional Union (CU), whose leadership, work, and fund-raising paralleled that of the Congressional Committee. When asked to account for the monies she had raised for the Congressional Committee and to separate the NAWSA fund-raising from the CU funds, Paul maintained that she couldn't separate the finances or the activities.[18]

It is obvious that at some point the CU had decided to set themselves up in opposition not only to the government, which kept them from their rights, but also to the mainstream suffrage organizations. Shaw and the NAWSA leadership still feared a split in the ranks. Surviving papers document how, for months, the NAWSA women worked relentlessly trying to find some compromise and avoid a division. Organizational papers clearly represent the hours and days of discussions, meetings, and attempts to resolve the differences and find some common ground. Lengthy reports and letters followed how the NAWSA leadership kept trying until they, most especially Shaw, had to conclude that the CU was not negotiating in good faith.

No matter what Shaw and the NAWSA did, the feared break in the movement under her watch appeared inevitable. Worn down by endless but fruitless negotiations that were stealing the time and energy that should have been used on direct suffrage work, finally the NAWSA leaders believed they had no choice but to sever the connection between Paul and Burns and the NAWSA Congressional Committee. To Shaw, it was a question of integrity, both financial and organizational. The leaders then had to scramble to keep their Congressional Committee functioning in the midst of this turmoil, bringing in Ruth Hanna McCormick and Antoinette Funk, both from Illinois.[19]

In Shaw's view, Alice Paul had become a difficult and dangerous leader, not honest, democratic, or straightforward. She would not show up for meetings that others, including her own colleagues, had worked hard to arrange, would not agree to understandings others had given hours to hammering out, and would not offer any of her own constructive alternatives. Now the Congressional Union made clear their decision to follow the practice of the Pankhursts, holding the party in power responsible for woman suffrage and to actively campaign against, in this case, the Democrats. The CU certainly realized that this position was at odds with the nonpartisan stand of the NAWSA, but they still applied to be an auxiliary of the NAWSA. This forced a vote among the NAWSA, a vote the CU lost. Next came complaints that the Congressional Union had copied the NAWSA's membership lists, sent out letters on NAWSA stationery, and phrased their fund-raising appeals in a way that made it easy to mistake the CU for the NAWSA Congressional Committee. When asked about this, Lucy Burns stated "that if it happened at all it was a mistake." In a year when seven states had woman suffrage on the ballot and when the NAWSA and numerous state organizations already had more than their hands full with campaign plans, it was this intrasuffrage controversy that created the most angst for the veteran Shaw.[20]

Shaw and many in the NAWSA felt as though the CU was working as hard to undermine the established suffrage movement as they were to promote women's enfranchisement. They couldn't see the sense of this strategy. At the core, the CU didn't want anything more progressive or radical than the NAWSA. The CU wasn't more inclusive than the NAWSA or more committed to class or race equality. Where they did differ was on tactics. Though the CU (and later the National Women's Party) argued that they did differ from the NAWSA in their emphasis on the federal or Susan B. Anthony Amendment—an argument many historians have accepted—as always, the sources provide a more complicated situation.

Early in 1914, the Congressional Union stepped up the conflict with the NAWSA, spreading the story that the NAWSA had dismissed Alice Paul and Lucy Burns from the Congressional Committee without a fair hearing. While some of the board wanted to reopen the issue and invite Alice Paul to yet another meeting, Shaw had had enough. She refused to give any more energy to the CU and wrote to the Official Board, "We think the thing has gone too far, with the days and nights spent by Mrs. Medill McCormick with Miss Paul and the almost unhuman [*sic*] treatment which was tendered her, we think it is quite sufficient and that we should consider the incident closed, and go on with our work." While such an approach was consistent with how Shaw handled many conflicts, she again underestimated the determination and persistence of her challengers. Shaw defended her decision by stating, "All I have ever asked for, or will ever ask for, is the opportunity to keep on as I have been keeping on for years, doing constructive, effective work, and people may say what they please; it is a matter for my own conscience." The newspapers began to get some hint of the split on January 19, 1914.[21]

Even before all this turmoil, Anna Howard Shaw had worked out her 1914 schedule carefully because she knew that the demands the seven state campaigns would take on the NAWSA resources, and on her personally, would be great. She expected to stay close to the New York headquarters early in the year, limiting her speaking to the Northeast before turning the headquarters' responsibilities over to Mary Ware Dennett when she did resume traveling. February and March included a southern speaking tour, a meeting with new and more moderate white southern leaders, and several weeks of rest in Florence Villa, Florida. In April, Anna, Lucy, and nieces Eleanor Shaw and Grace Green were to sail to Italy, where Shaw was determined to introduce a suffrage resolution at the International Council of Women. This would be a shorter than usual European trip because Shaw had committed to speaking in all the campaign states, except Harriet Taylor Upton's Ohio. The annual convention would be in Tennessee after the election. This was the plan that Anna, with Lucy, had carefully crafted.[22]

This ambitious but well-thought-through schedule was soon headed for a major revision. On her sixty-seventh birthday, when frigid temperatures, 75 mph winds, and a storm that left 9.7 inches of snow crippled rail and street travel in the Northeast, the train carrying Shaw and Carrie Chapman Catt was hours late when it finally reached Jersey City. As they descended onto an icy platform, Shaw slipped on the ice, injuring her ankle. Shaw, who either hated or mistrusted hospitals, insisted on being taken to her hotel room. Only a serious injury would stop Shaw. Unfortunately this was serious. Her ankle was broken so severely that she would have to stay off it and in her hotel room for at least six weeks.[23]

When the severity of the fracture and the news of her accident became public, so many people came forward to offer her all types of assistance that Shaw facetiously recommended this injury to those who doubted that they had friends. Old friends, including Carrie Chapman Catt, wanted her to convalesce in their homes. Others sent flowers or fruits or arranged for entertainment. Shaw put on her usual brave public face, but privately she was frustrated by this confinement that derailed her plans. She particularly regretted not being able to attend the board meeting in Alabama where many of the newer and more progressive southern leaders she had mentored were to join them.[24]

Yet one person saw opportunity where others saw misfortune. Journalist and writer Elizabeth Jordan had pleaded with Shaw to write her life story. Not surprisingly, the public was increasingly fascinated by Dr. Anna Howard Shaw. A year before, Shaw had met with Jordan about such a book and even came up with an outline of the chapters. However Jordan soon realized Shaw was not someone who would voluntarily take the time to sit and write about herself. There was also the fact that, as gifted as she was as a speaker, Shaw was equally uninspired as a writer. Now Jordan saw that this was probably the only time and the only way to get Shaw's story in her own words into a book. Consequently from mid-February until the end of March, while Shaw recuperated, Jordan arranged to come every morning with a stenographer and have Shaw dictate the story of her life.[25]

Even as she recovered, the CU's activities demanded her attention. The CU's accusations against the NAWSA brought the CU numerous converts, some preferring the more exciting direct action strategy, some frustrated by the slow progress under the NAWSA leadership, and some who had long opposed Shaw. Many suffragists wrote to Shaw and other officers questioning the NAWSA's stand. Confined as she was, Shaw's responses to these questions were perhaps lengthier and more thoughtful than they would have been otherwise.

To Annie G. Porritt, she apologized for the extent of her ramblings, yet this surviving letter captured Shaw's thinking at the time. After expressing regret over the dissension, Shaw argued that the CU policy of attacking both friendly and unfriendly Democrats was a form of militancy. She used the example of how this policy led to physical attacks in England on friends such as Philip Snowden. To Shaw, this was more dangerous than all the work of the antisuffragists. She continued explaining how Paul embraced the label of militant, endorsed all that the Pankhursts advocated, and had tried to bring Mrs. Pankhurst to D.C. when her presence would have damaged the progress the NAWSA had made. On the accusation that she and the NAWSA were jealous of the success of the CU's spectacles, Shaw wrote that she would be happy to turn all this over to them since "I think Miss Paul is pre-eminently fitted to carry on that line of work," which Shaw contrasted with the "real work." Shaw was not convinced that the time and energy spent on such lavish displays brought commensurate results. In turn Shaw suspected that Paul resented that Shaw didn't fully approve of the great parade in 1913.[26]

Shaw closed her letter by returning to the issue at hand, the policy of working against a man because of his party rather than his actions or stands. Shaw explained that the American and the British systems were not comparable and that the CU had been naive to believe that it would get the amendment through Congress in 1913. In closing, Shaw reiterated her view that suffragists needed to get enough states first to bring pressure on Congress and the president.[27]

If her injury and the CU issues weren't enough, Shaw had a putatively more personal crisis on her hands. On December 23, 1913, the *New York Times* had carried the first notice of Shaw's decision not to cooperate with the Delaware County (Pennsylvania) tax assessor on determining the worth of her property. In the midst of all the upheaval with the Congressional Union the previous year, and perhaps in an effort to divert some of the newspapers' attention from that, Shaw had become embroiled in this high-publicity conflict. In this case all evidence suggests that Shaw created this drama. In the *Times* article Shaw explained that she had decided to resist "taxation without representation," the position that her grandmother, Nicolas Grant Stott, Mary S. Anthony, and many other women in the United States and Great Britain had taken. Shaw urged other women to do the same. Shaw did not refuse to pay her taxes, as many soon assumed, but simply and legally declined to provide the assessor with a list of her property.[28]

Since Shaw refused to provide documentation of her possessions, the assessor put a value of $30,000 on Shaw's property and stocks. Shaw was a bit disingenuous when she protested that she wasn't worth one-tenth of that amount. Certainly Shaw was worth more than $3000. Why such a protest? Shaw may have been attempting to hide her true worth from not only the tax assessor but from her suffrage colleagues and the general public. Given Upton's charges against her, Shaw may have been especially sensitive about any information that might have shown her to have grown wealthy from her position.[29]

More press coverage followed when, in March, Shaw's ankle had finally healed enough for her to attend the rescheduled birthday celebration. The celebration included a modern dance performance by Ruth St. Denis's troupe that some considered risqué. Shaw had an unexpected but typically humorous reaction, another indication that she was throwing caution to the wind at this point in her tenure. "Such dancing! It made me wild to try it. One paper said they looked at me to see if I did not feel abashed at the bare feet and partly nude bodies of the Egyptian dancers, but I was looking as if I longed to do it myself." Now that she was at least partially mobile, she was able to keep her speaking engagement at Yale, though she went to significant lengths not to be photographed in a wheelchair. The students helped carry her to the stage. She also helped conceive of and plan a May 2nd National Suffrage or Women's Independence Day that was to be organized across the country by local women.[30]

As if the unexpected hadn't already complicated this year enough, Shaw confronted another dissenter when she finally could return to the NAWSA headquarters. Mary Ware Dennett had turned against her. It is hard to imagine how this change came as much of a surprise. Shaw had become very close to Dennett, had confided in her, relied on her ability to run the headquarters during all the times Shaw was on the road, and had very much defended Dennett when other board members raised questions about this NAWSA officer's work. Although Dennett had continued to be a very efficient leader of the growing staff, she had become disillusioned with the NAWSA work. As far back as 1912, she had written out her frustrations in a letter to Shaw. At those times her issues were philosophical, policy, and strategy disagreements, not personal conflicts. Shaw had been understanding of Dennett's discontent and accepting of these differences, but she had convinced Dennett to stay in the position, especially since Dennett was a single mother with two children to support. Now Dennett was openly unhappy with Shaw personally. Dennett felt betrayed.[31]

The issue that caused the breach was a change the board had made in the Literature Committee that Shaw had backed but Dennett opposed. However, many larger political differences were behind the final break between Dennett and Shaw. The relationship that had allowed Shaw to be as successful a president of the NAWSA as she had been was now apparently beyond repair.[32]

Again Shaw chose to just move on. It is almost as if Shaw expected such hostile breaks. Shaw often seemed oblivious to any steps she might have taken to understand and smooth the relationships among the diversity of women with whom she worked. She valued and expected loyalty, not unquestioning loyalty, but a directness and honesty that meant bringing differences out in the open. Shaw complained about what she saw as petty distractions, the gossip and the backbiting. The question is whether Shaw could distinguish between legitimate criticisms and petty complaints. She saw herself as a relatively uncomplicated personality and expected others to be as transparent as she believed herself to be.

Shaw's focus now was on Europe. This year Shaw had a particular mission: persuade the International Council of Women to adopt a woman suffrage resolution, a dream Susan B. Anthony and Elizabeth Cady Stanton had

had when they founded the organization. Appreciating the importance of this event and perhaps knowing how reluctantly Shaw parted with her own money, Shaw's new protégé, Katherine Dexter McCormick, and her mother had arrived in New York to take the protesting Shaw to the dressmakers. Mrs. Dexter and Mrs. McCormick paid for the two beautiful gowns, black silk stockings, and black satin slippers that would ensure that Shaw was elegantly garbed for this mission.[33]

After stops in Algiers and a landing in Naples, Shaw and Lucy proceeded to Rome. Shaw was clearly more anxious about this effort than she was at most such international gatherings. Shaw felt she was representing the many women who had founded the movement and the International Council of Women. Elizabeth Cady Stanton and Susan B. Anthony hadn't made suffrage a central principle in 1888 because they feared that would be too radical a stand for many of the international leaders. Shaw and her allies had decided this was the time to bring the suffrage issue to a vote; after Shaw's speech and much debate, the ICW finally endorsed woman suffrage. Though exceptionally self-critical of her efforts in Rome, Shaw fulfilled her responsibility in a speech reviewed positively by the *New York Times*. In analyzing her efforts in Europe she pondered that it "was good as far as suffrage is concerned. . . . Thought only of Aunt Susan and Mrs. Avery but I was not as wise in the way I did it as I should have been. Impulsiveness has always been my fault, but I am glad I did it."[34]

One senses that Shaw was growing impatient generally, impatient with progress at home, impatient with the NAWSA, impatient with Congress. The goal felt so close, yet Shaw may have feared she wouldn't see the end. The suffrage leaders now increased their pressure on President Wilson and Congress to act on the federal amendment. Speaker of the House Clark declared his support for woman suffrage, while the president argued that he couldn't take a stand since the issue was not in the Party's platform. Demands for suffrage resources grew; the NAWSA declared August 15, Lucy Stone's birthday, to be "Suffrage Self-Sacrifice Day," urging women throughout the country to contribute monies on that day for the fall campaigns. They hoped to raise $50,000.[35]

Shaw also recorded that money was tight for her personally. As a result of her accident, Shaw had been forced to take out a $1200 loan the previous spring, and she was anxious to repay it. Shaw confessed that she was always cross when she owed anyone a cent. It wasn't that she didn't have $1200, but records indicate that Shaw consistently invested whatever surplus money she had and that she would not touch the principal of any of her investments. She preferred to take out short-term loans when she needed extra monies. This information suggests that Shaw was still relying on lecturing income in addition to her Thomas-Garrett Fund salary.[36]

And then, out of the blue, that seemingly long-resolved issue of salaries reappeared. On July 13, Katherine Dexter McCormick, now treasurer of the NAWSA, wrote to M. Carey Thomas, asking her "if you do not think it would be wise to move an amendment to our National constitution which would make paid workers in the National Association not eligible for membership on the official board." What was this proposal? Was this aimed at Shaw? If it was it would have constituted a shocking proposal coming from one of Shaw's trusted lieutenants. But Thomas responded with support, and Shaw also declared her endorsement of the idea. Shaw, it turns out, wasn't the target; Mary Ware Dennett was. Nevertheless it seems incongruous that they both could get behind such a move.[37]

This development demonstrates how challenging it is to pull together all the pieces of Shaw's and the NAWSA's financial arrangements. Analyzing them is an even greater task. Certainly the five years covered by the original Thomas-Garrett Fund had ended in 1912. After that, according to the budget reports of the organization, the salaries of the other officers were paid from the regular NAWSA fund. However, no salary for the president ever appears on any official budget reports. But in a letter to Jane Addams, Thomas confided that she had continued to raise money for Shaw's salary in a very private arrangement.[38]

Thomas's, and assumedly Shaw's, decision to keep this agreement confidential, followed by Katharine Dexter McCormick's recommendation, argues that the class lines between those who could volunteer their time and those who needed pay were remarkably resistant to modification. Even though Shaw had never been paid directly from the NAWSA treasury, the fact that she was paid and that she had a quite modern sense of expecting to be appropriately compensated for her time and her expenses had caused problems throughout her presidency. Upton's charge that Shaw had been corrupted arose from this situation. Upton didn't appear to believe that Shaw had "earned" her salary. Mary Gray Peck, among others, had accused Shaw of financial dishonesty and mockingly had suggested to the California women that they could keep Shaw out of the state if they refused to pay her expenses. Yet no sources suggest that Shaw benefited inappropriately from suffrage work. Today we know that M. Carey Thomas was less than scrupulous with how she used other people's money, using it to live a luxurious lifestyle. Shaw's own finances are rather transparent. She was, as noted, very frugal, and her only "extravagance" was her home, Alnwick Lodge. Yet how can one reconcile Shaw acquiescing to a change that would allow only wealthy women to hold the true power of the organization to which she had given so much of her life?[39]

Shaw started her campaigning this year in South Dakota. This state was always hard to face after the first horrendous campaign there with Anthony and Catt in 1890. On September 7th, one of her last days in this state, Shaw rode six hours on a freight train to a town only to arrive and find no one to meet her. The next day she finally reached the end of her usually amazing patience with the rigors and problems of such campaigning. In the semi-shorthand she used in her diary, Shaw wrote, "The meeting here was the limit. I do not think So Dak women have improved one inch since 1890. They don't know how to get up a meeting anymore than their grandmothers did. . . . Farewell Redfield forever with joy." Yet the sixty-seven-year-old activist still had fifty-six days on the road until she was home.[40]

As Shaw and other workers crisscrossed Montana, Nevada, North Dakota, South Dakota, Ohio, Missouri, and Nebraska, they encountered a new challenge in the form of CU women who were working against all Democrats, among whom were some of the suffrage movement's strongest supporters. The NAWSA, in contrast, had proposed a "blacklist" of those who had actively opposed suffrage. To add to her frustration, on October 25th, Shaw, for the first recorded time, completely lost her voice. She was forced to cancel days of speaking and to rest. In the end, election day brought two victories, Montana and Nevada, two more suffrage states for the campaign map and two more diamonds for the pin that Anthony had passed on to Shaw.[41]

Only when she returned from these travels, as the charges and countercharges between Dennett and the board continued to be exchanged, did Shaw write to Thomas about the "very bitter and ugly letter" she had received from Mrs. Dennett: "The import of which was that I am entirely controlled by money. That I sold the organization out to you two years ago at Philadelphia, and that this year I had sold out the association and the cause to Mrs. Stanley (Katherine Dexter) McCormick and that I was simply the tool in your hands. She accused me of having a personal gain in it." Once again Shaw faced losing a friend and an important suffrage worker over money issues.[42]

In a sense there was truth to the accusation. It is disingenuous to believe that the wishes of the wealthy benefactors of the NAWSA had no influence on Shaw. On the other hand it isn't clear that Shaw ever changed her views on any significant issues. It is hard not to long for the thousands of lost letters between Lucy and Anna at these points in Shaw's story. How did Shaw work out the ethics of these arrangements? Did they change over the years? Although Shaw's 1909 recruitment of Alva Belmont to the NAWSA was the most public starting point of these complex relationships, for Shaw they went back much farther. Shaw had to accept a salary from the Garrett and Thomas Fund in 1907 to be able to do the work of the NAWSA president. The National Headquarters relied on Belmont's support for several years. Shaw received, as Susan B. Anthony had before her, "gifts" to use at her discretion. For Shaw the most substantial came from Pauline Agassiz Shaw. It had been with that $20,000 that Shaw had first had the resources to back her views on how and where the NAWSA work should be done. Whether the other board members recognized it or not, resources—of money, time, connections to power, or even a home in which to house the headquarters—had been the muscle they had all utilized to promote their ideas for the suffrage efforts. Until victory was achieved there could never be too much money, and all the leaders raised funds in whatever way they could. For example, at the mass meeting held on November 6, 1914, the suffrage women raised $105,000, with contributions that ranged from a few pennies up to one large contribution of $5000.[43]

It is hard to know precisely what Shaw's detractors meant by their charges of corruption and personal gain. Perhaps they thought Shaw should have accepted only "gifts," not demanded a salary. Or taken just enough money to keep herself fed, clothed, and housed at a minimal level, as Susan B. Anthony had. Peck, a major source of these accusations, left no specific examples. Although Shaw left very meticulous records of her finances during these years, as had Susan B. Anthony before her, even going to great lengths to document how she used the money from Pauline Agassiz Shaw, her financial relationship to the movement made her consistently vulnerable to such charges. It is also clear that Shaw didn't want her colleagues or the public to know just how much money she did have.[44]

All these conflicts were catching up to Shaw. Over the previous summer, Shaw met with Thomas and various other suffrage leaders to plan for the upcoming work and convention to be held in Nashville, Tennessee, after the election. Once again Shaw faced the NAWSA Convention wary of what it would bring for her. Shaw had left home with "great dread and yet my heart was not as heavy as it ought perhaps to have been." Among the strongest allies in the Shaw-Thomas camp were the two Mrs. McCormicks, Ruth Hanna McCormick of Illinois and Katherine Dexter McCormick of Boston. Their shared focus was primarily on building a well-directed Congressional program, while also encouraging strong southern support from a new generation of suffrage leaders, women such as Patti Ruffner Jacobs of Alabama and Lila Meade Valentine of Virginia. Though her injury had kept Shaw from the Official Board meeting and Southern Conference the previous March, Shaw had been actively mentoring new (white) leaders from the southern states. No doubt she hoped to foster a new generation of southern suffragists to counter the power and positions of Kate Gordon and Laura Clay.[45]

Thomas and Shaw discussed possible changes among the board. After volunteering that she would work on constitutional changes, Shaw shifted gears and wrote cryptically, "If you and those who stand with you think it best for me to stand for reelection I will not make it harder by opposing it. I only want you to know that I am trusting you to let me know when it is not best for me to continue." It isn't clear who did "stand with" Thomas. It was clear that Shaw was ready to exit the office of the presidency.[46]

A sequence of events leading up to the convention convinced both Thomas and Shaw that she should stand for reelection again. The two friends shared a drawing room on the journey to Tennessee, while the Southern Suffrage Association, organized by Kate Gordon, held its pre-NAWSA meeting in Chattanooga. Also arriving by train was a group of women from Illinois who were coming with the express plan to work against the NAWSA, Anna Howard Shaw, and Ruth Hanna McCormick. Upton headed another opposition group. This year they planned to force Shaw into the position of president emeritus and put a limit on any one person's presidential term. Again this was no ideological opposition, but came from southern conservatives, Illinois women, and Harriet Upton. Since no one in the opposition seemed able to keep their plans secret, Shaw's supporters, probably with the direction of Thomas, soon knew of them. Shaw's camp then preempted them by opening the convention with a resolution thanking Shaw for agreeing to serve for another year. Other motions on term limits and salaries were tabled. It isn't clear whether it was fortunate or unfortunate that Shaw's opposition took an underhanded means rather than a direct approach. It is possible that Shaw would have retired if she had been able to do it on her own terms and with dignity and honor, all of which she had earned.[47]

As much as this type of opposition annoyed Anna Howard Shaw, it was just one more minor disturbance in a year that had seen many larger problems. Knowing that Dennett, who had been the administrative center of the headquarters, would be gone, Shaw now faced the news that her first vice president and possible successor, Jane Addams, would not run for reelection. Soon Addams would focus on other issues, founding the Women's Peace Party. In the end, after the elections, Shaw ended up with a relatively new team of officers.[48]

One would have imagined that the NAWSA and its leader had enough controversy at this point, but in what many have seen as a serious misstep, the NAWSA complicated its own work and played into the CU's accusations by backing what has become known as the Shafroth Amendment. Perhaps the brainchild of Ruth Hanna McCormick, but backed by the NAWSA Board and introduced in the Senate by the longtime suffrage supporter Senator Shafroth of Colorado, this legislation was, at its core, an initiative and referendum measure through which the signatures of 8 percent of the voters would force a state legislature to place woman suffrage before all the voters in a general election. Since state and national workers had spent so much time persuading legislators to give voters such an opportunity, the younger suffrage workers imagined that this would be an easier way to increase the number of states backing woman suffrage.[49]

Almost immediately this "sensible" solution proved to be a confusing distraction for the NAWSA, as well as fodder for the opposition both within and from outside the suffrage movement. The CU immediately argued that the NAWSA was abandoning the Anthony Amendment. From the start, Shaw was ambivalent at best toward this amendment, but support from many of the younger board members was so strong that she went along with the plan.[50]

Now at the convention, the NAWSA delegates' concerns over the Shafroth Amendment were directed at Shaw. According to the *History of Woman Suffrage*, "The feeling aroused by the discussion of the Shafroth amendment was manifested in the election, where 315 delegates were entitled to vote and 283 votes were cast. Dr. Shaw received 192 votes for president and the rest were blank, as even delegates who opposed this amendment would not vote against her." There is no record of Shaw's reaction to this vote. Not surprisingly, Shaw was relieved to see both the convention and the year close.[51]

Yet January 1, 1915, brought little relief for Shaw. It was in her words, "a day of joy and grief." Shaw had received the news that her brother James was ill several days earlier. She had gone to New York in case "he wanted her." James was the oldest of her remaining siblings, the one who had believed in her when she had first chosen her nontraditional path, but also the brother Shaw recalled as always youthful and full of the enthusiasm of a curious child. On New Year's Day, Shaw first received word that her brother was holding his own. Then by noon came the call that he had passed peacefully at the age of seventy-six. Shaw boarded the train in New York and journeyed to Boston to attend his funeral. Shaw wrote, "It is the break in our last group, soon we will all be gone. I wonder why we ever came. It has not been easy for any of us. Life is such a mystery and yet across the sea men are slaughtering each other like sheep." Several days later Anna was startled to find out that her brother had left a will in which she was coheir with his second wife.[52]

Days later, in Washington, D.C., Shaw listened as the House of Representatives finally held the first full house debate on woman suffrage. Few of the suffragists expected Congress to pass the measure on its initial consideration. Shaw was disappointed but not overly so when on January 13, 1915, the House of Representatives defeated woman suffrage 204 to 174. In spite of this outcome, Shaw knew the momentum had changed, but she worried about how the emerging international developments might threaten that progress.[53]

The backdrop for everything was now the war in Europe. Though the United States had, and would continue to have, a policy of official neutrality for the next few years, war news dominated the front pages of newspapers. In 1915 the international alliances women had built with each other had to change. Transatlantic travel was no longer safe. When Shaw considered the year ahead, there was no plan for her annual voyage to Europe, nor did she expect to send any NAWSA representative to any such gatherings. In a humorous break amid the grim assessment, Shaw suggested that she would happily pay for Alice Paul's voyage over to Europe if she could be assured she wouldn't return.[54]

As if the fates knew that their time was limited, Massachusetts, New Jersey, Pennsylvania, and most importantly, New York, the eastern states with large populations and significant Congressional delegations, finally had woman suffrage on the ballot for the fall. The *Evening Post* put the matter succinctly when it proclaimed, "Suffrage War Climax Now in the East: Atlantic Coast States on Firing Line, Franchise a Presidential Issue in 1916." Shaw planned to devote herself to these eastern campaigns from April until November. First she would travel south to rest in Florida followed by several weeks fulfilling the southern commitments she had had to cancel because of her broken ankle the previous spring. With Shaw on the road, Katherine Dexter McCormick assumed running the New York Headquarters in place of Mary Ware Dennett.[55]

Perhaps her brother's death had shaken Shaw, or perhaps she was thinking of how hard she would push herself for the next eight months, but at the beginning of February, on the day she was scheduled to depart from Alnwick Lodge, she and Lucy went to their lawyer's office. It was only prudent that this couple, who had shared a life for over a quarter of a century but who enjoyed none of the automatic legal benefits accorded a married couple, would put their affairs in order. In her diary, Shaw solemnly and ruefully recorded that she and Lucy both signed their wills.[56]

Now Shaw went a step further, one that had to have been quite unusual for 1915. To protect Lucy's future economic security, especially in light of Shaw's ongoing battle with the county assessor, "in the year of our Lord one thousand nine hundred and fifteen . . . Anna H. Shaw of New York, formerly of Moylan . . . Singlewoman" sold her land, home, and all other buildings, and rights to Lucy E. Anthony for the "sum of one dollar." Neither woman left any explanation for or comments on this transaction. In her diary Shaw noted only, "At noon I said my silent farewell to Alnwick Lodge for a time at least." One has to suspect that Shaw had made the decision to pull out the stops this year in hopes that 1915 would end with a significant victory.[57]

With the rest of the NAWSA, Shaw was still struggling to convince suffragists and the general public that the Shafroth Amendment was not a substitute for the Susan B. Anthony Amendment. Shaw was working from Florida in March when Harriot Stanton Blatch's Women's Political Union withdrew as an auxiliary organization of NAWSA in part as a reaction to this confusion. Though these splits depressed Shaw, she was heartened by the positive and sympathetic coverage her talks received in Fort Worth, Dallas, Greenville, Mississippi, and other southern stops. At the end of this trip, Shaw wrote from Atlanta, "It has certainly been a triumphant trip, such as I never had before.[58]

Yet no period of positive news seems to have lasted long in these tumultuous years. On April 3, 1915, while Shaw was still in the South, M. Carey Thomas's longtime companion, Mary Garrett, died. This death may have been expected; Garrett had endured many years of ill health. Although it is possible that the events that unfolded during the rest of the year were already in play, it seems that Garrett's death may have been the final factor on the decisions both Thomas and Shaw made later in 1915. Thomas's biographer has argued that Mary Garrett's wishes were the reason Thomas had taken on public suffrage work in the first place, but it is hard to determine whether Thomas had remained active only or primarily to honor the interest of the woman who was not only her partner but also a major benefactor to Bryn Mawr, the suffrage movement, and Thomas personally.[59]

Shaw returned to the North in April, where she immediately threw all of her energy into campaigning. On May 2, she headed the suffrage parade in Philadelphia. In her speech at the Opera House Shaw argued that here in the State of Pennsylvania she also felt a tremendous positive change from just a year ago. After a brief stop at Bryn Mawr College to console a tired and grieving Thomas, Shaw went on to New York; the suffragists there presented her with a Saxon car to use in her suffrage travels. It seems that the half-century of depending only on the rails was coming to a close.[60]

Anna Howard Shaw gave, by one estimate, fifteen thousand speeches over her long public career. She spoke to the Chautauqua audiences almost every year and addressed the great suffrage rallies in London, New York, Philadelphia, Chicago, and Washington, D.C. She represented American women at numerous international conferences and was the first woman to preach in three of the great cathedrals of Europe. In every one of the forty-eight states she had taken to the podium, to great outdoor gatherings and in small towns. Though Shaw herself listed the 1893 sermon at the Chicago Columbian Exposition and the one in 1912 in Stockholm as the two orations with which she was most satisfied, scholars have come to a different conclusion. Looking back over all the speeches given by American women in the twentieth century, it was the speech that Shaw gave on June 21, 1915, in Ogdensburg, New York, that they have deemed her most important. It is considered the third most important address by an American woman and the twenty-seventh most significant American speech in the twentieth century. Its title is "The Fundamental Principle of a Republic."[61]

The central theme that Shaw developed in this speech was one that she had used for years, but its meaning was heightened during this time of war. Shaw spoke of the incredible vision that the founders had for this republic, but how we have never been able to completely live up to their vision. She reasoned that if we believe in this idea of the republic, we need to support its highest development. Tracing the exclusion of different groups from the franchise, Shaw argued how at this time it was women who were excluded and that this exclusion could not rationally be reconciled with the ideal. Addressing the traditional argument that women could not have an equal claim to citizenship since they didn't serve in time of war, Shaw drew on her own and her mother's experiences during the Civil War. She asked whether the women who picked up the work that men had left when they went off to war and the mothers who had borne and raised the soldiers were not also serving and contributing to the war effort. In her emotional closing Shaw based her claim for equal rights on the sacrifices of mothers who saw the children to whom they had given their life's work die for their country. After so many years of inspiring her audiences, Shaw still had her gift.[62]

Through the rest of this hectic summer, the name of Anna Howard Shaw stayed in the headlines. Starting on July 11th and lasting until July 25th, the papers gave attention to the saga of Dr. Shaw's little car that had been seized in the controversy over her taxes. In the end, the Delaware County Suffrage Society paid the $230 to buy the car and return it to the suffrage leader. Later, in August, when Shaw condemned the lynching of Leo Frank, the Jewish businessman abducted and murdered in Georgia, the *New York Times* carried her comments.[63]

In the midst of this campaign season in which every suffragist was doing as much as she possibly could and into which Shaw had thrown herself with an agenda of meetings and rallies that rivaled her earliest days on the lecture circuit, Harper Brothers published her autobiography, *The Story of a Pioneer*. This book was no deep self-reflective tome replete with feminist theory; it was very much a written version of many of Shaw's most significant memories and favorite anecdotes. Its saving grace is that this book was dictated, rather than written, by Shaw. Her long experience of creating visions with the spoken word was evident in the liveliness and vivid images of the tales of her early years. She gave her inimitable voice to what remains the only narrative record of those years that span her childhood through her emergence as a public persona in the late 1880s. That part of her book, which Eleanor Flexner cites as important social history, captures not just Shaw's particular struggle as she created possibilities for herself in an era when women were first pushing down traditional barriers but also the shared realities of many women and children who were pioneers on the remaining frontiers of the United States. These are the stories of the wives isolated on farms during the Civil War, of families who were never warm in winter or without hunger much of the year and whose days repeated themselves over and over again in a sameness that deadened hope and erased opportunities, and of young people who settled for the best that a community could offer in education or work or marriage or who found the means to escape and/ or build a better life, a stronger community, and a new economy. Shaw's story traces the changes that came with industry, new educational institutions, and the growth of the railroads. It was an American story that was accessible and entertaining.[64]

"Vale!" The title of the last chapter of the book captures what the book became once Shaw started describing her role in the suffrage movement: a grateful celebration and a farewell to the cause that had been and still was what gave meaning to her life. A large part of the honoring goes to Susan B. Anthony. It isn't that Shaw mythologized only Anthony; she extends no criticism to anyone in the movement, though a few people were perhaps obvious in their absence: Alice Paul, Abigail Duniway, and Harriot Stanton Blatch, for example. There is little mention of some of the women who had been close to Shaw at first but with whom she later had breaks, women such as Harriet Taylor Upton and Laura Clay.

In many ways this book was and still is propaganda for the suffrage movement and the NAWSA. Shaw had never planned to write such a book; when explaining this to a sister suffragist, she maintained that her injury had weakened her resolve against such a project. Perhaps the lasting worth of this book, which was well received by readers and reviewers, is that it captured Shaw's stories in her own voice. During 1915, *Story of a Pioneer* only added to Shaw's mystique and visibility.[65]

Shaw continued her incomparable contributions to the eastern campaigns, including marching in the fifty-thousand-strong parade in New York City. At one point after so many weeks on the road, she was so tired that she became forgetful, and yet her spirits were high and her sense of humor intact. "If you see a head lying about anywhere with no brains in it you will know it is mine. I am scattering my things about everywhere. I simply am no good any more. I left my glasses either in Long Branch or Newark. Have written back to both places, . . . I don't know whether I shall reach home with a rag on my back or not."[66]

Shaw came to the decision to retire from the NAWSA presidency sometime in the midst of all this activity. It may have been as early as the year before when Shaw learned that Mrs. Frank Leslie left $1,000,000 to Carrie Chapman Catt for suffrage work. It could have been when so many blank votes were cast at the last convention, or it may have been related to Mary Garrett's death. By the end of the campaign, when she went to Atlantic City, she was ready to state that it was to "celebrate her freedom." There she joined M. Carey Thomas and spent several days resting next to the Atlantic Ocean before they motored to New York City to await the results of the votes in Pennsylvania, New York, and Massachusetts.

Shaw must have hoped that she would go out in a blaze of glory, but she was disappointed. Woman suffrage did not win in any of the big four states that year. Shaw was quite sanguine about the outcomes. In the margins of the defeats, Shaw and other leaders saw progress that gave them hope and reasons to reassure the disappointed suffrage workers. Once again, Shaw used her eloquence to bolster the spirits of the exhausted and disheartened workers. Shaw could always project unflagging confidence and radiate a contagious optimism in her public appearances. She joined the other leaders at the Great Jubilee Meeting at the Academy of Music and then again the next day at Cooper Union, where the movement reaffirmed its determination by raising over $100,000 for the next campaign.[67]

Anna Howard Shaw announced her decision not to run for another term after the voting results were in. At the age of sixty-eight, after twenty-five years as a NAWSA officer, and close to twelve as president, Shaw decided that she had fulfilled her promise to Susan B. Anthony. The beloved but constraining hand of Susan B. Anthony was no longer keeping Shaw in an office for which her determination was total but for which her talents were less than a complete match. The public reason Shaw gave was that she was needed in the field and in the campaigns, speaking to the unconverted. From the time she made her announcement through the end of the NAWSA Convention, the *New York Times* and many other papers showered Shaw with praises. The press called her "genius," and "without a double." Tributes flooded in from around the globe.[68]

At that 1915 NAWSA Convention in Washington, D. C., Shaw turned the leadership position back to Carrie Chapman Catt. Yet even with her resignation, Shaw continued to be a shrewd negotiator. She not only took the expected title of Honorary President and retained a seat on the Official Board, but she also insisted on still having a desk at the National Headquarters. The NAWSA also quietly dropped its support for the Shafroth Amendment and recommitted itself to the original suffrage amendment.[69]

On the final night of the convention, the night to honor Anna Howard Shaw for all her service to "the cause," M. Carey Thomas, most appropriately, was directing the pageantry. The hall was filled, flowers were everywhere, and while these annual suffrage gatherings had long become less about symbols and more about business, there was a sense that this night would be extraordinary. With the white-haired elder stateswoman seated at the center of the stage, a procession of leaders, beginning with Thomas herself carrying a laurel wreath, followed by a garland-bearing Harriet Laidlaw and all the state presidents with their arms filled with large bouquets, proceeded to pay homage to Shaw until flowers all but enveloped her.[70]

Shaw had been part of the struggle for women's rights for almost as long as most of the audience could remember, since before many of them were born. The miles she had traveled were beyond calculation, and the people who had heard her numbered in at least the hundreds of thousands. Thomas, who had raised the funds for the salary that permitted Shaw to be the full-time NAWSA president, arranged the final gift of the movement to Shaw, an annuity that would give her an income for the rest of her life. Always stronger in the face of adversity than in celebration, Shaw was so moved that she was almost unable to speak. Finally, she regained her voice and thanked all the members of the convention for the honor of serving as their leader.[71]

In the days following the convention, Shaw, almost before she could begin to consider how her life would now change, took care of the business at hand. She needed to move out of her office. As she gathered the remains of the many years at 505 Fifth Ave., she began to feel ill. Alone in New York, she knew she wanted, as always, to get home to Alnwick Lodge and Lucy. Before boarding the train, she wired Lucy to bring her longtime physician, Dr. Jennie Medley, to meet her when she arrived. Shaw, who had faced so many illnesses and trials alone while traveling, pushed herself one more time to make it safely home. Dr. Medley first diagnosed the grippe, but Shaw's fever continued to rise. The grippe became pneumonia; Anna Howard Shaw fell into a coma.[72]

While Anna Howard Shaw was ill, Carrie Chapman Catt was assessing the state of the NAWSA, the movement as a whole, and the worldwide atmosphere. The NAWSA was almost entirely a different organization than the one Catt had turned over to Shaw in 1904. Thanks to Shaw's determination, perseverance and risk-taking, the NAWSA had survived and thrived. With Catt, an admirer of Shaw's but almost her opposite as a leader, it would continue the fight. For weeks, though, it wasn't clear whether Shaw would be there to move forward with the NAWSA as it sought to finish the work of enfranchising women.

CHAPTER 8

A Worker to the End
(1916–1919)

I have been a slave all my days and I am not going to be so any
longer. I am going to declare my freedom from bondage to
meetings and all sorts of things that do not leave me a chance to
find happiness in my life. We have both been hampered because of
our work and because we have not had money enough. . . . When
have I taken days off just for my pleasure? I have simply lectured
and worked at my desk and I have not gone off to the mountains
with friends or to the seashore or on motor trips or anywhere just
for good times. I am going to do it and so are you.

Over the course of her long working life, very few things stopped
Anna Howard Shaw.[1] Though illnesses plagued her from the time she was
in her forties, Shaw generally would manage to stave them off to keep them
from disrupting her schedule. On a number of trips to Europe, she spent
days confined to her cabin with some malady. Most often she was able to
get home to Lucy. Ironically, the peripatetic orator was most vulnerable to
respiratory illnesses, ankle injuries, and headaches. The last were so common
that Susan B. Anthony once remarked that a headache seemed necessary for
Shaw to give her best speeches. Now, however, Shaw may have taken this
ability to push through illnesses too far. For weeks at the end of her years as
president of the National American Woman Suffrage Association it looked
as though Anna Howard Shaw indeed had given her life to the cause.

Yet once again, Shaw pulled through, and the choices she made during
the remainder of her life provide important insights into her character and
the place she had in the public arena. Official retirement, although at first it
brought a lessening of her administrative responsibilities, in the end allowed
Shaw the freedom to broaden her involvements. During these last years, much
of the public, from the youngest suffrage supporter up to the U.S. president,
saw her as an elder stateswoman, a role Shaw enthusiastically embraced.[2]

Shaw reached her beloved Alnwick Lodge before her pneumonia turned critical. During all her nomadic years, Shaw had written of her yearning to spend time at her home. Now, once the immediate crisis passed, she had no choice. As she regained some strength, she could look out over the winter landscape of the rural Rose Valley and her Forest of Arden, a grove that had grown from all those trees she had brought back from her suffrage travels. When she could finally leave the bed, she could move to her favorite space at the top of the stairs, which she and Lucy named "Peter Pan," and its view of the ravine and the stream at its bottom. Alnwick Lodge represented all that Shaw had achieved since her hungry years in Michigan and Massachusetts. Under Lucy's care, her will again triumphed over her compromised physical health, but this recovery was much slower and longer than any since 1895. Her recovery seemed stalled.

Shaw was physically recovering for certain. Yet for many weeks, her spirit lagged. The spark was gone, and it wasn't clear whether the veteran activist would ever be able to step into a public role again. The prospect of a limited life, of a well-earned though still self-indulgent retirement, actually appeared to be draining Shaw. For a woman who had always defined herself through her work, the demanding work of traveling and speaking, if she couldn't continue to contribute to the fight for enfranchisement to which she had devoted her life, should she resign herself to her final and absolute rest?[3]

Lucy realized, perhaps more than Shaw herself, the depth of this internal struggle. Though part of the doctor's orders forbade reading Shaw any of the many letters of concern that she had received, Lucy was worried, worried enough to finally disregard the doctor's rule. She chose to read parts of one particular letter. It was the one from Carrie Chapman Catt.[4]

Over the years, these two great leaders, each respecting and admiring the other's talents, had felt their closeness ebb as the movement's political intricacies pulled them into competing alliances. Although Catt was an astute observer of Shaw's personal and political limitations, she was also one of Shaw's foremost admirers. Without ever saying as much, Catt and Shaw knew that in the fight for women's citizenship, they equaled each other in dedication.[5]

All this was evident in Catt's letter. It started, "I wish daily that I could express in words my feeling but I never have been able to do so, and it is now hopeless. I should like, were I possessed of the gift, to tell you what you have been to the movement and to all of us in it." Catt went on to honor Shaw as the only real orator that the entire international movement had produced. Carefully, Catt wrote of how she regretted that Shaw had to be president, and how that position had brought Shaw enemies that she shouldn't have had. She concluded, "I am glad you are free from it now. I want you to have the love and gratitude which was Miss Anthony's lot in her last twenty years—and you will I am sure you will."[6]

Apparently Lucy and Catt both knew Shaw better than her doctors. It was Catt's tribute that brought Shaw around. In her reply, Lucy described how Catt's testimonial produced a marked improvement: "So you see an incentive for getting well was most necessary and I really believed it was supplied . . .—the sympathy expressed, the appreciation and the call to arms came at the right moment."[7]

Shaw dictated an equally heartfelt reply. In it, she revisited certain moments in the struggle when she and Catt had been able to express their affection for one another. Shaw wrote of the thousands of times she had felt great pride when watching Catt's splendid leadership at the international and national meetings along with her sadness over the barrier that seemed to have kept them from the frank friendship that they had once shared. At this time when they were so reminded of their mortality, these two longtime suffrage warriors expressed the great love and respect they had for each other, sentiments that they needed to say then but which they would keep private in the remaining years of their shared struggle.[8]

M. Carey Thomas took a different tact. "You *simply and absolutely must obey orders* [with two additional lines under "must"]. . . . You owe this to your doctor and nurses and friends—and to the *CAUSE*. You have no right to throw away a life that was given back to suffrage. . . . A relapse will be fatal and really dishonorable to your work." Yet even Thomas felt that the time had come when she needed to express something more. So formal was this friendship that Shaw and Thomas never even called each other by their first names, but this time Thomas closed the letter with, "I love you and am so thankful that you are here in this good old earth for us to love."[9]

With the encouragement of these and many other friends, Shaw's will to live returned. When the doctors and Lucy felt she was well enough to travel, she went south to continue her recovery in Florence Villa, Florida, among her good friends and the warm weather. She remained in Florida from her sixty-ninth birthday in mid-February until mid-April. After Florida, Shaw traveled first to South Carolina and then up to Atlantic City, for some sea air.[10]

By May 5th she was at Bryn Mawr College. This was the first time since 1906 that Thomas and Shaw met when it wasn't a president-to-president meeting. Yes, Shaw was still the honorary president of the NAWSA, but she no longer had either the power or the responsibilities she had carried for those many years. Now she and Thomas needed to establish a different basis for their relationship; it seemed as though Thomas, too, was willing to give up her power role in the NAWSA while continuing to be Shaw's friend and financial overseer. Thomas had assumed responsibility for raising the annuity for Shaw, a task that was still unsettled throughout that year.[11]

By the summer of 1916, on one level it was almost as if the health crisis had never happened. Shaw was back to work fighting for suffrage. Yet each breakdown changed Shaw on a less obvious level. On one hand, it truly did seem as though only work could define and sustain her, but now she would write more frequently to Lucy about the leisure they could have when the battle was over. Shaw tried to find some of the limits and moderation that she had never accepted before this time. "I don't want any more meetings before I go west; I have not the energy for them, nor the nerve force. I must have peace and quiet and good cheer or I will go under again. The rest of my life I plan to live in the freest and easiest way possible."[12]

Within the NAWSA, Shaw's illness had forced a rather swift and clean transition. Shaw's absence from the scene allowed Catt to define her own leadership team and processes. In spite of Shaw's admiration for Catt, she hadn't been Shaw's first choice for NAWSA President; Shaw was wary of Catt's closest friend, Mary Hay, whom she referred to as the "Big Boss." Shaw had urged Harriet Laidlaw to run for the office. Not surprisingly, given Shaw's and Catt's different styles and strengths, Catt found some major problems with the organization, especially with the work of the Congressional Committee in Washington, D.C. Nevertheless Shaw quickly came to accept Catt's decisions and gave her full support to the new administration. Indicative of her new attitude were her comments to Lucy that she thought Catt was doing well and the young people were "splendid." Her role was to "speak and inspire" and share her views when requested by Catt.[13]

What was most striking about the media coverage of suffrage at this point was how each story on woman suffrage was literally surrounded by news on the war in Europe. It was as though woman suffrage was the only domestic issue that could compete with the global conflict. While Woodrow Wilson sought reelection as the candidate who kept the United States out of war, most people realized that such neutrality would probably not last. Since international gatherings were difficult if not impossible by this time, women had to work diligently in new ways to keep their connections to each other. Shaw was still chair of the Suffrage Department of the International Council of Women. When she wrote to her colleagues in June of 1916, she stated her ideas about the connection between women's rights and the world war. She then closed with, "My earnest prayer is that the day may not be far distant when the women of the world may again gather in convention to plan for an aggressive campaign in behalf of those things which build up a nation and exalt and develop human character."[14]

Carrie Chapman Catt could always read the political winds well. Early in 1916 she knew that the country was on the cusp of war just as the suffrage movement was closing in on its goal. She understood how the cessation of activism during the Civil War had set back the movement. At this point the NAWSA was in a catch-22: to stop active campaigning could halt the momentum, but not to give all to a war effort would brand the women as unpatriotic. Not knowing how long they had until a war declaration, Catt called an emergency NAWSA convention for the beginning of September 1916 in the oceanside resort of Atlantic City. This was the first meeting Shaw attended in her new role as honorary president.[15]

"The Crisis," the title Catt gave her speech, captured her analysis of the times within the movement and the country. Shaw had allowed the state organizations a great deal of autonomy, but Catt decided it was time to centralize the work of the NAWSA. In her speech, after paying tribute to all the women and men, Shaw prominently among them, who had given so much to the cause, Catt articulated an eloquent call to action and unity. This, Catt believed, was not the time to continue with the status quo; it was the time to seize the moment. Only renewed and reenergized efforts could bring women to victory. Catt asked for the loyalty of the women, specifically that they trust her and NAWSA, coordinate their local efforts closely with Catt's "Winning Plan," and support an increased effort in Washington, D.C.[16]

Signaling the prominent place of suffrage in the national political landscape, President Wilson spoke to the NAWSA for the first time at this convention. Still endorsing only state-by-state suffrage, he closed his address by urging the women to be patient. Catt had asked Shaw to reply to the president's address. In a masterful stroke, she turned to President Wilson at the close of her talk, and with one of her "irresistible smiles," stated that women *had* been patient and that they hoped that their long wait would be ended under his administration.[17]

In the final session of this last prewar convention, Shaw spoke on the appropriate theme of Americanism. After questioning how Americanism could be different from others' nationalisms, Shaw concluded with a statement certainly inspired by her own life. "The highest ideal of a republic is not a long bread line nor a soup kitchen but such opportunity that people can buy their own bread and make their own soup. Opportunity must be for all, men and women alike, and the peoples of every nationality."[18]

When Shaw resumed campaigning after the 1916 convention, she vacillated between optimism and despair. She feared that the work of the CU had set the movement back years, but she felt "long or short we have got to win and I am in it either till we do or I fall in the fight, for there is where the angel of death will find me." Though June had already brought defeat in Iowa, the November elections in West Virginia and South Dakota—though defeats also—had margins that were lower than expected, so Shaw and the movements still felt they were making progress. In a development that took even the most astute women leaders by surprise, suffragist Jeanette Rankin was elected the first ever U.S. Congresswoman.[19]

As the year—a year she had doubted she would have—ended, Shaw returned to Florence Villa where she and Lucy had decided they would rent a furnished cottage on Mary Jewett's property as their winter home. Shaw had grown to love this private spot in central Florida. Once again she had a sanctuary removed from the public eye where she could drop her professional persona and be herself. With pleasant weather, Shaw could have a rose garden, eat fresh local fruit all winter, breathe the warm air, and have the active outdoor life that she had always found restorative. To her old friend, Clara Osborn, Shaw explained she and Lucy had just decided to stay in Florida until about April 7th, abandoning their earlier plan to spend the rest of the winter traveling to California. Shaw said she needed to rest more than travel. "[W]e will settle down in the midst of one of the most beautiful spots I know in Florida." Shaw recognized that she should have headed south even earlier, but in the self-deprecating humor that signaled how relaxed she was, she continued, "We get the idea that the world cannot get along without us, and bye and bye we learn they can quite well and in fact have been impatient to get rid of us."[20]

In Florence Villa, Shaw came as close to retirement as she was willing to allow herself. Shaw was a more-than-welcomed guest, as Mary Jewett remembered: "[N]o greater entertainment, when she was in a talking mood, could be found than to sit with her and share her thoughts." There, Shaw indulged in two pleasures reminiscent of her early log cabin days in rural Michigan: "[S]he was a fire worshiper almost, and nobody could build a better fire than she, and to mend her clothes, which she saved the rest of the year for Florida evenings; all this while somebody read aloud or just talked, or better yet, got her started to talking." A determined and successful gardener, Shaw also returned to other youthful pastimes—she remained strong enough to wield an axe and steady enough to build a desk for her winter office.[21]

On February 14, 1917, in Florence Villa, Shaw celebrated her seventieth birthday. Close to two hundred letters, gifts, and congratulations from her long-time suffrage colleagues through President Wilson celebrated her life. Shaw felt so happy and honored that she wanted to share this joy with her oldest friend so she sent Clara Osborn a check for $100.[22]

Yet with all these celebratory notes came an ominous request from NAWSA President Catt to join her in Washington, D.C., for a small conference that month. Catt wanted Shaw to help decide how the NAWSA should respond to a declaration of war. The CU, soon to be renamed the National Women's Party, had already started picketing the White House in January.

In this atmosphere, the longtime leaders could feel that victory was in their reach, but the spread of war threatened all confidence in a known future. Shaw, Catt, and the other members of the NAWSA Executive Council gathered at the new NAWSA headquarters on Rhode Island Ave. to develop a plan. Suffrage momentum had already increased. In January, North Dakota had passed presidential suffrage, followed by Indiana and Ohio in February. Nebraska, Michigan, and Rhode Island would follow in April. Even the women of the southern state of Arkansas gained primary suffrage in 1917. Then the NAWSA learned that the tremendously important state of New York would have suffrage on the ballot in November. In a telling nod to their significance at this crucial point, Secretary of War Newton Baker joined the women for part of the time. President Catt announced at the mass meeting at the close of the three-day conference that suffragists, two million strong, were ready to support the president and the war effort in whatever way they could. They had rejected the idea that they would suspend suffrage activities, arguing that they could do both political and war work. Although many were pacifists or antiwar at their cores, they also agreed not to publically oppose the war. Though Shaw had been reluctant to leave her Florida retreat to attend the gathering, Catt reassured Shaw that her address to the gathering more than justified her coming.[23]

After this conference, Shaw returned to her "comfortably lazy" existence in Florida for several more weeks. Before she left Florida for her month-long lecture tour through seven southern states, Shaw drew up a new will. On March 26, 1917, Shaw signed, and three of her friends from Florida witnessed, a will that again left the bulk of her estate to Lucy E. Anthony. Shaw did, however, address issues that were new since her 1915 will, including her annuity, her autobiography, and its proceeds. She also took care to make bequests to three of her nieces to be "expended toward a college education," preferably at Bryn Mawr College.[24]

Even in the South where veteran suffrage leaders Kate Gordon and Laura Clay remained hostile to the federal amendment and railed against Catt, Shaw, and the NAWSA, and where writers and editors called Shaw as well as Susan B. Anthony and Jane Addams "n . . . -lovers," Shaw sensed a turning of the tide. In each state that she visited, Shaw found that southerners celebrated woman suffrage and welcomed her. On an organizational level, most of the "new women of the New South," were on board with the direction of the NAWSA.[25]

The United States entered the World War on April 6, 1917. Shaw's still active but less intense public life soon faced a drastic revision. On April 20, 1917, she received what was essentially a draft notice. A telegram from Walter Gifford of the Council of National Defense asked her to come to Washington as soon as possible to meet with him and Secretary of War Baker. The 1916 National Defense Act included the creation of the Council for National Defense "in order that an emergency would not find us without a central agency to direct the national mobilization back of the fighting army." Shaw had been appointed to the Woman's Committee of this Council for National Defense. She was not asked, she was told this, just as she was also told that she had been chosen as its chair.[26]

It was a tremendous tribute to Shaw's standing among the general public that President Wilson called on her to lead this effort. For the first time in U.S. history, there was a governmental body composed completely of women and focused on women. The creation of this committee also recognized the influence that women had at this point in U.S. history.

Nevertheless Shaw's appointment was politically complicated. It was a de facto governmental endorsement of the suffrage movement and an un-expected blow to a different women's organization, the National League for Woman's Service (NLWS). The NLWS had assumed that they would be coordinating women's war efforts, but the NLWS had strong links to the antisuffragist organizations. Further, the president's appointment was, at least in part, a political move. Not only did the Wilson administration want the support and work of the suffrage women, but also it didn't want such a large organization of women, many of whose leaders were some level of pacifist and many, such as Jane Addams, who were opposing the war or supporting the NWP pickets.[27]

An honor or not, this was a horrific demand on a woman who had barely recovered her health. Shaw had only begun to acknowledge that she had to accept some physical limitations and set a calmer pace for her life. After her meetings in Washington, Shaw went to Moylan to caucus with Lucy and her nieces about what this new development meant for their lives and their plans. From Shaw's letters, it is evident that not all members of her family supported her decision to put again the demands of the country above her personal welfare. In a letter written from the NAWSA Headquarters in New York, referring back to what had clearly been a trying evening with Lucy and her niece, Grace Green, Shaw thanked Lucy for her steadfast support. Although the other suffrage leaders were thrilled with her appointment, Shaw saw that only Catt, another Woman's Committee appointee, under-stood the burden that this was placing on both of them.[28]

That quickly, Shaw's so-called retirement ended. She was once again living a life of pressing meetings and overwhelming demands. Less than two weeks after Shaw had received the original telegram from Gifford and one week after she had met with the Secretary of War and the head of the Council for National Defense, she chaired a meeting with the diverse group of women who would make up this committee. In addition to Shaw, they included suffragists Catt; Antoinette Funk; and Katharine Dexter McCormick; along with Mrs. Philip North Moore of the National Council of Women; Mrs. Josiah Evans Cowles from the General Federation of Women's Clubs; Maude Wetmore of the National League for Women's Service; Mrs. Joseph Lamar of the National Society of Colonial Dames; Agnes Nestor, International Glove Workers' Union (representing labor women at Shaw's request); writer Ida Tarbell; and Hannah Patterson, who would be director of the executive office. There were no African American women on the committee. A total of fifteen women served in the executive office in the building unfortunately known as "Little Playhouse," the only available space in the capital.[29]

Now that the government had recruited and assembled this group of very capable women, as scholars who have studied this committee noted, they seemed uncertain about what they really wanted the women to do. Some speculation is that the women were appointed only as window dressing or to serve as rubber stamps for policies and initiatives from other agencies. The committee recognized that they were an advisory body, but they also considered themselves to be the most appropriate conduit, the "channel" in their words, between the federal government and the women of the country. To this end, Shaw and the others pledged unity and set about constructing what they saw as the most efficient structure through which to pass information from the federal government to women in all the states. They knew they already had the networks to do this and that their established structures would be far more efficient than any the government could construct in wartime.[30]

Appreciating the totality of the U.S. war effort in World War I is difficult for those who have experienced only the U.S. wars of the twenty-first century, where relatively few families have borne the greatest burden and many have remained removed from the immediate impact of the war's demands. In 1917, everyone was expected to contribute. For the Women's Committee this meant that for each state and territory, the national committee chose a state chair, who then organized a committee division at that level. Additionally, the national committee determined an honorary committee composed of the presidents of seventy-three national women's organizations. This list included religious, labor, educational, service, political, and professional groups—from the Girl Scouts and National Council of Jewish Women though the National Women's Trade Union League and National Women's Medical Association. So broad was this coalition that there were probably few issues on which they would have agreed except for the war work and the importance of women's contributions.[31]

Shaw was torn over the war and this work. She had always been against war, but she was a patriot. Politically, she knew that the suffrage movement could proceed during these years only if women clearly carried more than their share of the war work, a process complicated by the stands taken by the pacifists among them, such as Jane Addams and the National Women's Party, which refused to cooperate with a government that hadn't given their members the right to vote. She also knew that she would be sacrificing her health and her finances for this period of her life. There was no pay for this work even when it required taking up residence in Washington, D.C. for weeks or months at a time. The working woman in Shaw did request reimbursement for her expenses, though such monies were very slow in coming.[32]

On June 19, 1917, on the second page of the *Washington Post*, among a piece on U.S. Food Administrator Herbert Hoover's plan for housewives, four articles on the Red Cross fund-raising drive, and one on the Liberty Loans, was an announcement of the meeting of the women presidents with the Woman's Committee. This one page from one day gives a sense of the speed with which all these issues and groups needed to come together. Shaw had no illusions about the difficulties they all faced. She wrote to Lucy that "I am dreading next week so much I hardly dare think of it, but like 'Silas' I have got to do whether I want to or not."[33]

Shaw stayed in Washington during the summer of 1917, going to M. Carey Thomas's Atlantic City apartment on the weekends when she could. She felt lonely and isolated but once again bound to the work. Shaw and the Woman's Committee had created a comprehensive program and structure. The frustrations for Shaw and her coworkers were that the men running the other agencies with whom the women needed to coordinate their work could not or would not grant the Woman's Committee much responsibility. To Shaw it seemed that the men couldn't accept working with women as their equals or recognize that the women had developed an efficient organization.[34]

While Shaw labored through the summer for the U.S. government, members of the National Women's Party not only continued to picket the White House but escalated their rhetoric against the president. Shaw found the confrontational tactics and personal affronts to a wartime president offensive and politically counterproductive. To Shaw, when the NWP began to sharpen the accusations against President Wilson, they were acting as agents provocateurs. Then came the arrests, detentions, hunger strikes, and force-feeding at the Occoquan Workhouse. Shaw did not condone the treatment the women received. She and others in the NAWSA recognized, though, that Paul had very much wanted to create conditions to call a hunger strike. Additionally, after receiving a report from a colleague who visited the workhouse and knowing how Paul used the media, she questioned whether the conditions were as difficult as NWP women described them to be.[35]

Such suspicions were founded in Shaw's assessment of Paul and her NWP compatriots. She saw the NWP as neither diverse nor democratic, and she found Paul's personal self-promotion hard to swallow. The NWP and Paul infuriated Shaw by their attempts to revise suffrage history to glorify their leaders and their work. Two points of their propaganda especially outraged her. First was the claim that the NAWSA had ignored the federal amendment until Alice Paul came along in 1912 to reinvigorate that work. Shaw knew that she and many others in the NAWSA had never lost sight of the federal amendment as the ultimate goal. But worse yet was the NWP's position that Alice Paul was Susan B. Anthony's heir in the struggle and that Paul's contributions were comparable to those of the great leader. To Shaw and the NAWSA loyalists who had struggled to make woman suffrage respectable—who remembered how Susan B. Anthony, Lucy Stone, and other pioneers had been treated in public; how they had been ignored by the Congress and presidents; and how they had persisted decade after decade to bring woman suffrage into the mainstream of political issues—to even suggest that Paul, in her few years of activism, had made any equivalent contribution to the movement was outrageous, the claim of someone with an unrealistic sense of her importance. Anthony had given over fifty years to the cause; Paul had at best five active years in the American movement at this point. At times, Shaw wasn't even sure that Paul could be considered sane.[36]

As the summer of 1917 wore on, the New York campaign weighed on Catt and Shaw even as they struggled to establish the guidelines for the Woman's Committee. The women leaders had agreed it would be respectable and realistic to wait until two months before the vote on woman suffrage to turn their activities from the war work to the New York campaign. Fully cognizant of what a victory in New York could mean, Shaw was committed to give as much of her time and talents to New York as she could.[37]

Shaw and many other suffrage workers, young and old, once again poured into the most populous state in the country. While the media highlighted the most public events of the campaign, such as the vast number of supporters at the "monster" march of October 27, overwhelmingly the energy of the thousands of workers went into the district-by-district, precinct-by-precinct organizing, especially in New York City. The wartime rhetoric added new accusations aimed at undermining the suffrage support. One *New York Times* headline read "Suffrage Victory Laid to Germans . . . Sees Plot to End War." It didn't help that Alice Paul had been arrested and sentenced to jail in October.[38]

On November 6, 1917, the state of New York passed woman suffrage. This time there was enough money, publicity, and workers. In the end, those resources and the superior organizing produced the victory that is still considered the tipping point in the struggle. By 102,353 votes, the Empire State, the home state of both Elizabeth Cady Stanton and Susan B. Anthony, finally became the first great eastern state to grant women the franchise and full citizenship.[39]

What this victory meant and what it had cost, only Shaw and a few other veterans truly knew. Tears of joy and relief streamed down her face that night as the results were announced. So many times, over so many years, and in so many places, Shaw had had to suppress her own disappointment, maintain her public optimism, and use her eloquence to rally demoralized and exhausted suffrage workers when they faced defeat. Now she could hardly speak when she learned of this triumph. Perhaps only Carrie Chapman Catt could fully share and appreciate Shaw's joy on that night of such a victory. Thousands of women and many of their male allies had worked for years to produce this success; none had put in the time that Catt and Shaw had. But beyond the intellectual understanding of how the number of enfranchised women and the number of congressional votes would change the political climate, Shaw felt this accomplishment in her heart and in her soul. This night after the ballots had been counted and the victory announced at Times Square, Shaw found the winning of New York a vindication of her life's work and the life's work of her beloved mentor, Susan B. Anthony.[40]

Analysts have argued that the emphasis on war work helped rather than hurt the suffrage movement. Shaw agreed. And while bringing the New York delegation into the suffrage fold almost guaranteed success, this was not the end of the fight. It really only made the remaining work different. It would not be an easy path, but the fight for the federal amendment was now at a new level. For the suffrage leaders, the focus shifted even more toward Washington. They still had to get the Anthony Amendment through Congress and through states' ratification, while continuing to shoulder their diverse war responsibilities. These were the contradictory feelings that the NAWSA brought to its 1917 convention in Washington, D.C., in December. The victories of the last year, especially New York's, were appropriately celebrated, but even these had to be muted by the uncertainties of war.[41]

At the beginning of 1918, Shaw, writing to Lucy, sensed the end of the struggle for peace and for woman suffrage. She urged Lucy to join her in putting forth their greatest efforts. "Then, wild oats for both of us in our own way the rest of our lives. We will have earned freedom from worry and can rest and go about the earth if we have anything left to do it with." Shaw sounded almost carefree and certainly exuberant with her plans to "raise chickens and potatoes and enjoy the glory of our grove and Forest of Arden, and the glorious sunsets, and the beauty of the world from Peter Pan and the upper porch, and walk up and down the lower veranda reciting snatches of poetry and singing—sing, sing for the joy of singing."[42]

On January 10, 1918, Shaw, now a Washington political insider, had lunch with Speaker of the House Champ Clark and his wife before proceeding with them to the Capitol. It was from her place in the speaker's box that she listened to the members of the House of Representatives debate the Susan B. Anthony Amendment. On this day in January, seventy years after the Seneca Falls Convention, the House of Representatives voted 274 to 136 for the Susan B. Anthony Amendment. They just made the two-thirds needed to pass the legislation for which so many women—and men—had fought for so many years. This was the first of the final three steps by which women would achieve equal citizenship. "A great day! How I wish Aunt Susan had been here and yet she must know. Heaven could not be heaven if such a thing could happen and she not know it." Next would have to come the Senate vote and states' ratification.[43]

Shaw seemed to have conflicting impulses at this point. On one hand, she was still expanding her public roles beyond her commitment to suffrage and the Woman's Committee of the National Council. On January 21, Shaw was the first woman elected to the League to Enforce Peace Executive Committee. Founded in 1914 with the goal of establishing an international organization to ensure world peace, this organization was part of a larger movement that believed war could be avoided through negotiation and mediation.[44]

On the other, she was more reflective about her life's journey. After the congressional vote she made her way to the Florence Villa cottage. As a respite from all the official business that followed her there, from all the requests for help and complaints about discrimination and inefficiencies, Shaw took some time to write to old friends such as Clara Osborn. To this dear old friend she reflected on the time that had passed since they had enjoyed the blackberry patch outside Shaw's family's cabin or smelled her mother's hop vine and sweet briar.[45]

Shaw was soon back in the North, juggling her numerous responsibilities. "May the Lord have mercy on me," was her comment to Lucy when she gave an overview of her schedule for the summer. Washington was notoriously hot and humid in the summer, and in those pre–air-conditioning days, fans could help only so much. Shaw was a diligent worker, handling the frustrating red tape and assorted bureaucracies, as she and her committee tried to find the means to make this work more efficient and to allow women's voices to be heard. In many cases Shaw herself had to be the channel through which complaints of sexist discrimination in workplaces or racist discrimination in women's war work were addressed. It was not unusual for a government official to receive a packet of letters accompanied by a note from the chair of the Woman's Committee, requesting that his agency, which had the power the Woman's Committee did not, remedy this problem. If that tactic didn't work, Shaw didn't hesitate to bring the matter to the attention of President Wilson. One example that illustrates how Shaw brought her principles to bear on this work came when the YMCA refused to hire as camp hostesses women who were Catholic or Jewish. In this case, Shaw was effective in having the war department threaten the YMCA with the suspension of this responsibility if they didn't change their policy.[46]

Over that summer Shaw continued balancing the Woman's Committee work, suffrage responsibilities, and all the domestic activities that were just as much recreation as labor to her. In her letters to Lucy or others she wrote of trying to find some few days or weekends to escape back to Moylan, where she hoped to work on her garden. She didn't even want to go to Lily Dale, where she had spoken every summer for longer than she could remember; she just wanted to be at Alnwick Lodge and complete some work on her home. The thought of that made her happy. In one letter, after discussing both war and suffrage issues, Shaw closed with, "Please get a pint of Linseed oil so as to have it when I come to mix the green paint for the veranda if I can stay long enough after the attic is done."[47]

Shaw found only a few days to work at Moylan that summer. In Washington, she was successful in working to restructure the National Defense work in ways that made women equal to men. In September of that year, all the work was brought under the direction of a six-person Field Division, and Shaw was one of its three women. It was an extraordinary accomplishment to have a governmental body with gender balance in 1918.[48]

The strain of juggling numerous jobs was wearing on other leaders also. At the end of September, Shaw found Catt fearfully depressed. There was pressure on the NAWSA because the U.S. Senate was once again set to vote on the Susan B. Anthony Amendment. The NAWSA had agreed not to have a convention this year as a war measure, but Catt felt like giving up her post and calling a convention so the NAWSA could elect a new president. Now it was Shaw's turn to support and console Catt. Even though President Wilson finally came out publicly for the Susan B. Anthony Amendment, the September 30, 1918, Senate vote was two votes short of the needed two-thirds majority.[49]

On November 11, 1918, the war came to an end, blessedly sooner than expected for so many in the United States who had feared a long and devastating conflict. In Europe the war had been so much longer and the effects incomparably greater. Even though Shaw saw that the work of the Woman's Committee should and could continue, the cessation of the fighting lightened her burden immeasurably. She had led another major struggle for women. Within a month, on December 2, 1918, President Wilson urged the country to support woman suffrage in recognition of American women's war work.[50]

As 1918 drew to a close, there was a shared sense that everyone could breathe again. The end of the war should have brought Shaw another opportunity for something resembling retirement. Of course, it didn't. She was even more fully in the public's eye than she had been before. Her schedule for the next year wasn't exactly blank. The Woman's Committee work was ongoing, and the NAWSA scheduled a Jubilee Convention to be held in St. Louis in March. Shaw had agreed to join an impressive group of people who were organizing a conference highlighting the need for a national antilynching law. Lobbying the U.S. Senate continued as suffrage supporters searched to find the votes they needed to win in that chamber; the February 10, 1919, vote in the Senate had been only one "yea" short. Shaw did stick with her commitment to attend to her health, spending time in Florida before she began her work again.

"Oh it is good to be free. I feel young again," she wrote when the Woman's Committee finally submitted their resignations, even as she acknowledged how much the war work had taken out of her. "We must get all there is in life for us the next few years," she added. Shaw seemed more relaxed than she had been for many years.[51]

It had been fifteen months since the last NAWSA National Convention. At the gathering in St. Louis, Shaw continued her usual roles, giving her invocation and presiding at sessions, but the culmination of this long struggle was so close that the meeting gave less attention to rhetoric and more to the practical details. Even in the midst of the optimism about peace and suffrage, even as Shaw was honored as a pioneer and for all her war work, Shaw felt a loneliness at this convention. The women who had been her models and mentors were gone, and she was no longer directing the struggle.[52]

Shaw continued to plan with Lucy and M. Carey Thomas for a long voyage for the next spring, yet it seemed that she had worked too long to know how to stop. In April, she toured Texas before going on to engagements in New Jersey and New York. Her friends in Europe were on her mind. For all their sakes, she hoped that the peace would be a lasting one and that the sacrifices so many had made would mean that they would never see such a conflict again. Such was her state of mind when former President Taft and Harvard President Lowell, on behalf of the League to Enforce Peace, strongly urged her to join them on a tour to help convince the nation to support the president's peace plan and the League of Nations. In the end, Shaw agreed to give three weeks, after May 20, to this tour. As pulled as she was to finding a means to guarantee a lasting peace, she had other commitments to fulfill before she undertook another speaking tour.[53]

Shaw spoke at the first National Conference on Lynching, held at Carnegie Hall, May 5 and 6, 1919. Her role and her speech added one more piece to the puzzle that is her lifelong record on race. Without a doubt this was a crucial period of time for the crusade against lynching and the struggle for racial equality. Booker T. Washington had died in 1914, and the NAACP added a new and more radical voice to the chorus of organizations of women and men who had been challenging the growth of Jim Crow. The voices of African Americans had persisted in their calls for extending the franchise, even though at various times Shaw and the white-dominated suffrage movement had turned deaf ears to their calls and for equality in the war mobilization. Shaw had spoken out on lynching and had advocated for Black women during the war, but without ever fully confronting the segregation of the South. This urgent conference, called by the NAACP, and from which they published their report, "Thirty Years of Lynching, 1889–1919," gave Shaw what would be her final opportunity to contribute to this cause.[54]

In her speech, Shaw named lynching as "public murder" and addressed the central justification given for lynching, the protection of white women's honor. She argued that "protecting womanhood is a mere camouflage for the exhibition of barbarism." Of course she, as a woman who had fought and was still fighting, for the enfranchisement of women, argued that, "If this country wants to protect its women, let them give us the power to protect ourselves." She was not afraid to state how race framed women's sexual realities, and Shaw specifically spoke of how the "colored" woman had no power to protect herself from white men.[55]

In a timely recognition of Shaw's war work, on May 19, 1919, she became the first woman to be honored with the Distinguished Service Medal, the government's highest civilian award. Informed of this honor several weeks earlier when she had received a telegram from the Secretary of War, Shaw had immediately shared this news with Lucy Anthony and M. Carey Thomas. Yet as was often the case, her thoughts turned toward her mentor, and she wished that Susan B. Anthony could be with her at this time. The photographs of the ceremony held on the steps of the State War and Navy Building, Washington, D.C., saw Shaw, distinguished not only by her sex but also by her age, surrounded by younger military men. As would be expected, Shaw had little time to revel in this honor. Soon after the ceremony, Shaw joined President Taft and Harvard President Lowell on a tour sponsored by the League to Enforce Peace.[56]

Only a few days after she joined Taft and Lowell in Illinois, Shaw fell ill. This time she didn't make it home. Again it was pneumonia that kept Shaw in a Springfield hospital for several weeks. As soon as she was minimally better, Shaw returned to Alnwick Lodge. It seemed that once again she escaped the worst.[57]

The U.S. Senate finally passed the Susan B. Anthony Amendment while Shaw was convalescing. This was the next-to-last hurdle for the issue to which Shaw had dedicated her life. The bedridden Shaw so longed to be among her sister suffragists and their allies who were rejoicing in Washington. Knowing this, Catt and others continued to write to her, urging her to rest and take care of herself while also reassuring her they knew that in spirit she was among them.[58]

By the end of June Shaw felt so much better and stronger that she was even able to write a few letters, including a surviving note to Harriet Laidlaw. On June 29, she celebrated her recovery by driving into Philadelphia to meet her friend and colleague, Caroline Reilly, who was coming for a visit. In great spirits and very much herself, Shaw was full of energy and plans, but after an evening of good company, Lucy and Caroline awoke to find that Shaw had suffered a terrible relapse on Monday, June 30. That morning she had a high fever and chills that led to a physical collapse. The next morning, Caroline Reilly reported that Shaw, with nurses in constant attendance, was resting comfortably, and her doctor assured them that she was "out of danger."[59]

On Tuesday, as Reilly maintained the vigil with Lucy, Shaw again seemed a bit better. That evening she even asked Lucy to read to her as was their custom. After only a short time Lucy saw a change. The veteran campaigner was confused. She believed that she needed to catch a train. She struggled to communicate with Lucy; it was clear that the great orator was losing her ability to speak. Shaw was increasingly frustrated and so persistent in her attempts to get up, to find her ticket and leave, that even Lucy's repeated assurances that she had time to rest before the trip couldn't calm her. Finally her doctor administered a sedative, and Shaw slept the night of July 1.[60]

Shaw regained consciousness again for only a few minutes on the morning of July 2. Lucy would not leave her side. As she saw Shaw begin to slip away, Lucy sent for other members of the family, while Caroline Reilly wrote a brief note "to Dr. Shaw's closest and dearest friends," believing that, though they hoped for the best, they should know that she was "desperately sick." With the nurses, Lucy, and Caroline there, Anna Howard Shaw breathed her last in her beloved Alnwick Lodge. "She left us at seven in the evening, looking out towards the setting sun and at her beautiful Forest of Arden, which she planted herself and loved so much."[61]

Lucy immediately sent a telegram to Shaw's longtime Michigan friend, the Rev. Caroline Bartlett Crane, asking her to come and conduct a simple memorial service. Many years before and several times since, Shaw had told Crane that she wanted her to preside at such time, but Anna had never shared this plan with Lucy. Yet Lucy knew this was what Shaw would have wanted. As Lucy, Caroline Reilly, and others from close by first contacted friends and then officials of the various organizations of which Shaw had been a part, condolences and tributes poured in from all over the country and the world. Newspapers announced the passing of this woman who had become such an admired public figure.[62]

Anna Howard Shaw was memorialized in news items, obituaries, and editorials in large and small communities across the country. On July 3, the *San Antonio Evening News* called her the "Mother of Suffrage" and devoted five articles to Shaw, accompanied by a large photograph from her last visit to that city. In Fort Wayne, Indiana, her death was on the front page. The *Trenton Evening Times* editorialized as to how womanly it was that Shaw should determinedly persist until her work was completed. Yet among the hundreds of tributes none were as powerful as those of the

New York Times, the newspaper that had for so many years been a thorn in the side of suffragists.[63]

On July 3, the *Times* announced Shaw's death in a long article that retold her life story from her immigrant childhood through her recent role in the National Conference on Lynching. They characterized her life as "remarkable as it was rare" in its dedication to human betterment. The next day, along with three articles, was an editorial tribute to Shaw as a great and genuine American. After honoring her with a comparison to Lincoln, the editorial stated,

> Her spell was not to be evaded. Even in conversation her voice had the indefinable quality which makes the orator; and no one could look into those speaking eyes, or see that majestic head, without being aware that he was in the presence of an unusual human being. Sanity, liberality, cheerfulness, and that humorous patience that one finds exemplified but seldom, except in the case of such a man as Balfour, all went to the making of a great American. Anna Howard Shaw lives in the hearts of those who knew her and in those of that far wider circle that came under the magic of her personality and character, even if it were but for an hour.[64]

At five o'clock on Saturday afternoon, July 5, 1919, the Rev. Crane presided over a simple funeral service at Alnwick Lodge. Shaw's body lay in the space she called "Peter Pan," "under a blanket of delicate rosebuds, a tribute from the National Woman Suffrage Association." Wreaths from President and Mrs. Wilson, the Council of National Defense, and the League to Enforce Peace, among others, filled not only that room but the entire home. Among family and friends, Carrie Chapman Catt, as head of the official delegation from the NAWSA, was eloquent in her moving tribute to her longtime friend and sister suffragist. The ceremony included the Twenty-third Psalm and poems by George Eliot and Alfred Lord Tennyson. As was her long time wish, her remains were cremated and scattered at Moylan.[65]

In the NAWSA pamphlet "The Passing of Anna Howard Shaw," Ida Husted Harper wrote that Shaw died of overwork and died for her country. "Dr. Shaw died in the fullness of her power and there is none to inherit it. She was seventy-two years old but her wonderful voice was as rich and musical as in her youth, and her keenness of mind and force of expression seemed to increase with every year."[66]

We have no records of how those closest to Shaw mourned her death, but soon Lucy E. Anthony, M. Carey Thomas, Harriet and James Laidlaw, and numerous others began the work of committing Shaw to history. As Lucy distributed small items that had been special to Dr. Shaw to her closest friends, a committee organized to create several memorials to her. At the Victory Convention of the National American Woman Suffrage Association,

Chicago, February 12–18, 1920, the gathering passed a resolution establishing "an official joint memorial to Dr. Anna Howard Shaw—at Bryn Mawr College a Foundation in Politics and at the Women's Medical College of Pennsylvania a Foundation in Preventive Medicine—as a fitting continuation of her lifework."[67]

Shaw's handwritten last will was quite straightforward, leaving the bulk of her estate, unusual in its size and composition, to Lucy. It took almost two years for her estate to be appraised. In February of 1921, the *New York Times* carried a very small article recording the total appraisal of $32,613 and the special bequests to her nieces and grandnieces.[68]

Though Shaw had protested that she wasn't worth one-tenth of the $30,000 the assessor had determined her estate to be in 1914, when her estate was finally settled, it was worth over that amount even without Alnwick Lodge. The largest part of her assets was in stocks. Shaw had saved well for her own and Lucy's old age. Though Lucy was not old at this point, Shaw and suffrage had been her work and her life.[69]

Lucy recorded her thoughts when she wrote on the last page of Shaw's last datebook. "ON this the last night of the last day of the year which took away my precious love—her friendship—and to serve her was the joy of my life. She was the most unselfish—the best friend one could have—in as much as I helped in the little I have to make her life easier perhaps that much am I glad I have lived."[70]

As tributes to Shaw continued over the years—a middle school in Philadelphia was named after her as was a dormitory in North Carolina—Lucy Anthony engaged Susan B. Anthony's biographer, Ida Husted Harper, to write Shaw's story. Lucy, more than anyone else, was determined that Shaw should have a biography. As had her Aunt Susan, Lucy understood that you couldn't assume that historians would write an accurate history of the struggle. Also in the family tradition, she had saved letters, clippings, and other memorabilia. Now she brought out and reread herself all the letters—six thousand of them—that Shaw had written to her over the thirty years of their relationship. Lucy was so anxious to have this biography that she invited Harper to live at Moylan as she worked on this volume, which was to be completed by the end of 1926.[71]

Unfortunately, there were various delays, and when Lucy and M. Carey Thomas finally read the working draft, they were sorely disappointed. Ida Husted Harper, now in her seventies, seemed unable to synthesize all the materials into the compelling narrative Lucy and M. Carey Thomas expected. Together they decided to end their agreement, but legal and personal complications followed. Consequently, the relationships among Anthony, Thomas, and Harper were strained, with Harper threatening to bring a suit against Anthony. Next Lucy hoped perhaps that Elizabeth Jordan, who had worked with Shaw on her autobiography, might take up the project, but that too fell through. As the 1930s proceeded, Lucy continued her search for an author for Shaw's story.[72]

Through the 1920s and 1930s Shaw held her own in the country's memory. It was during this period that suffrage pioneers wrote their own and the movement's histories, newspapers carried retrospectives, and numerous authors examined the lives of the women, including Shaw, who so contributed to the expansion of citizenship. Shaw's story was always celebrated in her hometown of Big Rapids and, also in Michigan, Albion College remembered her as their most eminent alumnus through the 1930s. Her autobiography was reprinted in 1928, and in 1929 the publisher brought out a special edition for schools.[73]

As Lucy grew older, the issue of Shaw's story weighed on her. She blamed herself for the failed Harper biography. She became so desperate that she reread and reconsidered the Harper work. Unfortunately, Lucy and Shaw's niece, Nicolas Shaw Fraser, had destroyed many of the original letters. When Lucy finally sent the remaining sources to Mary Dillon at Northwestern University, Dillon decided that they were too compromised to use as a basis for a new biography.[74]

On August 29, 1943, in the midst of another world war, the Liberty cargo ship *Anna Howard Shaw* was launched from the South Portland, Maine, shipyard. It seemed so appropriate that this ship was sponsored by the director of the U.S. Department of Labor Women's Bureau. Mary Anderson, herself a single, self-supporting woman and an immigrant, had risen through the ranks of women's organizations to hold this significant government post. Anderson recounted all of Shaw's own seagoing and war-related connections at this dedication. Her naming of this ship after Dr. Shaw with whom she had worked early in her rise to power marked the last national recognition of Anna Howard Shaw for fifty years.[75]

Within the next year, Lucy E. Anthony died, having survived Shaw by twenty-five years. Although Carrie Chapman Catt lived until 1947 and Alice Stone Blackwell until 1950, soon all their stories would begin to fade from our national memory. In a postwar era that witnessed a tremendous backlash against women generally and feminism in particular, the women who struggled for women's equality faded from the national memory. In an era that condemned as abnormal any woman who wanted more than a domestic life, few people celebrated as heroic the remarkable life of this pioneering woman and the struggle to which she had committed her life. Such erasures not only robbed women of their history, but also girls of role models who had created remarkable lives for themselves and had fought for opportunities and equality.[76]

Anna Howard Shaw and Women's History

History matters, but, as we well know, history doesn't just happen. Over the many years of researching Anna Howard Shaw, I was driven by a quest to understand not only the life of this remarkable woman but also how women's history transformed this transgressive, irreverent pioneering woman into an incompetent and conservative leader—that is, when our scholarship didn't ignore her entirely. In the end, this book argues that knowing Anna Howard Shaw's life is important for our history.[1]

It has been a long struggle to bring Shaw's story front and center. First, while Susan B. Anthony clearly had passed on to her niece, Lucy, a keen awareness that the women who had led the long fight for women's rights and suffrage would have to be responsible for writing its history, Lucy died frustrated that she had not been able to bring into print the story of the woman she called her "precious love." This problem was compounded by the fact that, as other suffragists wrote their versions of the movement, those who knew and valued Shaw's contributions remained silent. Consequently, certain perspectives, especially those of Alice Paul and her Congressional Union/National Women's Party colleagues and those of the anti-Shaw insurgents, especially Mary Gray Peck, stood relatively unquestioned. Both camps greatly influenced Eleanor Flexner, who, in turn, became the foundational source for the post-1960s scholarship. Even as the last decades of research has brought impressive breadth and depth to our understandings of women's rights activism, the strategies of the National Women's Party have continued to capture the popular imagination while Flexner's views have dominated the scholarly analyses.[2]

It is wonderful on one level that these portrayals of certain events and individuals have captured the imaginations of contemporary students, writers, and filmmakers and have renewed interest in the U.S. suffrage movement. On the other hand, when such works appear as conclusive, as if the story of women's struggle for the franchise is fully known, the process of assessing

Shaw's place (and many others') in that history and her contributions to the expansion of women's rights has been in part a fight to keep open doors that are quickly closing. This closing is especially ironic knowing that Shaw's story had greater cultural currency before the resurgence of women's history.[3]

Such concerns drove me to want to produce *the book* on Anna Howard Shaw, of course. Shaw has shadowed my life. For twenty years I have worked in the building at Albion College where Shaw lived as a student. Her name is on the door to my office; images of her are on the walls. She lived most of her adult life in my hometown of Philadelphia and frequently visited the campus where I first studied as an undergraduate. It is getting to be an old joke, among my students, family, and colleagues, that I can relate anything and everything to Anna Howard Shaw. Yet as I complete this manuscript, my hopes are more modest. I hope this biography will interrupt the repetition of questionable conclusions about Shaw and her leadership and inspire us to ask more questions about Shaw, suffrage, and late nineteenth and early twentieth century womanhood. After all this research and analysis, I am left with my own questions about her and her contributions. If this volume increases interest in Shaw and the suffrage movement and spurs more research on both, it will have made a contribution.[4]

There is more to Shaw's story than fits into this biography. There are more sources—generous colleagues forward Shaw-related finds to me regularly. There are other aspects of Shaw's work that need examinations. No doubt some historians will question the conclusions of this volume and Shaw's significance. But just having that debate will be a major step forward. What is left is considering what we gain from studying Anna Howard Shaw's life. On a very basic level, Shaw's life reminds us of the complexity of history. Although having a compelling and accessible narrative is great, it can't be at the expense of a full examination of the best data and a thorough application of relevant feminist theory.

Feminist theory demands at its most basic level the consideration of all aspects of privilege, all aspects of oppression, and all the intersections and interactions among these factors in studies of women. We have a long scholarship recognizing the distinctive paths and consciousnesses of women of color and working-class women who have overcome substantial barriers to achieve positions of influence in politics, the professions, or other arenas. Shaw's background as a woman who rose from poverty and rural isolation, her lifelong identity as a working woman, particularly as a woman who *needed* to work, and her obvious standing as a woman-identified woman, can't be ignored in evaluating her suffrage contributions.[5]

As an early and unusual "new woman," Shaw challenges simplistic ideas about gender in her era. Tracing how Shaw pushed, exploited, and expanded the accepted limits of her era's womanhoods uncovers the shifting boundaries and weaknesses of the nineteenth-century sex/gender system. In an era when imposed gender standards varied by class and race, Shaw was always caught in those tensions. Her life pushes us to consider just how complex the intersections of class, race, and sex are. Shaw had race privilege, but she had to earn the respectability that other white women gained almost automatically from marriage or class status. Using her status as an ordained minister and medical doctor to compensate, she then also cloaked her calls for change and reform in patriotic idealism. Shaw was hardly alone in her experience of early patriarchal abandonment. Her rise reveals the significance of understudied but nevertheless gendered factors such as women's own understandings of their bodies, the necessity of self-protection, and the impact of accessible and affordable transportation for women's activism. Happenstance played a role. If one Methodist elder hadn't promoted women as preachers at the same time the railroad and a public high school came to Big Rapids, Michigan, for example, Shaw's life might have taken an entirely different path.[6]

Anna Howard Shaw loved and honored women. The breadth and diversity of her relationships are obvious. And just as there is no easy term to describe Shaw's social/economic position, even today we have no adequate terms to describe who Susan B. Anthony, Lucy E. Anthony, Persis Addy, and Frances Willard were to Shaw. While analyzing sexual expression in women's lives is a significant part of lesbian and women's history, Judith Bennett argues the necessity of studying "lesbian-like" behaviors and relationships in the absence of clear data in that area. Shaw's identification of Susan B. Anthony, whom she called "Aunt" and viewed as a mother, as the emotional center of her life may seem psychologically suspect in the post-Freudian period, but it also forces a larger reconceptualization of women's, lesbians', and/or women-identified women's relationships. Since Shaw saw nothing questionable about claiming that bond, her life contests the primacy of the romantic dyad in women's lives and why same-sex relationships can't simply be conceived as some sort of parallel to heterosexual marriage. Yet, given the compromised nature of much of Shaw's correspondence, we are left wondering how Shaw conceptualized her other relationships and if her heirs' decisions to destroy her letters resulted from the midcentury morbidification of the love between women, to use Faderman's phrase.[7]

We have the document in which Shaw names Susan B. Anthony as her great "passion," but few statements describing other connections, especially her partnership with Lucy. From early in Shaw's relationship, Lucy was "home." Certainly Shaw viewed Susan B. and Lucy E. Anthony as family in an era when laws reserved that term for affiliations based on biology or marriage. Ninety years after Shaw's death, recognition of "alternative families" remains uneven at best. In most places in the United States, members of such families are still denied the legal rights and automatic benefits that accrue to state-recognized unions and units, forcing many families to use wills, powers of attorney, and other measures to claim or protect their medical decision-making powers, economic assets, and other marital and familial rights. In the early 1900s Shaw and Lucy E. Anthony were already using some of these means to safeguard their partnership, their family, and their money.

Shaw's two wills and other legal papers document her consciousness of her financial responsibilities to Lucy. They frame how clearly and strongly Shaw conceived of herself as the economic provider of her family, while demonstrating how she valued and honored Lucy as both homemaker and business partner. Shaw also sought to empower her nieces and grandnieces by providing most of them with some financial resources, especially for education. Shaw's wishes and actions show how she circumvented patriarchal assumptions and state definitions of family long before there were formal legal and political challenges. Wills are a great source for examining such intentions. More research is needed to determine how innovative Shaw was in this area and how widespread such uses of wills were. Most probably Shaw had been inspired by Mary Anthony's will that left monies to her biological niece Lucy, as well as to Shaw, whom she considered an adopted niece. A quarter-century after Shaw's death, Lucy, in turn, while leaving most of her estate to her surviving sister, also left bequests to both Anthony and Shaw nieces.[8]

Shaw's early life and her relationships with women have, at least, received some recent scholarly attention.

It is hard to overestimate how significant a problem the lack of attention is to her suffrage leadership and NAWSA presidency. Shaw was a nationally recognized leader of the suffrage movement for thirty years. She was the longest-serving president of the NAWSA. She was "conscripted" out of retirement by the U.S. President to head the first governmental entity that was by, for, and about women. At the time of her death she was a beloved elder stateswoman who was still campaigning for women, racial equality, and peace. Shaw had major influence within the NAWSA and in the public's view of suffrage and women's issues from 1888 until her death.

Yes, her tenure saw tensions, but what Flexner and most others since have ignored, is that the upheavals of Shaw's presidency were not just personality clashes or the results of incompetent leadership. A close exploration of the rich and diverse sources of the years 1904–1915 document needed change and real, measurable progress. Always deeply committed to universal and full suffrage, Shaw stood firm on this principle even as many other white suffrage leaders, northerners as well as southerners, progressives as well as conservatives, waived. One could argue that the internal strife that took place under Shaw's presidency wasn't a response to Shaw's ineffective administration, but a response to her effort to exert her power as NAWSA president, challenge the status quo, and change the organization. It is impossible to know how much of the opposition that she faced was exasperated by her status as an outsider, but the issue needs to be brought into the light. This is not to argue that Shaw didn't contribute to these conflicts. It is clear that she did not have great interpersonal skills, at least not those expected of the middle-class ladies. Even Carrie Chapman Catt, who admired Shaw, considered her "scraggy." The other side of Shaw's proudly claiming that she wasn't a lady might have been her own defensiveness around more privileged women. Shaw had to contend with a board she had inherited, which was composed of women who considered themselves her social superiors and several of whom—Avery, Upton, and probably Clay—felt they were better suited for this post than Shaw.

Should Shaw be criticized for clashing with a board that Carrie Chapman Catt described as "deadwood"? This board was hardly unified on basic principles and included at least two women, Clay and Gordon, who supported white supremacy, opposed universal suffrage, and never backed the federal amendment. Additionally, as Susan B. Anthony had predicted, this board was not loyal to Shaw. These women had resisted innovations under Carrie Chapman Catt, a much stronger organizational leader, even before challenging Shaw.

The financial demands of the suffrage efforts and the intricate web of the NAWSA monies—the official treasury, the Thomas-Garrett Fund, the various Anthony funds, and the private donations to specific individuals and to specific efforts—complicated all of the interactions among these women. Since Shaw drew her salary and expenses from these sources, only some of which were open to full scrutiny, she was vulnerable to questions of personal gain and slippery accounting from women who had never had to earn their livings or depend on waged positions. Many of these concerns came inevitably with the transition of the NAWSA from a voluntary association to a centralized, professional organization. Nevertheless, the board members felt, correctly, that their power had been undercut from the time that Susan B. Anthony began to work with M. Carey Thomas and Mary Garrett and continued as wealthy women such as Alva Belmont joined the movement and based their financial support on personal connections as much as on a dedication to the larger cause.[9]

The entire argument about whether Shaw and Catt or Paul can claim responsibility for the renewed NAWSA focus on the federal amendment is problematic only because no NAWSA president ever abandoned that focus. As her predecessors had, Shaw understood that the women needed to gain suffrage in a critical mass of states before there could be effective pressure on Congress and the president. As noted, Shaw worked to prepare the NAWSA for that transition from at least as early as 1908.

Credit for the success of the NAWSA after 1910 must also be shared among Shaw and the other officers in the headquarters, Mary Ware Dennett and Jessie Ashley, whose politics were among the most radical of the NAWSA. It is hard to reconcile the amicable relationship Shaw had with these two younger women for several important years with the tempestuous and disastrous work atmosphere that existed with Shaw, Potter, and Peck. The former seemed much more consistent with Shaw's general approach to interpersonal and working relationships. While she didn't get along with everyone and often appeared indifferent to personal feelings, she did try to keep conflicts to a minimum and often advised other suffrage workers to ignore personal slights or statements. Shaw mostly would become annoyed by what she saw as obstructionist behavior. As her confrontation with the board in 1910 illustrated, she would stand her ground, alone, when she felt she was right. She tended to be naive, assuming loyalty and trusting others, until proven wrong.

Again in contrast to many scholarly conclusions, Shaw had a plan, at least from the time she could devote herself full-time to the leadership, but she also understood and respected the power of state and local women leaders. After the first campaign that she oversaw as president—the 1906 Oregon effort—she shifted the NAWSA away from directing state work to assisting local women through training, finances, publicity and press work, and her own speeches in those states where the NAWSA had specifically been invited to contribute. As Graham argued, Shaw was committed to a democratic process and such a process is often a bit chaotic.[10]

Another commonly held view is that women such as Florence Kelley and Rachel Foster Avery left the board because Shaw was ineffectual. At this point we don't have the sources with which to answer that question. What is clear is that Shaw was a change agent whose life experiences had acclimated her to discord and adversity in the pursuit of what she knew was right. Certainly there seems to be enough evidence to indicate the overwhelmingly negative conclusions about Shaw's leadership have been premature. Shaw wasn't the perfect leader, but the growth that took place in the NAWSA after 1910 belies the accepted judgments about Shaw's leadership.

Shaw spent much more of her public life on stage than she did behind a desk. For over a quarter of a century before Alice Paul and decades before Harriot Stanton Blatch became active figures in the U.S. suffrage movement, Shaw had traveled to thousands of venues and had spoken to hundreds of thousands of people. Local newspapers furthered Shaw's reach by covering her appearances and discussing her arguments. With this knowledge suffrage and women's activism research needs to reconsider the influence of Shaw as a representative of the movement for women's rights and of the "new woman." Who Shaw was, from her sturdy matronly build to her lively, mischievous humor, contrasted with the severe earnestness of Susan B. Anthony and other well-known suffragists. Though O'Neill argues that Shaw best fulfilled the stereotype of the angry feminist, few sources support that conclusion. It makes more sense that average people across the country could identify with this hearty immigrant and daughter of the frontier.[11]

Her forte was the spoken rather than the written word, and her audiences were the average citizens rather than the intellectuals. Can we claim to understand the ideas of the woman suffrage movement without a systematic study of the content of the thousands of speeches Anna Howard Shaw gave? They are worthy of a volume in their own right. Some scholarship has excerpted certain sentences and statements—often used out of context—occasionally seriously misread, to support various analyses about the movement. On gender, motherhood, race, universal suffrage, and imperialism, to name a few topics, Shaw's positions and analyses were at odds with the putative dominant ideas among her colleagues. Given that Shaw's views probably reached more individuals through her lectures, media coverage, and NAWSA publications, what weight should they be given? Shaw's speeches and views are still a rich vein to mine.[12]

Economics remains a decidedly dry and perhaps "unsexy" topic in our history. The biographies we do have seldom give more than a cursory discussion to how these women met their basic needs, acquired wealth, or managed their monies. Horowitz's *The Passion and Power of M. Carey Thomas* and DuBois's biography of Harriot Stanton Blatch stand as two important exceptions. Nor is there much analysis of how the bases of women's financial situations influenced their attitudes toward fiscal matters. Some of the very early second-wave discussions that first named the system of heterosexism focused on its economic implications, but feminist scholarship has failed to fully continue that discussion and research. Lisa Tetrault's groundbreaking article on the postbellum lyceum hopefully will inaugurate more such analyses. We still struggle to find even the vocabulary to adequately differentiate among the varying realities and consciousnesses of married, partnered, and single women; wage-earning versus non–wage-earning women; and women with earned versus acquired wealth, just to name a few permutations. Perhaps in no other area does Shaw's life remind us to carefully examine the material realities of women's lives.[13]

Shaw's and the NAWSA'a views and actions concerning race-related matters warrant further study. First, it is clear that the complexity of such issues argues that use of the term "racist" is too blunt a term to use without qualification. It lumps together, in this case, women who were unequivocally and publically opposed to racial equality; women who ignored racial issues; and women who attempted, however inadequately or inconsistently, to change the racial landscape. Shaw refused the increasingly racist strategies of the senior southern suffragists while recruiting and promoting more moderate southern white women. In her rhetoric she called for equality for all regardless of race. Yet her actions never matched her oratory. Taking certain stands as she might have at the 1911 convention would have brought race issues out into the open in the NAWSA, but Shaw feared a race-based schism in the movement. African American women and other women of color were kept on the margins of the movement. As W. E. B. Du Bois argued then and Louise Newman argued in her 1999 book, *White Women's Rights*, the privileged cannot effectively legislate for the disenfranchised. Without women of color in leadership positions, the NAWSA and Shaw could not recognize their needs and views. Nevertheless, the 1912 NAWSA Convention in Philadelphia with Dr. Du Bois giving the keynote address showcased a very different stand than the 1903 meeting in New Orleans. We do not know how much credit Shaw deserves for Du Bois's presence, but it did take place under her leadership.[14]

There are legitimate complications for Shaw's standing in our history. With the somewhat contradictory nature of her life—both outrageous and respectable—Shaw is a difficult subject, a "disorderly woman." Her journey highlights difference, the great gulf between the womanhood of someone who had to defend herself with a gun in a dark forest in the middle of the night and a woman who has never been far enough outside of patriarchal protection to need such a weapon or such chutzpah. The fact that Shaw's early life took her so far outside of the hegemonic view of femininity is certainly linked to her ability to construct an autonomous woman's life and to lead a movement of women during a time of incredible societal change. In many ways, her standpoint—Shaw acted as if she already had all the rights and freedoms for which women were fighting—enhanced her ability to envision transforming the suffrage movement as well as determine how women could best serve the United States during the Great War.

Shaw wasn't the first woman to achieve ordination or a medical degree, nor was she even one of the earliest women speakers. She was not a theorist in the traditional sense of writing major works for publication. She was not one of the founding mothers of the suffrage movement, nor was she present when woman suffrage was finally achieved. Nevertheless she devoted her life and her outstanding abilities to the cause of woman suffrage. Denying the immensity of Shaw's contributions demands ignoring a great deal of documentation. Although one book and one view can hardly answer all the questions concerning Anna Howard Shaw's place in U.S. and woman suffrage history, hopefully this biography, by bringing new sources and new evidence into the discussion and by reframing the issues, has kept the inquiry open. Perhaps now Shaw can stand again, as she stood in her lifetime, as the embodiment of the "new woman," as the voice of the second generation of the suffrage movement, and as the true political heir of Susan B. Anthony.

NOTES ON SOURCES

The research for this book spanned eighteen years and consequently witnessed many changes in searching for and accessing sources. In the end, it combines traditional historical methods with the easier availability of certain materials, books, photographs, and public documents that are now digitized and searchable online. This essay presents the process of that research. It starts with an examination of the general sources on Shaw and, in many ways, follows my own process of uncovering and contextualizing Shaw's life. However, it is not an exhaustive discussion of all the sources used in this book.

Any discussion of Anna Howard Shaw's life must start with her autobiography, *The Story of a Pioneer* (New York: Harper and Brothers, 1915). It remains the major source for information about her family and her early years. This book isn't a traditional autobiography; Shaw did not physically write it. As discussed in Chapter 7, in 1914 Shaw dictated this series of recollections and reflections to journalist Elizabeth Jordan, who arranged and edited the material. The first part of the book is remarkably accurate given that Shaw told these stories without notes decades after the events took place. After Shaw enters the women's rights movement, however, the book follows themes rather than time. It is neither chronological nor comprehensive. A more important consideration is that Shaw "wrote" the book at the end of her NAWSA presidency and at the height of the suffrage organizing movement. It is very much a celebration of that movement and the leaders who were close to Shaw, especially Susan B. Anthony. Though Shaw mentions that there were disagreements and tensions within the movement, she is generous in her praise of all the women involved. On the other hand, some women, such as Alice Paul, are not mentioned at all. In spite of its limitations, it is a wonderful and rich source.

The collected papers of Anna Howard Shaw and Lucy E. Anthony that are part of Series X of the Mary Earhart Dillon Collection, 1863–1955 (Schlesinger Library, Radcliffe Institute, Harvard University) are the foundational materials for this biography. These 210 folders of letters, photographs, diaries, and other memorabilia cover the years from Shaw's first teaching certificates in 1865 through the launching of the SS *Anna Howard Shaw* in 1943. The

"Finding Aid" provided by the Radcliffe Institute traces the history of the collection and describes its scope and content. The guide also notes that the collection doesn't fully capture either woman's life; the original six thousand letters between Shaw and Lucy E. Anthony and one thousand between Shaw and Susan B. Anthony were eventually destroyed by Shaw's heirs.

Among the most important remaining items are Shaw's reminiscences of her early childhood. While *Story of a Pioneer* highlights the adventures of Shaw's early life, these writings recall the hard and unhappy beginnings of a sickly child. The diaries and appointment books not only trace Shaw's travels for thirty years, but they also contain records of the lectures she gave, the people she met, and, in some cases, the money she earned. Dr. Mary Jewett's recollections of Shaw in Florida give a glimpse into the rare "leisure" of Shaw's later life. Though a good section of the collection is taken up with transcriptions of Shaw's speeches, sermons, and lectures, the quality and quantity of those records are inferior to those in Linkugel's dissertation (discussed later).

The next most significant source is the unpublished biography that Ida Husted Harper, coeditor of *History of Woman Suffrage* and Susan B. Anthony biographer, wrote during the 1920s. Harper had known and worked with Shaw during Shaw's life. They also had their disagreements. After Shaw's death, Lucy E. Anthony shared with Harper all the letters and materials she had saved from her thirty-year partnership with Shaw. Harper drew liberally from these letters, so much so that parts of the draft are simply excerpts from Shaw's letters. Harper added some material related to Shaw's early life based on the stories of Lucy E. Anthony and others. The draft follows Shaw's life but continues Shaw's approach of ignoring the conflicts within the NAWSA. Though Harper never completed the book, it is a valuable source because it contains at least some parts of the many letters Shaw wrote home. The existing draft belongs to the Bentley Library of the University of Michigan.

In 1972, Ralph Wakefield Spencer wrote a dissertation on Anna Howard Shaw at the Boston University School of Theology, "Doctor Anna Howard Shaw: the evangelical feminist" (PhD Dissertation, Boston University, 1972). As his title indicates, Spencer's focus was on Shaw as a religious as well as a political figure. Nevertheless, his book considers most aspects of Shaw's life based on a considerable number and range of sources from those in Shaw's papers through newspaper articles, Methodist history, and materials from other archival collections. Spencer's analyses are impressive given that women's history had barely emerged as a field when he wrote this dissertation.

The other major bodies of work on Anna Howard Shaw are the 1960 dissertation by Wil A. Linkugel, "The Speeches of Anna Howard Shaw" (PhD, University of Wisconsin, 1960), and the 1991 book, *Anna Howard Shaw: Suffrage Orator and Social Reformer* (New York: Greenwood Press,

1991), that he wrote with Martha Watson. As scholars of rhetoric, the authors consider Shaw's speeches, sermons, and lectures. Linkugel's dissertation includes over one thousand pages of Shaw's words, a far more complete compilation than is included in her papers. They present and analyze a range of her speeches using rhetorical analyses. The focus isn't on the content of her talks, which have yet to be fully mined for insights into Shaw's positions on the issues within the women's movement and beyond.

All the photographs from Anna Howard Shaw's Papers at the Schlesinger Library have been digitized and are accessible at the Harvard Visual Information Access website, http://via.lib.harvard.edu/via/deliver/advancedsearch?_collection=via (accessed May 3, 2013). Additional collections of photographs of Shaw included those at the Library of Congress, http://lcweb2.loc.gov/pp/pphome.html (accessed May 3, 2013), Carrie Chapman Catt Albums at Bryn Mawr College, http://triptych.brynmawr.edu/cdm4/catt.php (accessed May 3, 2013), and the Laura Clay scrapbooks at the Kentucky Digital Library, http://kdl.kyvl.org/cgi/f/findaid/findaid-idx?c=kyead;idno=kukavpa46m4 (accessed June 5, 2013).

Though literate, the Shaw family hardly had the leisure or perhaps the consciousness to leave written documents such as diaries and journals for future generations. As a result, there are only public records to supplement Shaw's statements about her family's background and her early life. Through the now online British and U.S. census documents, as well as International Genealogical Index (IGI) records and other related sources available through the city records or the Tyne and Wear Archives, it is possible to verify the births/christenings, deaths, and residences of the Stott and Shaw families from Alnwick and Newcastle in Northumberland County to New Bedford, Massachusetts, onto Green Township, Michigan.

There are certain late-eighteenth- and early-nineteenth-century records from Alnwick Manuscripts online at communities.northumberland.gov.uk/Alnwick_C13.htm (accessed May 3, 2013) that further place the Stott family in this town. The 1822 history of Alnwick, William Davison's *A Descriptive and Historical View of Alnwick* (Alnwick: n.p., 1822) fills in additional details. Unfortunately, beyond the census, the Shaws didn't leave many records in Newcastle. Visits to both Alnwick and Newcastle provided a clearer sense of the geography of this area and the locations in Newcastle of the Shaw residences. The ship's manifest documents the family's voyage from Liverpool to New York (Records of the U.S. Customs Service, National Archives).

In Lawrence, Massachusetts, the Immigrant City Archives holds the city directories, maps, and histories from the years the Shaws lived there. Especially important is the description of the public school system in Maurice B. Dorgan's *History of Lawrence, Massachusetts* (Lawrence, Mass.: The author, 1924). Though it wasn't possible to locate the Shaw home in Lawrence, the school Shaw probably attended is still standing (personal observation by author).

The log cabin that housed the Shaw family for twelve years in Green Township, Michigan, no longer stands, but the land that belonged to the family can be identified by the Bureau of Land Management Records and maps available at the Mecosta County Historical Museum. This organization also houses records about the area's development and the growth of its educational system. The Civil War records that trace the enlistments and service of Shaw's father and brothers are online and available at www.ancestry.com (accessed May 3, 2013). Shaw's papers include her teaching certificates for Mecosta County after 1865. The earliest photographs of Anna Howard Shaw are part of Harvard University Library's Visual Information Access system.

Anna Howard Shaw left an increasingly durable mark on institutional and other records once she became a public figure. The first of these were quite local. After her teaching certificates came her licensing as a local preacher recorded in the Big Rapids District Methodist Church Records and her attendance at Albion College (United Methodist Church Archives and Albion College Archives, Albion College). Her papers contain her first sermons as well as the earliest letters between Shaw and her lifelong friend, Clara Osborn.

Similarly, Boston University School of Theology Library houses documentation from Shaw's years there, including a copy of her thesis, as well as the records of the Hingham parish where she served during her last year of seminary and of Anna Oliver's petition for ordination. Official papers concerning Shaw's efforts for ordination are in her papers. Drew University Archives house the records from the 1880 Annual Conference of the Methodist Episcopal Church. Shaw left the story of her ordination in two forms; the first is in her autobiography and the second and more extensive version is the one she told young activist, Ray Costelloe, now part of the Shaw Papers.

There are few records concerning Persis Crowell Addy and her father, Prince Crowell, though East Dennis has reconstructed his family home. Jim Coogan's *Sail Away Ladies: Stories of Cape Cod Women in the Age of Sail* (East Dennis, Mass.: Harvest Home Books, 2003) recounts the story of Addy's marriage and honeymoon. She and her family members are buried in the Dennis Quivet Cemetery (personal observation).

In his dissertation, Ralph Spencer included a thorough analysis of Shaw's pastoral efforts at the Wesleyan Methodist Church in East Dennis that complements Shaw's account in her autobiography. The Congregational Church in Dennis, now the Dennis Union Church, houses Shaw's Communion Service (personal observation) and keeps her memory alive. Rev. Elaine Buker provided this author with a number of programs and newspaper articles that commemorate Shaw's work on Cape Cod.

The most useful secondary sources on Shaw for this early period are Beverly Ann Zink-Sawyer's *From Preachers to Suffragists: Woman's Rights and Religious Conviction in the Lives of Three Nineteenth-Century American Clergywomen*, 1st ed. (Louisville: Westminster John Knox Press, 2003) and Mary D. Pellauer's *Toward a Tradition of Feminist Theology: The Religious Social Thought of Elizabeth Cady Stanton, Susan B. Anthony, and Anna Howard Shaw* (Chicago Studies in the History of American Religion, Brooklyn, N.Y.: Carlson, 1991). There are also important works that discuss the emergence of the Lyceum and Chautauqua movements and women as public speakers: J. Matthew Gallman, *America's Joan of Arc: The Life of Anna Elizabeth Dickinson* (New York: Oxford University Press, 2006); John R. McKivigan, *Forgotten Firebrand: James Redpath and the Making of Nineteenth-Century America* (Ithaca: Cornell University Press, 2008); and Angela G. Ray, "What Hath She Wrought? Woman's Rights and the Nineteenth-Century Lyceum" (*Rhetoric & Public Affairs* 9, no. 2 [2006]: 183–213).

The important scholarly works that provide the context for analyzing Shaw's relationships and personal life include Estelle Freedman's "Separatism as Strategy: Female Institution Building and American Feminism, 1870–1930" (*Feminist Studies* 5, no. 3 [1979]: 512–529) and Kathryn Kish Sklar's "Hull House in the 1890s: A Community of Women Reformers" (*Signs* 10, no. 4 [1985]: 658–677) on the importance of networks for women activists; Carroll Smith-Rosenberg's *Disorderly Conduct: Visions of Gender in Victorian America*, 1st ed. (New York: A. A. Knopf, 1985) and this author's *Spinsters and Lesbians: Independent Womanhood in the United States* (New York: New York University Press, 1996) on single and "new women"; and John D'Emilio and Estelle Freedman's *Intimate Matters: A History of Sexuality in America*, 1st ed. (New York: Harper and Row, 1988) and Leila Rupp's *Sapphistries: A Global History of Love between Women* (Intersections, New York: New York University Press, 2009) on women's intimate relationships.

Central to the next period of Anna Howard Shaw's life was her struggle to find what she felt was the best use of her talents. Her attendance and graduations from Boston University School of Medicine Medical School, as well as the history of that institution, are online at http://www.bumc.bu.edu/busm/BUSM-About.html and http://www.homeoint.org/history/king/3–05.htm (both accessed May 3, 2013). Flyers from her papers (Anna Howard Shaw, Dillon Collection) record her interactions with the leading women's rights activists from Boston. Most important for this transition from a pastor to a full-time lecturer and activist are the letters between Shaw and the different members of the Stone-Blackwell family. Newspapers articles that place Shaw in Michigan during some of this time as well as letters from

Frances Willard, Mary Livermore, and Clara Barton attest to her efforts to launch her career beyond Massachusetts. These letters note the tensions between Shaw and the Massachusetts Woman Suffrage Association leaders. Those from Frances Willard reveal the contrasting ease of that friendship. Basic information on these women is contained in Edward T. James, Janet Wilson James, Paul S. Boyer, and College Radcliffe's *Notable American Women, 1607–1950: A Biographical Dictionary* (Cambridge, Mass.: Belknap Press of Harvard University Press, 1971). Additionally, biographies of Willard and Livermore place these women in U.S. history: Ruth Bordin and Birgitta Anderson, *Frances Willard: A Biography* (Chapel Hill: University of North Carolina Press, 1986); and Wendy Hamand Venet, *A Strong-Minded Woman: The Life of Mary Livermore* (Amherst: University of Massachusetts Press, 2005).

After Shaw met Susan B. Anthony and Lucy E. Anthony, Shaw's work begins to be recorded in *The History of Woman Suffrage* and documented in the correspondence among these women. The surviving letters and fragments of the letters among these women attest to the almost instantaneous commitment Shaw made to the elder Anthony, even as they struggled to work out the details of their affiliation. Concurrently, these letters trace the complex relationship between Shaw and Lucy E. Anthony. Ida Husted Harper's biography of Anthony, *The Life and Work of Susan B. Anthony* (Indianapolis: Hollenbeck Press, 1908) includes additional relevant material.

Susan B. Anthony's papers from this period are at the Library of Congress (Susan B. and Mary S. Anthony Papers, 1846–1934, Library of Congress). Anthony's letters and particularly her diaries shed light on her gradual withdrawal from the most active parts of the NAWSA work and her reliance on her younger lieutenants, especially Shaw. Nevertheless both Anthony's and Shaw's own diaries contradict Shaw's statement in her autobiography that she and Anthony were hardly separated after they met. These papers also record Anthony's financial matters.

Although no other letters can compensate for those that were destroyed, the intact correspondence of nearly two years between Shaw and Harriet Cooper are important (Sarah Brown Ingersoll Cooper Papers, 1813–1921, Ithaca, N.Y., Division of Rare and Manuscript Collections, Cornell University Library). They chronicle the California campaign in a way that demonstrates the key role Shaw played in it, how she and Susan B. Anthony developed strategies, and how Shaw actively and aggressively recruited other leaders such as Carrie Chapman Catt and Mary Hay to work in California. On other levels they record Shaw's concerns for how monies were spent and her determination that her own work be self-supporting rather than a drain on the California suffrage organizations. Because Shaw was also trying to mentor Harriet Cooper, these letters show the delicate line that women had to maintain between intimate friendships and political relationships. Further, these letters also cover the time when Shaw lost both of her parents and had her first recorded bout with pneumonia. They follow her recovery at her summer cottage in Wianno. Because Shaw describes her daily life we have a glimpse of her nontraditional life and physical regime at The Haven, as well as her life in Philadelphia.

Similarly, Shaw's attitudes toward U.S. colonization of Cuba emerge in her letters to "Home Folks," from her 1901–1902 Caribbean trip (Anna Howard Shaw, Dillon Collection) and are congruent with those of her "White Man's Burden" speech (in Linkugel, "Speeches").

The records from Shaw's land dealings on Cape Cod are online and available from the Barnstable County Offices in Barnstable, Massachusetts. The Osterville Historical Society has several books that describe the history of this area and the development of the section named Wianno. There is also information online about the home Anna and Lucy shared with Rachel Foster Avery in Somerton, Pennsylvania. It is possible to trace at least some of the homes Shaw and Lucy rented in Philadelphia. Approximately half of them are still standing, and it is possible to see the progression from row homes through the spacious Mt. Airy twin that was their last rental (personal observation).

The increasingly large number of newspaper articles about Shaw's appearances argues that she was well known by the beginning of the last decade of the nineteenth century (Anna Howard Shaw Papers). Letters from Carrie Chapman Catt during this period of apprenticeship for both future NAWSA presidents record their respect for each other. Catt importantly addresses the already emerging jealousy of some older suffrage workers toward this younger "star."

Anna Julia Cooper's much discussed response to Shaw's speech, "Woman versus the Indian," marks the beginning of Shaw's long struggle with the issue of racism within the nation and the NAWSA: Anna J. Cooper, Charles C. Lemert, and Esme Bhan, *The Voice of Anna Julia Cooper: Including a Voice from the South and Other Important Essays, Papers, and Letters, Legacies of Social Thought* (Lanham, Md.: Rowman and Littlefield, 1998); and Vivian M. May, "Thinking from the Margins, Acting at the Intersections: Anna Julia Cooper's a Voice from the South" (*Hypatia* 19, no. 2 [2004]: 74–91).

After Anna Howard Shaw was elected President of the National American Woman Suffrage Association, the quantity and quality of sources about her changed dramatically. While the research for the first part of this biography often involved searching for any available sources, for the rest of the book the process meant sorting through a tremendous range of materials and making choices about which were the most important.

In addition to all the materials in her own papers, important sources covering the earliest days of Shaw's NAWSA presidency include the Ella Hawley Crossett Papers (Susan B. Anthony Memorial, Inc., "Susan B. Anthony Memorial, Inc., Papers, 1834–1960," University of Rochester Special Collections), which contains both the official letters Shaw sent to all state suffrage presidents as well as more personal letters. The NAWSA Papers (Library of Congress), Catherine Waugh McCulloch's papers (Dillon Collection, Schlesinger Library), and the Laura Clay Papers (University of Kentucky) contain materials that span these years. McCulloch's correspondence is significant because she was an independent voice in the movement. Clay's records include numerous letters from Kate Gordon, Harriet Taylor Upton, and other leaders, as well as memorabilia related to the issues of Southern white suffragists.

After Susan B. Anthony's death in 1906, M. Carey Thomas emerged as Shaw's closest colleague in the movement. Though Thomas edited her papers before her death (M. Carey Thomas Papers, Bryn Mawr College Special Collections), breaks in the suffrage-related materials in this collection aren't obvious. What remains is the largest intact collection of letters to and from Anna Howard Shaw, covering 1906 to her death in 1919 and really beyond, because Thomas was involved in establishing memorials for Shaw and efforts to publish a biography. These are the best sources for tracing Shaw's political decisions and personal feelings over these years of her leadership, especially her dealings with other NAWSA officers after the 1910 board turnover.

The Thomas collection records how Thomas and her partner, Mary Garrett, handled the fund-raising that became the Thomas-Garrett Fund. All the related personal and business correspondences track Shaw's money-related concerns. Thomas's letters to other women working in the NAWSA as well as those to Shaw document the roles she played—the official one as head of the College Equal Suffrage League (CESL) in the movement as well as the unofficial ones as advisor and sometime "manager" for Shaw.

Though hardly as extensive, the letters from Carrie Chapman Catt to Mary Gray Peck (Carrie Chapman Catt Papers, Manuscript Division, Library of Congress, Washington, D.C.) were invaluable for their insights into the Peck-led anti-Shaw "insurgency" as well as for Catt's candid analyses of Shaw's and Thomas's actions during the important transitional period, 1909 to 1911. Similarly, the letters from the Garrison Family Papers, Isabel Howland Papers, and Annie Porritt Papers (Sophia Smith Collection, Smith College, Northampton, Mass.) shed light on financial concerns, racial issues, and political splits in the NAWSA.

The Mary Ware Dennett, Frances Squire Potter, Harriet Burton Laidlaw Papers (Schlesinger Library, Radcliffe Institute, Harvard University) are among the collections that reveal significant aspects of Shaw's presidency.

The Potter Papers give more background on Frances Squire Potter and Mary Gray Peck with whom Shaw had the most far-reaching internal conflict. Mary Ware Dennett replaced Potter as Corresponding Secretary in 1910. Though the one biography of Dennett, Constance M. Chen's *"The Sex Side of Life:" Mary Ware Dennett's Pioneering Battle for Birth Control and Sex Education* (New York: New Press, 1996) highlights Dennett's eventual break with Shaw, her letters document four extremely productive years, 1910–1914, of NAWSA growth and success, much of which must be credited to Dennett's talents, her hard work, and her ability to translate Shaw's visions into actions. Laidlaw's records trace another political friendship that grew during the last years of Shaw's leadership. Shaw had confided in Dennett for many years, but after their 1914 conflict, Harriet Laidlaw assumed more of that role. The NAWSA-related letters in Jane Addams's papers (Jane Addams Papers, 1860–1960, Swarthmore, Pa., Peace Collection, Swarthmore College Special Collections) are few, but they note the longer relationship between M. Carey Thomas and Addams and the rather minimal connection between Shaw and Addams, supporting the idea that Thomas engineered Addams's 1911 election as NAWSA vice president.

The official correspondence, National American Woman Suffrage Association Records (Manuscript Division, Library of Congress, Washington, D.C.) contains both the tedious and the remarkable discussions among the NAWSA officers and particularly the state presidents. Though the Library of Congress theoretically houses copies of all the extant *Proceedings* of the annual conventions of the NAWSA, they are more easily accessed at the Schlesinger Library.

Many private and public holdings of materials concerning the later years of the suffrage movement contain at least some letters by or about Shaw. Although researchers have identified many of these sources, it was not possible to examine all of them for this biography. On the other hand, the searchable databases of the *New York Times* (Proquest.com) and the *Washington Post* (via Ancestry.com) eased tracking the coverage of both Shaw's work and that of the rest of the movement (both websites accessed May 3, 2013).

From the 1890s until her death, Anna Howard Shaw was part of the international women's movement via first the International Council of Women and then the International Suffrage Alliance. Rupp's *Worlds of Women: The Making of an International Women's Movement* (Princeton, N.J.: Princeton University Press, 1997) and Bosch's *Politics and Friendship: Letters from the International Woman Suffrage Alliance, 1902–1942* (Columbus: Ohio State University Press, 1990) cover Shaw's roles in the politics and friendships of these organizations.

In addition to the works by and about Anna Julia Cooper discussed above, Terborg-Penn's *African American Women in the Struggle for the Vote, 1850–1920*

Blacks in the Diaspora (Bloomington: Indiana University Press, 1998) remains the most complete discussion of African American women's organizing for the franchise. Giddings's recent *Ida: A Sword among Lions: Ida B. Wells and the Campaign against Lynching* (New York: Amistad, 2008) covers Wells's work on women's issues. W. E. B. Du Bois devoted several issues of the *Crisis*, published by the National Association for the Advancement of Colored People (NAACP), to discussions of woman suffrage (June 1912, September 1912, and November 1917). While there are other writings on this topic, these are the most significant.

Similarly, Spruill's *New Women of the New South: The Leaders of the Woman Suffrage Movement in the Southern States* (New York: Oxford University Press, 1993) is the foundational text on the white women suffragists from the Southern states. Mead's *How the Vote Was Won: Woman Suffrage in the Western United States, 1868–1914* (New York: New York University Press, 2004) brings new research and analyses to the work in the west. Hoganson's "'As Badly Off as the Filipinos': U.S. Women's Suffragists and the Imperial Issue at the Turn of the Twentieth Century" (*Journal of Women's History* 13, no. 2 [2001]: 9) examines how suffrage leaders differed in their responses to American imperialism.

The primary and secondary sources on Shaw and U.S. women generally during World War I are strong. The National Archives has microfilmed the minutes of the Woman's Committee of the Council for National Defense. Emily Blair's *The Woman's Committee United States Council of National Defense: An Interpretative Report* (Washington, D.C.: Government Printing Office, 1920) summarizes the Woman's Committee's work. In her *Frontiers* article and her thesis, Barbara R. Finn analyzes Shaw's leadership in "Anna Howard Shaw and Women's Work" (*Frontiers: A Journal of Women Studies* 4, no. 3 [1979]: 21–25); and "The Thought of Anna Howard Shaw as Reflected in Her Correspondence as Chairman of the Woman's Committee of the National Council of Defense, 1917–1918" (Thesis, George Washington University, 1978). Brownell's "The Woman's Committees of the First World War: Women in Government, 1917–1919" (PhD Dissertation, Brown University, 2002) covers the women's committees generally. Steinson, in *American Women's Activism in World War I* (New York: Garland Publishers, 1982), and Jensen, in *Mobilizing Minerva: American Women in the First World War* (Urbana: University of Illinois Press, 2008), consider women's activism and mobilization.

Shaw's will, the deeds for Alnwick Lodge, Lucy E. Anthony's will, and related maps and materials were obtained from the Delaware County Courthouse in Media, Pennsylvania, or through the Delaware County Archives in Lima, Pennsylvania. Rachel Foster Avery's will was found in the Bucks County Courthouse in Doylestown, Pennsylvania.

The foundational histories of the U.S. suffrage movement remain the early works of Flexner, in *Century of Struggle: The Woman's Rights Movement in the United States* (Cambridge: Belknap Press of Harvard University Press, 1959); Kraditor, in *The Ideas of the Woman Suffrage Movement, 1890–1920* (New York: Norton, 1981); and O'Neill, *Everyone Was Brave: A History of Feminism in America* (New York: Quadrangle/The New York Times Book Co., 1976). Sara Hunter Graham's *Woman Suffrage and the New Democracy* (New Haven: Yale University Press, 1996) is tremendously important for Shaw scholarship because it was the first publication to argue that Shaw's presidency was not the doldrums but the beginning of a "suffrage renaissance." Others who have begun to revise the suffrage narrative are Ellen Carol DuBois's *Harriot Stanton Blatch and the Winning of Woman Suffrage* (New Haven.: Yale University Press, 1997) and Michael McGerr's "Political Style and Women's Power, 1830–1930" (*Journal of American History* 77, no. 3 [1990]: 864–885).

NOTES

Introduction

1. "ANNA HOWARD SHAW," New York Times (1857–Current file), July 4, 1919, 6, http://0-www.proquest.com.library.albion.edu/ (accessed December 3, 2009).

2. Anna Howard Shaw, *The Story of a Pioneer* (New York: Harper and Brothers, 1915), 74–80.

3. Carrie Chapman Catt and Nettie Rogers Schuler, *Woman Suffrage and Politics: the Inner Story of the Suffrage Movement* (New York: C. Scribner's, 1926), 268.

4. Shaw, *Story of a Pioneer*.

5. Trisha Franzen, "Singular Leadership: Anna Howard Shaw, Single Women and the U.S. Woman Suffrage Movement," *Women's History Review* 17, no. 3 (2008).

6. Shaw receives critical attention in the three early books on the movement: Eleanor Flexner, *Century of Struggle: The Woman's Rights Movement in the United States* (Cambridge: Belknap Press of Harvard University Press, 1959); Aileen S. Kraditor, *The Ideas of the Woman Suffrage Movement, 1890–1920* (New York: Norton, 1981); and William L. O'Neill, *Everyone Was Brave: A History of Feminism in America* (New York: Quadrangle/The New York Times Book Co., 1976). There have been very few history articles on Shaw, and she is absent from many recent books on the suffrage movement. See, for example, Linda K. Kerber, Alice Kessler-Harris, and Kathryn Kish Sklar, *U.S. History as Women's History: New Feminist Essays*, Gender & American Culture (Chapel Hill: University of North Carolina Press, 1995); and Louise Michele Newman, *White Women's Rights: The Racial Origins of Feminism in the United States* (New York: Oxford University Press, 1999). Two books on the international women's movement give Shaw more attention. See Leila J. Rupp, *Worlds of Women: The Making of an International Women's Movement* (Princeton, N.J.: Princeton University Press, 1997); and Mineke Bosch with Annemarie Kloosterman, eds., *Politics and Friendship: Letters from the International Woman Suffrage Alliance, 1902–1942* (Columbus: Ohio State University Press, 1990). Other major works on Shaw have focused on her rhetorical style or religion. See Wil A. Linkugel and Martha Watson, *Anna Howard Shaw: Suffrage Orator and Social Reformer*, Great American Orators, No. 10 (New York: Greenwood Press, 1991); Mary D. Pellauer, *Toward a Tradition of Feminist Theology: The Religious Social Thought of Elizabeth Cady Stanton, Susan B. Anthony, and Anna Howard Shaw*, Chicago Studies in the History of American Religion (Brooklyn, N.Y.: Carlson, 1991); and Beverly Ann Zink-Sawyer, *From Preachers to Suffragists: Woman's Rights and Religious Conviction in the Lives of Three Nineteenth-Century American Clergywomen*, 1st ed. (Louisville, Ky.: Westminster John Knox Press, 2003). On the issue of Shaw's marginalization,

see, for example, Jean H. Baker, *Votes for Women: The Struggle for Suffrage Revisited*, Viewpoints on American Culture (Oxford: Oxford University Press, 2002); and Catherine Lunardini and Christine A. Clinton, *The Columbia Guide to American Women in the Nineteenth Century*, Columbia Guides to American History and Cultures (New York: Columbia University Press, 2000).

7. Trisha Franzen, *Spinsters and Lesbians: Independent Womanhood in the United States* (New York: New York University Press, 1996).

8. Sara Hunter Graham, *Woman Suffrage and the New Democracy* (New Haven: Yale University Press, 1996); Michael McGerr, "Political Style and Women's Power, 1830–1930," *Journal of American History* 77, no. 3 (1990); Kimberly Jensen, "'Neither Head nor Tail to the Campaign': Esther Pohl Lovejoy and the Oregon Woman Suffrage Victory of 1912," *Oregon Historical Quarterly* 108, no. 3 (2007); and Rebecca J. Mead, *How the Vote Was Won: Woman Suffrage in the Western United States, 1868–1914* (New York: New York University Press, 2004).

9. Most of the stories from Shaw's childhood come from her autobiography or other writings. No members of her family left memoirs of any type. Public documents can verify the basics of her family's life, but there are no personal sources to support Shaw's views of life before Albion College except Clara Osborn's letters and interviews.

10. Sara Alpern, *The Challenge of Feminist Biography: Writing the Lives of Modern American Women*, Women in American History (Urbana: University of Illinois Press, 1992); Susan Ware, "The Book I Couldn't Write: Alice Paul and the Challenge of Feminist Biography," *Journal of Women's History* 24, no. 2 (2012): 13–36, http://o-muse.jhu.edu.library.albion.edu/ (accessed July 5, 2012); and Helen Lefkowitz Horowitz, *The Power and Passion of M. Carey Thomas* (New York: Alfred A. Knopf, 1994).

11. Early in the reemergence of women's history, Lerner went so far as to state that Shaw "represented the very essence of middle-class respectability." Gerda Lerner, *The Woman in American History* (Menlo Park, Calif.: Addison-Wesley Publishing Co., 1971), 161. On how whiteness determined the basic direction of the women's movement, see Newman, *White Women's Rights*.

12. Anna Howard Shaw to Eleanor Garrison, December 11, 1911, Garrison Family Papers, 1694–2005, MS 60, Box 127, File 13, Sophia Smith Collection, Smith College, Northampton, Massachusetts. Some of the contradictions between Shaw's public persona and her life can be seen in the contrasting conclusions of Faderman and Watson. Lillian Faderman, "Acting 'Woman' and Thinking 'Man': The Ploys of Famous Female Inverts," *GLQ: A Journal of Lesbian and Gay Studies* 5, no. 3 (1999); and Martha Watson, *Lives of Their Own: Rhetorical Dimensions in Autobiographies of Women Activists*, Studies in Rhetoric/Communication (Columbia: University of South Carolina Press, 1999).

13. Nancy F. Cott et al., "Considering the State of U.S. Women's History," *Journal of Women's History* 15, no. 1 (2003); Ellen Carol DuBois, *Woman Suffrage and Women's Rights* (New York: New York University Press, 1998); and Franzen, "Singular Leadership." Lisa Tetrault provides an important expansion of this discussion, arguing that even "middle-class" suffragists struggled financially. Lisa Tetrault, "The Incorporation of American Feminism: Suffragists and the Postbellum Lyceum," *Journal of American History* 96, no. 4 (2010).

14. Flexner discusses Shaw's early hardships and O'Neill notes that both Shaw and Charlotte Perkins Gilman were raised in poverty. Flexner, *Century of Struggle*, 106; and O'Neill, *Everyone Was Brave*, 141.

15. Linkugel and Watson, *Anna Howard Shaw*.

16. For discussions of "new women" and ever-single women, see Carroll Smith-Rosenberg, *Disorderly Conduct: Visions of Gender in Victorian America* (New York: Oxford University Press, 1985); June Sochen, *The New Woman: Feminism in Green-wich Village, 1910–1920* (New York: Quadrangle Books, 1972); Joanne J. Meyerowitz, *Women Adrift: Independent Wage Earners in Chicago, 1880–1930*, Women in Culture and Society (Chicago: University of Chicago Press, 1988); Kathy Lee Peiss, *Cheap Amusements: Working Women and Leisure in Turn-of-the-Century New York* (Phila-delphia: Temple University Press, 1986); Kathryn Kish Sklar, "Hull House in the 1890's: A Community of Women Reformers," *Signs: Journal of Women in Society and Culture* 10, no. 4 (1985): 658–677; Lee Virginia Chambers-Schiller, *Liberty, a Better Husband: Single Women in America: The Generations of 1780–1840* (New Haven: Yale University Press, 1984); and Trisha Franzen, "Rehabilitating Anna: The Remarkable Life of the Rev. Dr. Anna Howard Shaw," Singlewomen Seminar, 14th Berkshire Conference on the History of Women, Minneapolis, Minnesota, June 15, 2008.

17. Leila J. Rupp, *Sapphistries: A Global History of Love between Women*, Inter-sections (New York: New York University Press, 2009), 200. Ginzberg states, in her recent biography of Elizabeth Cady Stanton, that Susan B. Anthony similarly headed a family, providing a home and singlehandedly supporting her mother and sister. Lori D. Ginzberg, *Elizabeth Cady Stanton: An American Life* (New York: Hill and Wang, 2009), 140. However, Anthony scholars document a different ar-rangement. Records show that Lucy Read Anthony, after Anthony's father died, had purchased the home with the proceeds from the sale of the family farm (Judith E. Harper, *Susan B. Anthony: A Biographical Companion*, ABC-CLIO Biographical Companion (Santa Barbara, Calif.: ABC-CLIO, 1998), 19. The National Susan B. Anthony Museum and House website states that Mary then bought the house from her mother in 1873, http://susanbanthonyhouse.org/timeline.php (accessed April 14, 2013). Further most sources state that Mary S. Anthony was a longtime schoolteacher and public school principal who worked until 1883, after her mother's death. Harper, *Susan B. Anthony*, 19; and Kathleen Barry, *Susan B. Anthony: A Bi-ography of a Singular Feminist* (New York: New York University Press, 1988), 222. My own reading of Susan B. Anthony's diaries at the Library of Congress gave me the impression that Mary had worked and had her own money (Susan B. Anthony, and Mary S. Anthony, "Susan B. Anthony Papers, 1846–1934," Library of Congress).

18. Bederman argues that "manliness" was replaced by "masculinity" during this time period. It makes sense that something similar occurred with "womanliness." Gail Bederman, *Manliness & Civilization: A Cultural History of Gender and Race in the United States, 1880–1917*, Women in Culture and Society (Chicago: University of Chicago Press, 1996).

19. Shaw, *Story of a Pioneer*, 55; Angela G. Ray, "What Hath She Wrought? Wom-an's Rights and the Nineteenth-Century Lyceum," *Rhetoric & Public Affairs* 9, no. 2 (2006): 183–214; and Beverly Ann Zink-Sawyer, "The Preachers and the Suffragists: The Role of Preachers in the Ideological Transformation of the Woman Suffrage Movement in the United States" (PhD Dissertation, Vanderbilt University, 1997).

While Shaw voted for the anti-*Woman's Bible* resolution, it is hard to find out what role she played in the controversy beyond that.

20. Wil A. Linkugel, "The Speeches of Anna Howard Shaw" (PhD Dissertation, University of Wisconsin, 1960); and Linkugel and Watson, *Anna Howard Shaw*.

21. For Anderson, O'Reilly, and Newman, see Franzen, *Spinsters and Lesbians*. Both Cooper and Bethune were married, but both marriages were short and didn't really bring either woman many economic benefits. In her 1991 article, Gordon discusses the higher rate of marriage among Black reform leaders than among white reformers. Linda Gordon, "Black and White Visions of Welfare: Women's Welfare Activism, 1890–1945," *Journal of American History* 78, no. 2 (1991): 559–590. Additionally Brown found that Black women had greater solidarity across class lines than white women did during the post–Civil War era. Elsa Barkley Brown, "To Catch a Vision of Freedom: Reconstructing Southern Black Women's Political History, 1865–1880," in *Unequal Sisters: A Multicultural Reader in US Women's History*, eds. Vicki L. Ruiz and Ellen Carol DuBois, 3d ed. (New York: Routledge, 2000).

22. Not surprisingly given her era, there are many contradictions in Shaw's public and private writings and actions concerning race. Many of her most obviously racist comments have been analyzed in books such as Rosalyn Terborg-Penn, *African American Women in the Struggle for the Vote, 1850–1920*, Blacks in the Diaspora (Bloomington: Indiana University Press, 1998), 115, 116–117, 126; and Barbara Hilkert Andolsen, *"Daughters of Jefferson, Daughters of Bootblacks": Racism and American Feminism* (Macon, Ga: Mercer University Press, 1986). Few scholars have acknowledged her antiracist and anti-imperialist positions, statements or actions. See, for example, Kristin Hoganson, "'As Badly Off as the Filipinos': U.S. Women's Suffragists and the Imperial Issue at the Turn of the Twentieth Century," *Journal of Women's History* 13, no. 2 (2001); and Flexner, *Century of Struggle*, 219. Throughout her life, Shaw was engaged in discussions over race. See, for example, Anna Howard Shaw to Lucy E. Anthony, November. 20, 1903, Anna Howard Shaw Papers, Folder 506; and Anna Howard Shaw, "Votes for All: A Symposium," *Crisis* 15 (November 1917): 19.

23. Kraditor, *Ideas of the Woman Suffrage Movement*, 8.

24. Interestingly, in *Alice Paul and the American Suffrage Campaign*, the authors argued that Alice Paul had been neglected until twenty years ago. Katherine H. Adams and Michael L. Keene (Urbana: University of Illinois Press, 2008), xi–xix. Using simple quantitative measures such as counting findings each applicable decade up to 2003 from FirstSearch, WorldCat, and American History and Life, I found that Alice Paul had been neglected until about 1970, but that Elizabeth Cady Stanton and Anna Howard Shaw had also received little scholarly attention. Since 1970, Susan B. Anthony and Elizabeth Cady Stanton appeared the most in these searches. Shaw, Paul, and Carrie Chapman Catt appeared significantly less frequently, but there was no significant difference among them. A simple WorldCat search shows that Anna Howard Shaw has 18 (or 20 percent) fewer references than Alice Paul and 62 (or 47 percent) fewer references than Carrie Chapman Catt. Perhaps the easiest method for quantifying the research on Shaw is by noting that there is no biography of her, though there was a children's book about her published in 2001. Don Brown, *A Voice from the Wilderness: The story of Anna Howard Shaw* (Boston: Houghton-Mifflin, 2001). Other recent books that focus on Shaw have been in the fields of rhetoric or religion.

25. Flexner, *Century of Struggle*, 237–239, 248–249.

26. Ibid., 249, 258. There is no smoking gun among Flexner's papers, but over the course of my research, it became clear that Flexner's views were very similar to those of Mary Gray Peck, one of the surviving suffrage leaders Flexner interviewed during her research. While Flexner recognized that Peck was far from objective, and was, by the time she spoke with her, "on the verge of losing her marbles," she only conceded how much Peck adored Carrie Chapman Catt, not her animosity toward Shaw. As noted in Chapter 6, Peck ignored or underplayed Shaw's contributions to the movement to an "appalling"—to use Catt's term—degree. Yet Flexner didn't acknowledge this and how this attitude may have tainted Peck's overall assessment of the movement. Eleanor Flexner Papers, 1895?-1995, item description, dates, 73-65—89-M152, Folders 6 and 57, Schlesinger Library, Radcliffe Institute, Harvard University, Cambridge, Massachusetts.

27. Kraditor, *Ideas of the Woman Suffrage Movement*, 9; Flexner, *Century of Struggle*, 248; and O'Neill, *Everyone Was Brave*, 120–121.

28. Marjorie Julian Spruill, *New Women of the New South: The Leaders of the Woman Suffrage Movement in the Southern States* (New York: Oxford University Press, 1993), 136; Ellen Carol DuBois, *Harriot Stanton Blatch and the Winning of Woman Suffrage* (New Haven: Yale University Press, 1997); and Linda Ford, "Alice Paul and the Politics of Nonviolent Protest," in *Votes for Women: The Struggle for Suffrage Revisited*, ed. Jean H. Baker (New York: Oxford University, 2002), 116. Sarah Evans mentions Shaw after she finished her twelve years as NAWSA president, and Louise Newman never mentions Shaw at all. Sara M. Evans, *Born for Liberty: A History of Women in America* (New York: Free Press, 1989); and Louise Newman, *White Women's Rights*). Graham, *Woman Suffrage and the New Democracy*; Rupp, *Worlds of Women*; and Bosch, *Politics and Friendship*. See, for example, Jean Marie Eggleston, "A Study of the Development of Dr. Anna Howard Shaw—Reformer and Orator" (MS Thesis, Northwestern University, 1934). Nancy Aldinger Nakai, "The President Reverend Doctor, Anna Howard Shaw" (Thesis, University of Hawaii, 1980); S. J. Edwards, "Anna Howard Shaw and Lucy Elmina Anthony: 'That You Could See the Inside of My Love'" (Thesis, Slippery Rock University of Pennsylvania, 1997); and Leslie Collins Hester, "Rebellious Revelry: The Rhetorical Functions of Anna Howard Shaw's Humor" (Thesis, California State University, 2007).

29. A recent example is Brownell's dissertation on the Woman's Committees of World War I where she refers to the NAWSA as being "moribund" at the end of Shaw's presidency. There is no credible evidence that the NAWSA was near death in 1915. Penelope Noble Brownell, "The Woman's Committees of the First World War: Women in Government, 1917–1919" (PhD Dissertation, Brown University, 2002).

30. Graham, *Woman Suffrage and the New Democracy*; First Unitarian Church of Des Moines, "1st Women's Suffrage Parade: Boone, Iowa, October 1908," http://www.ucdsm.org/BooneParade.php (accessed April 14, 2013); and "IOWA SEES SUFFRAGETTES: 600 Led by the Rev. Anna Shaw Parade for Boone's Benefit," New York Times (1857–Current file), October 30, 1908, 6, http://0-www.proquest.com.library.albion.edu/ (accessed December 3, 2009).

31. Spruill, *New Women of the New South*; Elna C. Green, "The Rest of the Story: Kate Gordon and the Opposition to the Nineteenth Amendment in the South,"

Louisiana History: The Journal of the Louisiana Historical Association 33, no. 2 (1992); Paul E. Fuller, *Laura Clay and the Woman's Rights Movement* (Lexington: University of Kentucky Press, 1975); Clavia Goodman, *Bitter Harvest: Laura Clay's Suffrage Work*, Kentucky Monographs 3 (Lexington, Ky.: Bur Press, 1946); B. H. Gilley, "Kate Gordon and Louisiana Woman Suffrage," *Louisiana History: The Journal of the Louisiana Historical Association* 24, no. 3 (1983); and Elna C. Green, *Southern Strategies: Southern Women and the Woman Suffrage Question* (Chapel Hill: University of North Carolina Press, 1997).

32. See Ellen Carol DuBois, *Feminism and Suffrage: The Emergence of an Independent Women's Movement in America, 1848–1869* (Ithaca: Cornell University Press, 1980); and Trisha Franzen, "A Friendship of Power and Politics: Anna Howard Shaw, M. Carey Thomas and the U.S. Woman Suffrage Movement" (unpublished manuscript).

33. "CHARGES MISUSE OF SUSAN ANTHONY FUND: Suffrage Delegate's Criticism Tearfully Refuted by Dr. Shaw at Convention. SHE IS AGAIN PRESIDENT Proposal to Move the National Headquarters to Chicago Results in an Acrimonious Debate," New York Times (1857–Current file), October 24, 1911, 10, http://0-www.proquest.com.library.albion.edu/ (accessed December 3, 2009); and Harriet Taylor Upton and Lana Dunn Eisenbraun, *Harriet Taylor Upton's Random Recollections* (Warren, Ohio: Harriet Taylor Upton Association, 2004).

34. Mary Gray Peck, *Carrie Chapman Catt, a Biography* (New York: H. W. Wilson Co., 1944), 224–226, 265; and Graham, *Woman Suffrage and the New Democracy*.

35. Collins Hester, "Rebellious Revelry," and Ida Husted Harper, "Unpublished Manuscript, Biography of Anna Howard Shaw" (Ann Arbor: Bentley Library, University of Michigan, n.d.), 173.

36. "DR. SHAW PUBLISHES STORY OF HER LIFE: Writes Entertainingly of Her Early Struggles as a Rural Pastor. WON AUDIENCE OF SAILORS Book Filled with Reminiscences of Women Who Were Pioneers in Suffrage Movement," New York Times (1857–Current file), September 12, 1915, http://0-www.proquest .com.library.albion.edu/ (accessed December 3, 2009). Shaw was generally great press. Shaw appears to have "created" publicity at certain times. One clear example is when she resisted paying taxes in Pennsylvania and the tax assessor seized the car the New York suffragists had given her. See Special to the *New York Times*, "BOND FOR DR. SHAW'S AUTO: If Suffrage Leader Furnishes $300, Gift Car Will Go Free," New York Times (1857–Current file), July 22, 1915, 9, http://0-www.proquest .com. library.albion.edu/ (accessed December 3, 2009).

Chapter 1. The Development of a Dissenter, 1847–1870

1. Anna Howard Shaw, Series X of the Mary Earhart Dillon Collection, 1863–1955, handwritten memoir fragment, n.d., A-68, Folder 352, Schlesinger Library, Radcliffe Institute, Harvard University.

2. "Ann Howard Shaw," Registration of Birth, March 27, 1847, General Register Office, Newcastle upon Tyne, U.K.

3. Tim Lambert, "A Brief History of Newcastle Upon Tyne," http://www .localhistories.org/newcastle.html (accessed April 7, 2013); and Anna Howard Shaw, *The Story of a Pioneer* (New York: Harper and Brothers, 1915), 1–6.

4. Ibid.

5. The Shaw family stayed with family names for the daughters in the family. Eleanor and Nicolas in particular were passed on from two generations before Anna Howard Shaw's generation to two generations after. Shaw never commented on her name except for wishing they had named her Valentine. Note by Lucy E. Anthony in Ida Husted Harper, "Unpublished Manuscript, Biography of Anna Howard Shaw" (Ann Arbor: Bentley Library, University of Michigan, n.d.), after page 73.

6. Shaw, *Story of a Pioneer*, 6–7; and Newcastle City Council Libraries and Information Service, "Photograph, 13 Churchill St. Newcastle-Upon-Tyne, Dept. of Environmental Health, 1938," http://222.tynesidelifeandtimes.org.uk/photo/034907.htm (accessed April 7, 2013).

7. Records on the Shaw family are confusing. In her autobiography, Shaw mentions that one other Shaw son, Peter, died in the Crimean War. A search of existing records has produced no sources on him. Although several Shaws fought, were wounded, or died in the Crimean War, I have found no record of a Peter Shaw. In a later record, Shaw's father is mentioned as one of three sons of John and Eleanor Shaw. Shaw, *Story of a Pioneer*, 3. Chapman Brothers, *Portrait and Biographical Album, Mecosta County, Mich.* (Chicago: Chapman Brothers, 1883), 462. Handwritten memoir fragment, n.d., Shaw Papers; "Eleanor Robinson" Christening Record, July 10, 1774, Sion Meeting House, Alnwick, Northumberland, http://www.familysearch.org (accessed April 7, 2013); Chapman Brothers, *Portrait and Biographical Album*, 464–465; Public Records Office, *Census Returns of England and Wales, 1841, Newcastle, Northumberland*, 43888; and William Davison, *A Descriptive and Historical View of Alnwick*, 2d ed., Alnwick, 1822.

8. Shaw, *Story of a Pioneer*, 27. *Big Rapids Pioneer*, February 24, 1881; "Married," *Pioneer Magnet*, February 9, 1881, http://files.usgwarchives.org/mi/mecosta/newspapers/magnet2.txt (accessed April 7, 2013); Mecosta County History, "Tenth Michigan Cavalry," Photograph of the Officers, Archives of Michigan, State of Michigan photograph, http://seekingmichigan.org/u?/p4006coll3,37 (accessed April 7, 2013).

9. William Davison, "A Descriptive and Historical View of Alnwick"; personal observation by author, June 23, 2006; "Return of Men and Carts (1798)," Alnwick Manuscripts, http://communities.northumberland.gov.uk/007552.htm (accessed April 7, 2013); and "Northumberland Militia List (1762)," Alnwick Manuscripts, http://communities.northumberland.gov.uk/008340.htm (accessed April 7, 2013). In the 1851 census there were fifteen Stotts in the town of Alnwick but none over the age of forty. Office of Public Records, *Complete Returns for England and Wales, 1851*; and Shaw, *Story of a Pioneer*, 14, 80–81, and 268–269.

10. Personal communication, Dr. Christopher Hagerman, Albion College. The Alnwick Congregational Church, aka Sion Meeting House, opened June 30, 1816. The congregation had previously met in Bondgate Hall, a house belonging to Robert Widdrington Esq., Hauxley Davison, "A Descriptive and Historical View of Alnwick." Baptismal Records of the children of James and Nicolas Stott, International Genealogical Index, http://www.familysearch.org (accessed April 7, 2013); and "List of Poor People in Alnwick Parish (January 14, 1823)," Alnwick Manuscripts, http://communities.northumberland.gov.uk/007132FS.htm1823 (accessed April 7, 2013).

11. Shaw, *Story of a Pioneer*, 6–7.

12. Davison, A Descriptive and Historical View of Alnwick"; The Duchess's Community High School, "The School—a Brief History," http://www.dchs-alnwick.org/school/index.php?sectid=101&subsectid=58 (accessed April 14, 2013); personal communication, Gemma Bates, Collections and Archives Assistant, The Northumberland Estates, July 28, 2006.

13. Harper, "Unpublished Manuscript," 2.

14. "Thomas Shaw and Nicolas Stott," Marriage Record, January 31, 1835, St. Andrews Parish Records, Tyne and Wear Archives.

15. Blenheim was a busy commercial street of stone houses with some storefront businesses. The Shaws possibly lived in the same building where Thomas had his business. There is no documentation about the home that they owned at this time. Public Records Office, *Census Returns of England and Wales, 1841, Newcastle, Northumberland*; 43888; St. John Parish, Northumberland; Tim Lambert, "A Brief History of Newcastle Upon Tyne"; Baptismal Records, Children of Thomas and Nicolas Shaw, International Genealogical Index, http://www.familysearch.org (accessed April 7, 2013); and Earl Morse Wilbur, *A History of Unitarianism* (Cambridge: Harvard University Press, 1945).

16. Shaw, *Story of a Pioneer*, 6.

17. Ibid., 7.

18. Elizabeth T. Hurren, "Poor Law versus Public Health: Diphtheria, Sanitary Reform, and the 'Crusade' against Outdoor Relief, 1870–1900," *Social History of Medicine* 18, no. 3 (2005); and Fred Lewes, "The GRO and the Provinces in the Nineteenth Century," *Social History of Medicine* 4, no. 3 (1991).

19. "Elizabeth Nicolas Shaw," Birth Registration, General Register Office, *England and Wales Civil Registration Indexes*, London, England: General Register Office (Oct-Nov-Dec 1849, v. 25), 419; and Death Record, General Register Office. *England and Wales Civil Registration Indexes*, London, England: General Register Office (Jul-Aug-Sep 1851, v. 25), 255. "Seventh Census of the United States, 1850," National Archives Microfilm Publication M432, 1009 Rolls; Records of the Bureau of the Census, Record Group 29, National Archives, Washington, D.C., *Lynn, Essex, Massachusetts*, Roll M432_311, Page 245, Image 63.

20. Office of Public Records, *Complete Returns for England and Wales, 1851. Alnwick, Northumberland*; Shaw, handwritten memoir fragment, n.d.; and Shaw, *Story of a Pioneer*, 4.

21. Ibid., 8.

22. "Passenger Lists of Vessels Arriving at New York, New York, 1820–1897," National Archives Microfilm Publication M237, 675 Rolls; Records of the U.S. Customs Service, Record Group 36, National Archives, Washington, D.C., 1851; Arrival New York, United States, Microfilm Serial M237, Microfilm Roll M237_106, Line 42, List Number 1482. Shaw didn't remember the name of the ship correctly in her autobiography. She remembered it as the *John Jacob Westervelt* but records show *Jacob A. Westervelt*. Shaw, *Story of a Pioneer*, 7–11.

23. Ibid., 11.

24. Ibid., 12.

25. Ibid., 12; Miriam Forman-Brunell, *Girlhood in America: An Encyclopedia* (Santa Barbara, Calif.: ABC-CLIO, 2001); Ruth Birgitta Anderson Bordin, *Frances Willard:*

A Biography (Chapel Hill: University of North Carolina Press, 1986); Helen Lefkowitz Horowitz, *The Power and Passion of M. Carey Thomas* (New York: Alfred A. Knopf, 1994); and Barbara Welter, "The Cult of True Womanhood: 1820–1860," *American Quarterly* 18, no. 2 (1966).

26. Maurice B. Dorgan, *History of Lawrence, Massachusetts, with War Records* (Lawrence, Mass.: the author, 1924), 45–49; and *Lawrence City Directory* (Lawrence, Mass.: J. H. Barnes, 1857).

27. Shaw, *Story of a Pioneer*, 12–20; Bureau of the Census, *Eighth Census of the United States, 1860*, Washington, D.C., National Archives and Records Administration, 1860. *Lawrence Ward 1, Essex, Massachusetts*, Roll M653_498, Page 12, Image 14; "Map of Lawrence, Massachusetts, 1855"; personal observation by the author, Immigrant City Archives, Lawrence Massachusetts; and *Lawrence Directory—1853–54* (Lawrence, Mass.: The Courier Office, 1853).

28. Dorgan, *History of Lawrence*, 128; and Shaw, *Story of a Pioneer*, 13–14.

29. Personal observation; Dorgan, *History of Lawrence*, 89; "A reason perhaps why Dr. Anna Howad [*sic*] could not spell," undated fragment in Harper, "Unpublished Manuscript."

30. Shaw, *Story of a Pioneer*, 13.

31. Ibid., 15–16.

32. Ibid., 15–18. As with the previous story, there is no easy way to verify this story. A search of the 1860 Census data for the area surrounding the Shaw home does not show any house that was the residence for unrelated women. Bureau of the Census, *Eighth Census of the United States, 1860*, Washington, D.C., National Archives and Records Administration, 1860. *Lawrence Ward 1, Essex, Massachusetts*, Roll M653_498, Page 12, Image 14.

33. Shaw argues that her father invented the process that eliminated his type of work. There is no record that any such development took place in Newcastle or Lawrence. Karen A. Guffey, "From Paper Stainer to Manufacturer: J. F. Bumstead and Co., Manufacturers and Importers of Paper Hangings," in Richard C. Redmond, Elizabeth Sander, and Penny J. Nylander, eds. *Wallpaper in New England* (Boston: Society for the Preservation of New England Antiquities, 1986), 29–40; *Lawrence City Directory*, 1857; Dorgan, *History of Lawrence*, 171; Thomas Shaw—Land Record, March 1, 1857, *United States, Bureau of Land Management, Michigan Pre-1908 Homestead & Cash Entry Patent and Cadastral Survey Plat Index*. General Land Office Automated Records Project, 1994, Ancestry.com. *Michigan Land Records* (database online). Provo, Utah: The Generations Network, Inc., 1997.

34. Chapman Brothers, *Portrait and Biographical Album*; and Donald Dickmann and Larry A. Leefers, *The Forests of Michigan* (Ann Arbor: University of Michigan Press, 2003).

35. Shaw, *Story of a Pioneer*, 20–21.

36. Ibid., 21.

37. Ibid., 21–26.

38. Ibid., 26.

39. Ibid., 27–28.

40. Ibid., 28.

41. Ibid., 30–33.

42. Ibid., 40–42.

43. Ibid., 41–42.

44. On mid-nineteenth-century gender ideology, see, for example, Forman-Brunell, *Girlhood in America*; and Mary P. Ryan, *The Empire of the Mother: American Writing about Domesticity, 1830 to 1860* (New York: Institute for Research in History/Haworth Press, 1982).

45. Shaw, *Story of a Pioneer*, 34.

46. Exactly when Thomas Sr. joined the family is unclear. The 1860 census lists all the family, but Shaw argues that he didn't join the family for eighteen months. Similarly there is the question of James's departure and return. The 1860 census of Massachusetts taken on July 19 lists James Shaw as a patient in the Massachusetts General Hospital in Boston, but he was also listed with the family in Michigan on the June 16, 1860 census. Thomas Jr. is also listed as being still in Lawrence in 1860. Shaw, *Story of a Pioneer*, 42. Bureau of the Census, *Eighth Census of the United States, 1860*, Washington, D.C., National Archives and Records Administration, *Green, Mecosta, Michigan*, Roll M653_554, Page 0, Image 115; Bureau of the Census. *Eighth Census of the United States, 1860*, Washington, D.C., National Archives and Records Administration, *Lawrence Ward 1, Essex, Massachusetts*, Roll M653_498, Page 3, Image 5; and Bureau of the Census, *Eighth Census of the United States, Boston Ward 5, Suffolk, Massachusetts*, Roll M653_521, Page 515, Image 516.

47. Shaw, *Story of a Pioneer*, 43–44.

48. Ibid., 43–44.

49. Shaw, *Story of a Pioneer*, 51–53; "Record of Service of Michigan Volunteers 1861–65" (1903); Colton Carpenter and Eleanor Shaw, December 3, 1861, Marriage Records of Mecosta County, http://files.usgwarchives.net/mi/mecosta/vitals/marriages/dbn-aug2008-can-carr.txt (accessed April 7, 2013); Mecosta County Teaching Certificate, 1865, Anna Howard Shaw, Series X of the Mary Earhart Dillon Collection, 1863–1955, A-68, Folder 352.

50. Shaw, *Story of a Pioneer*, 52–53.

51. Ibid., 52–53.

52. Chapman Brothers, *Portrait and Biographical Album*, 462–464; Shaw, *Story of a Pioneer*, 54–55.

53. Ibid., 55; Joyce Antler, "After College, What? New Graduates and the Family Claim," *American Quarterly* 32, no. 4 (Fall 1980): 409–434; and Christopher Lasch, "Jane Addams: The College Woman and the Family Claim," in The New Radicalism in America (1889–1963): The Intellectual as a Social Type (New York: Alfred A. Knopf, 1966).

54. "Portrait of Anna Howard Shaw with a Young Man, R. L. ca. 1860–1870," photograph (Harvard University Library Visual Information Access); and "Two Portraits of Anna Howard Shaw, ca. 1860–1870," photographs (Harvard University Library Visual Information Access).

55. "Anna Howard Shaw with Others, 1860–1865," photograph (Harvard University Library Visual Information Access). The Osborn family moved to Big Rapids from Owego, New York, sometime between 1860 and 1870. Clara was the second daughter and third child of L. J. and Mary Osborn. L. J. (Levi) was a tailor. Bureau of the Census, *Eighth Census of the United States, 1860*, Washington, D.C., National Archives and Records Administration, 1860, *Owego, Tioga, New York*, Roll M653_867, Page 0, Image 407; and Bureau of the Census, *Ninth Census of the United States,*

1870, Washington, D.C., National Archives and Records Administration, *Big Rapids Ward 1, Mecosta, Michigan*, Roll M593_690, Page 19, Image 39; Winifred Leith, "Will Tell Her Story of Dr. Shaw," *Grand Rapids Herald*, December 4, 1921; and Mary Hurlbut Cordier, *Schoolwomen of the Prairies and Plain: Personal Narratives from Iowa, Kansas, and Nebraska, 1860s-1920s* (Albuquerque: University of New Mexico Press, 1992).

56. Shaw, *Story of a Pioneer*, 64.

57. Among Shaw's papers are teaching certificates for "Annie H. Shaw" from 1865 (handwritten document from Township of Richmond, County of Mecosta), 1869, and 1871, printed certificates from Mecosta County. Anna Howard Shaw Papers, Folder 352. There is a significant body of research documenting women's activism during this period across race, class, and region. See, for example, Lucy Eldersveld Murphy and Wendy Hamand Venet, *Midwestern Women: Work, Community, and Leadership at the Crossroads*, Midwestern History and Culture (Bloomington: Indiana University Press, 1997); Claire Goldberg Moses and Heidi I. Hartmann, *U.S. Women in Struggle: A Feminist Studies Anthology*, Women in American History (Urbana: University of Illinois Press, 1995); Nancy A. Hewitt, *Southern Discomfort: Women's Activism in Tampa, Florida, 1880s-1920s*, Women in American History (Urbana: University of Illinois Press, 2004); Joyce Ann Hanson, *Mary Mcleod Bethune & Black Women's Political Activism* (Columbia: University of Missouri Press, 2003). On women teachers in the West, see, for example, Cordier, *Schoolwomen of the Prairies and Plains*; and Polly Welts Kaufman, *Women Teachers on the Frontier* (New Haven: Yale University Press, 1984).

Chapter 2. The Road to Independence (1871–1880)

1. Anna Howard Shaw, *The Story of a Pioneer* (New York: Harper and Brothers, 1915), 63.

2. Bureau of the Census, *Ninth Census of the United States, 1870*, Washington, D.C., National Archives and Records Administration, *Green, Mecosta, Michigan*, Roll M593_690, Page 60, Image 121. Shaw's father, Thomas Shaw, is listed as a farmer whose real estate was now worth $1500 and whose personal property was valued at $360. Henry, her youngest brother, was a farm worker. Her mother, Nicolas, was "keeping house." One of Shaw's older brothers, Jack (John), married with three children, was listed just before his father as a farmer with real estate valued at $2000, suggesting that his father had given or sold him part of the original family farm of 160 acres. Thomas Jr. was also married with one child, farming close by on land valued at $1000, perhaps by virtue of another parental gift or transaction. Mary was living in the town of Big Rapids, eight miles away, with her husband, William Green, a successful lumberman, and their first child. Their property was valued at $16,600 Bureau of the Census, *Ninth Census of the United States, 1870*, Washington, D.C., National Archives and Records Administration, *Green, Mecosta, Michigan*, Roll M593_690, Page 60, Image 123. Anna's oldest brother James was in Nebraska. Bureau of the Census, *Ninth Census of the United States, 1870*, Washington, D.C., National Archives and Records Administration, *Fremont, Dodge, Nebraska*, Roll M593_828, Page 319, Image 638. Eleanor Shaw Colton's widower had taken their one child with him when he remarried and relocated. Eleanor Shaw Colton is

buried with her parents in Big Rapids. On her gravestone she is listed by her birth rather than her married name (personal observation by author).

3. Nancy Folbre, "The Unproductive Housewife: Her Evolution in Nineteenth-Century Economic Thought," *Signs* 16, no. 3 (1991).

4. Charles Harold Lyttle, *Freedom Moves West: A History of the Western Unitarian Conference, 1852–1952* (Boston: Beacon Press, 1952). For the paths of more privileged "new women," see, for example, Helen Lefkowitz Horowitz, *The Power and Passion of M. Carey Thomas* (New York: Alfred A. Knopf, 1994); Victoria Brown, *The Education of Jane Addams, Politics and Culture in Modern America* (Philadelphia: University of Pennsylvania Press, 2004); and Paul E. Fuller, *Laura Clay and the Woman's Rights Movement* (Lexington: University of Kentucky Press, 1975).

5. Shaw devotes a significant number of pages in her autobiography to this decade. Shaw, *Story of a Pioneer*, 54–123. The records for this period of Shaw's life are more extensive than for the first twenty-three years. They include the following sources: United Methodist Church (U.S.) Michigan Conference, "Minutes of the Michigan Annual Conference of the United Methodist Church, 1875–1884" (Albion College Archives); *Albion College Catalog, 1874–75* (Albion College Archives); and Annie Howard Shaw, "Rest" (Boston University, 1878). Letters from this decade include those from Shaw to Clara Osborn. *Letters, 1873–1919*, Anna Howard Shaw, Series X of the Mary Earhart Dillon Collection, 1863–1955, A-68, Folder 527, Schlesinger Library, Radcliffe Institute, Harvard University. "Sermon No. 1," 1871, Wil A. Linkugel, "The Speeches of Anna Howard Shaw" (PhD Dissertation, University of Wisconsin, 1960), 11–24; and "Women in the Ministry," in Linkugel, "Speeches," 414–421.

6. Shaw, *Story of a Pioneer*, 55.

7. Ibid., 55.

8. It isn't clear whether the railroad reached Big Rapids in 1869 or 1871. Willis Frederick Dunbar, *All Aboard! A History of Railroads in Michigan* (Grand Rapids, Mich.: W. B. Eerdmans Publishing Co., 1966); *History of Ottawa County, Michigan* (Chicago: H. R. Page, 1882), 33; and Chapman Brothers, *Portrait and Biographical Album, Mecosta County, Mich.* (Chicago: Chapman Brothers, 1883), 252.

9. See, for example, Amy G. Richter, *Home on the Rails: Women, the Railroads and the Rise of Public Domesticity* (Chapel Hill: University of North Carolina Press, 2005); and Karen M. Morin, "Frontiers of Femininity: A New Historical Geography of the Nineteenth-Century American West," in *Space, Place, and Society* (Syracuse, N.Y.: Syracuse University Press, 2008).

10. Big Rapids, Michigan, High School Homepage, http://www.brps.k12.mi.us/alumni/ (accessed April 11, 2013).

11. The most complete source of information on Marianna Thompson is from her daughter's papers at the Texas State Archives. "Erminia Thompson Folsom, Papers," in *Erminia Thompson Folsom, 1856–1965* (Austin: Texas State Archives); and Shaw, *Story of a Pioneer*, 55. On the lyceum, see Lisa Tetrault, "The Incorporation of American Feminism: Suffragists and the Postbellum Lyceum," *Journal of American History* 96, no. 4 (2010).

12. Shaw, *Story of a Pioneer*, 56.

13. Ibid., 56–67; Mary P. Ryan, "The Power of Women's Networks: A Case Study of Female Moral Reform in Antebellum America," *Feminist Studies* 5, no. 1 (1979);

and Estelle Freedman, "Separatism as Strategy: Female Institution Building and American Feminism, 1870–1930," *Feminist Studies* 5, no. 3 (1979).

14. West Michigan Methodist Episcopal Conference, "Conference Reports, 1839–1875," in *West Michigan Conference of the United Methodist Church* (Albion, Mich.: Albion College Library Special Collections).

15. James E. Kirby, Russell E. Richey, and Kenneth E. Rowe, *The Methodists, Denominations in America*, No. 8 (Westport, Conn.: Greenwood Press, 1996); and Carl J. Schneider and Dorothy Schneider, *In Their Own Right: The History of American Clergywomen* (New York: Crossroad Publishing Co., 1997).

16. Paul Wesley Chilcote, *John Wesley and the Women Preachers of Early Methodism*, Atla Monograph Series (Metuchen, N.J.: Scarecrow Press, 1991); Catherine A. Brekus, *Strangers & Pilgrims: Female Preaching in America, 1740–1845*, Gender and American Culture (Chapel Hill: University of North Carolina Press, 1998); and John O. Foster, *Life and Labors of Mrs. Maggie Newton Van Cott*, Women in American Protestant Religion, 1800–1930 (New York: Garland Publishing, 1987).

17. Shaw, *Story of a Pioneer*, 58–63. There is very little material on Dr. Peck in the West Michigan United Methodist Archives. West Michigan Methodist Episcopal Conference, "Conference Reports, 1839–1875," and "Big Rapids District Reports, 1863–1890," in *West Michigan Conference of the United Methodist Church* (Albion, Mich.: Albion College Library Special Collections).

18. Shaw, *Story of a Pioneer*, 58–63.

19. Ibid., 61–62.

20. Ibid., 62–65.

21. Ibid., 62. Since her parents had no money, it is logical that her brother-in-law made this offer.

22. Ibid., 64–65.

23. Ibid., 64–66.

24. Ibid., 64–66; Mary Ashton Rice Livermore, *The Story of My Life: Or, the Sunshine and Shadow of Seventy Years* (Hartford, Conn.: A. D. Worthington and Co., 1897); and Wendy Hamand Venet, *A Strong-Minded Woman: The Life of Mary Livermore* (Amherst: University of Massachusetts Press, 2005).

25. This licensing of a woman was a local decision that never came to the entire West Michigan Conference. Anna Howard Shaw is not mentioned in any of the minutes of the West Michigan Conference from 1868 to 1876. "Conference Reports, 1839–1876." The confirmation of her licensing in the Big Rapids District Conference as a Local Preacher on July 26, 1873, with renewals through 1875, is contained in a letter from J. C. Floyd of Evart, Michigan, to Rev. C. L. Barnhart, March 22, 1880, Shaw Papers, A-68, Folder 354.

26. Shaw, *Story of a Pioneer*, 66–68.

27. Helen Lefkowitz Horowitz, *Alma Mater: Design and Experience in the Women's Colleges from Their Nineteenth-Century Beginnings to the 1930s* (Amherst: University of Massachusetts Press, 1993); and Barbara Miller Solomon, *In the Company of Educated Women: A History of Women and Higher Education in America* (New Haven: Yale University Press, 1985).

28. Keith J. Fennimore, *The Albion College Sesquicentennial History: 1835–1985* (Albion, Mich.: Albion College, 1985).

29. *Albion College Catalog, 1874–75*, and *Albion College Catalogue, 1875–76*, Albion College Archives, Albion, Mich.

30. Shaw, *Story of a Pioneer*, 66–72.

31. Ibid., 81–82.

32. Fennimore, *Albion College Sesquicentennial History*, 210; and Ida Husted Harper, "Unpublished Manuscript, Biography of Anna Howard Shaw" (Ann Arbor: Bentley Library, University of Michigan, n.d.), 23; and "Dr. Anna Howard Shaw," by Della P. Pierce, M.D., included in Harper, "Unpublished Manuscript."

33. This and other sources confirm that Anna Howard Shaw was lecturing on temperance in the early 1870s, though the origin of her commitment to this cause isn't clear. Although the Temperance Movement had a long history, the Women's Christian Temperance Movement (WCTU) was founded in 1874. Sara M. Evans, *Born for Liberty: A History of Women in America* (New York: Free Press, 1989), 127; and Harper, "Unpublished Manuscript," 23.

34. Ibid., 24.

35. Ibid., 73–74.

36. Among the photographs of Anna Howard Shaw in the VIA of Harvard University Library is a series of five portraits of the young Shaw. The first is most probably the earliest and least composed, but the last one shows a confident and mature young woman. "Portraits of a Young Anna Howard Shaw, ca. 1865–1875" (Harvard University Library Visual Information Access). On Dickinson's and Cather's short hair, see J. Matthew Gallman, "America's Joan of Arc: The Life of Anna Elizabeth Dickinson" (Oxford: Oxford University Press, 2006); and Phyllis C. Robinson, *Willa, the Life of Willa Cather* (Garden City, N.Y.: Doubleday, 1983). On early dress reforms, including a call for women to cut their hair, see Gayle V. Fischer, *Pantaloons and Power: Nineteenth-Century Dress Reform in the United States* (Kent, Ohio: Kent State University Press, 2001).

37. Pierce, "Dr. Anna Howard Shaw," in Harper, "Unpublished Manuscript." Edward H. Clarke, *Sex in Education: Or, a Fair Chance for the Girls*, Medicine & Society in America (New York: Arno Press, 1972); and Julia Ward Howe, *Sex and Education: A Reply to Dr. E. H. Clarke's "Sex in Education,"* American Women: Images and Realities (New York: Arno Press, 1972).

38. Shaw, *Story of a Pioneer*, 81.

39. Ibid., 83. Clifford explores some of the challenges and strategies of women who were isolated from communities of women. Geraldine Jonçich Clifford, *Lone Voyagers: Academic Women in Coeducational Universities, 1870–1937* (New York: Feminist Press at the City University of New York, 1989).

40. Shaw, *Story of a Pioneer*, 85.

41. Ibid., 85–88.

42. Ibid., 89–90.

43. Ibid., 89–92. Vincent Kuharic, "Prince Sears Crowell, Sea Captain," http://www.zoupe.com/crowell/theman.php (accessed April 14, 2013); and Jim Coogan, *Sail Away Ladies: Stories of Cape Cod Women in the Age of Sail* (East Dennis, Mass.: Harvest Home Books, 2003).

44. Shaw, *Story of a Pioneer*; Albert G. Boyden, *History and Alumni Record of the State Normal School, Bridgewater, Mass., to July, 1876* (Boston: Noyes and Snow, 1876); and Coogan, *Sail Away Ladies*.

45. Shaw, *Story of a Pioneer*, 92–93; and Addy gravestone, Dennis Quivet Cemetery (personal observation of the author, November 14, 2008).

46. Harper, "Unpublished Manuscript," 28.

47. The scholarship on nineteenth-century relationships among U.S. women is extensive. For overviews, see, for example, John Freedman, Estelle B. D'Emilio, *Intimate Matters: A History of Sexuality in America*, 1st ed. (New York: Harper and Row, 1988); and Leila J. Rupp, *A Desired Past: A Short History of Same-Sex Love in America* (Chicago: University of Chicago Press, 1999). Nevertheless, the debate over how to name these relationships has never been resolved. Trisha Franzen, "United States," in Bonnie Zimmerman, *Lesbian Histories and Cultures: An Encyclopedia, Encyclopedia of Lesbian and Gay Histories and Cultures*, vol. 1 (New York: Garland Publishing, 2000).

48. Shaw, *Story of a Pioneer*, 97–107.

49. Ibid., 100–107.

50. Joint Commission on the Origin of American Methodism, *Origin of American Methodism: Report of the Joint Commission Representing the Methodist Episcopal Church, the Methodist Episcopal Church, South, and the Methodist Protestant Church* (Chicago: Methodist Book Concern, 1916). There is a story that Anna Howard Shaw was not asked back to Hingham after she revitalized the parish during her final year in seminary. Helen Beal Woodward, "The One Who Got Away," n.d., Anna Howard Shaw documents, School of Theology Archives, Boston University, Boston, Massachusetts. The records of the parish tell a different story. On May 1, 1877, Shaw was first invited to become pastor. On January 27, 1878, the church leaders at Hingham "Voted that we request Sister Shaw to return another year as Preacher." Then in May 1878, the church voted to employ a Brother Comstock. These records suggest that Shaw left Hingham voluntarily. Shaw is vague on this. "Hingham Massachusetts Administration Quarterly Conference, 1865–1896," School of Theology Library Archives, Boston University; and Shaw, *Story of a Pioneer*, 91–93, 106; Elizabeth Cady Stanton, *Declaration of Sentiments: Seneca Falls Convention, July 1848* (Tucson, Ariz.: Kore Press, 2004).

51. Shaw, *Story of a Pioneer*, 107–121.

52. Ibid., 107–112. Ralph Wakefield Spencer's 1972 dissertation on Anna Howard Shaw contains his findings from an examination of the East Dennis Parish Records. Spencer found no records to corroborate or contradict Shaw's accounts. R. W. Spencer, *Dr. Anna Howard Shaw: The Evangelical Feminist* (PhD Dissertation, Boston University, 1972).

53. Shaw, *Story of a Pioneer*, 122–130; and R. Costelloe, n.d., "Ordination" (of AHS after Ladee told story to her), Shaw Papers, A-68, Folder 354.

54. "BISHOP GILBERT HAVEN DEAD: A NOBLE AND ENERGETIC CAREER ENDED—HIS SERVICES TO HIS CHURCH AND HIS COUNTRY," New York Times (1857–Current file), January 4, 1880, 1, http://0-www.proquest.com.library.albion.edu/ (accessed December 4, 2009). Ida Husted Harper and Susan B. Anthony, *The History of Woman Suffrage, Volume IV, 1883–1900* (Indianapolis: Hollenbeck Press, 1902), 266.

55. H. Mathews, "Record" New England Conference, April 3, 1880, Shaw Papers, A-68, Folder 354.

56. Frances Lyons-Bristol forwarded the materials of the 1880 General Conference

to me (F. Lyons-Bristol, Reference Archivist, The General Commission on Archives and History of The United Methodist Church, 1880 General Conference Records, 2009).

57. Shaw, *Story of a Pioneer*, 122–130; and Costelloe, "Ordination."

58. In her autobiography, Shaw is vague about which of her congregations gave her the service. Since she considered the Wesleyan Church to be her primary congregation, it would have made sense that they gave it. However, today the communion service is on display at the Dennis Union Church (personal observation, November 2008). Shaw, *Story of a Pioneer*, 122–130.

59. Shaw, *Story of a Pioneer*, 121–130; and Costelloe, "Ordination," 1–10.

60. On self-supporting women during the colonial era, see, for example, Clare A. Lyons, *Sex among the Rabble: An Intimate History of Gender & Power in the Age of Revolution, Philadelphia, 1730–1830* (Chapel Hill: Published for the Omohundro Institute of Early American History and Culture, Williamsburg, Virginia, by the University of North Carolina Press, 2006).

Chapter 3. Finding the Cause (1881–1889)

1. Anna Howard Shaw, "The Heavenly Vision," March 25, 1888, in Wil A. Linkugel, "The Speeches of Anna Howard Shaw" (PhD Dissertation, University of Wisconsin, 1960), 28.

2. Shaw really belonged to the pioneering generation of new women. Though there were some women born before 1840, such as Susan B. Anthony, who carved out independent lives for themselves, their numbers were few. With each decade over the rest of the century, increasing numbers of women found the means to live outside the roles designated by the patriarchal family. In many ways the women saw themselves as creating another type of family. See Carroll Smith-Rosenberg, *Disorderly Conduct: Visions of Gender in Victorian America*, 1st ed. (New York: A. A. Knopf, 1985); Trisha Franzen, *Spinsters and Lesbians: Independent Womanhood in the United States* (New York: New York University Press, 1996). Among the most significant changes involved women's presence in the waged workforce. W. Elliot Brownlee and Mary M. Brownlee, *Women in the American Economy: A Documentary History, 1675 to 1929*, A Yale Paperbound (New Haven: Yale University Press, 1976).

3. Sara M. Evans, *Born for Liberty: A History of Women in America* (New York: Free Press, 1989). Eleanor Flexner, *Century of Struggle: The Woman's Rights Movement in the United States* (Cambridge: Belknap Press of Harvard University Press, 1959); and Rosalyn Terborg-Penn, *African American Women in the Struggle for the Vote, 1850–1920*, Blacks in the Diaspora (Bloomington: Indiana University Press, 1998); Jack M. Balkin, "How Social Movements Change (or Fail to Change) the Constitution: The Case of the New Departure," *Suffolk Law Review* 39, no. 27 (2005).

4. Evans, *Born for Liberty*; Claire Goldberg Moses and Heidi I. Hartmann, *U.S. Women in Struggle: A Feminist Studies Anthology*, Women in American History (Urbana: University of Illinois Press, 1995); and Helen Lefkowitz Horowitz, *The Power and Passion of M. Carey Thomas* (New York: Alfred A. Knopf, 1994).

5. Ralph Wakefield Spencer, "Dr. Anna Howard Shaw: The Evangelical Feminist" (PhD Dissertation, Boston University, 1972). Unfortunately, the 1880 census did not record the worth of people's personal property or real estate. This is the last census

that is useful for this research. The 1890 census was destroyed by an accidental fire. Shaw doesn't appear on the 1900 census, and the 1910 information adds nothing new to this research.

6. Shaw wrote that Mary died in 1883. According to Chapman Brothers, she died in 1881 and Henry Shaw died in 1883. Anna Howard Shaw, *The Story of a Pioneer* (New York: Harper and Brothers, 1915), 139–140; and Chapman Brothers, *Portrait and Biographical Album, Mecosta County, Mich.* (Chicago: Chapman Brothers, 1883), 271.

7. Not long after Anna left Big Rapids, the elder Shaws had joined Mary's household. Shaw, *Story of a Pioneer*, 138–140.

8. Chapman Brothers, *Portrait and Biographical Album*, 270; and Jan Cortez, "George W. Green," Mecosta County Genealogical Society, http://www.migenweb .org/mecosta/bios/wgreen.html (accessed April 14, 2013).

9. Shaw, *Story of a Pioneer*, 131–147.

10. Ibid., 141; John Preston Sutherland, MD, "Boston University School of Medicine," in William Harvey King, MD, LLD, *History of Homeopathy and Its Institutions in America*, http://www.homeoint.org/history/king/3-05.htm (accessed April 14, 2013); and *Portrait and Biographical Album*, 478.

11. "History," Boston University School of Medicine, http://www.bumc.bu.edu/ medicine/introduction/history/ (accessed April 14, 2013).

12. Given these experiences it was jarring to read a later description of Shaw as having been narrowly educated and inexperienced in life. It is hard to imagine that any of the women who would be Shaw's suffrage peers had had such a wide range of involvements or worked with a greater diversity of people. Rheta Childe Dorr, *Susan B. Anthony, the Woman Who Changed the Mind of a Nation* (New York: AMS Press, 1970).

13. Gloria Moldow, *Women Doctors in Gilded-Age Washington: Race, Gender, and Professionalization* (Urbana: University of Illinois Press, 1987).

14. Shaw, *Story of a Pioneer*, 146, 141, 151.

15. Spencer, "Dr. Anna Howard Shaw," 148; and Shaw, *Story of a Pioneer*, 149.

16. Shaw, *Story of a Pioneer*, 146–147; "Broadside: East Dennis Club, 1880–81, Speakers Course, Including Mary A. Livermore, Julia Ward Howe and Rev. Annie Shaw" (1880), Anna Howard Shaw Papers, Folder 147, Series X of the Mary Earhart Dillion Collection, Schlesinger Library, Radcliffe Institute, Harvard University; and Lucy Stone to Anna Howard Shaw, May 7, 1884, Shaw Papers, Folder 531.

17. Shaw, *Story of a Pioneer*, 101–104.

18. James E. Kirby, Russell E. Richey, and Kenneth E. Rowe, *The Methodists, Denominations in America: No. 8* (Westport, Conn.: Greenwood Press, 1996), 88–89; Angela G. Ray, "What Hath She Wrought? Woman's Rights and the Nineteenth-Century Lyceum," *Rhetoric & Public Affairs* 9, no. 2 (2006): 183–214; and Lisa Tetrault, "The Incorporation of American Feminism: Suffragists and the Postbellum Lyceum," *Journal of American History* 96, no. 4 (2010).

19. John R. McKivigan, *Forgotten Firebrand: James Redpath and the Making of Nineteenth-Century America* (Ithaca: Cornell University Press, 2008). 119–120.

20. J. Matthew Gallman, *America's Joan of Arc: The Life of Anna Elizabeth Dickinson* (Oxford: Oxford University Press, 2006); and "Portraits of Anna Howard Shaw, ca. 1879–1890," photographs (Harvard University Library Visual Information Access).

21. Shaw, *Story of a Pioneer*, 260. Anna Howard Shaw clearly agreed with women such as Dr. S. Josephine Baker that women professionals shouldn't draw attention to themselves through their dress. Trisha Franzen, *Spinsters and Lesbians: Independent Womanhood in the United States* (New York: New York University Press, 1996), 69. Portraits of Anna Howard Shaw, ca. 1879–1890; and Shaw *Story of a Pioneer*, 112.

22. "Two Group Portraits, Outside, of Members of the Blackwell Family with Mrs. Christianson Beaufort, Professor and Poet William Herbert Carruth, Lawyer Cora Benneson, Benjamin H. Goodridge, and Suffragist Anna Howard Shaw, Ca 1877–1882," photographs (Harvard University Library Visual Information Access); and Shaw, *Story of a Pioneer*, 138.

23. Shaw came to the attention of the Stone-Blackwell family by the early 1880s when her ordination and other activities in East Dennis were mentioned in the *Woman's Journal*, February 12, 1881, January 21, 1882, November 24, 1883.

24. See, for example, Flexner, *Century of Struggle*; and Aileen S. Kraditor, *The Ideas of the Woman Suffrage Movement, 1890–1920* (New York: W. W. Norton, 1981).

25. Holly Berkley Fletcher, "Gender and the American Temperance Movement of the Nineteenth Century," in *Studies in American Popular History and Culture* (New York: Routledge, 2008), 79–125.

26. Ruth Bordin, *Frances Willard: A Biography* (Chapel Hill: University of North Carolina Press, 1986).

27. Shaw, *Story of a Pioneer*, 157; and Spencer, "Dr. Anna Howard Shaw," 88–91, 166.

28. "Two Group Portraits, Outside, of Members of the Blackwell Family," and "Anna Howard Shaw, Lucy E. Anthony and Alice Stone Blackwell Camping in Canada," photographs (Harvard University Library Visual Information Access).

29. Anna Howard Shaw to Lucy E. Anthony, October 16, 1890, Shaw Papers, Folder 502.

30. "The School Excursion," *Big Rapids Pioneer*, August 12, 1886; "Notice," *Big Rapids Pioneer*, August 26, 1886; and "Miss Annie Shaw," *Big Rapids Pioneer*, September 9, 1886.

31. Anna Howard Shaw to Lucy Stone, February 1, 1887, Shaw Papers, Folder 532; Mary A. Livermore to Anna Howard Shaw, September 15, 1886, and Clara Barton to Anna Howard Shaw, December 7, 1886, Shaw Papers, Folder 536.

32. Shaw, *Story of a Pioneer*, 157–158. The negotiations and regular correspondence extended from January through August. See, for example, Anna Howard Shaw to Lucy Stone, January 6, 1887; Anna Howard Shaw to Lucy Stone, February 1, 1887; Anna Howard Shaw to Alice Stone Blackwell, March 3, 1887; and Anna Howard Shaw to Alice Stone Blackwell, May 4, 1887; Anna Howard Shaw to Henry Blackwell, May 4, 1887; all in "General Correspondence: Anna Howard Shaw," National American Woman Suffrage Association Records, Box 27, Manuscript Division, Library of Congress, Washington, D.C.

33. In a nondated statement from Anna Howard Shaw to Executive Committee of the Massachusetts Woman Suffrage Association in 1887, Shaw is explicit about the pay rates and dates of her employment with them. In this case she states that she would be "paying my own expenses." Anna Howard Shaw to Executive Committee MWSA, n.d., 1887. Tetrault, "The Incorporation of American Feminism."

For scholarship on singlewomen, see, for example, *Women's History Review* 17, no. 3 (2008), Special Issue, "Winner or Losers: Single Women in History 1000–2000."

34. "Rev. Anne H. Shaw, Lecturer," press packet, n.d., Shaw Papers, Folder 417.

35. Frances Willard to Anna Howard Shaw, November 22, 1888, Folder 534; Ida Husted Harper, "Unpublished Manuscript, Biography of Anna Howard Shaw" (Ann Arbor: Bentley Library, University of Michigan, n.d.), 45–46; Wil A. Linkugel and Martha Watson, *Anna Howard Shaw: Suffrage Orator and Social Reformer*, Great American Orators, No. 10 (New York: Greenwood Press, 1991); and Linkugel, "Speeches," 110. No sources document how the Shaw-Willard friendship changed when Shaw chose to work with Anthony.

36. Ida Husted Harper and Susan B. Anthony, *The History of Woman Suffrage, Volume IV, 1883–1900* (Indianapolis: Hollenbeck Press, 1902), 128.

37. Ida Husted Harper, *The Life and Work of Susan B. Anthony* (Indianapolis: Hollenbeck Press, 1908). Susan always could count on her family for support. She considered her parents' farm and later the house her widowed mother purchased as her home. She also spent time in Kansas at the home of her brother, Daniel Read Anthony.

38. Ibid.

39. Anna Howard Shaw to Lucy Stone, February 1, 1887, Shaw Papers, Folder 531; Harper and Anthony, *History of Woman Suffrage*, 640; "Rachel Foster Avery," in Edward T. James et al., *Notable American Women, 1607–1950: A Biographical Dictionary* (Cambridge: Belknap Press of Harvard University Press, 1971), 71–72; and "Anthony-Avery Papers, 1882–1908," in Department of Rare Books, Special Collections and Preservation (Rochester, N.Y.: River Campus Libraries, University of Rochester).

40. Harper and Anthony, *History of Woman Suffrage*, 128; and Shaw, *Story of a Pioneer*, 189.

41. Mary Earhart Dillon, *Frances Willard: from Prayers to Politics* (Chicago: University of Chicago Press, 1944), 196; Harper and Anthony, *History of Woman Suffrage*, 128–133; and Shaw, *Story of a Pioneer*, 159.

42. Anna Howard Shaw to Lucy E. Anthony, April 27, 1888, Shaw Papers, Folder 502; Bureau of the Census, *Ninth Census of the United States, 1870*, Washington, D.C., National Archives and Records Administration, *Fort Scott Ward 3, Bourbon, Kansas*, Roll M593_429, Page 455, Image 173; and Bureau of the Census, *Tenth Census of the United States, 1880*, Washington, D.C., National Archives and Records Administration, *Rochester, Monroe, New York*, Roll T9_863, Family History Film 1254863, Page 365.2000, Enumeration District 88, Image 0426.

43. Anna Howard Shaw to Lucy E. Anthony, April 27, 1888, Shaw Papers, Folder 502.

44. Susan B. Anthony to Lucy E. Anthony, n.d., quoted in Harper, "Unpublished Manuscript," 54.

45. Anna Howard Shaw to Lucy E. Anthony, February 11, 1889, Shaw Papers, Folder 502.

46. Anna Howard Shaw to Lucy E. Anthony, May 21, 1889, and Anna Howard Shaw to Lucy E. Anthony, May 24, 1889, Shaw Papers, Folder 502.

47. The Park Street address is the one that is listed on her publicity flyers. Shaw Papers, Folder 417; Anna Howard Shaw to Lucy E. Anthony, October 21, 1889,

Shaw Papers, Folder 502; WCTU Franchise Department Leaflet, October 19, 1889, with handwritten note from Lucy E. Anthony as secretary, Shaw Papers, Folder 417; and "Monroe County Library, http://www.libraryweb.org/rochimag/SBA/Other.htm#4 (accessed April 14, 2013).

48. "Famous Clan of Shaws Meet Today after Many Years," *Washington Times*, August 7, 1911.

49. Anna Howard Shaw to Lucy Stone, July 18, 1888, in Spencer, "Dr. Anna Howard Shaw," 155.

Chapter 4. Apprenticeship in the National American Woman Suffrage Association (1890–1903)

1. "Let No Man Take Thy Crown," Anna Howard Shaw, February 1894, in Wil A. Linkugel, "The Speeches of Anna Howard Shaw" (PhD Dissertation, University of Wisconsin, 1960), 69.

2. Dorinda Riessen-Reed, *The Woman Suffrage Movement in South Dakota* (Vermillion, S.D.: Governmental Research Bureau, State University of South Dakota, 1958).

3. Anna Howard Shaw, *The Story of a Pioneer* (New York: Harper and Brothers, 1915), 189–216.

4. Anna Howard Shaw to Lucy E. Anthony, September 9, 1890, Anna Howard Shaw Papers, Folder 502, Schlesinger Library, Radcliffe Institute, Harvard University; and Anna Howard Shaw to Lucy E. Anthony, January 16, 1890, Shaw Papers, Folder 502.

5. Early PR brochures, photographs, newspaper clippings, and Anna Howard Shaw to Lucy E. Anthony, October 16, 1890, Shaw Papers, Folders 417 and 503. Susan B. Anthony urged Shaw to abandon her religious title and association with Methodism. By the time she became NAWSA president, Shaw most often used her medical title, becoming Dr. Shaw.

6. Shaw, *Story of a Pioneer*, 169–188.

7. Both Kraditor and O'Neill discuss the family backgrounds of the suffrage leaders. Aileen S. Kraditor, *The Ideas of the Woman Suffrage Movement, 1890–1920* (New York: W. W. Norton, 1981); William L. O'Neill, *Everyone Was Brave: A History of Feminism in America* (New York: Quadrangle/The New York Times Book Co., 1976).

8. There is a wide literature on the experiences of different classes and races of women in the West during this period. See, for example, Jane E. Simonsen, *Making Home Work: Domesticity and Native American Assimilation in the American West, 1860–1919* (Chapel Hill: University of North Carolina Press, 2006); Quintard Taylor and Shirley Ann Wilson Moore, *African American Women Confront the West: 1600–2000* (Norman: University of Oklahoma Press, 2003); Elizabeth Jameson and Susan H. Armitage, *Writing the Range: Race, Class, and Culture in the Women's West* (Norman: University of Oklahoma Press, 1997); and Lillian Schlissel, *Women's Diaries of the Westward Journey*, Studies in the Life of Women (New York: Schocken Books, 1992).

9. Shaw, *Story of a Pioneer*, 169–188.

10. John Milton Cooper, *Pivotal Decades: The United States, 1900–1920* (New York:

W. W. Norton, 1990); John Whiteclay Carosso and Vincent P. Chambers, *The Tyranny of Change: America in the Progressive Era, 1900–1917*, St. Martin's Series in Twentieth Century United States History (New York: St. Martin's Press, 1980); and Christine Stansell, *The Feminist Promise: 1792 to the Present*, 1st ed. (New York: Modern Library, 2010).

11. Laura Briggs, *Reproducing Empire: Race, Sex, Science, and U.S. Imperialism in Puerto Rico*, American Crossroads, 11 (Berkeley: University of California Press, 2002); Kristin L. Hoganson, *Fighting for American Manhood: How Gender Politics Provoked the Spanish-American and Philippine-American Wars*, Yale Historical Publications (New Haven: Yale University Press, 1998); Gail Bederman, *Manliness and Civilization: A Cultural History of Gender and Race in the United States, 1880–1917* (Chicago: University of Chicago Press, 1996); and Kristin L. Hoganson, *Consumers' Imperium: The Global Production of American Domesticity, 1865–1920* (Chapel Hill: University of North Carolina Press, 2007).

12. Alys Eve Weinbaum, "Writing Feminist Genealogy: Charlotte Perkins Gilman, Racial Nationalism, and the Reproduction of Maternalist Feminism," *Feminist Studies* 27, no. 2 (2001); and Paul Buhle et al., *The Concise History of Woman Suffrage: Selections from the Classic Work of Stanton, Anthony, Gage, and Harper* (Urbana: University of Illinois Press, 1978), 347; and Bederman, *Manliness and Civilization*.

13. Shaw, *Story of a Pioneer*, 195–204, 248–252.

14. Susan B. Anthony and Ida Husted Harper, *History of Woman Suffrage, Volume IV* (Rochester, N.Y.: Susan B. Anthony: Charles Mann, 1902); and Anna Howard Shaw, "Indian versus Women," *Women's Tribune*, May 9, 1891.

15. Shaw, "Indian versus Women."

16. Ibid.

17. Ibid.

18. Anna J. Cooper et al., *The Voice of Anna Julia Cooper: Including a Voice from the South and Other Important Essays, Papers, and Letters*, Legacies of Social Thought (Lanham, Md.: Rowman and Littlefield, 1998).

19. Although many people have repeated this incident with varying interpretations of the facts and Cooper's perspective, any discussion and analysis is limited and somewhat speculative since Cooper's is the only record of the incident involving Shaw and Wimodaughsis. Further, there are no other discussions of the exchange from that period. Additionally some scholars have argued that Cooper was being sarcastic or ironic in her praise of Shaw and Anthony. Others have seen the entire incident differently going so far as to attribute to Shaw the blatant racism that Cooper praises her for confronting and moving the entire incident to Kentucky. A central problem is that most scholars don't seem to have read Shaw's speech. This is an example of the "cherry picking" of phrases and quotations that mar many of the discussions about Shaw's positions. See Barbara Hilkert Andolsen, *"Daughters of Jefferson, Daughters of Bootblacks": Racism and American Feminism* (Macon, Ga.: Mercer University Press, 1986); Vivian M. May, "Disciplinary Desires and Undisciplined Daughters: Negotiating the Politics of a Women's Studies Doctoral Education," *NWSA Journal* 14, no. 1 (2002); and Vivian M. May, "Thinking from the Margins, Acting at the Intersections: Anna Julia Cooper's a Voice from the South," *Hypatia* 19, no. 2 (2004). On Shaw's connection to Wimodaughsis, see Gloria Moldow, *Women Doctors in Gilded-Age Washington: Race, Gender, and Professionalization* (Urbana:

University of Illinois Press, 1987), 140–141. Ida Husted Harper, *The Life and Work of Susan B. Anthony* (Indianapolis: Hollenbeck Press, 1908), 700.

20. Cooper, *Voice of Anna Julia Cooper*.

21. When first considering this issue, I assumed Cooper had been present to hear Shaw's speech. It was late in this research that I received a copy of Shaw's talk through the generosity of Kristin Mapel Bloomberg, After comparing the texts, I began to doubt that Cooper had actually heard Shaw's entire talk since most of Cooper's essay has nothing to do with what Shaw said. A full intertextual analysis is beyond this work. Harper, *History of Woman Suffrage*, 182–183; Cooper, *Voice of Anna Julia Cooper*, 105; and Shaw, "Indian versus Women."

22. There is evidence that Anna Howard Shaw spoke at Black women's clubs and sought to include women of all races on the NAWSA programs after she became NAWSA president, but there is no indication that she had anywhere near the level of interactions or contacts among the communities of African American leaders that Susan B. Anthony or Jane Addams had.

23. Kathi Kern, *Mrs. Stanton's Bible* (Ithaca: Cornell University Press, 2001).

24. "God's Women," in Linkugel, "Speeches," 368–382; and Wil A. Linkugel and Martha Watson, *Anna Howard Shaw: Suffrage Orator and Social Reformer*, Great American Orators, No. 10 (New York: Greenwood Press, 1991), 131–138.

25. "Shaw publicity," 1890, Shaw Papers, Folder 417; and "Appointment Books," 1893–1919, Shaw Papers.

26. Anna Howard Shaw to Lucy E. Anthony, n.d., 1890, South Dakota. Shaw Papers, Folder 502. Nothing in the surviving papers explains Lucy's illness. Lucy frequently attended the NAWSA Conventions but only occasionally joined Shaw during some of the state campaigns.

27. Anna Howard Shaw to Lucy E. Anthony, September 24, 1891, Shaw Papers, Folder 503. Though Henry James had coined the term *Boston Marriage* in the mid-1880s to describe the relationship between two unmarried, middle-class women, there is no source that indicates that Shaw or Lucy were familiar with or ever used that term.

28. See photograph in Shaw, *Story of a Pioneer*, 80. The records following Rachel Foster Avery's life after she married are scant, and there is little information about her husband's work or their financial arrangements.

29. Anna Howard Shaw to Lucy E. Anthony, September 25, 1891; Anna Howard Shaw to Lucy E. Anthony, September 27, 1891, Shaw Papers, Folder 503.

30. Anna Howard Shaw to Lucy E. Anthony, November 10, 1892, Shaw Papers, Folder 503. Records suggest that both Shaw and Anthony bought land on this stretch of sea coast. Barnstable County Registry of Deeds, April 19, 1893, Book 205, Page 1 from Barnstable County.

31. Ida Husted Harper, "Unpublished Manuscript, Biography of Anna Howard Shaw" (Ann Arbor: Bentley Library, University of Michigan), 59–60.

32. "Exciting Methodist Questions," *New York Times* (1857–Current file), May 18, 1880, 1, http://o-www.proquest.com.library.albion.edu/ (accessed December 5, 2009). Anna Oliver would die later in 1892 at the age of 52. Donald W. Haynes, "Wesleyan Wisdom: A Turning Point for Women in Our Journey," *United Methodist Reporter*, March 5, 2009. Oliver and Shaw weren't the only leading women Buckley

challenged. According to the *New York Times* he had also objected to Frances Willard's efforts.

33. Anna Howard Shaw, "Woman's Right to Suffrage," *Chautauqua Assembly Herald*, August 9, 1892.

34. Ibid., 817.

35. Shaw, *Story of a Pioneer*, 256–259.

36. Mary Wright Sewall and Women Conf Author: World's Congress of Representatives. *The World's Congress of Representative Women: A Historical Résumé for Popular Circulation of the World's Congress of Representative Women, Convened in Chicago on May 15, and Adjourned on May 22, 1893, under the Auspices of the Woman's Branch of the World's Congress Auxiliary* (Chicago: Rand, McNally and Co., 1894). Several African American women were invited speakers at the World Congress of Representative Women, including Fannie Barrier Williams, Frances Watkins Harper, Anna Julia Cooper, Fannie J. Coppin, Sarah J. Early, and Haile Q. Brown.

37. There is significant scholarship on the racism and ethnocentrism of the Columbian Exposition going back a number of decades. See, for example, Elliott M. Rudwick and August Meier, "Black Man in the 'White City': Negroes and the Columbian Exposition, 1893," *Phylon (1960-)* 26, no. 4 (1965); and Christopher Robert Reed, *All the World Is Here! The Black Presence at White City*, Blacks in the Diaspora (Bloomington: Indiana University Press, 2000). The sources on the exclusion of and protests by Black women have almost as long a history. See Ann Massa, "Black Women in the 'White City,'" *Journal of American Studies* 8, no. 3 (1974); Gayle Gullett, "'Our Great Opportunity': Organized Women Advance Women's Work at the World's Columbian Exposition of 1893," *Illinois Historical Journal* 87, no. 4 (1994); Shaw, *Story of a Pioneer*, 175–178.

38. Anna Howard Shaw, "Lift Your Standards High," in Linkugel, "Speeches," 49–68.

39. Kern, *Mrs. Stanton's Bible. Sarah Brown Ingersoll Cooper Papers, 1813–1921* (Ithaca: Division of Rare and Manuscript Collections, Cornell University Library). Shaw was writing to Harriet Cooper during this time.

40. 1893 Appointment Book, Shaw Papers, Folder 397.

41. Either Shaw or Lucy Anthony wrote Shaw's rates in the appointment books during these years. See 1893 Appointment Book, "Anna Shaw Dates," and Contract with the Brockway Lecture Bureau, October 5, 1895, Shaw Papers, in *Series X of the Mary Earhart Dillon Collection*, Schlesinger Library, Radcliffe College. John R. McKivigan, *Forgotten Firebrand: James Redpath and the Making of Nineteenth-Century America* (Ithaca: Cornell University Press, 2008), 120; Lisa Tetrault, "The Incorporation of American Feminism: Suffragists and the Postbellum Lyceum," *Journal of American History* 96, no. 4 (2010): 1027–1056; and Shaw, *Story of a Pioneer*, 158.

42. Shaw, *Story of a Pioneer*, 158. On the financial situations of these other leaders, see Victoria Brown, *The Education of Jane Addams*, Politics and Culture in Modern America (Philadelphia: University of Pennsylvania Press, 2004); Elizabeth Anne Payne, *Reform, Labor, and Feminism: Margaret Dreier Robins and the Women's Trade Union League*, Women in American History (Urbana: University of Illinois Press, 1988); Ellen Carol DuBois, *Harriot Stanton Blatch and the Winning of Woman*

Suffrage (New Haven: Yale University Press, 1997); Ruth Birgitta Anderson Bordin, *Frances Willard: A Biography* (Chapel Hill: University of North Carolina Press, 1986); and Charlotte Perkins Gilman, *The Living of Charlotte Perkins Gilman: An Autobiography*, Wisconsin Studies in American Autobiography (Madison: University of Wisconsin Press, 1991).

43. Appointment Books, 1893–1896, Shaw Papers, Folders 397–400.

44. Ida Husted Harper and Susan B. Anthony, *The History of Women Suffrage, Volume IV, 1883–1900* (Indianapolis: Hollenbeck Press, 1902), 814; Frederick Douglass and Philip Sheldon Foner, *Frederick Douglass on Women's Rights*, Contributions in Afro-American and African Studies, No. 25 (Westport, Conn.: Greenwood Press, 1976); and Shaw, *Story of a Pioneer*, 177.

45. Susan B. Anthony had teased Shaw that, given her expanded physique, she might not be able to mount the mule by herself. Of course nothing made the proud and stubborn Shaw push herself more than such a challenge, something Anthony probably knew well; Shaw managed to get on her mule without assistance. George Fiske, "Anna Howard Shaw, Susan B. Anthony, and Others Riding in Yosemite: Group Portrait of Men and Women on Horses," photograph (Harvard University Library Visual Information Access, 1895). The University of Rochester Special Collections also has a number of photographs from this first of Shaw's trips to California. Harper, "Unpublished Manuscript," 106; and "Dr. Shaw's Circus Stunts," New York Times (1857–Current file), February 12, 1914, 24, http://0-www.proquest.com.library.albion.edu/ (accessed December 6, 2009).

46. The letters between Harriet Cooper and Anna Howard Shaw number over one hundred and fill four folders and, unlike most other Shaw correspondence, they were never edited. Sarah Brown Ingersoll Cooper Papers, #6543, Box 7, Folders 12–15, Division of Rare and Manuscript Collections, Cornell University Library; Appointment Books, 1895–96, Shaw Papers, Folders 399–400.

47. Anna Howard Shaw to Harriet Cooper (dictated), July 15, 1895, in Cooper Papers, Box 7, Folders 12.

48. Shaw, *Story of a Pioneer*, 267–268.

49. "An Adamless Eden of Women in Bloomers," *New York World*, August 25, 1895, 1; Shaw, *Story of a Pioneer*, 267–268; and Anna Howard Shaw to Harriet Cooper, August 30, 1895, Cooper Papers, Box 7, Folder 12.

50. Though the Census of 1890 was destroyed in a fire, the Veterans Schedules and City Directories documented that Shaw's parents and two brothers remained in Michigan. "General Index to Pension Files, 1861–1934, Washington, D.C., National Archives and Records Administration"; Anna Howard Shaw to Clara Osborn, August 30, 1891; Anna Howard Shaw to Lucy E. Anthony, February 13, 1891; Anna Howard Shaw to Lucy E. Anthony, February 18, 1892; Shaw Papers, Folders 527 and 503; Anna Howard Shaw to Harriet Cooper, September 17, 1895, Cooper Papers, Box 7, Folder 12.

51. The financial arrangements among Susan B., Mary S., and Lucy Read Anthony were more complex. Deborah had purchased the Rochester home when she sold the family farm following her husband's death. Mary worked consistently as a school-teacher and then school principal while also caring for her increasingly infirm mother and various nieces and nephews. Although Ginzberg suggests that Susan supported Mary and Lucy, that is clearly an overstatement. Susan never had a steady income

and much of what she did earn went to the cause. Lori D. Ginzberg, *Elizabeth Cady Stanton: An American Life* (New York: Hill and Wang, 2009), 140. For whatever reason, Shaw never seemed close to Tom's daughter, Margaret, perhaps because she had both her mother and father. Harper, "Unpublished Manuscript," 117.

52. Flexner ignores Shaw's presence in the 1895–1896 California campaign. Eleanor Flexner, *Century of Struggle: The Woman's Rights Movement in the United States* (Cambridge: Belknap Press of Harvard University Press, 1959), 215–217. On the other hand, Shaw wanted to make her trips to California pay for themselves and not cost the California suffrage organizations any money. Her friendly letters to Harriet Cooper often went into great detail over the best arrangements. See, for example, Anna Howard Shaw to Harriet Cooper, October 6, 1895, Box 7, Folder 12.

53. As noted above (n. 50) Shaw's letters went into great detail on finances. She already knew that some people thought she charged too much.

54. Anna Howard Shaw to Harriet Cooper, July 30, 1895; and Anna Howard Shaw to Harriet Cooper, November 11, 1895, in Cooper Papers, Box 7, Folder 12. At this point there are about three letters a week from Anna Howard Shaw to Harriet Cooper. See, for a different view of the California campaign, Rebecca J. Mead, *How the Vote Was Won: Woman Suffrage in the Western United States, 1868–1914* (New York: New York University Press, 2004).

55. Harper and Anthony, *History of Woman Suffrage*, 480–482; Shaw, *Story of a Pioneer*, 270–277; and Harper, *Life of Susan B. Anthony*, 863–893.

56. "They Met Death Together," New York Times (1857–Current file), December 12, 1896, 8, http://0-www.proquest.com.library.albion.edu/ (accessed December 6, 2009).

57. On July 14, 1897, Susan B. Anthony wrote in her diary that she had been at home for nine months, which was longer than she had been home for thirty or forty years. Susan B. Anthony Papers, Box 3, Reel 4, Manuscript Division, Library of Congress, Washington, D.C.

58. Although Shaw drifted away from the temperance movement and her closeness to Willard diminished, neither woman left any comments on the change in their relationship. Shaw, *Story of a Pioneer*, 207–208.

59. "The White Man's Burden," in Linkugel, "Speeches," 971–990.

60. Kristin Hoganson, "'As Badly Off as the Filipinos': U.S. Women's Suffragists and the Imperial Issue at the Turn of the Twentieth Century," *Journal of Women's History* 13, no.2 (Summer 2001): 9–33; and "The White Man's Burden," in Linkugel, "Speeches," 971–990.

61. Anna Howard Shaw to "Home Folks," in Harper, "Unpublished Manuscript," 143–189.

62. Shaw wrote long descriptions of her travels on this trip that Lucy then forwarded to various family members and friends. Anna Howard Shaw to "Home Folks," compiled in Harper, "Unpublished Manuscript," 143–189.

63. Shaw, *Story of a Pioneer*, 352.

64. Anna Howard Shaw to Lucy E. Anthony, April 17, 1901, Shaw Papers, Folder 506.

65. Harper, *History of Suffrage*, 352.

66. Harper, *Life of Susan B. Anthony*, 1171.

67. Ibid., 285; and Mary Gray Peck and National American Woman Suffrage

Association, *Carrie Chapman Catt, a Biography* (New York: H. W. Wilson Co., 1944), 106. Eleanor Flexner stated that Anthony chose Catt over Shaw, establishing this as the orthodox view for modern suffrage scholarship.

68. Peck, *Carrie Chapman Catt*, 17–85.

69. Harper, *History of Woman Suffrage*; Peck, *Carrie Chapman Catt*, 104–135; and Susan B. Anthony to Laura Clay, April 15, 1900, *Clay, Laura (1849–1941) Papers, 1882–1941*, Collection Number: 46M4 Special Collections, University of Kentucky, Lexington, Kentucky. Harper and Anthony, *History of Women Suffrage*.

70. Harper and Anthony, *History of Woman Suffrage*, 61.

71. Anna Howard Shaw, in Harper, "Unpublished Manuscript," 206; Datebook, 1903, March 1903, in Harper, "Unpublished Manuscript," 207; Anna Howard Shaw to Lucy E. Anthony, April 17, 1903, Shaw Papers, Folder 507.

72. Ida Husted Harper, *History of Woman Suffrage*, V. 5 (New York: National American Woman Suffrage Association, 1922), 82–83.

73. Shaw, *Story of a Pioneer*, 311–313.

Chapter 5. Compromised Leadership

1. Anna Howard Shaw to Susan B. Anthony, February 3, 1904, in Ida Husted Harper, "Unpublished Manuscript, Biography of Anna Howard Shaw" (Ann Arbor: Bentley Library, University of Michigan, n.d.), 118.

2. Shaw wrote, "Such a sick head, I think the worst I ever had. I do not see how I can keep up this way. It is so hard not to be well and have to work. Today Lucy and Nicolas took such good care of me." Diary 1904, January 10, 1904, Shaw Papers, Series X of the Mary Earhart Dillon Collection, 1863–1955, A-68, Folder 380, Schlesinger Library, Radcliffe Institute, Harvard University.

3. Roosevelt did create some stir when he invited Booker T. Washington to dine at the White House in 1901. Jacqueline M. Moore, *Booker T. Washington, W. E. B. Du Bois, and the Struggle for Racial Uplift*, African American History Series (Questia. com: Scholarly Resources, 2003 [accessed April 14, 2013]).

4. John Whiteclay Chambers and Vincent P. Carosso, *The Tyranny of Change: America in the Progressive Era, 1900–1917*, St. Martin's Series in Twentieth Century United States History (New York: St. Martin's Press, 1980).

5. Rosalyn Terborg-Penn, *African American Women in the Struggle for the Vote, 1850–1920*, Blacks in the Diaspora (Bloomington: Indiana University Press, 1998); Elizabeth Anne Payne, *Reform, Labor, and Feminism: Margaret Dreier Robins and the Women's Trade Union League*, Women in American History (Urbana: University of Illinois Press, 1988); Susan Levine, "Labor's True Woman: Domesticity and Equal Rights in the Knights of Labor," *Journal of American History* 70, no. 2 (1983); and Paula Baker, "The Domestication of Politics: Women and American Political Society, 1780–1920," *American Historical Review* 89, no. 3 (1984).

6. Jacqueline Van Voris, *Carrie Chapman Catt: A Public Life* (New York: Feminist Press at the City University of New York, 1987); Susan E Marshall, *Splintered Sisterhood: Gender and Class in the Campaign against Woman Suffrage.* (Madison: University of Wisconsin Press, 1997); and Carrie Chapman Catt and Nettie Rogers Shuler, *Woman Suffrage and Politics: The Inner Story of the Suffrage Movement* (New York: C. Scribner's Sons, 1926).

230 NOTES TO CHAPTERS 4 AND 5

7. See, for example, Christine Stansell, *The Feminist Promise: 1792 to the Present*, 1st ed. (New York: Modern Library, 2010); and Ellen Carol DuBois, *Harriot Stanton Blatch and the Winning of Woman Suffrage* (New Haven: Yale University Press, 1997).

8. Why the Avery family moved to Europe isn't clear. What is clear is that Cyrus Miller Avery was a disappointment to Shaw, Susan B. Anthony, and Lucy Anthony. Anna Howard Shaw to Lucy E. Anthony, August 8, 1905, Shaw Papers, Folder 506.

9. Susan B. Anthony to William Lloyd Garrison Jr., January 4, 1905, Garrison Family Papers, 1694–2005, MS 60, Folder 26, Sophia Smith Collection, Smith College, Northampton, Massachusetts. It isn't clear what action the Garrisons took in response to Anthony's letter.

10. Anna Howard Shaw to Eleanor Garrison, December 10, 1911, Garrison Family Papers, 1694–2005, MS 60, Box 127, File 13, Sophia Smith Collection, Smith College, Northampton, Massachusetts. Shaw had written about this earlier, of how hard it was to "hobnob" with society women. Ida Husted Harper and Susan B. Anthony, *The History of Women Suffrage, Volume IV, 1883–1900* (Indianapolis: Hollenbeck Press, 1902), 352.

11. Harper, "Unpublished Manuscript," 64, 106, 156. Harper makes this argument, but it isn't clear that any depressive episodes were severe enough to keep Shaw from her work except perhaps in December 1909.

12. Anna Howard Shaw to Isabel Howland, March 5, 1899, Box 2, Folder 46, Isabel Howland Papers, Sophia Smith Collection, Smith College, Northampton, Massachusetts.

13. This is an interesting note because it further complicates any easy analysis of Anna Howard Shaw's relationship with Lucy; in this case, Shaw shared a bed with Susan B. and not Lucy. Diary 1904, February 7, 1904, Shaw Papers, Folder 380.

14. Anna Howard Shaw, *The Story of a Pioneer* (New York: Harper and Brothers, 1915), 286; Susan B. Anthony to William Lloyd Garrison Jr., February 1904, Garrison Family Papers, Folder 21; and Paul E. Fuller, *Laura Clay and the Woman's Rights Movement* (Lexington: University of Kentucky Press, 1975), 113–115.

15. 1904 Appointment Book, Shaw Papers, Folder 506.

16. See, for example, Leila J. Rupp, *Worlds of Women: The Making of an International Women's Movement* (Princeton, N.J.: Princeton University Press, 1997); and Patricia Greenwood Harrison, *Connecting Links: The British and American Woman Suffrage Movements, 1900–1914* (Westport Conn.: Greenwood Press, 2000).

17. Harper, "Unpublished Manuscript"; and Harriet Taylor Upton and Eisenbraun Lana Dunn, *Harriet Taylor Upton's Random Recollections* (Warren, Ohio: Harriet Taylor Upton Association, 2004).

18. Geoffrey Blodgett, "Alice Stone Blackwell," in Edward T. James et al., *Notable American Women, 1607–1950: A Biographical Dictionary* (Cambridge: Belknap Press of Harvard University Press, 1971), 156–158.

19. Philip R. Shriver, "Harriet Taylor Upton," in James, *Notable American Women*, 500–501; and Upton and Dunn, *Harriet Taylor Upton's Random Recollections*.

20. Paul S. Boyer, "Laura Clay," in James, *Notable American Women*, 346–348; and L. E. Zimmerman, "Kate M. Gordon," in James, *Notable American Women*, 66–68.

21. Susan B. Anthony to William Lloyd and Ella Garrison, January 29, 1904, Garrison Family Papers, 1694–2005, MS 60, Folder 26. In *Bitter Harvest*, Upton

is quoted as describing Clay as a bulldog. Clavia Goodman, *Bitter Harvest: Laura Clay's Suffrage Work*, Kentucky Monographs 3 (Lexington, Ky.: Bur Press, 1946). See also Fuller, *Laura Clay and the Woman's Rights Movement*. Clay's scrapbooks from this period are online. *Laura Clay Photographic Collection, Ca. N.D.—1933*, Kentuckiana Digital Library. There is less research on Kate Gordon and even tracing her family is difficult. B. H. Gilley, "Kate Gordon and Louisiana Woman Suffrage," *Louisiana History: The Journal of the Louisiana Historical Association* 24, no. 3 (1983); Elna C. Green, "The Rest of the Story: Kate Gordon and the Opposition to the Nineteenth Amendment in the South," *Louisiana History: The Journal of the Louisiana Historical Association* 33, no. 2 (1992).

22. Anna Howard Shaw to "State Presidents," November 7, 1904, Ella H. Crossett Papers, Special Collections, University of Rochester Library, Rochester, New York; and Sara Hunter Graham, *Woman Suffrage and the New Democracy* (New Haven, Conn.: Yale University Press, 1996).

23. Ellen DuBois argues that the term for most of the NAWSA leaders should be *elite*, to designate the women who didn't have to work for a living. Ellen Carol DuBois, *Woman Suffrage and Women's Rights* (New York: New York University Press, 1998), 178–179. The suffrage movement had recognized that some women needed to earn a living only to the extent of paying salaries to clerical and field workers. See, for example, DuBois, *Harriot Stanton Blatch*, 113.

24. Harper, "Unpublished Manuscript," 118–119.

25. Both Frances Squire Potter and Mary War Dennett were divorced, self-supporting mothers when they ran the NAWSA headquarters.

26. Harper, "Unpublished Manuscript," 118–119. For how some other NAWSA officers viewed Shaw's need to work, see Mary Gray Peck, quoted in Rebecca J. Mead, *How the Vote Was Won: Woman Suffrage in the Western United States, 1868–1914* (New York: New York University Press, 2004), 217, n. 58.

27. Shaw had already reached the personally significant amount of $10,000.00 in 1896. Harper, "Unpublished Manuscript," 100. See Kraditor and O'Neill on the class backgrounds of these women. Aileen S. Kraditor, *The Ideas of the Woman Suffrage Movement, 1890–1920* (New York: Norton, 1981); and William L. O'Neill, *Everyone Was Brave: A History of Feminism in America* (New York: Quadrangle/The New York Times Book Co., 1976).

28. It is pretty clear that Shaw underestimated both her living expenses and the expenses of being the NAWSA president. The fact that Shaw agreed to this lesser amount ended up causing problems later. See Rachel Foster Avery to M. Carey Thomas and Mary Garrett, February 12, 1909, M. Carey Thomas Papers, Special Collections Department, Bryn Mawr College Library.

29. Moynihan's biography of Duniway contains some of this background. Ruth Barnes Moynihan, *Rebel for Rights, Abigail Scott Duniway*, Yale Historical Publications, 130 (New Haven: Yale University Press, 1983).

30. The *History of Woman Suffrage* doesn't give a title, but "Our Ideal" is handwritten on the copy included in Shaw's papers. In the Linkugel dissertation, the title is "Heroic Service in the Case of the Truth." Ida Husted Harper, *History of Woman Suffrage, Volume V* (Rochester, N.Y.: Susan B. Anthony: Charles Mann, 1922), 125; Shaw Papers, Folder 428; and Wil A. Linkugel, "The Speeches of Anna Howard Shaw" (PhD Dissertation, University of Wisconsin, 1960), 433–474.

31. Linkugel, "Speeches," 433–474.

32. Harper, *History of Suffrage V*, 124.

33. Ibid., 145. On Florence Kelley, see Kathryn Kish Sklar, *Florence Kelley and the Nation's Work* (New Haven: Yale University Press, 1995).

34. There is no evidence that any African American woman spoke at the 1906 convention, but Fannie Barrier Williams spoke at the 1907 Chicago Convention. This note is important also as an indication that after the entire "Woman versus the Indian" exchange, Shaw and Anna Julia Cooper remained in contact with each other. Anna Howard Shaw to Catherine W. McCulloch, November 13, 1905, Catharine Waugh McCulloch, Series VI of the Mary Earhart Dillon Collection, 1869–1945, A-68, Folder 164, Schlesinger Library, Radcliffe Institute, Harvard University; Anna Howard Shaw to Emily Howland, September 26, 1905, Isabel Howland Papers, Sophia Smith Collection, Smith College, Northampton, Massachusetts; "Race Suicide Heresy," *Washington Post*, April 12, 1905.

35. It is possible that Shaw's ideas for speakers were opposed by the more conservative members of the board. There is no record of how these decisions were made.

36. Shaw, *Story of a Pioneer*, 295–298.

37. Additionally Shaw, Anthony, and Thomas had all participated in the celebration of Elizabeth Cady Stanton's eightieth birthday. "Elizabeth Cady Stanton," New York Times (1857–1922), November 13, 1895, http://o-www.proquest.com.library .albion.edu/ (accessed July 15, 2012); and "In Honor of Mrs. E. C. Stanton," New York Times (1857–1922), November 12, 1895, http://o-www.proquest.com.library .albion.edu/ (accessed July 15, 2012).

38. Shaw, *Story of a Pioneer*, 295–296.

39. The two most complete sources on Thomas are M. Carey Thomas and Marjorie Housepian Dobkin, *The Making of a Feminist: Early Journals and Letters of M. Carey Thomas* (Kent, Ohio: Kent State University Press, 1979); and Helen Lefkowitz Horowitz, *The Power and Passion of M. Carey Thomas* (New York: Alfred A. Knopf, 1994). Kathleen Waters Sanders, *Mary Elizabeth Garrett: Society and Philanthropy in the Gilded Age* (Baltimore: Johns Hopkins University Press, 2008), 3.

40. Horowitz, *Power and Passion*; and Shaw, *Story of a Pioneer*, 225–226. Both M. Carey Thomas and Mary Garrett became life members after the convention in 1906, though Mary Garrett had contributed to the NAWSA as early as Catt's first presidency. MCT to Elizabeth Hauser, April 7, 1906, M. Carey Thomas Papers, Special Collections Department, Bryn Mawr College Library. This fund, which was raised by the next year, went by various names. For the sake of clarity, I will refer to it as the Thomas-Garrett Fund.

41. Harper, *History of Woman Suffrage*, 167–168; and Ida Husted Harper, *The Life and Work of Susan B. Anthony* (Indianapolis: Hollenbeck Press, 1908), 1401–1409.

42. "Others Will Follow," 1906 Convention Presidential Address, in Linkugel, "Speeches," 475–511.

43. Shaw devotes a full chapter of her autobiography to the "Passing of Aunt Susan" in Shaw, *Story of a Pioneer*, 218–238. Scholars, especially Graham argue that such stories re-created Anthony as the suffrage "saint." Sara Hunter Graham, *Woman Suffrage and the New Democracy* (New Haven, Conn.: Yale University Press, 1996), 47–52.

44. Diary 1906, March 9, 1906, Shaw Papers, Folder 382.

45. Ibid., March 12, 1906. Though Anthony died on March 13, Shaw wrote this entry beginning on the page printed "March 12, 1906."

46. Harper, *Life of Susan B. Anthony*, 1440.

47. Harriet Taylor Upton to Laura Clay, July 6, 1906, Laura Clay Papers, Box 3, Folder 39, University of Kentucky Library Special Collections, Lexington, Kentucky. Anna Howard Shaw to Lucy E. Anthony, September 27, 1906, in Harper, "Unpublished Manuscript," 259–260.

48. Anna Howard Shaw to Lucy E. Anthony, September 27, 1906, in Harper, "Unpublished Manuscript," 259–260.

49. Marjorie Julian Spruill, *New Women of the New South: The Leaders of the Woman Suffrage Movement in the Southern States* (New York: Oxford University Press, 1993), 120–122.

50. Ibid.

51. By 1907 there were three funds that had some claim as memorials to Susan B. Anthony. The first involved a building for women students at the University of Rochester, the second was the one announced by Rachel Foster Avery called the Susan B. Anthony Memorial Fund, and the third was the one that Thomas and Garrett handled called the Susan B. Anthony Memorial Guarantee Fund. M. Carey Thomas to Mrs. William M. Ivins, April 27, 1907, M. Carey Thomas Papers; and Harper, *History of Suffrage V*, 235, 253.

52. Anna Howard Shaw to Ella Hawley Crossett, May 13, 1908, Susan B. Anthony House, Inc., Papers, Suffrage Manuscript Collections, University of Rochester Library, Rochester, N.Y.

53. "The New Man," in Linkugel, "Speeches," 969.

54. Ibid; and Nancy Folbre, "The Unproductive Housewife: Her Evolution in Nineteenth-Century Economic Thought," *Signs* 16, no. 3 (1991): 463–484.

55. Harper, *History of Suffrage V*, 229; and Strom Sharon Hartman, "Leadership and Tactics in the American Woman Suffrage Movement: A New Perspective from Massachusetts," *Journal of American History* 62, no. 2 (1975).

56. In her autobiography, Shaw puts this event in 1908, while in the unpublished biography Harper seems to put it in 1906. A number of M. Carey Thomas's letters determine that the fund was completed May 1, 1907. Shaw, *Story of a Pioneer*, 295–296; Harper, "Unpublished Manuscript," 146; and M. Carey Thomas to various benefactors, April 27, 1907, M. Carey Thomas Papers.

57. Diary 1905, Shaw Papers, Deed, February 27, 1905, Between Henry Lewis and Anna Howard Shaw, 1905 Deed Book, 46–48, Register of Deeds, Delaware County Courthouse, Media, Pennsylvania; and 1906 Map of Upper Providence Township, Delaware County Archives, Lima, Pennsylvania.

58. It is ironic that Shaw writes little about this home in her autobiography. Her other sources document how long she and Lucy wanted such a home and how happy Shaw was to finally have it. They had discussed the naming of their home in 1906. There are many photographs of Alnwick Lodge on file at Harvard. Shaw, *Story of a Pioneer*, 268.

59. Harper, "Unpublished Manuscript," 284; photographs (Harvard University Library Visual Information Access).

60. Anna Howard Shaw to Clara Osborn, December 26, 1907, Shaw Papers, Folder 527.

61. Ibid.; and Map of Upper Providence Township, Delaware County Archives, Lima, Pennsylvania, land records, map at Delaware County Archives.

62. This was also the beginning of mass meetings, especially in New York. There is a photograph among the Harvard collection that shows a march and identifies it as one welcoming Shaw to her hometown. The buildings in the photograph didn't match those in Shaw's hometown of Big Rapids, Michigan. That same photograph was used by the Boone County Historical Society when members planned a reenactment of the 1908 march, http://www.uiowa.edu/~humiowa/BooneSuffrageMarch .html (accessed April 14, 2013) and http://www.celebratesuffrage2008.org/History .php (accessed April 14, 2013). DuBois, *Harriot Stanton Blatch*, 123.

63. *Buffalo Express* report quoted in Harper, *History of Suffrage V*, 216.

64. Ibid., 236.

65. Anna Howard Shaw to Lucy E. Anthony, November 1908, quoted in Harper, "Unpublished Manuscript," 293.

Chapter 6. Creating Her Vision

1. "Is Democracy a Failure?" Anna Howard Shaw, March 2, 1911, in Wil A. Linkugel, "The Speeches of Anna Howard Shaw" (PhD Dissertation, University of Wisconsin, 1960), 563.

2. "Suffrage Headquarters: Reporters Get a Private View of New National Offices," New York Times (1857–Current file), September 18, 1909, 3, http://0-www.proquest .com.library.albion.edu/ (accessed December 7, 2009). Eleanor Flexner, *Century of Struggle: The Woman's Rights Movement in the United States* (Cambridge: Belknap Press of Harvard University Press, 1959), 256. Less noted is that the NAWSA had also opened an office in Washington, D.C., earlier that year. "Suffragettes in Capital: Mrs. Avery Will Run Washington Headquarters after Feb. 1," New York Times (1857–Current file), January 21, 1909, 18, http://0-www.proquest.com.library.albion .edu/ (accessed December 7, 2009).

3. For example, Anna Howard Shaw wrote to M. Carey Thomas on April 8, 1909, requesting that her salary come directly from Thomas and Garrett rather than go through the NAWSA Treasurer, Harriet Taylor Upton. M. Carey Thomas Papers, Reel 57, Special Collections Department, Bryn Mawr College Library. Trisha Franzen, "Singular Leadership: Anna Howard Shaw, Single Women and the U.S. Woman Suffrage Movement," *Women's History Review* 17, no. 3 (2008). Carrie Chapman Catt admitted that Shaw was "scraggy." Carrie Chapman Catt to Mary Gray Peck, December 6, 1911, Carrie Chapman Catt Papers, Manuscript Division, Library of Congress, Washington, D.C.

4. Charlotte Perkins Gilman, *The Living of Charlotte Perkins Gilman: An Autobiography*, Wisconsin Studies in American Autobiography (Madison: University of Wisconsin Press, 1991); and William L. O'Neill, *Everyone Was Brave: A History of Feminism in America* (New York: Quadrangle/The New York Times Book Co., 1976).

5. "Think Husbands Aren't Mainstays: Audience Votes an Emphatic 'No' to the Question: 'Do They Support Their Wives?'" New York Times (1857–Current file), January 7, 1909, 9, http://0-www.proquest.com.library.albion.edu/ (accessed December 7, 2009); Ann Crittenden, *The Price of Motherhood: Why the Most Important*

Job in the World Is Still the Least Valued (New York: Metropolitan Books, 2001); Ellen Key, *The Renaissance of Motherhood: Transl. from the Swedish by Anna E. B Fries* (New York: Source Book Press, 1914); Ellen Carol DuBois, *Woman Suffrage and Women's Rights* (New York: New York University Press, 1998), 194.

6. Anna Howard Shaw to M. Carey Thomas, April 8, 1909, M. Carey Thomas Papers, Reel 57.

7. Alys Eve Weinbaum, "Writing Feminist Genealogy: Charlotte Perkins Gilman, Racial Nationalism, and the Reproduction of Maternalist Feminism," *Feminist Studies* 27, no. 2 (2001). Most probably neither Alice Stone Blackwell nor Florence Kelley wavered in their support of universal suffrage.

8. Thomas and Garrett had the power to disperse the remaining balance of the fund, known as both the Susan B. Anthony Guarantee Fund and the Garrett-Thomas Fund, each year from 1907 to 1912. As the leader of the College Equal Suffrage League, Thomas had an official position within the association. Trisha Franzen, "A Friendship of Power and Politics: Anna Howard Shaw and M. Carey Thomas and the U.S. Woman Suffrage Movement" (unpublished).

9. Franzen, "A Friendship," and Ralph Wakefield Spencer, "Dr. Anna Howard Shaw: The Evangelical Feminist" (PhD Dissertation, Boston University, 1972), 281.

10. Shaw had written to Thomas on October 26, 1908, and December 26, 1908, about wanting a Washington, D.C., headquarters. M. Carey Thomas Papers, Reel 57, Rachel Foster Avery to Catharine W. McCulloch, 1909, Catharine Waugh McCulloch, Series VI of the Mary Earhart Dillon Collection, 1869–1945, A-68, Schlesinger Library, Radcliffe Institute, Harvard University.

11. "Suffragettes in Capital," *New York Times*, January 21, 1909.

12. Christopher Lasch, "Alva Erskine Smith Vanderbilt Belmont," in *Notable American Women 1607–1950*, ed. Edward T. James (Cambridge: Belknap Press of Harvard University, 1971). Belmont consolidated her social position through the marriage of her daughter, Consuelo, to the Duke of Marlborough.

13. Anna Howard Shaw to Lucy E. Anthony, June 17, 1909, Ida Husted Harper, "Unpublished Manuscript, Biography of Anna Howard Shaw" (Ann Arbor: Bentley Library, University of Michigan, n.d.), 297.

14. Anna Howard Shaw to M. Carey Thomas, March 12, 1909, Reel 57; and M. Carey Thomas to Anna Howard Shaw, March 13, 1909, Reel 35, M. Carey Thomas Papers.

15. Anna Howard Shaw to M. Carey Thomas, March 22, 1909, M. Carey Thomas Papers, Reel 57.

16. Maud Wood Park, "The Row at the National," undated essay, National American Woman Suffrage Association Papers.

17. See Frances Boardman Squire Potter Papers, 1879–1923, Schlesinger Library, Radcliffe Institute, Harvard University.

18. "Urges Suffragists to become Militant," New York Times (1857–Current file), June 15, 1909, 8, http://0-www.proquest.com.library.albion.edu/ (accessed December 7, 2009).

19. Ida Husted Harper, *History of Woman Suffrage, Volume V* (Rochester, N.Y.: Charles Mann, 1922), 243.

20. Ibid., 243.

21. Ibid., 243–265.

22. Ibid., 264.

23. Ibid., 255; Anna Howard Shaw to Isabella Howland, August 10, 1909, Isabel Howland Papers, Sophia Smith Collection, Smith College, Northampton, Massachusetts.

24. Anna Howard Shaw to Ella Hawley Crossett, August 9, 1909, August 1, 1909, Susan B. Anthony House, Inc., Papers, Suffrage Manuscript Collections, University of Rochester Library, Rochester, N.Y.

25. Belmont's efforts were followed closely by the press. Over the summer of 1909, especially in August, the *New York Times* had more than fifteen articles on Mrs. Belmont's suffrage activities. See, for example, Special to The *New York Times*, "Governor at Mrs. Belmont's," New York Times (1857–Current file), August 27, 1909, 1, http://o-www.proquest.com.library.albion.edu/ (accessed December 7, 2009). "Suffragettes at Newport," New York Times (1857–Current file), August 3, 1909, 6, http://o-www.proquest.com.library.albion.edu/ (accessed December 7, 2009). "Suffragists Meet at Marble House," New York Times (1857–Current file), August 25, 1909, 1, http://o-ww.proquest.com.library.albion.edu/ (accessed December 7, 2009).

26. "Suffrage Headquarters," New York Times (1857–Current file), September 18, 1909, 3, http://o-www.proquest.com.library.albion.edu/ (accessed December 7, 2009).

27. Some of this tension is seen in the letters between Shaw and the New York State leaders, especially with Ella Crossett. Susan B. Anthony House, Inc., Papers. See also Ellen Carol DuBois, *Harriot Stanton Blatch and the Winning of Woman Suffrage* (New Haven: Yale University Press, 1997); and Jacqueline Van Voris, *Carrie Chapman Catt: A Public Life* (New York: Feminist Press at the City University of New York, 1987).

28. "Suffragists to Aid Girl Waist Strikers," New York Times (1857–Current file), December 9, 1909, 3, http://o-www.proquest.com.library.albion.edu/ (accessed December 7, 2009). Not all went smoothly. Many of the working women questioned the efforts of the wealthy suffrage leaders. "Women Socialists Rebuff Suffragists," New York Times (1857–Current file), December 20, 1909, 5, http://o-www .proquest.com.library.albion.edu/ (accessed December 7, 2009).

29. Not surprisingly, many materials from this particular period are missing from Shaw's papers. Fuller writes that the move from Warren, Ohio, to New York City was a deliberate effort on Shaw's part to take control away from Harriet Taylor Upton, as well as an opportunity for Shaw to give Lucy E. Anthony more responsibility. Paul E. Fuller, *Laura Clay and the Women's Rights Movement* (Lexington: University of Kentucky Press, 1975), 114–117.

30. M. Carey Thomas to Mary Garrett, November 5, 1909, M. Carey Thomas Papers, Reel 15, Special Collections Department, Bryn Mawr College Library.

31. The correspondence among the other Board members doesn't really heat up until December. Much of the correspondence is in the Laura Clay Papers and discussed in Fuller's biography of Clay. It appears that Mary Gray Peck would write to Harriet Upton who would in turn correspond with Laura Clay. Most of the other major leaders of the NAWSA show up in the correspondence. For example, Harriet Taylor Upton to Laura Clay, December 3, 1909, Laura Clay Papers, Box 6, Folder 92; and Harriet Taylor Upton to Laura Clay, December 17, 1909, Laura Clay Papers,

Box 6, Folder 95; Kate Gordon to Laura Clay, December 7, 1909, Box 6, Folder 94, Laura Clay Papers; and Fuller, *Laura Clay*, 114–118. Catt's response to Potter is surprisingly casual and she jokes about "Miss Peck and I are making love to one another." Carrie Chapman Catt to Frances S. Potter, December 7, 1909, Carrie Chapman Catt Papers, Manuscript Division, Library of Congress, Washington, D.C.

32. Anna Howard Shaw and M. Carey Thomas appear to have been trying to deal with the issues at Headquarters during November, which seems in part to have involved Shaw taking over some of Thomas's responsibilities in the CESL and Lucy E. Anthony doing work for the CESL. M. Carey Thomas to Anna Howard Shaw, November 22, 1909, Reel 149; M. Carey Thomas to Caroline Lexow, November 22, 1909, M. Carey Thomas Papers, Reel 149; and M. Carey Thomas to Caroline Lexow, November 29, 1909, M. Carey Thomas Papers, Reel 149. See M. Carey Thomas to Rachel Foster Avery and Florence Kelley, December 3, 1909, and M. Carey Thomas to Harriet Taylor Upton, December 16, 1909, and M. Carey Thomas Papers. Maud Wood Park argues that Shaw was jealous of Potter's abilities as a speaker. See, Park, "Row at the National."

33. A possible scenario includes an alliance among Kelley, Potter, and Peck who were the three NAWSA most allied with other labor and progressive era organizations.

34. Diary 1910, January 1–3, 1910, Anna Howard Shaw Papers, 384; Fuller, *Laura Clay*, 193, n.10; and Shaw to Catherine Waugh McCulloch, January 12, 1910, Catharine W. McCulloch, Series VI of the Mary Earhart Dillon Collection, 1869–1945, A-68, Folder 165, Schlesinger Library, Radcliffe Institute, Harvard University.

35. Ibid.

36. See Harriet Taylor Upton to Laura Clay, January 13, 1910, Box 6, Folder 98, January 20, 1910, Box 6, Folder 99, February 16, 1910, Box 6, Folder 101, and March 10, 1910, Laura Clay Papers, Box 6, Folder 105, and April 4, 1910, Box 6, Folder 108, Laura Clay Papers. There are numerous similar letters.

37. Diary 1910, March 17, 1910, Shaw Papers, Folder 384. Anna Howard Shaw to M. Carey Thomas, February 2, 1910, M. Carey Thomas Papers, Reel 250.

38. Ida Husted Harper, ed., *History of Woman Suffrage, 1910–1920*, vol. III (New York: National American Woman Suffrage Association, 1922), 264–309.

39. *Forty-Second Annual Report of the National American Woman Suffrage Association, Given at the Convention, Held at Washington, D.C., April 14 to 19, Inclusive* (New York: The Association, 1910).

40. Though the *Proceedings* stated that, at the opening of the 1910 convention, all the officers were present except the second vice president, Florence Kelley; Alice Stone Blackwell, one of the auditors, was absent also. Mary Gray Peck, not an officer but the headquarters secretary, had to leave the convention upon the illness and death of her mother. Ibid.; Harper, *History of Woman Suffrage Volume V*.

41. *Proceedings*, 93–94.

42. "Two Suffragist Officers Resign," and "Mrs. Potter's Retirement Starts Afternoon's Row," *Washington Herald*, April 20, 1910, 2; "Young Blood Needed," *Washington Herald*, April 21, 1910, 3; and "A Card from Mrs. Avery and Mrs. Upton," *Woman's Journal*, April 30, 1910, 71.

43. Anna Howard Shaw to M. Carey Thomas, April, 1910, M. Carey Thomas Papers, Reel 57.

44. On Easter 1910, Shaw wrote of her despair. Later that month Shaw wrote to Rachel trying to sort things out. Harper, "Unpublished Manuscript," 298.

45. There are a number of letters in the M. Carey Thomas Papers concerning this event through May 1910. See, for example, M. Carey Thomas to Lucretia Blankenburg, May 11, 1910, M. Carey Thomas Papers, Reel 149. There was much brouhaha over the role Upton and Avery could play in the elections of their successors. See Anna Howard Shaw to Catherine McCulloch, June 3, 1910, Catharine Waugh McCulloch Papers, A-68; Anna Howard Shaw to State Presidents, December 1, 1910, Shaw Papers. See Anna Howard Shaw to Aletta Jacobs, Mineke with Annemarie Kloosterman Bosch, ed., *Politics and Friendship: Letters from the International Woman Suffrage Alliance, 1902–1942* (Columbus: Ohio State University Press, 1990), 113–114.

46. Harper, "Unpublished Manuscript," 321–322, 298, 305. It does seem that Rachel Foster Avery was in some kind of decline; one year after this event she more or less disappeared from the public record except for an appearance at the 1917 NAWSA Convention where she was "warmly introduced" by Anna Howard Shaw. Harper, *History of Woman Suffrage, 1910–1920*, 540. Further, Shaw included a photograph of her with Avery's child in her autobiography. She wrote only positively about Rachel Foster Avery and all these other women in that volume. Anna Howard Shaw, *Story of a Pioneer* (New York: Harper and Brothers, 1915).

47. Shaw had written this intent in her diary at the beginning of the year. Diary 1910, January 1, 1910, Shaw Papers, Folder 483.

48. The official history says very little about this controversy and Harper's unpublished biography notes only that there were the expected adjustments. Harper, *History of Woman Suffrage, 1910–1920*, 310, 315; and Harper, "Unpublished Manuscript," 192–194.

49. See, for example, Kathi Kern, *Mrs. Stanton's Bible* (Ithaca: Cornell University Press, 2001).

50. It seemed that the use of the term *insurgents* to designate those opposed to Shaw originated with Mary Gray Peck. Flexner, *Century of Struggle*, 249.

51. Harper, *History of Woman Suffrage, 1910–1920*. Most of the information from this period comes from the Dennett Papers. See, for example, "Dennett, Mary Ware, 1872–1947. Papers," (Cambridge: Schlesinger Library, Radcliffe College). The one biography of Mary Ware Dennett talks little about the years where there was a very productive and positive working relationship and friendship between Shaw and Dennett. Constance M. Chen, *"The Sex Side of Life": Mary Ware Dennett's Pioneering Battle for Birth Control and Sex Education* (New York: New Press, 1996).

52. Anna Howard Shaw to Lucy E. Anthony, June 10, 1910, in Harper, "Unpublished Manuscript," 308.

53. For Catt on Shaw, see, for example, Carrie Chapman Catt to Mary Gray Peck, September 27, 1910, Carrie Chapman Catt Papers, Manuscript Division, Library of Congress, Washington, D.C.

54. Kate Gordon to Official Board, August 22, 1910, Mary Ware Dennett Papers; Anna Howard Shaw to Official Board, November 13, 1910, Shaw Papers.

55. Harper, "Unpublished Manuscript," 198, 201–202.

56. "Public Indifference Held Responsible," New York Times (1857–Current file), April 1, 1911, 3, http://www.proquest.com.library.albion.edu/ (accessed December

8, 2009); and "Anna Howard Shaw to Member of Official Board," April 17, 1911, Shaw Papers, Folder 538.

57. Kate Gordon to Mary Ware Dennett, June 6, 1911, Mary Ware Dennett Papers. It is unclear if anything united the insurgents except their opposition to Anna Howard Shaw. Kate Gordon to Insurgent Members, July 3, 1911, Catharine Waugh McCulloch, Series VI of the Mary Earhart Dillon Collection, 1869–1945, A-68, Schlesinger Library, Radcliffe Institute, Harvard University.

58. Harper, "Unpublished Manuscript."

59. Shaw, *Story of a Pioneer*, 175; and "Started by Dr. Anna Shaw," *Washington Post*, July 17, 1911, 5.

60. "Warrior Brothers Visit Dr. Anna Shaw," *Philadelphia Ledger*, August 5, 1911; and "Famous Clan of Shaws Meet Today after Many Years," *Washington Times*, August 7, 1911. Harper, "Unpublished Manuscript," 205–206.

61. Anna Howard Shaw to Catherine McCulloch, August 3, 1911; and Anna Howard Shaw to Member of the Official Board, September 29, 1911, Catherine McCulloch Papers. Shaw continued to receive a salary for her suffrage work. M. Carey Thomas and Mary Garrett continued to raise monies for this but they did it quietly and apart from the NAWSA. M. Carey Thomas to Jane Addams. "Jane Addams Papers, 1860–1960," Swarthmore, Pennsylvania, Peace Collection, Swarthmore College Special Collections.

62. Harper, *History of Woman Suffrage, 1910–1920*, 329.

63. Fuller, *Laura Clay*, 123–127; *Woman's Journal*, October 21, 1911, October 28, 1911; and Catherine McCulloch to Sophonisba Breckinridge, October 28, 1911, Catharine Waugh McCulloch Papers, A-68.

64. Ibid.; and Harper, *History of Woman Suffrage, 1910–1920*, 324–332. "Charges Misuse of Susan B. Anthony Fund," New York Times (1857–Current file), October 24, 1911, 10, http://0-www.proquest.com.library.albion.edu/ (accessed December 9, 2009).

65. Catherine Waugh McCulloch to Madeline Breckinridge McDowell, January 12, 1912, McCulloch Papers.

66. Anna Howard Shaw to M. Carey Thomas, October 28, 1911, November 17, 1911, M. Carey Thomas Papers, Reel 57. In the November letter Shaw also comments on the continuing repercussions from the 1910 convention and refers to an article by Mary Gray Peck written about Shaw and Thomas. She may be referring to an article that was published that December that includes, among other comments, the only analysis from this period that dismisses the importance of Anna Howard Shaw's speaking. Mary Gray Peck, "Some American Suffragists," *Life and Labor* (December, 1911): 368–373.

67. Carrie Chapman Catt to Aletta Jacobs, July 16, 1910, in Bosch, *Politics and Friendship*, 110–112.

68. Carrie Chapman Catt to Mary Gray Peck, December 13, 1911, and December 26, 1911, Carrie Chapman Catt Papers, Manuscript Division, Library of Congress, Washington, D.C.

69. Harper, "Unpublished Manuscript," 211.

70. Ibid., 338.

71. "Crusade in Skirts: Women Plead with Congress for the Ballot," *Washington Post*, March 14, 1912, 2; M. Carey Thomas to Ruth Hanna McCormick, April

5, 1919, M. Carey Thomas Papers; Harper, *History of Woman Suffrage, 1910–1920*, 667–668; "Suffrage Army out on Parade," New York Times (1857–1922), May 5, 1912, 1, http://0-www.proquest.com.library.albion.edu/ (accessed December 9, 2009); "Woman Suffrage on Film," New York Times (1857–1922), June 16, 1912, 18, http://0-www.proquest.com.library.albion.edu/ (accessed December 9, 2009); Robert P. J. Cooney Jr., *Winning the Vote: The Triumph of the Woman Suffrage Movement* (Santa Cruz, Calif.: American Graphic Press, 2005). Anna Howard Shaw, "If I Were President," *McCall's*, June 1912.

72. Harper, *History of Woman Suffrage, 1910–1920*, 705–707; Anna Howard Shaw to Jane Addams, August 16, 1912, Jane Addams Collection, Reel 6, Folder 1192, Swarthmore College, Swarthmore, Pennsylvania.

73. Diary 1912, Shaw Papers, Folder, 386; Anna Howard Shaw to M. Carey Thomas, September 2, 1912, M. Carey Thomas Papers, Reel 57.

74. "Dr. Anna Howard Shaw Gives Remarkably Interesting Address on the Suffrage Movement," *Kalamazoo Gazette*, September 11, 1912; "Rev. Anna Shaw," *Albion Recorder*, September 16, 1912.

75. "Woman of World Prominence Here," *Sunday Oregonian*, September 29, 1912; Kimberly Jensen, "'Neither Head nor Tail to the Campaign': Esther Pohl Lovejoy and the Oregon Woman Suffrage Victory of 1912," *Oregon Historical Quarterly* 108, no. 3 (2007); and Mrs. Solomon Hirsch to Anna Howard Shaw, quoted in Harper, "Unpublished Manuscript," 229. Shaw felt she had done a good job in Oregon. See Anna Howard Shaw to M. Carey Thomas, October 11, 1912, M. Carey Thomas Papers, Reel 57; and Diary 1912, October 15, 1912, Shaw Papers, Folder 386.

76. "Suffragists Gain Four More States," New York Times (1857–Current file), November 7, 1912, 7, http://0-www.proquest.com.library.albion.edu/ (accessed December 9, 2009); and "400,000 Cheer Suffrage March," *New York Times* (1857–Current file), November 10, 1912, 1, http://0-www.proquest.com.library.albion.edu/ (accessed December 9, 2009).

Another example of the myth-making that underplays Shaw's work, the documentary, *One Woman, One Vote*, subtly credits Harriot Stanton Blatch for the victories of this year while attributing the defeats to Shaw. Ruth Pollak, Susan Sarandon, Felicia M. Widmann, PBS Video, Educational Film Center, *One Woman, One Vote*, Alexandria, Virginia: PBS Video, 1995.

77. Harper, *History of Woman Suffrage, 1910–1920*, 332–363; *Forty-Fourth Annual Report of the National American Woman Suffrage Association Given at the Convention, Held at Philadelphia, Pa., November 21 to 26, 1912* (New York: The Association, 1912).

78. Ibid.

79. See W. E. B. Du Bois, "Forward Backward," *Crisis* 2 (October 1911): 243–244; and "The Suffering Suffragettes," *Crisis* 4 (June 1912): 76–77. It isn't clear whether Du Bois deliberately used the *suffragette* term. He also consistently referred to Shaw as "Mrs." Shaw. It was probably Jane Addams, who was head of the Chicago NAACP branch, who arranged for Du Bois to speak. That Du Bois rather than a woman suffragist such as Ida B. Wells-Barrett was asked highlights the complexities of and tensions within the African American activist communities. See, for example, Paula Giddings, *Ida: A Sword among Lions: Ida B. Wells and the Campaign against Lynching* (New York: Amistad, 2008), 441–443; and David L. Lewis, *W. E. B. Du Bois—The Fight for Equality and the American Century, 1919–1963* (New York: H. Holt, 2000).

80. Du Bois, "Suffering Suffragettes"; and Garth E. Pauley, "W. E. B. Du Bois on Woman Suffrage: A Critical Analysis of His Crisis Writings," *Journal of Black Studies* 30, no. 3 (2000). Yellin had written on these same issues in 1973. Jean Fagan Yellin, "DuBois' 'Crisis' and Woman's Suffrage," *Massachusetts Review* 14, no. 2 (1973). Harper, in the official history, doesn't mention any of these issues and barely notes the 1912 speech. Harper, *History of Woman Suffrage, 1910–1920*.

81. Ibid.; and W. E. Burghardt DuBois, "Disfranchisement" (New York: National American Woman Suffrage Association, 1912), *Forty-Fourth Annual Report*.

82. *Public Ledger*, November 22, 1912, quoted in Linkugel, "Speeches," 590. Anna Howard Shaw to M. Carey Thomas, December 1912, M. Carey Thomas Papers, Reel 57.

Chapter 7. Unanticipated Challenges

1. Anna Howard Shaw to Annie G. Porritt, March 5, 1914, Annie Gertrude Webb Porritt Papers, Sophia Smith Collection, Smith College, Northampton, Massachusetts.

2. Though these years saw major NAWSA successes, there is little in the scholarship analyzing those events. Most attention goes to the emergence of the Congressional Union/National Women's Party. See Eleanor Flexner, *Century of Struggle: the Woman's Rights Movement in the United States* (Cambridge: Belknap Press of Harvard University Press, 1959), 248–275.

3. Since the unification of the major suffrage organizations, at least some leaders of the NAWSA had been trying to establish a Washington, D.C., headquarters, as noted in earlier chapters.

4. Ida Husted Harper, "Unpublished Manuscript, Biography of Anna Howard Shaw" (Ann Arbor: Bentley Library, University of Michigan, n.d.), 235; Diary January 1913, Anna Howard Shaw Papers, Folder 387. Among the core group of suffragists there were several repeated surnames such as Miller, of course, but also Paul, Avery, and McCormick. Susan Look Avery was the mother of Lydia Avery Coonley-Ward, but they are not related to Rachel Foster Avery. This letter was written on October 21, 1912, by Harriet Taylor Upton to Dr. Cora Smith (Eaton) King, who sent it "to Mrs. Emma Smith Devoe of Seattle, who sent it to Abigail Scott Duniway . . . who sent it around Portland and no one knows where else." Upton also described Shaw as "a little, humped, yellow faced, sour-looking woman." M. Carey Thomas enclosed a copy of the letter when she wrote to Emma M. Perkins, December 21, 1912, M. Carey Thomas Papers.

5. Harper, "Unpublished Manuscript," 237; Anna Howard Shaw to Lucy E. Anthony, January 26 (?), 1913, Shaw Papers, Folder 508.

6. It is fascinating to consider that M. Carey Thomas had once been Woodrow Wilson's boss when she had been dean at Bryn Mawr while he was a faculty member. On the planned parade, see "Motive for Pageant," *Washington Post*, January 13, 1913, 2; "Will Ride as Heralds," *Washington Post*, January 27, 1913, 2; and "Suffragists Plan Big Reception for Pilgrim Army Here Friday," *Washington Post*, February 26, 1913.

7. Ida Husted Harper, ed., *History of Woman Suffrage, 1910–1920*, vol. III (New York: National American Woman Suffrage Association, 1922), 280; *Forty-Second Annual Report of the National American Woman Suffrage Association, Given at the Conven-*

tion, Held at Washington, D.C., April 14 to 19, Inclusive (New York: The Association, 1910), 203; and Diary 1911, September 30, 1911, Shaw Papers, Folder 385.

8. On February 27, the entire page 5 of the *Washington Post* was taken up with articles related to the suffrage parade, *Washington Post*, February 27, 1913, 5; "Cavalry Save Suffrage Parade from Hoodlums," *World*, March 4, 1913, 1; "Sum Up Day's Work: Two Thousand Suffragists in Rally after Parade," *Washington Post*, March 4, 1913, 3.

9. Shaw wrote that she didn't want to come down too harshly on the young women because she understood that they had been disappointed in lack of concrete results from the great march. Shaw felt the time to reprimand them hadn't come yet. Anna Howard Shaw to Annie G. Porritt, March 5, 1914, Annie Gertrude Webb Porritt Papers; Harper, "Unpublished Manuscript," 240.

10. Paula Giddings, *Ida: A Sword among Lions: Ida B. Wells and the Campaign against Lynching* (New York: Amistad, 2008), 513–522.

11. Ibid; and Harper, *History of Woman Suffrage, 1910–1920*, 366–369.

12. Ibid., 366.

13. Harper, "Unpublished Manuscript," 242–243. A series of photographs from the collection of the International Suffrage Alliance documents that scene in Budapest (Harvard University Library Visual Information Access).

14. Ibid., 243; Anna Howard Shaw, *The Story of a Pioneer* (New York: Harper and Brothers, 1915), 331–334.

15. Harper, "Unpublished Manuscript," 245.

16. Diary 1913, October 21, 1913, Shaw Papers, Folder 387; Harper, *History of Woman Suffrage, 1910–1920*, 364; "Fair Cohorts Meet," *Washington Post*, November 30, 1913, 1; and "Anna Howard Shaw Still Leader," *New York Times*, December 5, 1913, 3.

17. Harper, "Unpublished Manuscript," 252; and Anna Howard Shaw to Lucy Burns, November 19, 1913, National American Woman Suffrage Association Records, Manuscript Division, Library of Congress, Washington, D.C.

18. See, for example, Lucy Burns to Anna Howard Shaw, December 17, 1913; and Anna Howard Shaw to Member of Official Board, December 18, 1913, National American Woman Suffrage Association Records, Manuscript Division, Library of Congress, Washington, D.C.

19. See, as a small sampling of these documents, "Post-Convention Executive Committee Meeting," December 8, 1913; Mary Ware Dennett to Official Board, December 19, 1913; and Anna Howard Shaw to Lucy Burns, December 20, 1913, NAWSA Records.

20. Ruth Hanna McCormick to Anna Howard Shaw, March 21, 1914, NAWSA Records; Diary 1914, January 1, 1914, Anna Howard, Folder 389; and Harper, "Unpublished Manuscript."

21. Anna Howard Shaw to Annie G. Porritt, March 5, 1914, Annie Gertrude Webb Porritt Papers. There are many pages on this conflict in the NAWSA Papers at the Library of Congress. See, for example, Anna Howard Shaw to Official Board, January 14, 1914, National American Woman Suffrage Association Records. "Suffragists Quick to Deny Break," New York Times (1857–Current file), January 19, 1914, 7, http://0-www.proquest.com.library.albion.edu/ (accessed December 10, 2009).

22. Diary 1914, January 1914, Shaw Papers, Folder 388.

23. "Dr. Anna Shaw Hurt in Station," New York Times (1857–Current file),

February 15, 1914, 1, http://o-www.proquest.com.library.albion.edu/ (accessed December 10, 2009).

24. Diary 1913, September 30, 1913, Shaw Papers, Folder 387; Elizabeth Garver Jordan, *Three Rousing Cheers* (New York: London, D. Appleton-Century Co., 1938); and Anna Howard Shaw to M. Carey Thomas, February 28, 1914, M. Carey Thomas Papers, Reel 57.

25. Jordan, *Three Rousing Cheers*, 330–336.

26. Anna Howard Shaw to Annie G. Porritt, March 5, 1914, Annie Gertrude Webb Porritt Papers.

27. Ibid.

28. "Dr. Shaw Defies a Tax Collector," New York Times (1857–Current file), December 13, 1913, 6, http://o-www.proquest.com.library.albion.edu/ (accessed December 10, 2009); "Women's Tax Fight Will Be Passive," New York Times (1857–Current file), December 30, 1913, 18, http://o-www.proquest.com.library .albion.edu/ (accessed December 10, 2009); "Miss Shaw's Taxes," New York Times (1857–Current file), January 14, 1914, 10, http://o-www.proquest.com .library.albion.edu/ (accessed December 10, 2009); Juiliana Tutt, "'No Taxation without Representation' in the American Woman Suffrage Movement," *Stanford Law Review*, 2010/05// 2010, 1473; and "Dr. Shaw Held Disobedient," *Washington Post*, January 16, 1914, 3.

29. Anna Howard Shaw to Rosamond Danielson, March 11, 1914, Shaw Papers.

30. Linda J. Tomko, *Dancing Class: Gender, Ethnicity, and Social Divides in American Dance, 1890–1920* (Bloomington: Indiana University Press, 1999), 56–57; Anna Howard Shaw to State Presidents, February 23, 1914; No name note, March 4, 1914; Anna Howard Shaw to State Presidents, February 25, 1914, National American Woman Suffrage Association Records, Manuscript Division, Library of Congress, Washington, D.C.; Diary 1914, March 18, 1914, Shaw Papers, Folder 388; and Harper, "Unpublished Manuscript," 252–253, 263–264.

31. Ibid.; and Mary Ware Dennett to Official Board, April 4, 1914, Mary Ware Dennett Papers.

32. Diary 1914, April 15, 1914, April 16, 1914, Shaw Papers, Folder 388.

33. M. Carey Thomas Papers; Diary 1914, April 1914, Shaw Papers, Folder 388.

34. "Sees Suffrage Gains," *Washington Post*, May 114, 1914, 4; and "Cheer Her Suffrage Plea," *Washington Post*, May 16, 1914, 4; Diary 1914, June 1, 1914, Shaw Papers.

35. "Again to Ask Ballot," *Washington Post*, June 27, 1914, 4; "Clark for Women," *Washington Post*, June 28, 1914, 4; "Ready for Invasion," *Washington Post*, June 29, 1914, 7; and "Sacrifice for Suffrage," New York Times (1857–1922), June 30, 1914, 4, http://o-www.proquest.com.library.albion.edu/ (accessed December 11, 2009).

36. Diary 1914, August 18, 1914, Shaw Papers, Folder 388.

37. Katharine D. McCormick to M. Carey Thomas, July 13, 1914, M. Carey Thomas Papers.

38. M. Carey Thomas to Jane Addams, December 12, 1912, in the Jane Addams Collection (DG 001), Swarthmore College Peace Collection, Box 7, Folder 531.

39. Rebecca J. Mead, *How the Vote Was Won: Woman Suffrage in the Western United States, 1868–1914* (New York: New York University Press, 2004), 216, n. 58.

40. Diary 1914, September 8, 1914, Shaw Papers.

41. Diary 1914, October 25, 1914, Shaw Papers.

42. Anna Howard Shaw to M. Carey Thomas, November 3, 1914, M. Carey Thomas Papers, Reel 57.

43. "Suffragists Raise $105,619 at Rally," New York Times (1857–Current file), November 7, 1914, 5, http://o-www.proquest.com.library.albion.edu/ (accessed December 11, 2009).

44. Both Anthony and Shaw regularly recorded their income and expenditures in their diary/datebooks. See, for example, Susan B. Anthony diaries, Susan B. Anthony Papers, Box 3, Reel 3–4, Manuscript Division, Library of Congress, Washington, D.C.; and Shaw Diaries, Shaw Papers, Folders 385–388.

45. Anna Howard Shaw to Catherine McCulloch, February 21, 1914, Catharine Waugh McCulloch, Series VI of the Mary Earhart Dillon Collection, 1869–1945; A-68, Schlesinger Library, Radcliffe Institute, Harvard University. In this letter Shaw also declares herself a "mugwamp [sic]." Anna Howard Shaw to M. Carey Thomas, March 14, 1914, M. Carey Thomas Papers, Reel 57; and "Mrs.Belmont's Wire Stirs Suffragists," New York Times (1857–Current file), March 8, 1914, C5, http://o-www.proquest.com.library.albion.edu/ (accessed December 10, 2009).

46. Anna Howard Shaw to M. Carey Thomas, July 8, 1914, M. Carey Thomas Papers, Reel 57.

47. Diary 1914, November 6, 1914, Shaw Papers, Folder 388; and Harper, "Unpublished Manuscript," 294–295.

48. Jane Addams's relationship with Shaw and the NAWSA is understudied. One letter between Carrie Chapman Catt and Mary Gray Peck suggests that Catt expected "JA" to become the next NAWSA president. Why Addams resigned one year before Shaw retired is unclear; a recent biography of Madeline Breckridge sheds some light on this topic. Melba Porter Hay, *Madeline McDowell Breckinridge and the Battle for a New South* (Lexington: University Press of Kentucky, 2009).

49. "New Move for Suffrage," New York Times (1857–Current file), March 21, 1914, 2, http://o-www.proquest.com.library.albion.edu/ (accessed December 10, 2009); Ruth Hanna McCormick to Anna Howard Shaw, March 21, 1914, National American Woman Suffrage Association Records. The amendment was also called the Shafroth-Palmer Amendment.

50. Bess Booth to Ruth Hanna McCormick, March 29, 1914, National American Woman Suffrage Association Records; and Anna Howard Shaw to Catherine Mc-Culloch, April 14, 1914, Catharine Waugh McCulloch, Series VI of the Mary Earhart Dillon Collection, 1869–1945.

51. Proceedings, *Forty-Sixth Annual Convention, National American Woman Suffrage Association, Day Sessions, Representatives Hall, State Capitol, Evening Mass Meeting, Ryman Auditorium, Nashville, Tenn., November Eleventh to Seventeenth Inclusive, 1914* (1914); Harper, *History of Woman Suffrage, 1910–1920*, 424; and Harper, "Unpublished Manuscript," 298–300.

52. Diary 1915, January 3, 1915, Shaw Papers, Folder 389. In the end, the amount Shaw received from her brother's estate was a little over $1200. Will of James S. Shaw, Register of Probate, Suffolk County, Massachusetts, V. 1074, p. 97, #167663.

53. "Suffrage Meets Defeat in House," *Washington Post*," January 13, 1915, 1.

54. Anna Howard Shaw to Lucy E. Anthony, April 10, 1915, in Harper, "Unpublished Manuscript," 379.

55. "Suffrage War Climax Now in the East," *Evening Post*, February 25, 1915, 1; and Shaw, *Story of a Pioneer*, 317.

56. Diary 1915, February 1, 1915, Shaw Papers, Folder 389. It isn't clear if there are any earlier records in which women partners employed these legal moves to take care of each other financially.

57. "Asks Suffrage in Jersey," *Washington Post*, January 26, 1915, 2; Deed, Anna Howard Shaw to Lucy Anthony, February 1, 1915, Register of Deeds, Book 460, 76, Delaware County Courthouse, Media, Pennsylvania.

58. "Anna Howard Shaw Says There Is No Dissension Between New York and National Suffragists," New York Times (1857–Current file), March 21, 1915, X4, www.proquest.com. library.albion.edu/ (accessed December 11, 2009); "Dr. Anna Shaw Predicts Men of South Will Disapprove of Anti-Suff Congressmen," *Fort Worth Star Telegram*, March 31, 1915; "Eminent Suffrage Leader in Dallas," *Dallas Morning [illegible]*, April 2, 1915; and "Dr. Anna Shaw's Brilliant Address, *Greenville Democrat*, April 5, 1915; Harper, "Unpublished Manuscript," 379.

59. "Miss Mary Garrett Dies," New York Times (1857–Current file), April 4, 1915, 8, http://0-www.proquest.com.library.albion.edu/ (accessed December 11, 2009); and Helen Lefkowitz Horowitz, *The Power and Passion of M. Carey Thomas* (New York: Alfred A. Knopf, 1994).

60. "Rev. Dr. Shaw Heroine of Big Suffrage Day," *Philadelphia Sunday Morning [illegible]*, May 2, 1915.

61. "'I Have a Dream' Leads Top 100 Speeches of the Century," News Release, December 15, 1999, University of Wisconsin, http://www.news.wisc.edu/misc/speeches/ (accessed April 14, 2013). "The Fundamental Principle of a Republic," in Wil A. Linkugel, "The Speeches of Anna Howard Shaw" (PhD Dissertation, University of Wisconsin, 1960), 258–292.

62. Linkugel, "Speeches," 258; Wil A. Linkugel and Martha Watson, *Anna Howard Shaw: Suffrage Orator and Social Reformer*, Great American Orators, No. 10 (New York: Greenwood Press, 1991).

63. This episode warranted seven *New York Times* articles and was covered by other papers as well. See, for example, "Seizes Suffragist's Motor," *Washington Post*, July 11, 1915, 10; "Dr. Shaw's Auto Saved: 'Eastern Victory' Bought for $230 by Suffragists at Tax Sale," New York Times (1857–1922), July 25, 1915, 13, http://0-www.proquest.com.library.albion.edu/ (accessed December 11, 2009). "Dr. Shaw Scorns Chivalry That Made Leo Frank Hang," *Tribune*, August 20, 1915; and Robert P. J. Cooney Jr., *Winning the Vote: The Triumph of the Woman Suffrage Movement* (Santa Cruz, Calif.: American Graphic Press, 2005).

64. "Dr. Shaw Publishes Story of Her Life," New York Times (1857–1922), September 12, 1915, 5, http://0-www.proquest.com.library.albion.edu/ (accessed December 11, 2009).

65. "Delightful Reminiscences of a Girl Pioneer," New York Times (1857–1922), September 26, 1915, SM12, http://0-www.proquest.com.library.albion.edu/ (accessed December 11, 2009); and "Two Hundred Leading Books of the Year," New York Times (1857–Current file), November 28, 1915, BR1, http://0-www.proquest.com.library.albion.edu/ (accessed December 11, 2009).

66. Anna Howard Shaw to Lucy E. Anthony, August 31, 1915, Shaw Papers, Folder 508.

67. "Dr. Anna Shaw Says Fight Will Continue until Suffrage Wins," *New York Times*, November 3, 1915, 5; Diary 1915, November 2, 1915, November 3, 1915, Shaw Papers, Folder 389.

68. Harper, "Unpublished Manuscript," 312; "Without a Double," New York Times (1857–Current file), November 23, 1915, 12, http://o-www.proquest.com .library.albion.edu/ (accessed December 11, 2009).

69. Harper, *History of Woman Suffrage, 1910–1920*, 456–460.

70. Ibid.

71. Ibid.

72. Harper, "Unpublished Manuscript," 332–333.

Chapter 8. A Worker to the End (1916–1919)

1. Anna Howard Shaw to Lucy E. Anthony, Ida Husted Harper, "Unpublished Manuscript, Biography of Anna Howard Shaw" (Ann Arbor: Bentley Library, University of Michigan), 344.

2. On one level scholars have studied and analyzed the last years of Shaw's life, especially her service as the chair of the Women's Committee of the Council for National Defense, more than her NAWSA presidency. See, for example, Barbara R. Finn, "Anna Howard Shaw and Women's Work," *Frontiers: A Journal of Women Studies* 4, no. 3 (1979); and Barbara J. Steinson, *American Women's Activism in World War I* (New York: Garland Publishers, 1982). Even Lemons's *The Woman Citizen*, though it focuses on the following decades, devotes a number of pages to Shaw and the work of the council. J. Stanley Lemons, *The Woman Citizen: Social Feminism in the 1920's* (Urbana: University of Illinois Press, 1973).

In the first decades after Shaw's death, she was remembered as a heroic woman pioneer and leader of the suffrage movement. See, for example, Helen Christine Bennett, *American Women in Civic Work* (New York: Dodd, Mead, 1919); Sarah Knowles Bolton, *Lives of Girls Who Became Famous*, rev. and enl. ed. (New York: Thomas Y. Crowell Co., 1925); Mabel Ansley Murphy, *Greathearted Women: Biographies of Sixteen Women Leaders of American and English Life* (Philadelphia: The Union Press, 1920).

3. After she recovered, Shaw went back and wrote in her diary about her illness. Diary 1916, January 1, 1916, Anna Howard Shaw Papers in the Woman's Rights Collection, 1908–1943, WRC 1036–1040, Folder 390, Schlesinger Library, Radcliffe Institute, Harvard University.

4. Diary 1916, January 1916, Shaw Papers, Folder 390; and Harper, "Unpublished Manuscript," 332–337.

5. Certainly Rachel Foster Avery had been the first of Susan B. Anthony's protégés, but she disappeared from suffrage and most public records after 1911. Harper, "Unpublished Manuscript," 235–236.

6. Carrie Chapman Catt to Anna Howard Shaw, quoted in Harper, "Unpublished Manuscript," 334–335. Catt was generally on target about the movement, but her argument that the presidency didn't bring Shaw "fresh prestige" was a questionable conclusion. It is unclear whether Shaw would have garnered the press coverage that she did if she hadn't served as the head of the premier suffrage organization.

7. Lucy E. Anthony to Carrie Chapman Catt, quoted in Harper, "Unpublished Manuscript," 335.

8. Harper, "Unpublished Manuscript," 235–238.

9. M. Carey Thomas to Anna Howard Shaw, January 4, 1916, in M. Carey Thomas Papers, Special Collections Department, Bryn Mawr College Library, Reel 35.

10. Diary 1916, February 14, 1916, April 9, 1916, Shaw Papers, Folder 390.

11. See, for example, minutes of Anna Howard Shaw Fund, July 10, 1916, M. Carey Thomas Papers; M. Carey Thomas to Anna Howard Shaw, telegram, November 15, 1916; M. Carey Thomas to Anna Howard Shaw, November 28, 1916, M. Carey Thomas Papers; and Anna Howard Shaw to Clara Osborn, December 20, 1916, Shaw Papers, Folder 527.

12. Anna Howard Shaw to Lucy E. Anthony; Harper, "Unpublished Manuscript," 344.

13. Carrie Chapman Catt was, at first, concerned about the role Anna Howard Shaw would play in the NAWSA as honorary president. Carrie Chapman Catt to Mary Gray Peck, February 2, 1916, Carrie Chapman Catt Papers, Manuscript Division, Library of Congress, Washington, D.C. Anna Howard Shaw to Harriet B. Laidlaw, H. B. (Harriet Burton) Laidlaw Papers, 1851–1958, October 12, 1915, A-63, Schlesinger Library, Radcliffe Institute, Harvard University, Cambridge, Massachusetts; and *Oral History Interview with Lucy Somerville Howorth, June 20, 22, and 23, 1975.* Interview G-0028, Southern Oral History Program Collection (#4007), University Library, The University of North Carolina at Chapel Hill, 2004.

14. Mineke Bosch with Annemarie Kloosterman Bosch, ed., *Politics and Friendship: Letters from the International Woman Suffrage Alliance, 1902–1942* (Columbus: Ohio State University Press, 1990), 161–166; and Harper, "Unpublished Manuscript," 348–349.

15. Jacqueline Van Voris, *Carrie Chapman Catt: A Public Life* (New York: Feminist Press at the City University of New York, 1987), 142–145.

16. Ida Husted Harper, ed., *History of Woman Suffrage, 1910–1920,* vol. III (New York: National American Woman Suffrage Association, 1922), 480–512. The NAWSA also debated but in the end reiterated its position as a nonpartisan body, a position Shaw had strongly urged.

17. Ibid., 598.

18. Ibid., 511–512; and Harper, "Unpublished Manuscript," 353.

19. Anna Howard Shaw to Harriet Laidlaw, H. B. (Harriet Burton) Laidlaw Papers, 1851–1958, October 8, 1916, A-63, Schlesinger Library, Radcliffe Institute, Harvard University, Cambridge, Massachusetts.

20. Anna Howard Shaw to Clara Osborn, December 20, 1916, Shaw Papers, Folder 527; and Anna Howard Shaw to Lucy E. Anthony, December 25, 1916, Shaw Papers, Folder 509.

21. "Anna Howard Shaw—The Woman," talk given by Mary B. Jewett for the Florence Villa Club, February 1920, Shaw Papers, Folder 362.

22. Anna Howard Shaw to Clara Osborn, February 11, 1917, Anna Howard Shaw to Clara Osborn, March 11, 1917, Shaw Papers, Folder 527; and "Felicitates Dr. Anna Shaw," New York Times (1857–Current file), February 16, 1917, 6, http://o-www .proquest.com.library.albion.edu/ (accessed December 13, 2009).

23. "Suffrage Leaders Gather in Capital," *Washington Post,* February 19, 1917; "Suffrage Help in War," *Washington Post,* February 26, 1917; and Harper, "Unpublished Manuscript," 361.

24. "Last Will and Testament," Anna Howard Shaw, March 26, 1917, filed July 9, 1919, Register of Wills, Delaware County Courthouse, Media, Pennsylvania.

25. Marjorie Julian Spruill, *New Women of the New South: The Leaders of the Woman Suffrage Movement in the Southern States* (New York: Oxford University Press, 1993). The Laura Clay Papers at the University of Kentucky include a number of the very racist materials that specifically target Anna Howard Shaw. Laura Clay Papers, 1882–1941, University of Kentucky Library, Lexington, Kentucky.

26. Anna Howard Shaw to Lucy E. Anthony, April 21, 1917; Harper, "Unpublished Manuscript," 362–363; and Emily Newell Blair, *The Woman's Committee United States Council of National Defense: An Interpretative Report* (Washington: Government Printing Office, 1920).

27. There was quite a row over which women's groups should be in charge of the war work. The National League for Women's Service, which was endorsed by the National Association Opposed to Woman Suffrage, expected to take the lead, and even when their proposal was rejected by the Council for National Defense, they proceeded with registering women. Barbara J. Steinson, *American Women's Activism in World War I* (New York: Garland Publishers, 1982), 299–303.

28. Anna Howard Shaw to Lucy E. Anthony, April 29, 1917, Shaw Papers, Folder 509.

29. Blair, *Woman's Committee.*

30. Ibid.

31. Ibid., 9–12. Although there were no African American women on the Woman's Committee, African American women's groups were included in the larger gathering.

32. Diary 1917, April 26, 1917, Shaw Papers, Folder 391; and Harper, "Unpublished Manuscript," 424.

33. "75 Women Presidents Today Confer over Work of Women in War's Crisis," *Washington Post*, June 19, 1917; and Anna Howard Shaw to Lucy E. Anthony, June 20, 1917, Shaw Papers, Folder 509.

34. Ibid.; and Blair, *Women's Committee.*

35. Anna Howard Shaw to Harriet B. Laidlaw, August 16, 1917, September 23, 1917, Harriet B. Laidlaw Papers; and Carrie Chapman Catt to Mary Grey Peck, n.d., Eleanor Flexner Papers, 1895?-1995, 73-65—89-M152, Folder 37, Schlesinger Library, Radcliffe Institute, Harvard University, Cambridge, Massachusetts.

36. Anna Howard Shaw to Lucy E. Anthony, n.d.; Harper, "Unpublished Manuscript," 418, 439; Anna Howard Shaw, "Men of America on Trial for Democracy," *Public*, August 24, 1917; "Suffrage Women Threaten Wilson," *New* York Times (1857–Current file), November 12, 1917, http://0-www.proquest.com.library.albion.edu/ (accessed July 7, 2009). Alice Paul was serving her sentence during the New York state campaign. In spite of all the attention women's history and the popular media has given the NWP and the White House pickets, it is difficult to gauge just how much influence that group had. For example, in looking at the *New York Times* coverage for 1917, Alice Paul appears in the paper 26 times with one front-page article. Anna Howard Shaw appears 28 times with five front-page articles, and Carrie Chapman Catt is in 40 articles with two front-page stories.

37. Harper, "Unpublished Manuscript."

38. Special to the *New York Times* (November 19, 1917). "Suffrage Victory Laid

to Germans," New York Times (1857–1922), 11, retrieved November 4, 2011, from ProQuest Historical Newspapers, the *New York Times* (1851–2007), Document ID: 102376548.

39. "New Suffrage Drive Planned by Women," New York Times (1857–Current file), November 7, 1917, 3, http://0-www.proquest.com.library.albion.edu/ (accessed December 11, 2009); and "Suffrage Leaders Call for Reprisal," New York Times (1857–1922), November 21, 1917, 1, http://0-www.proquest.com.library .albion.edu/ (accessed December 11, 2009).

40. Carrie Chapman Catt to Lucy E. Anthony, n.d., Shaw Papers, 556, 1943; and Sara Hunter Graham, *Woman Suffrage and the New Democracy* (New Haven: Yale University Press, 1996), 113.

41. Harper, *History of Woman Suffrage, 1910–1920*, 512–549.

42. Anna Howard Shaw to Lucy E. Anthony, January 1, 1918, Shaw Papers; and Harper, "Unpublished Manuscript," 438.

43. Diary 1918, January 10, 1918, Shaw Papers, Folder 392.

44. Diary 1918, January 21, 1918, Shaw Papers, Folder, 392; and "Women in Campaign for Permanent Peace," New York Times (1857–1922), January 21, 1918, 11, http://0-www.proquest.com.library.albion.edu/ (accessed December 11, 2009).

45. Anna Howard Shaw to Clara Osborn, February 1918, Shaw Papers, Folder 527; and M. Carey Thomas to Anna Howard Shaw, March 3, 1918, M. Carey Thomas Papers, Reel 35.

46. Barbara Rittinger Finn, "The Thought of Anna Howard Shaw as Reflected in Her Correspondence as Chairman of the Woman's Committee of the National Council of Defense, 1917–1918" (Thesis, George Washington University, 1978); Anna Howard Shaw to Lucy E. Anthony, May 29, 1918, in Harper, "Unpublished Manuscript," 440; Anna Howard Shaw to Lucy E. Anthony, June 18, 1918, July 19, 1918, in Harper, "Unpublished Manuscript," 444.

47. Anna Howard Shaw to Lucy E. Anthony, August 21, 1918, in Harper, "Unpublished Manuscript," 445.

48. Diary 1918, September 17, 1918, in Harper, "Unpublished Manuscript," 445.

49. Anna Howard Shaw to Lucy E. Anthony, September 29, 1918, Shaw Papers, Folder 509.

50. Anna Howard Shaw to Lucy E. Anthony, December 4, 1918, Shaw Papers, Folder 509.

51. Anna Howard Shaw to Lucy E. Anthony, March 9, 1919, Shaw Papers, Folder 510.

52. Anna Howard Shaw to M. Carey Thomas, March 17, 1919, M. Carey Thomas Papers, Reel 57.

53. Anna Howard Shaw to Lucy E. Anthony, March 8, 1919, Shaw Papers, Folder 510; and Anna Howard Shaw to M. Carey Thomas, May 4, 1919, M. Carey Thomas Papers, Reel 57.

54. *Publications Relating to National Conference on Lynching* (New York: National Conference on Lynching, 1919).

55. "The Cowardice of the Mob," Anna Howard Shaw, in Wil A. Linkugel, "The Speeches of Anna Howard Shaw" (PhD Dissertation, University of Wisconsin, 1960), 991–996.

56. "Medal for Dr. Anna Shaw," New York Times (1857–1922), May 18, 1919, 10,

http://o-www.proquest.com.library.albion.edu/ (accessed December 11, 2009); and Anna Howard Shaw to M. Carey Thomas, May 19, 1919, M. Carey Thomas Papers, Reel 57.

57. Shaw's entry of May 27, 1919, ends with "I am enjoying the trip very much and am glad I could come." Harper, "Unpublished Manuscript," 470.

58. Telegram, Carrie Chapman Catt to Anna Howard Shaw in Springfield, Illinois, June 10, 1919, and Carrie Chapman Catt to Anna Howard Shaw, June 21, 1919, Shaw Papers, Folder 512.

59. Anna Howard Shaw to Harriet Laidlaw, June 27, 1919, Harriet Burton Laidlaw Papers; and Caroline J. Reilly to Carrie Chapman Catt, July 1, 1919, Sophia Smith Collection, Smith College, Northampton, Massachusetts.

60. Caroline J. Reilly to "Dear Friends," July 2, 1919, Carrie Chapman Catt Papers, Sophia Smith Collection; and Lucy E. Anthony, "To the dear and near friends of Dr. Anna Howard Shaw," September 10, 1919, Shaw Papers, Folder 556.

61. Ibid.; and Caroline J. Reilly to "Dear Friends," July 2, 1919, Carrie Chapman Catt Papers.

62. Lucy E. Anthony, "To the dear and near friends of Dr. Anna Howard Shaw," September 10, 1919, Shaw Papers, Folder 556.

63. "Latest Photo of 'Mother of Suffrage,'" "Dr. Shaw Gives Women of City Three Charges," "Death Ends Work of Leader among Suffrage Forces," "Mobilizing Women of Country in War Won Dr. Shaw D.S.C.," and "Dr. Shaw While Here Launched Work of Americanization," *San Antonio Evening News*, July 3, 1919, 3; "Dr. Anna Howard Shaw, Leader of Women, Dies," *Fort Wayne* News, July 3, 1919, 1; and "Dr. Anna Howard Shaw," *Trenton Evening News*, July 5, 1919, 6.

64. "Dr. Anna H. Shaw, Suffragist, Dies," New York Times (1857–1922), July 3, 1919, 12, http://o-www.proquest.com.library.albion.edu/ (accessed December 11, 2009; "Peace Appeal Last Work of Dr. Shaw," New York Times (1857–1922), July 4, 1919, 7, http://o-www.proquest.com.library.albion.edu/ (accessed December 11, 2009); and "Anna Howard Shaw," New York Times (1857–1922), July 4, 1919, 6, http://o-www.proquest.com.library.albion.edu/ (accessed December 11, 2009).

65. Lucy E. Anthony, "To the dear and near friends of Dr. Anna Howard Shaw," September 10, 1919, Shaw Papers, Folder 556.

66. Ida Husted Harper, "The Passing of Anna Howard Shaw" (New York: National Woman Suffrage Publishing Co., Inc., 1919).

67. "Anna Howard Shaw Memorial of the National American Woman Suffrage Association," National American Woman Suffrage Association Records, Manuscript Division, Library of Congress, Washington, D.C.

68. "Dr. Anna Shaw's Estate Is $32,613," New York Times (1857–Current file), February 8, 1921, 3, http://o-www.proquest.com.library.albion.edu/ (accessed December 11, 2009).

69. Ibid.

70. Written in Lucy Anthony's hand on December 31, 1919, in Shaw's 1919 Diary. Diary 1919, December 31, 1919, Shaw Papers, Folder 393.

71. "Agreement between Ida Husted Harper and Lucy E. Anthony," July 12, 1926, Shaw Papers, Folder 557.

72. Lucy E. Anthony to M. Carey Thomas, February 27, 1929, M. Carey Thomas Papers; and Archival Notes, Shaw Papers, Folder 350–351.

73. See, for example, Helen Christine Bennett, *American Women in Civic Work* (New York: Dodd, Mead, 1919). Albion College Dean of Women Audrey Wilder tried to get the autobiography republished. Audrey Wilder Papers, Local History Room, Albion Public Library.

74. "History of the Collection," Finding Guide, Shaw Papers.

75. "11 Women Hailed by Mrs. Roosevelt," New York Times (1857–Current file), March 9, 1935, http://o-www.proquest.com.library.albion.edu/ (accessed December 11, 2009); and American Merchant Marine at War, "Liberty Ships Built by the United States Maritime Commission in World War II," http://www.usmm.org/libertyships.html (accessed April 14, 2013).

76. "Miss Lucy Anthony, A Suffrage Leader," New York Times (1857–Current file), July 6, 1944, http://o-www.proquest.com.library.albion.edu/ (accessed December 11, 2009); and Trisha Franzen, *Spinsters and Lesbians: Independent Womanhood in the United States* (New York: New York University Press, 1996).

Epilogue

1. Judith M. Bennett, *History Matters: Patriarchy and the Challenge of Feminism* (Philadelphia: University of Pennsylvania Press, 2006).

2. Though Gerda Lerner expressed concerns about the emphasis on biography in women's history, within suffrage and other women's activist scholarship there haven't been that many biographies that critically analyze women's lives. Equally important would be reexaminations of the early biographies and autobiographies. Nancy F. Cott et al., "Considering the State of U.S. Women's History," *Journal of Women's History* 15, no. 1 (2003: 146). As I have argued in other parts of this book, Flexner, Kraditor, O'Neill, and other early suffrage historians appeared to have based their assessments of Shaw's presidency and her importance on materials written by authors who were supporters of Carrie Chapman Catt or Alice Paul, or influenced by such writers. To give just two examples, in the case of the former, Mary Gray Peck appears to have played a significant role beyond her own biography of Carrie Chapman Catt. Second, the National Women's Party supporter Rheta Childe Dorr wrote a Susan B. Anthony biography. In contrast, M. Carey Thomas never wrote about her role in the movement and later her papers were closed for decades after her death. Lucy E. Anthony's struggle to get a Shaw biography has already been discussed. On the dearth of post-1970 Shaw scholarship, I have wondered about the effect of O'Neill's harsh judgment about Shaw. Eleanor Flexner, *Century of Struggle: The Woman's Rights Movement in the United States* (Cambridge: Belknap Press of Harvard University, 1959); Aileen S. Kraditor, *The Ideas of the Woman Suffrage Movement, 1890–1920* (New York: Norton, 1981); William O'Neill, *Everyone Was Brave: A History of Feminism in America* (New York: Quadrangle/New York Times Book Co., 1976); Mary Gray Peck and Collection, National American Woman Suffrage Association, *Carrie Chapman Catt, a Biography* (New York: H. W. Wilson Co., 1944); and Rheta Childe Dorr, *Susan B. Anthony, the Woman Who Changed the Mind of a Nation* (New York: AMS Press, 1970).

3. Important here have been the films on the suffrage movement: *One Woman, One Vote, Not for Ourselves Alone,* and *Iron Jawed Angels.* Ruth Pollak, Susan Sarandon, Felicia M. Widmann, PBS Video, Educational Film, Center, *One Woman,*

One Vote (Alexandria, Va.: PBS Video, 1995); Ken Burns, Paul Barnes, Geoffrey C. Kellerman, and Sally Ward, *Not for Ourselves Alone: The Story of Elizabeth Cady Stanton and Susan B. Anthony* (Alexandria, Va.: PBS Home Video: Distributed by Warner Home Video, 1999), Visual Material; and Katja von Garnier et al., *Iron Jawed Angels* (New York: HBO Video, 2004).

The early books, articles, and lists tend to grant Shaw a prominent place. See "11 Women Hailed by Mrs. Roosevelt," New York Times (1857–Current file), March 9, 1935, http://o-www.proquest.com.library.albion.edu/ (accessed December 11, 2009); Dorothea Mary Northcroft, *American Girls of Adventure* (London: F. Muller, 1947); Helen Christine Bennett, *American Women in Civic Work* (New York: Dodd, Mead, 1919), among others. Even at Shaw's alma mater, there is a difference between how Shaw is considered in three books on Albion College. See Ann Hollinshead, *Eminent and Interesting Albionians: Volume I* (Albion, Mich.: Albion College Alumni Assoc., 1955); Robert Gildart, *Albion College, 1835–1960: A History* (Albion, Mich.: Albion College, 1961); Keith J. Fennimore, *The Albion College Sesquicentennial History: 1835–1985* (Albion, Mich.: Albion College, 1985).

4. Not surprisingly, most of the theses and dissertations on Shaw take a more positive view. See, for example, Ralph Wakefield Spencer, "Dr. Anna Howard Shaw: The Evangelical Feminist" (PhD dissertation, Boston University, 1972); Wil A. Linkugel, "The Speeches of Anna Howard Shaw" (PhD Dissertation, University of Wisconsin, 1960); and Leslie Collins Hester, "Rebellious Revelry: The Rhetorical Functions of Anna Howard Shaw's Humor" (Thesis, California State University, Fresno, 2007). One example of a different view of Shaw is Jensen's article on the Oregon campaign. Kimberly Jensen, "'Neither Head nor Tail to the Campaign': Esther Pohl Lovejoy and the Oregon Woman Suffrage Victory of 1912," *Oregon Historical Quarterly* 108, no. 3 (2007).

5. See, for example, Paula Giddings, *Ida: A Sword among Lions: Ida B. Wells and the Campaign against Lynching* (New York: Amistad, 2008); Elsa Barkley Brown, "Womanist Consciousness: Maggie Lena Walker and the Independent Order of Saint Luke," in *Unequal Sisters: A Multicultural Reader in U.S. Women's History*, ed. Ellen Carol DuBois and Vicki Ruiz (New York: Routledge, 1990); A'Lelia Perry Bundles, *On Her Own Ground: The Life and Times of Madam C. J. Walker* (New York: Washington Square Press, 2002); Michelle M. Tokarczyk and Elizabeth A. Fay, *Working-Class Women in the Academy: Laborers in the Knowledge Factory* (Amherst: University of Massachusetts Press, 1993); Gloria Moldow, *Women Doctors in Gilded-Age Washington: Race, Gender, and Professionalization* (Urbana: University of Illinois Press, 1987); and Annelise Orleck, *Common Sense and a Little Fire: Women and Working-Class Politics in the United States, 1900–1965*, Gender and American Culture (Chapel Hill: University of North Carolina Press, 1995); and Nancy A. Hewitt, "Taking the New Woman Hostage," *Journal of Women's History* 14, no. 1 (2002). In 1908, Jean Gordon, sister to NAWSA officer, Kate Gordon, gave a talk entitled, "Noblesse Oblige," in Ida Husted Harper, ed., *History of Woman Suffrage, 1910–1920*, vol. III (New York: National American Woman Suffrage Association, 1922), 231–232).

6. Just as Hewitt argues that "differences among white women have been submerged," Shaw's life questions just how widespread the dominant ideals of "woman" were. Hewitt, "New Woman,"156.

7. While Lillian Faderman and others position Anna Howard Shaw within lesbian history, they use a very broad definition of lesbian and lovers, naming Clara Osborn as well as Lucy E. and Susan B. Anthony, as Shaw's "lovers." All these women and more were "intimates" of Shaw's, and Shaw spoke of her deep affection and connections to these women. On the other hand, I have found nothing that could clearly be categorized as a sexual reference among all of Shaw's writings. Rupp grapples with some of these concerns. Lillian Faderman, *To Believe in Women: What Lesbians Have Done for America—A History* (Boston: Houghton Mifflin, 1999); Faderman, "Acting 'Woman' and Thinking 'Man': The Ploys of Famous Female Inverts," *GLQ: A Journal of Lesbian and Gay Studies* 5, no. 3 (1999); and Leila J. Rupp, *Sapphistries: A Global History of Love between Women*, Intersections (New York: New York University Press, 2009).

8. These public records are especially important sources for understanding families where no one left private diaries or other writings. See, for example, Beverly Greene Bond, "'The extent of the law': Free women of color in antebellum Memphis, Tennessee," in Janet L. Coryell, *Negotiating Boundaries of Southern Womanhood: Dealing with the Powers That Be*, Southern Women (Columbia: University of Missouri Press, 2000). Apparently in one line of Anna Howard Shaw's family there was some resentment that Shaw left money only to women. Although it is true that she didn't leave any money to her brothers or nephews, she also didn't leave money to her niece, Margaret Shaw (personal communication).

9. The feelings against the "salaried officers" continued with the old officers accusing them of "selling out . . . to the money power." See Kate Gordon to Catherine Waugh McCulloch, June 5, 1912, Catharine Waugh McCulloch Papers, in *Series VI of the Mary Earhart Dillon Collection*, Schlesinger Library, Radcliffe Institute, Harvard University.

10. Sara Hunter Graham, *Woman Suffrage and the New Democracy* (New Haven: Yale University Press, 1996), 29–30.

11. Shaw was attacked by certain writers in the South because of her support for the cause of African Americans and her friendship with Frederick Douglass. Many of these broadsides survive, and the Laura Clay Papers include a number of them. Laura Clay Papers, 1882–1941, University of Kentucky Library. On at least one occasion she was described as "very fat," but very few personal attacks on her survive. O'Neill names Susan B. Anthony as the most caricatured of the suffrage leaders. Wil A. Linkugel and Martha Watson, *Anna Howard Shaw: Suffrage Orator and Social Reformer*, Great American Orators, No. 10 (New York: Greenwood Press, 1991).

12. Will Linkugel collected Shaw's speeches for his 1960 dissertation. Aside from Linkugel and Watson analyses of Shaw's rhetoric, there are no analyses of her body of work. Linkugel, "Speeches"; Linkugel and Watson, *Anna Howard Shaw*; and Hester, "Rebellious Revelry."

13. Margaret Small, "Lesbians and the Class Position of Women," in Nancy Myron and Charlotte Bunch, *Lesbianism and the Women's Movement*, 1st ed., Diana Press Essay Series (Baltimore: Diana Press, 1975); Trisha Franzen, *Spinsters and Lesbians: Independent Womanhood in the United States* (New York: New York University Press, 1996). The studies of single women have recently gotten more attention. See "Special Issues: Single Women in History," *Women's History Review* 17, no. 3 (2008); and Roundtable on Singlewomen, Berkshire Conference on the History

of Women, Minneapolis, Minnesota, 2008. Lisa Tetrault, "The Incorporation of American Feminism: Suffragists and the Postbellum Lyceum," *Journal of American History* 96, no. 4 (2010). It is interesting to note that Rachel Foster Avery—who inherited a significant fortune from her father, later also inherited from her mother's estate, and married—died shortly after Shaw; however, Avery left a much smaller estate. Harriet Taylor Upton, a married woman and only child of a congressman, lost her home and was left rather impoverished during the Depression. In contrast, Lucy E. Anthony was able to hold onto Alnwick Lodge and two-thirds of the estate that Shaw left her until her own death in 1944, even though there is no evidence that she ever worked for wages after Anna Howard Shaw died. See Will and Related Documents, Rachel Foster Avery, Register of Wills, Buck County Courthouse, Doylestown, Pennsylvania; Harriet Taylor Upton and Eisenbraun Lana Dunn, *Harriet Taylor Upton's Random Recollections* (Warren, Ohio: Harriet Taylor Upton Association, 2004); and Will and Related Documents, Lucy E, Anthony, Register of Wills, Delaware County Archives, Lima, Pennsylvania.

14. W. E. Burghardt Du Bois, "Disfranchisement" (New York City: National American Woman Suffrage Association, 1912); and Louise Michele Newman, *White Women's Rights: The Racial Origins of Feminism in the United States* (New York: Oxford University Press, 1999).

INDEX

Adamless Eden, 83

Addams, Jane, 8, 80, 95, 153, 170, 201; NAWSA vice president, 134-135, 137-138, 140, 156; pacifism, 171-172

Addy, Persis Crowell, 44-46, 75, 187; bequest to Shaw, 53; records on, 196

African-Americans, 8, 70, 78, 95, 118, 139, 178, 225n11

African American women, 52, 74, 95, 192; Columbian Exposition, 78, 227n36; 1903 NAWSA Convention, 91, 93; 1912 NAWSA Convention, 139; 1913 Suffrage Parade, 144; sources, 202; treatment by railroads, 34, 73; Woman's Committee of the Council for National Defense, 172, 249n31. *See also* Black women

African Methodist Episcopal Church, 36

Albion, 40-42

Albion College, 3, 35, 183, 186; Shaw at, 39-42, 196

Alcott, Bronson, 55

Alcott, Louisa, 55

Alnwick, 17-18, 20, 195

Alnwick Castle, 17

Alnwick Lodge, 163, 165, 177; building, 112; photographs, 234n58; selling to Lucy E. Anthony, 158; Shaw's death at, 180-81

alternative families, 187

American Indians, 8, 118. *See also* Native Americans

American Woman Suffrage Association, 58, 60-65, 68

Anderson, Mary, 8, 95, 146, 183, 208n21

Andrews, Bishop, 47

Anna Howard Shaw Women's Center (Albion College), 3

Anthony, Daniel Read, 63

Anthony, Jacob Merritt, 63

Anthony, Lucy E.: background, 63; characteristics, 75; death, 183; efforts for Shaw biography, 182-183; relationship with Rachel Foster Avery, 62, 74; relationship with Shaw, 6, 64-65, 75-76, 81, 84, 102, 182; role in NAWSA, 84; role in NAWSA conflict, 123-126

Anthony, Lucy Read, 207n17

Anthony, Mary Elmira, 63

Anthony, Mary S., 87, 99, 107, 110, 112, 122, 150, 188, 198, 201n17

Anthony, Susan B., 68; background, 62, 116; character, 67-68, 74, 82; choice of successor, 89-90; death, 107-110; mentoring Shaw, 63-64, 77-79; as NAWSA president, 81; promoting Shaw as NAWSA president, 94, 97-98; Shaw relationship with, 6, 71, 75, 81, 87; Thomas-Garrett Fund, 11, 101, 105-106

Arizona Territory, 123, 136-138

Ashley, Jessie, 129-130, 132, 135, 140, 190

Ashton, Michigan, 37

Avery, Cyrus Miller, 62, 231n8

Avery, Rachel Foster, 87, 96, 110-111, 119, 189-190, 226n28; relationship with Shaw, 65-66, 76, 84, 112, 152, 239n46; relationship with Susan B. Anthony, 62, 64; role in NAWSA conflict, 125, 127-129

Baker, Jean, 10

Baker, Newton, 170

Baltimore, Maryland, 105-108

Barton, Clara, 59, 107, 198

Bay View Sunday School Assembly, 61

Beecher, Henry Ward, 56

Beecher, Rev. Lyman, 107

Belmont, Alva, 154, 189, 236n12; background, 119; opposition to, 125, 132; support for NAWSA headquarters, 120, 122; support for suffrage, 123-124

Bennett, Judith, 187

Bethune, Mary McLeod, 8, 208n21

Bible, 74, 79; women in, 74

Big Rapids, Michigan, 183, 187; family in,

TRISHA FRANZEN is a professor of women's and gender studies at Albion College and the author of *Spinsters and Lesbians: Independent Womanhood in the United States.*

WOMEN IN AMERICAN HISTORY

The University of Illinois Press
is a founding member of the
Association of American University Presses.

Composed in 10.5/13 ITC Galliard Pro
by Celia Shapland
at the University of Illinois Press
Manufactured by Thomson-Shore, Inc.

University of Illinois Press
1325 S. Oak Street
Champaign, IL 61820-6903
www.press.uillinois.edu